Managing Complexity
in Organizations

Managing Complexity in Organizations

A View in Many Directions

Edited by Michael R. Lissack
and Hugh P. Gunz

QUORUM BOOKS
Westport, Connecticut • London

Library of Congress Cataloging-in-Publication Data

Managing complexity in organizations : a view in many directions /
   edited by, Michael R. Lissack, Hugh P. Gunz.
      p.   cm.
   "A collection of work prepared for the two 1998 gatherings of the
'Managing the Complex' conference . . . . Complex-M and Managing the
Complex took place . . . in Toronto in April and in Boston in
October"—P.   .
   Includes bibliographical references and index.
   ISBN 1–56720–285–3 (alk. paper)
   1. Strategic planning—Congresses.   2. Organization—Congresses.
3. Industrial project management—Congresses.   4. Technological
complexity—Congresses.   I. Lissack, Michael.   II. Gunz, Hugh P.
HD30.28.M3452   1999
658.4'012—dc21   99–13621

British Library Cataloguing in Publication Data is available.

Library of Congress Catalog Card Number: 99–13621
ISBN: 1–56720–285–3

First published in 1999

Quorum Books, 88 Post Road West, Westport, CT 06881
An imprint of Greenwood Publishing Group, Inc.
www.quorumbooks.com

Printed in the United States of America

The paper used in this book complies with the
Permanent Paper Standard issued by the National
Information Standards Organization (Z39.48–1984).

10 9 8 7 6 5 4 3 2 1

Book design by Richard Freed.

Contents

Chapter 1

Introduction

Michael R. Lissack and Hugh P. Gunz

Vaclav Havel, the Czech president and playwright, said, "We have to abandon the arrogant belief that the world is merely a puzzle to be solved, a machine with instructions waiting to be discovered, a body of information to be fed into a computer." In dealing with management concepts, it is not only what we presently see that matters, but also the frame in which we place the present input. What we see is always a function of where we stand. The frames we use to make sense of the world are shaped by both our past experiences and our assumptions. Betting on serendipitous genius is not management but gambling.

This book is a collection of work prepared for the two 1998 gatherings of the Managing the Complex conference—a semiannual gathering for discussions about the relationships between managing organizations and the science of complex systems. Managing the Complex attracts managers, academics, consultants, and others interested in the possibility of applying the insights of the science of complex systems to day-to-day management problems. Many of the attendees are members of the Complex-M discussion list on the Internet—itself a virtual gathering place for discussions of complexity and management. The first two real-life gatherings of Complex-M and Managing the Complex took place in 1998, in Toronto in April and in Boston in October. More than 100 papers were prepared for these events. From these, 18 were chosen for this volume, plus an introductory chapter by Michael Lissack and concluding words from both of us.

In recent years there has emerged a collection of interdisciplinary scientific efforts known as the science of complex systems.

Complex systems, which consist of many interacting entities and exhibit properties such as self-organization, evolution, and constant novelty, exist in all the domains of our world. Complex systems are very difficult to comprehend by the standard, analytic approach of modern science. The science of complex systems attempts to discover general laws governing such systems by bringing together people and ideas from many disciplines. As yet, such general laws have not been found, but the efforts have yielded much deeper insights into the systems studied. The emerging theory of complex systems research has resulted in a growing movement to reinvigorate management. Theory, research, practice, and education can all benefit by adopting a more dynamic, systemic, cognitive, and holistic approach to the management process. As interest in the study of complex systems has grown, a new vocabulary is emerging to describe discoveries about wide-ranging and fundamental phenomena. Complexity theory research has allowed for new insights into many phenomena and for the development of new manners of discussing issues regarding management and organizations.

Complexity thinking provides insight at two levels. It introduces new *metaphors* for visualizing and thinking about organization and management, and it provides novel *models* for making sense of the world of organizations. Central to both are the concepts of *emergence* and *coherence.* At the second Managing the Complex gathering the attendees suggested that within management applications complexity thinking represents the solution to the quest for intentional (read purposive), emergent (arising from interactions) coherence (a making sense of the world). What people want, the attendees collectively said, is not knowledge, not certainty, not comfort, but meaning. Stories are generative mechanisms for creating a context for sense-making—for finding meaning. The logo "intentional, emergent coherence" was intended to be a reflection of the power of the interactions of stories, models, and meanings.

The metaphors and models derived from complexity can be used to both retrospectively make sense of observations and proactively help create a new, sensible environment. Thus, a shared language based on the insights of complexity can have an important role in a management context. The use of complexity theory metaphors can change the way managers think about the problems they face. Instead of competing in a game or a war, managers of a complexity thinking enterprise are trying to find their way on an ever-changing, ever-turbulent landscape. Such a conception of their organizations' basic task can, in turn, change the day-to-day decisions made by management.

Those decisions and the sense-making associated with them, in their own turn, affect the day-to-day lives of the remaining members of the organization, whose actions affect the organization's tasks, and so on through an ever-emergent spiral. Management can supply the intent, and the members can supply the emergent, but both must work together to create the coherent.

VOCABULARY

The most productive applications of complexity insights have to do with new possibilities for innovation in organizations. These possibilities require new ways of thinking, but old models of thinking persist long after they are productive. New ways of thinking don't just happen; they require new models that have to be learned. Managing the Complex—the conference and the book—is dedicated to helping both practicing managers and academics acquire, understand, and examine these new mental models.

There are a number of terms and concepts that the authors of this volume use that they assume the reader is familiar with but that can be obscure to anyone who is not. Here we introduce some of the more common; anyone used to the language of complexity theory can skip over the next three paragraphs.

Much complex behavior results from *nonlinearity*, a reference to a particular kind of interaction. Linear systems are "characterized by stable relationships between variables and respond to changes in their parameters, or to external 'shocks,' in a smooth and proportionate manner. . . . Nonlinear systems may be characterized by periods of both linear and nonlinear interactions. . . during [nonlinear] periods relationships between variables may change, resulting in dramatic structural or behavioral change....Nonlinear systems are consequently capable of generating very complex behavior over time" (Kiel and Elliott, 1997: 5). So, for example, we hope for a linear relationship between how far we press the accelerator pedal and how fast the car goes. What we do not want is a situation in which, when the pedal reaches a given point, the car suddenly starts slowing down. That would be an example of nonlinearity, and it is surprisingly common in natural systems (if not in automotive design).

The term *chaos* is reserved in complexity theory for behavior, that has the appearance of randomness, although it is not truly random. In theory, a chaotic system will follow a predictable path, given a given set of circumstances. However, the consequences of the nonlinear interactions that typically underlie chaotic behavior are that the slightest variation in any of these circumstances can cause a striking change in the system's behavior, making it, for all practical purposes, essentially unpredictable. That is not to say that everything about the system is unpredictable, however. One way in which chaotic and nonchaotic systems can be distinguished is in the kinds of *attractor* they display. Attractors are not what the term seems to imply on the surface: they do not attract. A system's attractor is the path it follows over time (strictly speaking, through the system's phase space). Chaotic systems display a particular kind of attractor, labeled *strange*, which has particular properties distinguishing it from other kinds of attractor. Closely linked with the concept of attractors is that of *fitness landscapes*, multidimensional maps of the "fitness" of a complex system, which are of particular interest, for example, to evolutionary biologists.

A number of scholars of complexity are interested in a particular kind of complex behavior that seems to exist at what has been called *the edge of chaos*, a critical state falling between comparatively straightforward, linear behavior and the wildness of chaos. It has sometimes been argued that, because many complex systems appear to evolve naturally into this condition, it could also be called *self-organized criticality*.

These terms result in a new language for business. Consider, for example, Table 1.1 drawn from Robin Wood's first draft of Chapter 7.

The language may seem unfamiliar, but the ideas behind it are very powerful. Such power makes the use of complexity ideas attractive to managers. To return to our main theme, consider next this lesson drawn from Cutler (Chapter 18):

There may be a trade-off between, on one hand, survivability within established structures and, on the other hand, performance. Maximization of performance may sometimes be impossible under conditions of optimized survivability within a structure of subordination. Anyone who has ever worked for anyone else probably knows this from personal experience. There is no reason that organizational performance should be any different in this respect. Indeed, the more complex any environment becomes, the more likely this may be, and the more frequently the contradictions may appear. The long (i.e., continuous) duration of unpredicted and unfamiliar decisional situations and the experience of high tension in the contemporary business environment, then combine to increase the stress on decisionmakers. As pointed out earlier, all other things being equal, this decreases their ability to learn from the environment against which their very success or failure will be judged. Such a condition today seems characteristic, if not fundamental. One solution is for organizational adaptation through learning to cease being a mechanism for responding to the environment, and for mergers and acquisitions to predominate in an attempt to control the environment. Yet mergers and acquisitions in the corporate world today are barely survival tools by which

Table 1.1
Some Strategic Management Definitions and Their New Science Equivalents

Term	Current Definition	New Science Meaning
Customer Value Proposition & Business Design	Organizations deliver a particular customer value proposition to a definable market in order to exist. The delivery of the customer value proposition relies upon a business design, which uses key business processes to harness the distinctive competencies and resources of the firm to deliver superior value to relevant markets. Customer value propositions and business designs compete and collaborate for customers, resources, infrastructures, and skills on strategic landscapes.	The network of relationships and dependencies between a firm and its neighbors in a business ecosystem with which it interacts or by which it can be impacted. Within each ecosystem are coevolving fitness landscapes that are defined by the boundaries between different business designs and the territories within which they compete and collaborate. A business design expresses the configuration of activities, know-how, resources, and infrastructure by an adaptive agent on a fitness landscape ("strategic landscape"). Business designs have been selected by evolution or design to offer the optimal trade-off between exploitation and exploration congruent with the expectations of stakeholders in the firm and the demands of the business environment.
Strategy	The chosen means by which an organization coherently anticipates and adapts itself to its environment so as to realize its vision and win against competitors. It is a frame of mind—a thinking process and learning concerned with long-term adaptation—with the survival and well being of the organization.	The process by which an organization generates, develops, and maintains a robust business design capable of both exploiting its current distinctive capabilities (its fitness function) on or near its current fitness peak and exploring its strategic landscape and business ecosystem for entrepreneurial opportunities beyond the lifecycle of its current business design (its sustainability function) away from its current fitness peak.
Direction	Who we are as a business enterprise and what we should be trying to achieve. The purpose and scope of an organization, together with its principles, success formulae and long-term aspirational goals.	The rules (both written and unwritten), by which a firm exploits and explores the landscape and business ecosystem: exploitation rules—what we must do to be economically viable and politically legitimate with our stakeholders—and exploration rules—the search rules that define how we will search the strategic landscape and business ecosystem/s and what we are looking for (scanning).

corporations and their components are driven—driven, moreover, not necessarily by any internal logic about the environment but by the environment itself unreflectively. Prominent chief executive officers (CEOs) frequently face, with respect to their subsidiaries, much the same problem Gorbachev faced with the republics. ... The difficult question for managers at the highest level is how to allow the[ir] subsidiaries the freedom to survive and be viable, while at the same time providing them incentives to stay within the overall corporate institution, yet without imposing upon them constraints that sub-optimize their survivability. Gorbachev tried and failed. Steve Jobs failed and returned.

In recognizing the challenges of navigating through complexity, scholars have offered complementary notions such as the science of muddling through, logical incrementalism, or "emergent strategies." The interactive complexity that is part of current management environments and practice often makes it hard to design the "best" system a priori—there are simply too many variables and issues to be considered. These challenges are magnified if the system itself is poorly understood and, furthermore, is put to use in varying and poorly understood environmental contexts. In such a situation, it becomes difficult, if not impossible, to design a system that takes into account all the contingencies that might arise. Thus, to the extent that current management literature does not examine the complexity perspective, it is missing what is likely to be the vital element for success in the twenty-first century.

THE PLAN OF THE BOOK

The book is organized into four main parts, each of which has a brief introduction for the chapters therein:

Part I: Overview: The three chapters in this part are intended to introduce the reader to the topic of how complexity science relates to modern management practice. They provide context for the parts on strategy, creativity, communications, and applications that follow.

Part II: Strategy: The three chapters in this part examine strategy from a complexity perspective and complexity from a strategy perspective.

Part III: Creativity and Communication: The four chapters in this part look at the intersection of complexity, creativity, and communication. The chapters seek to answer the question, What is it about the complexity perspective that alters the way we both approach problems and see and communicate about the world?

Part IV: Applications: Chapters 12 through 19 examine how complexity-influenced theories of management can actually affect day-to-day management practice. The domains examined range from telecommunications to windmills to Soviet power politics. The lessons drawn, however, are applicable day-to-day to most of us as managers.

In the study of complex systems, the idea of emergence is used to indicate the way that patterns, structures, or properties arise that do not seem adequately explained by referring only to the system's preexisting components and their interaction. Advice to managers stemming from complexity theory is itself an emergent phenomenon. Merely reading the chapters herein is not enough. What matters is the actions that result. What the authors who are gathered together here—and in person at the Managing the Complex conferences—hope to do is to influence your thinking enough to affect those actions. Such is the perspective of the attendees of Managing the Complex and of the authors of this volume.

REFERENCES

Kiel, L. D., and E. Elliott, eds. 1997. *Chaos Theory in the Social Sciences: Foundations and Applications.* Ann Arbor: University of Michigan Press.

Stern, C. W. and Stalk, G. (eds.). 1998. *Perspectives on Strategy: From the Boston Consulting Group.* New York: John Wiley and Sons.

Part I

Overview

The three chapters in this section are intended to introduce the reader to the topic of how complexity science relates to modern management practice. They provide context for the sections on strategy, creativity, communications, and applications that follow.

Michael R. Lissack's "Complexity and Management: It Is More than Jargon" lays the initial groundwork in providing context to the reader. Lissack introduces complexity science terms and their meanings and places them within the world of management. He contends, "At the overlapping boundaries of complexity science and organization science is where the importance of vocabulary, language, metaphors, and models comes into play." He echoes Jay Forrester: "While most people understand first-order effects, few deal well with second- and third-order effects. Unfortunately, virtually everything interesting in business lies in fourth-order effects and beyond" (Stern and Stalk, 1998). Ultimately, he concludes, "The future of organization science lies in Forrester's fourth-order effects.... If we wish to understand organizations and what makes them what they are, complexity science is perhaps not only our most potent tool but at present may be our only tool."

In his "Complexity—More than a Fad?" Tom Petzinger identifies for the reader why complexity science represents something more than the litany of management consulting buzzwords and fads. Petzinger notes the strength of the theory and substance that underlie complexity theory. At the same time, he cautions against expectations that complexity science is, in any form, a predictive science. The strength of complexity for managers is in its descriptive abilities. "Complexity describes the world *as it is*. Complexity is a way of describing what occurs in a system. By its very nature complexity does not predict an outcome.... Complexity is not about adding behaviors; it is about removing them. It is not the addition of another program; instead it signals a retreat from programs.... Any management seeking to use complexity as a tool to obtain particular results will abandon the concept very quickly. For this we should be highly grateful." To Petzinger, complexity is more than a fad, but it remains at risk of being falsely viewed as a panacea.

In "Complexity, Computational Ability, and the Corporation of the Future," Arnold J. Wytenburg argues that modern "corporations' ability to keep pace with change is a reflection of their capacity to make sense of the complexity, which simultaneously (1) comprises the environment in which they exist while (2) defining the extent, nature, form, and behavior of their participation within that environment. This modern market environment is what the 'new sciences' define as dynamic, complex, non-linear, and self-organizing." Wytenburg provides a history of organizational change as viewed from a systems perspective. By providing this type of history he helps the reader to locate complex systems thinking along the continuum of management concepts that have evolved as our market environments have evolved. But Wytenburg argues that systems thinking and complexity are especially relevant now, in the turbulent environments that characterize the passage to the twenty-first century. He concludes, "Together, the science of complexity theory, the principles of emergent behavior, and the discipline of systems thinking can enable organizations to see and understand a corporation simultaneously as being comprised of systems, as being a system in its own right, and as being part of a larger system that, taken together, comprise a market environment that is inherently complex, volatile, and unpredictable."

REFERENCE

Stern, C. W. and Stalk, G. (eds.). 1998. *Perspectives on Strategy: From the Boston Consulting Group*. New York: John Wiley and Sons.

Chapter 2

Complexity and Management: It Is More than Jargon

Michael R. Lissack

Every day, voices in the mass media tell us we live in a world in which complexity is rising and institutional orders are dissipating. In such a world, organizational science studies ways of fending off the forces of chaos that are, so to speak, always just around the corner. Management is portrayed as the process not only of fending off, but also of sometimes seizing hold of those very forces. The traditional management literature—the stuff from which most of our MBA-led generation is taught—tends to speak of an objective world where interactions can be described in linear terms, where words have singular meanings, and where prediction and control are paramount. The focus on control provides one perspective on "chaos" and the manifold changes occurring all around us. A contrasting perspective evolves from complexity science. Complexity theory challenges the traditional management assumptions by noting that human activity allows for the possibility of emergent behavior. In the study of emergence, complexity science and organization converge.

Organizations can be viewed as systems of interpretation and constructions of reality (Berger and Luckmann, 1966). In order to survive, organizations must find ways to interpret events so as to stabilize their environments and try to make them more predictable; organizations must also find ways to interpret events so as to be one with the environment, an environment that they choose. A central concern of organization science is that of understanding how people construct meaning and reality, and exploring how that enacted reality provides a context for action. When managers "enact" the environment, they as Weick (1995) put it "construct, rearrange, single out, and demolish many 'objective' features of their surroundings... they unrandomize variables, insert vestiges of orderliness, and literally create their own constraints." Through this process of sense-making and reality construction, people in an organization give meaning to the events and actions of the organization. This occurs at two principal levels—the individual and the organization.

Organizations often experience change as an "emergent" process. Casti (1997) defines "emergence" as an overall system behavior that comes out of the interaction of many participants—behavior that cannot be predicted or "even envisioned" from knowledge of what each component of a system does in isolation. This is the experience of change, yet this approach is scarcely found in the organization science literature. When emergent change is recognized within the literature, it is discussed superficially and metaphorically with the organizational whole as the unit of analysis (Alvesson, 1990, 1995; Comfort, 1994). Often the emergent nature of change as experienced by other members of the organization is overlooked. Change, instead, is treated as continuous, step-like, or even chaotic but with a definable scope and focus (Stacey, 1996). The experienced sense of change—that the whole is bigger than the sum of the parts and that the patterns observed and felt are unexpected—is not captured.

The study of complex systems, or, as some call it, complexity theory, is a rigorous and formal attempt to deal with this issue of emergent wholes. The past few years have found an increasing interest in this subject by organization science researchers. The year 1998 alone saw more than one dozen conferences and symposia with complexity and management as a theme. *Emergence: A Journal of Complexity Issues in Organizations and Management* began publication in 1999 and had several conferences planned. Hatch and Tsoukas (1997) note that "interpretative organization theory often challenges views of organizations produced by (traditional) research yet echoes the findings of complexity theory." Most other complexity-oriented writers would echo that observation (e.g., Stacey, 1996; Overman, 1996; Phelan, 1995). These writers tend to point out that both complex systems and organizations are

- non-linear, such that there is no proportionality between cause and effect,
- fractal, such that measurement is scale-dependent, and concepts are indeterminate,
- recursive between scale levels, such that it is easy to get lost,
- sensitive to initial conditions, such that the system is experienced as volatile,

- replete with feedback loops and potential bifurcation points, and
- subject to emergence.

As Levy (1994) phrased it:

By understanding industries as complex systems, managers can improve decision-making and search for innovative solutions.... Chaos [complexity] theory is a promising framework that accounts for the dynamic evolution of industries and the complex interactions among industry actors. By conceptualizing industries as chaotic systems, a number of managerial implications can be developed. Long-term forecasting is almost impossible for chaotic systems, and dramatic change can occur unexpectedly; as a result, flexibility and adaptiveness are essential for organizations to survive. Nevertheless, chaotic systems exhibit a degree of order, enabling short-term forecasting to be undertaken and underlying patterns can be discerned. Chaos [complexity] theory also points to the importance of developing guidelines and decision rules to cope with complexity, and of searching for non-obvious and indirect means to achieving goals.

Levy (1994) argues strongly that complexity theory and its metaphors have managerial implications. What is this complexity theory? As of 1999, it is less an organized, rigorous theory than a collection of ideas that have in common the notion that within dynamic patterns there may be underlying simplicity that can, in part, be discovered through the use of large quantities of computer power (Horgan, 1995; Casti, 1995, 1997) and through analytic, logical, and conceptual developments (Bar-Yam, 1997). It is also the discipline that has self-organized to examine the question of how coherent and purposive wholes emerge from the interactions of simple and sometimes non-purposive components. The theory includes such ideas as phase changes, fitness landscapes, self-organization, emergence, attractors, symmetry and symmetry breaking, chaos, quanta, the edge of chaos, self-organized criticality, generative relationships, and increasing returns to scale.

Some have chosen to distinguish the science components (both qualitative and quantitative) as the study of complex systems, while others allocate the word "complexity" to be inclusive not of the science but also of the more popular fad-like uses of complex systems terms. Whichever label one uses, the ideas of complexity are important. Witness this quote from Overman (1996) in his "New Science of Management":

Are traditional social science methods incapable of dealing with the complex and indeterminate problems facing management today? It is not so much the wedding of scientific logic and method to management theory and practice that is problematic, as it is the outdated models of scientific inquiry that slow our progress. The new sciences of chaos and quantum theory [complexity] offer valuable metaphors and methods that can challenge the management research agenda into the next century [with]... the image of self-organization, dissipative structures, and dynamic complexity.

Organization Science in a call for papers for a special issue on applications of complexity theory noted:

A number of findings now seem fairly well established, including the following: (1) Many dynamic systems do not reach an equilibrium (either a fixed point or a cyclical equilibrium). (2) Processes that appear to be random may actually be chaotic, in other words may revolve around identifiable types of "attractors." Tests exist that can detect whether apparently random processes are in fact chaotic. (3) Two entities with very similar initial states can follow radically divergent paths over time. The behavior of complex processes can be quite sensitive to small differences in initial conditions. This can lead to highly path-dependent behavior, and historical accidents may "tip" outcomes strongly in a particular direction. (4) Very complex patterns can arise from the interaction of agents following relatively simple rules. These patterns are "emergent" in the sense that new properties appear at each level in a hierarchy. (5) Complex systems may resist reductionist analyses. In other words, it may not be possible to describe some systems simply by holding some of their subsystems constant in order to study other subsystems. (6) Time series that appear to be random walks may actually be fractals with self-reinforcing trends. In such cases we may observe a "hand of the past" in operation. (7) Complex systems may tend to exhibit "self-organizing" behavior. Starting in a random state, they may naturally evolve toward order instead of disorder. (Anderson, 1996)

A short list of books would be sufficient for those unfamiliar with the field to get a decent handle on complexity. One might begin with *Complexity: The Emerging Science at the Edge of Order and Chaos* (Waldrop, 1992), which is an overview of the origins of complexity theory through the eyes of its explorers and the book with which to begin exploring this field. Although as early as 1986 there was an academic book published with the title *Complexity, Managers, and Organizations* (Streufert and Swezey, 1986), *Chaos: Making a New Science* (Gleick, 1987) is considered to be the classic work in the field and introduced laypersons to the complexities of complexity. *At Home in the Universe: The Search for the Laws of Self-Organization and Complexity* (Kauffman, 1995) explores what complexity theory might mean for the future of economics and organizations. *Leadership and the New Science: Learning about Organization from an Orderly Universe* (Wheatley, 1992) provides a broad survey of quantum mechanics as well as complexity theory and then extends its speculations to their relevance to leadership and organization. *Figments of Reality: The Evolution of the Curious Mind* (Stewart and Cohen, 1997) and *The Collapse of Chaos: Discovering Simplicity in a Complex World* (Cohen and Stewart, 1994) bring some history of simplicity to the exploration of chaos and complexity. *Complexity and Creativity in Organizations* (Stacey, 1996) illustrates applications of new science to organizational dynamics and change.

The supposed lessons from complexity theory turn up in more and more places. Take this item from the March 1996 issue of *Organizational Dynamics*:

Chaos theory also makes a profound point that corporate executives need to internalize: beyond a certain point, increased knowledge of complex, dynamic systems does little to improve our ability to extend the horizon of predictability for those systems. No matter how much we know about the weather, no matter how powerful the computers are, specific long-range predictions are not feasible. We can know, but we cannot predict.... Essentially, an organization must be flexible enough to adapt, creative enough to innovate, and responsive enough to learn. (Crossan, et al., 1996)

Or take this item from the *Wall Street Journal*:

Mr. Michels acts as an agent in a "self-organizing system," a phrase biologists use to describe organisms that continually adapt to the environment without losing their basic identity. Although it is tempting to dismiss the idea as management-by-metaphor, a few companies are beginning to recognize how closely their operations resemble such systems in the natural world—and how the lessons might be applied to the quest for success in the ever-changing market. (Petzinger, 1996a)

Complexity science has also caught the attention of a wide academic audience. Articles with such titles as "Hierarchical Selection and Organizational Adaptation" (Warglien, 1995), "Chaos and Transformation: Implications of Nonequilibrium Theory for Social Science and Society" (Loye and Eisler, 1987), "Complexity, Genuine Uncertainty, and the Economics of Organization" (Langlois and Everett, 1992), and "Chaos Theory and Organization" (Thietart and Forgues, 1995) have appeared in numerous journals, including *Industrial and Corporate Change, Behavioral Science, Human Systems Management, Journal of Management Inquiry, Academy of Management Review*, and *Organization Science*. While one might expect a lengthy article entitled "Complexity, Organization, and Stuart Kauffman's *The Origins of Order*" (Westhoff, Yarbrough, and Yarbrough, 1996) to appear in the *Journal of Economic Behavior and Organization*, it is a reflection of the breadth of the field to see reviews of *Emergent Complexity: The Evolution of Intermediate Societies* (Arnold, 1996) in *Ameri-*

can Antiquity and to read subscription notices for a journal entitled *Complexity and Chaos in Nursing.*

THE COMPLEXITY METAPHOR—SOME EXAMPLES

Complexity theory, as used in the previous discussion, has its own vocabulary and its own metaphors. One such metaphor is the notion of an edge of chaos. Its most fervent proponent is Kauffman. Through his research, Kauffman

> began to see that living systems operated at their most robust and efficient level in the narrow space between stability and disorder—poised at "the edge of chaos." It was here, it appeared, that the agents within a system conducted the fullest range of productive interactions and exchanged the greatest amount of useful information. People recognize this in everyday life: A slightly messy office is a productive one; rollicking families are happy; economies flourish under scant regulation. The edge of chaos, but not quite chaos itself. (Petzinger, 1996b)

In a complex world, strategy is a set of processes for monitoring the behaviors of both the world and the agents of the organization, observing where potential attractors are, and attempting to supply resources and incentives for future moves. It may be that command and control are impossible (at least in the absolute and in the aggregate), but the manager retains the ability to influence the shape of what complexity theory [and biology] refers to as "the fitness landscape" (Lane and Maxfield, 1995).

Identification of value-added knowledge as a task can be represented by the metaphor of search for optimal fitness on a landscape. The landscape is rugged, in that there are hills and valleys, and it is turbulent in that it co-evolves both with the outside environment and with the very participants (employees, customers, suppliers, regulators, competitors, etc.) who make up the essence of that landscape.

Kauffman carried out a number of studies of search on rugged landscapes that demonstrate that, when fitness is average, search is best carried out far away across the space of possibilities. But as fitness increases, the fittest variants are found ever closer to the current location in the space of possibilities (Kauffman, 1993).

On complex surfaces (i.e., rugged fitness landscapes with many hills and valleys) systems can become trapped on poor local optima (the wrong hill). Kauffman's research has developed a variety of approaches to "simulated annealing" to assist in getting organizations away from these local optima and moving toward a more "global optimum." Simulated annealing is an optimization procedure based on using an analogue of temperature, which is gradually lowered so that the system nearly equilibrates at each temperature and is gradually trapped into deep energy wells. The general concept lying behind simulated annealing is that at a finite temperature the system sometimes "ignores" some of the constraints and takes a step "the wrong" way, and hence increases energy temporarily. Ignoring constraints in a judicious way can help avoid being trapped on poor local optima (Kauffman, 1993: 111–112).

Within this language clearly is a "how." Kauffman recommends breaking up the organization into patches, yet he emphasizes that these patches must interact. This advice is different from the old management standby of the independent, self-sufficient business unit. In the nature and quantity of the interactions Kauffman finds that the organization as a whole can be moved toward a global optimum, even though each patch is acting selfishly. Interactions require language or some other mechanism of fairly continual communication. He stresses that the patches must be coupled. In management jargon, the pieces must communicate, and not just at quarterly review sessions.

The basic idea of patch procedure is simple: take a hard, conflict-laden task in which many parts interact, and divide it into a quilt of non-overlapping patches. Try to optimize within each patch. As this occurs, the couplings between parts in two patches across patch boundaries will mean that finding a "'good" solution in one patch will change the problem to be solved by the parts in adjacent patches. Since changes in each patch will alter the problems confronted by neighboring patches, and the adaptive moves by those patches in turn will alter the problem faced by yet other patches, the system is just like our model of co-evolving ecosystems. (Kauffman, 1995: 252–253)

Kauffman's other two procedural suggestions are to ignore some of the inputs coming into the organization (the theory seems to be that accommodating all inputs leads to freezing and that the necessary degrees of freedom to better find optima can be accomplished only by deliberately ignoring some of the inputs) and to recognize that too much data cease to be information (that which informs the agent or actor) but instead act like a brake on the system.

The annealing process can also be looked at as one of deliberately introducing noise into a system to see what happens. Guastello (1995: Chapter 4) refers to this as "the chaotic controller":

Chaotic control works counter-intuitively by first adding a small amount of low-dimensional noise into the system. The reasoning is that the amount of sensitivity to initial conditions is not uniform throughout the attractor's space; sensitivity is less in the basin of the attractor and least in its center.... Adding noise to the system allows the attractor to expand to its fullest range. (Guastello, 1995: Chapter 4)

This is a very different concept of noise from the statistical view (which suggests that noise should be discarded). Where traditional managers may have wished to delete the extraneous, the complexity research-educated manager may be attempting to cause the deliberate addition of noise at various places along the way. Of course, noise can still be noise, and search strategies must be able to separate wheat from chaff if the enterprise is to be at all successful.

Managers who can make use of the metaphors of complexity see their companies in a different light than those who do not and, in a sense, are competing in a different world (Lakoff and Johnson, 1995). Corporate managers may, for example, view their companies as being in a race—be it for success, market share, revenues, or survival. That metaphor influences the way they see the world and the way they manage their companies.

In the race metaphor, the landscape is fixed even if the course is not. One has an identified goal and a set of competitors. In the fitness landscape metaphor, the landscape itself is always changing. One's goals, course, and competitors are but factors that can and do affect the shape of the landscape itself. The objective is to climb to a non-local peak, and your peaks may be very different from those of your competitors.

In the race metaphor, information and data can be confused. Too much data lead to a loss of vision, a potential diversion from the goal, and the risk of overload. In the complexity metaphor, data are merely unused potential information. Information changes the landscape and data become information when they are ascribed value (whether correctly or not). Noise is a risk and a diversion in the race metaphor and a source of new understanding and potential information in the complexity metaphor. Table 2.1 illustrates some of the complexity theory metaphors.

Metaphor use can go too far if one forgets the "as if" qualities of the metaphors themselves. By 1995, the misplaced use of complexity and chaos terms had led to Kellert's (1995) article, "When Is the Economy Not Like the Weather? The Problem of Extending Chaos Theory to the Social Sciences." Of this rampant use of complexity concepts, Kellert notes

metaphorical extensions can serve as useful antidotes to previous importations of concepts and methods from linear dynamics. But the metaphorical use of chaos theory can be misused if terminology is construed too broadly, or if the criteria for chaos are interpreted too loosely. Nor-

Table 2.1
Some Complexity Theory Metaphors

Metaphorical Concept	Inference	Practical Application
fitness landscape	local vs. global optima	search strategies (for improvements)
fitness landscape	co-evolving deformations	be aware of feedback loops and interactions with all levels of stakeholders
attractor	behavior that passively follows a pattern	choice is more important than trying to influence predestined behavior
simulated annealing	use "chaos" to control "chaos"	a bit of bedlam can be a good thing for crowds, data flow, and information retrieval
simulated annealing	"noise" can add creativity	seek out controlled elements of noise, new voices, and outside perspectives
patches	selfish bits can be better than a holistic whole	subdivide the organizing into interactive pieces with constant communication
tau	too much data cause a clogging of the pipes	limit the quantity of simultaneous change that the organization attempts to recognize
generative relationships	seek tomorrow's returns in each encounter today	approach each encounter by asking how this will help me grow
increasing returns	knowledge-based components of economy differ from traditional	promote network and community effects whenever possible
sensitive dependence to initial conditions	prediction is impossible	control per se won't work

mative conclusions, such as the contention that chaos theory proves the optimality of laissez-faire capitalism, run into even more serious problems.

Kellert questions such treatments as that of Thietart and Forgues (1995): "Organizations are presented as nonlinear dynamic systems subject to forces of stability and forces of instability which push them toward chaos." As a metaphor, maybe; as a mathematical system, no. More recently the trend has been to assert that corporations are living organisms and can be understood through biology (cf. Kelly, 1994; Carr, 1996). The error lies in neglecting to distinguish the model—"nonlinear dynamic systems" or DNA—from the thing modeled—organizations. Metaphors not only illustrate for us what two domains have in common but also force us to think about how they differ. When map and territory get conflated, however, the observations about differences get lost. The risk is that the valuable contribution of the language and the metaphors disappears in the arguments over whether or not they "literally apply." Scott Barton (1994) perhaps phrased it best:

These definitions, although clearly metaphorical, bear little resemblance to the definition of chaos in the physical sciences. This paradigm, although new and exciting, offers no cure for the profound difficulties [management scientists] face in establishing reliability and validity in all of their research. Instead, it provides a new way of thinking about [organizational] systems. Ultimately, its value to [management science] will be a function of its ability to solve problems and understand phenomena more effectively than competing paradigms. As with all new paradigms, investigators need the latitude to be speculative at first... the concepts of chaos, nonlinear dynamics, and self-organizing systems can allow investigators to explore a variety of areas from new and promising angles, ones that many may have never before considered.

What these metaphors can do is provide access to new ideas and new analogies for use in confronting the unexpected and the unfamiliar.

When any aspect of our experience strikes us as worth understanding, either for the first time or in a new way, we begin to search for [analogous instances].... I would say that just as we turn to a dictionary for the definition of unknown words in terms of familiar words, so we look to phenomena of other sorts, whether natural or artificial, for analogs of things, qualities, and events—including aspects of our own experience and activity—that we wish to comprehend. (Leary, 1990)

COMPLEXITY SCIENCE AND ORGANIZATION
SCIENCE—A LONG RELATIONSHIP?

While complexity science may, thus far, have contributed only metaphors and models to the organization science literature, it would be foolhardy to write off such contributions as insignificant or minor. These metaphors and models are world-constituting for those who use them (Astley, 1985; Cilliers, 1999). Both complexity science and organization science have a common problem they wish to address—uncertainty. In their joint concern for uncertainty lies the basis for what is likely to be a very long relationship.

A lesson from complexity science is that it is always valuable to examine what occurs when foreground and background are shifted (Bechtel and Richardson, 1993; Mitchell, 1994; Bar-Yam, 1997). The added insight can suggest new relationships and new categories of thought. Management theory rarely takes up this challenge. Yet, much can be gained, for a different picture emerges when one reverses the prominence of the boxes and the arrows in the typical management and leadership models taught to most MBAs and popularized in business texts. These models are likely to use boxes and similar shapes to indicate reified entities—things that have an ontological status. They use arrows to indicate relationships, flows, and exchanges—items to which it grants no ontological basis other than fleetingness. By contrast, consider models that reverse the ontology. The relations, flows, and exchanges are deemed to be "real" and "extant," while the items formerly designated by shapes—the organization, its hierarchical structure, work climate, systems, mission, and strategy are afforded only the fleeting recognition of a snapshot in time. The analogy here is to a balance sheet or to those bad Polaroid pictures one takes on vacation. Each is but an inadequate reflection of a flowing reality temporarily stopped for the purpose of having a record created.

Consider the notion of "uncertainty." More than 30 years ago, Thompson (1967) was able to write, "uncertainty appears as the fundamental problem for complex organizations, and coping with uncertainty, as the essence of the administrative process." The intervening three decades have marked little progress. Connell and Nord (1996) write of the "Infiltration of Organization Science by Uncertainty and Values," making note of the increased emphasis on language and meaning. Gergen and Thatchenkery (1996) note that methods may be sought to generate "new realities." Jacobson and Jacques (1997) can write of "Destabilizing the Field" by introducing a post-structuralist approach to the questions of meaning within organizations. If the study of organizations is itself plagued by uncertainty and doubt, that is a reflection of the uncertainties felt by organizations themselves and the members thereof. Perhaps what is occurring is that, as time marches inexorably forward, we are encountering more of what Rittel described as "wicked problems"—"a class of social system problems which are ill formulated, where the information is confusing, where there are many clients and decision makers with conflicting values, and where the ramifications in the whole system are thoroughly confusing" (Churchman, 1967). Or perhaps we just feel like we are.

Organization science for 50 years has focused on "controlling uncertainty." Complexity science for the past 10 years has focused on how to understand it so as to better "go with the flow" and perhaps to channel that flow. In the possibilities created when we question whether the control or the uncertainty occupies the foreground lies the potential convergence of complexity science and organization science. John Seely Brown of Xerox PARC refers to such convergence items as "boundary objects."

At the overlapping boundaries of complexity science and organization science is where the importance of vocabulary, language, metaphors, and models comes into play. The possibility space of the organization is constrained by the language of interpretation available to it and its members—for in that language their reality will be constructed. Managers choose the environments they attend to, and their internal views shape these choices. The choice of frames (which endow meaning) and metaphors (which can provoke new images) within an organization can be determinative of what an organization can both extract and absorb from the environment around it. Kauffman (1996) refers to nearby possibilities as "the adjacent possible." The sequence of activities within and by an organization represents both movement within the possibility space and an enactment of how it defines the adjacent possible. In the interplay between language and activity, one finds both meaning and tension. Not only must organizations act, but their understanding of those actions—their sense-making—must be coherent if identity is to be preserved.

Weick, in his 1995 work on sense-making, notes that "as ways of talking and believing proliferate, new features of organizations are noticed." New features of the organizations' environments are surely noticed as well. The use of metaphor, in as simple a form as naming a situated activity, is a *generative* process. Any given label is also an invitation to see an object as if it were something else; through the resonance of possible connotations, new contextual meaning can be created. Word choice is thus a fundamental tool for the manager whose role is to shape and create contexts in which appropriate forms of self-organization can occur.

Complexity science words and models give new tools to business leaders. By actively seeking to guide language choice, managers can influence the perceptions and actions of the remaining members of the organization. The question is, which words? The key lies in remembering that the concept is of *word choice in usage,* and, as such, both "choice" and "usage" are important. These observations open the door for *leadership through languaging*—through word choice in usage (c.f. Pondy, 1976; Piccardo et al., 1990). Leaders' effectiveness lies in their ability to make activity *meaningful* for those they lead. They do this not by changing behavior, but by giving others a sense of understanding about what they are doing. Jay Conger, writing in Academy of Management Executive (1991), notes, "It is important that business leaders see their role as meaning makers. They must pick and choose from the rough materials of reality to construct pictures of great possibilities.... In the choice of words, values, and beliefs, you as a leader craft reality."

The adoption of complexity science terms into the day-to-day lingo of corporate managers is much more than a Wittgensteinian "language game" (c.f. Astley and Zammuto, 1992). Word choice in usage delimits possibility space and helps to determine the adjacent possible. Thus, it is an active process with real consequences and not just a symbolic toy. Management must deal with the consequences of languaging, and it is the managers' choice whether or not to do so in a purposeful manner. What complexity science metaphors do for an organization is give its members access to both new words and new possibilities for action. With the access to new actions comes the potential for new identity. The most prominent example of this is Monsanto, which not only adopted complexity science lingo but also reorganized the entire company around it.

Experience teaches us that thought does not express itself in words, but rather realizes itself in them. A word in context means both more and less than, the same word in isolation: more, because it acquires new context; less, because its meaning is limited and narrowed by the context. The sense of a word... changes in different minds and situations and is almost unlimited. It is not merely the content of a word that changes, but the way reality is generated and reflected in a word. (Vygotsky, 1986)

Monsanto's chairman, Robert Shapiro, grabbed hold of complexity science concepts and, in the immortal words of Microsoft, chose to embrace and extend. The result was a spin-off of Monsanto's chemical businesses and a headfirst rush into becoming the largest biotech company in the world.

In an ever-changing world, managers and organizational members alike are faced with daily challenges to maintaining identity, coherence, and purpose. Organizational science must address such challenges. Phil Anderson (1996), in Organization Science's call for papers for a special issue on complexity, noted: "Organizational scholars seldom come to grips with non-linear phenomena. Instead, we tend to model phenomena as if they were linear in order to make them tractable, and we tend to model aggregate behavior as if it is produced by individual entities which all exhibit average behavior." Bill McKelvey in his recent work (1998) notes:

Organization science must define organizational *microstates* in addition to defining the nature of aggregate behavior. For physicists, particles and microstates are one and the same—the microstates of physical matter are atomic particles and subparticles. For chemists and biologists, microstates are, respectively, molecules and biomolecules. For organization scientists, microstates are defined as *discrete random behavioral process events*.... The manner in which these kinds of activities are *exactly* carried out from one day to another, or from one person to another, or in one organization or another, is uninteresting to most organization scientists. The question is, should we assume they are all uniform or random.... Would we expect all people on all loading docks to inspect pallets exactly the same way or all software response persons to open all calls exactly the same way? Probably not—people, loading docks, product, software, customers, and so on, all differ...

Those studying aggregate firm behavior increasingly have difficulty holding to the traditional uniformity assumption about human behavior. Psychologists have studied individual differences in firms for decades (Staw, 1991). Experimental economists have found repeatedly that individuals seldom act as consistent rational actors (Hogarth and Reder, 1987; Camerer, 1995). Phenomenologists, social constructionists, and interpretists have discovered that individual actors in firms have unique interpretations of the phenomenal world, unique attributions of causality to events surrounding them, and unique interpretations, social constructions, and sense-makings of others' behaviors they observe (Silverman, 1971; Burrell and Morgan, 1979; Weick, 1979, 1995; Reed and Hughes, 1992; Chia, 1995, 1996). Although the effects of institutional contexts on organizational members are acknowledged (Zucker, 1988; Scott, 1995), and the effects of social pressure and information have a tendency to move members toward more uniform norms, values, and perceptions (Homans, 1950), there are still strong forces remaining to steer people toward idiosyncratic behavior in organizations and the idiosyncratic conduct of organizational processes.

In those idiosyncratic differences lie what makes an organization. To study such microstates is to study the very makeup of complex systems. Bruce Henderson, the late founder of BCG, was fond of quoting Jay Forrester: "While most people understand first-order effects, few deal well with second- and third-order effects. Unfortunately, virtually everything interesting in business lies in fourth-order effects and beyond" (Stern and Stalk, 1998). The future of organization science lies in Forrester's fourth-order effects and in McKelvey's microstates. If we wish to understand organizations and what makes them what they are, complexity science is perhaps not only our most potent tool but at present may be our only tool.

REFERENCES

Alvesson, M. (1990). "Organization, from Substance to Image?" *Organization Studies*, Vol. 11, No. 3, 373–394.

Alvesson, M. (1995). *Management of Knowledge-Intensive Companies*. Berlin and New York: Walter De Gruyter.

Anderson, P. (1996). Call for papers by *Organization Science*. Posted on the Internet.

Arnold, J. (1996). *Emergent Complexity: The Evolution of Intermediate Societies*. London: International Monographs in Prehistory.

Astley, W. (1985). "Administrative Science as Socially Constructed Truth." *Administrative Science Quarterly*, Vol. 30, 497–513.

Astley, W. and Zammuto, R. (1992). "Organization Science, Managers, and Language Games." *Organization Science*, Vol. 3, No. 4, 443–474.

Barton, S. (1994). "Chaos, Self-Organization, and Psychology." *American Psychologist*, Vol. 49, No.1 (January), 514.

Bar-Yam, Y. (1997). *Dynamics of Complex Systems*. Reading, MA: Addison-Wesley.

Bechtel, W. and Richardson, R. (1993). *Discovering Complexity*. Princeton, NJ: Princeton University Press.

Berger, P. and Luckmann, T. (1966). *The Social Construction of Reality*. New York: Doubleday.

Burrell, G. and Morgan, G. (1979). *Sociological Paradigms and Organizational Analysis*. London: Heinemann.

Camerer, C. (1995). "Individual Decision Making." In J.H. Kagel and A.E. Roth (Eds.), *The Handbook of Experimental Economics*. Princeton, NJ: Princeton University Press, 587–703.

Carr, C. (1996). *Choice, Chance, and Organizational Change: Practical Insights from Evolution for Business Leaders and Thinkers*. New York: AMACOM.

Casti, J. (1995). *Complexification, Explaining a Paradoxical World through the Science of Surprise*. New York: Harper Perennial.

Casti, J. (1997). *Would Be Worlds*. New York: John Wiley and Sons.

Chia, R. (1995). "From Modern to Postmodern Organizational Analysis." *Organization Studies*, Vol. 16, No. 4, 579–604.

Chia, R. (1996). *Organizational Analysis as Deconstructive Practice*. Berlin: Walter De Gruyter.

Churchman, C. (1967). "Wicked Problems." *Management Science*, Vol. 4, No. 14, B141–142.

Cilliers, P. (1999). *Complexity and Postmodernism: Understanding Complex Systems*. London: Routledge.

Cohen, J. and Stewart, I. (1994). *The Collapse of Chaos: Discovering Simplicity in a Complex World.* New York: Penguin.

Comfort, L. (1994). "Self-Organization in Complex Systems." *Journal of Public Administration Research and Theory,* Vol. 4, No. 3, 393–410.

Conger, J. (1991). "Inspiring Others, the Language of Leadership," *Academy of Management Executive,* Vol. 5, No. 1, 31–45.

Connell, A. and Nord, W. (1996). "Infiltration of Organization Science by Uncertainty and Values." *Journal of Applied Behavioral Science,* Vol. 32, No. 4, 407–427.

Crossan, M., et al. (1996). "The Improvising Organization, Where Planning Meets Opportunity." *Organizational Dynamics* (March).

Gergen, K. and Thatchenkery, T. (1996). "Organization Science as Social Construction, Postmodern Potentials." *Journal of Applied Behavioral Science,* Vol. 32, No. 4, 356–377.

Gleick, J. (1987). *Chaos.* London: Sphere.

Guastello, S. (1995). *Chaos, Catastrophe and Human Affairs.* Mahwah, NJ: Lawrence Erlbaum Associates.

Hatch, M. and Tsoukas, H. (1997). "Complex Thinking about Organizational Complexity, the Appeal of a Narrative Approach to Organizational Theory." Paper presented at the AMA meeting, Boston.

Hogarth, R. M. and Reder, M. W. (Eds.). (1987). *Rational Choice: The Contrast between Economics and Psychology.* Chicago: University of Chicago Press.

Homans, G. C. (1950). *The Human Group.* New York: Harcourt.

Horgan, J. (1995). "From Complexity to Perplexity." *Scientific American,* June, 104–109.

Jacobson and Jacques (1997). "Destabilizing the Field, Poststructuralist Knowledge-Making Strategies in a Postindustrialist Era." *Journal of Management Inquiry,* Vol. 6, No. 1, 42–59.

Kauffman, S. (1993). *The Origins of Order: Self Organization and Selection in Evolution.* Oxford: Oxford University Press.

Kauffman, S. (1995). *At Home in the Universe.* Oxford: Oxford University Press.

Kauffman, S. (1996). "Investigations." Santa Fe Institute Working Paper #96–08–072.

Kellert, S. (1995). "When Is the Economy Not like the Weather? The Problem of Extending Chaos Theory to the Social Sciences." In A. Albert (Ed.), *Chaos and Society.* Amsterdam: IOS Press.

Kelly, K. (1994). *Out of Control.* London: Fourth Estate.

Lakoff, G. and Johnson, M. (1980, 1995). *Metaphors We Live By.* Chicago: University Of Chicago Press.

Lane, D. and Maxfield, R. (1995). "Foresight Complexity and Strategy." Santa Fe Institute Working Paper #95–12–106.

Langlois, R. and Everett, M. (1992). "Complexity, Genuine Uncertainty, and the Economics of Organization." *Human Systems Management,* Vol. 11, 67–75.

Leary, D. (Ed.). (1990). *Metaphors in the History of Psychology.* New York: Cambridge University Press.

Levy, D. (1994). "Chaos Theory and Strategy, Theory, Application, and

Managerial Implications." *Strategic Management Journal*, Vol. 15 (Summer), 167–178.

Loye, D. and Eisler, R. (1987). "Chaos and Transformation, Implications of Nonequilibrium Theory for Social Science and Society." *Behavioral Science*, Vol. 32, 53–65.

McKelvey, W. (1998). "Thwarting Faddism at the Edge of Chaos: On the Epistemology of Complexity Research." Presented at the Workshop on Complexity and Organization, Brussels, Belgium, June 89.

Mitchell, W. (1994). *The Reconfigured Eye: Visual Truth in the Post-Photographic Era*. Cambridge: MIT Press.

Overman, E. (1996). "The New Science of Management, Chaos and Quantum Theory and Method." *Journal of Public Administration Research and Theory*, Vol. 6, No. 1, 75–89.

Petzinger, T. (1996a). "The Front Lines." July 12, *Wall Street Journal*.

Petzinger, T. (1996b). "The Front Lines." October 18, *Wall Street Journal*.

Phelan, S. (1995). "From Chaos to Complexity in Strategic Planning." Paper presented to the Academy of Management 55th Annual Meeting, Vancouver, Canada.

Piccardo, C. et al. (1990). "Car Makers and Marathon Runners, in Pursuit of Culture through the Language of Leadership." In P. Gagliardi (Ed.), *Symbols and Artifacts*. Berlin: Walter De Gruyter.

Pondy, L. (1976). "Leadership Is a Language Game." In M. Mccall and M. Lombardo (Eds.), *Leadership, Where Else Can We Go?* Greensboro, NC: Center for Creative Leadership.

Reed, M. and Hughes, M. (Eds.). (1992). *Rethinking Organization: New Directions in Organization Theory and Analysis*. London: Sage.

Scott, W. R. (1995). *Institutions and Organizations*. Thousand Oaks, CA: Sage.

Silverman, D. (1971). *The Theory of Organizations*. New York: Basic Books.

Stacey, R. (1996). *Complexity and Creativity in Organizations*. San Francisco: Berrett Koehler.

Staw, B. M. (Ed.). (1991). *Psychological Dimensions of Organizational Behavior*. Englewood Cliffs, NJ: Prentice-Hall.

Stern, C. and Stalk, G. (1998). *Perspectives on Strategy: From the Boston Consulting Group*. New York: John Wiley and Sons.

Stewart, I. and Cohen, J. (1997). *Figments of Reality: The Evolution of the Curious Mind*. Cambridge: Cambridge University Press.

Streufert, S. and Swezey, R. (1986). *Complexity, Managers, and Organizations*. London: Academic Press.

Thietart, R. and Forgues, B. (1995). "Chaos Theory and Organization." *Organization Science*, Vol. 6, No. 1, 19–31.

Thompson, J. (1967). *Organizations in Action, Social Science Bases of Administrative Theory*. New York: McGraw-Hill.

Vygotsky, L. (1962, 1986). *Thought and Language*. Edited by A. Kozulin. Cambridge: MIT Press.

Waldrop, M. (1992). *Complexity*. New York: Simon and Schuster.

Warglien, M. (1995). "Hierarchical Selection and Organizational Adaptation." *Industrial and Corporate Change*, Vol. 4, No. 1, 161–186.

Weick, K. (1979). *The Social Psychology of Organizing*. Reading: Addison-Wesley.

Weick, K. (1995). *Sensemaking in Organizations.* Thousand Oaks, CA: Sage Publications.

Westhoff, F., Yarbrough, B. and Yarbrough, R. (1996). "Complexity, Organization, and Stuart Kauffman's *The Origins of Order." Journal of Economic Behavior and Organization*, Vol. 29, No. 1.

Wheatley, M. (1992). *Leadership and the New Science: Learning About Organization from an Orderly Universe.* San Francisco: Berrett-Koehler.

Zucker, L. G. (1988). *Institutional Patterns and Organizations: Culture and Environment.* Cambridge, MA: Ballinger.

Chapter 3

Complexity—More than a Fad?

Tom Petzinger

Will complexity become a management fad?

Among the authors in this volume, I am qualified to answer few questions beside this: I am, after all, not a scientist. I never spent five minutes in grad school. I never wrote a scholarly word in my life. But I do see a lot of different kinds of business, up close and personal, every week of the year. For 20 years I've made my living talking to managers, owners, and entrepreneurs. The biologist Steve Jones (whose work you may know), once commented that "reality is all about getting your feet wet. The truth about snails, or anything else, is in the muck." Well, I make my living traipsing through the muck of modern management.

Some of the fears about faddism are well founded. As a category of professional people, managers are as vulnerable to fad and fashion as any teenager I've ever known. You hear people chide management for adopting the "flavor of the month." That's putting it generously. Managers are like my teenage daughter, who has an uncanny ability to forecast the very lipstick shade that will be popular in her school group *that day*, or my nephew, who never fails to realize when the hottest style in the Nike catalog is about to turn cold. Part of the reason that managers are so vulnerable to this behavior is that they need a constant stream of repairs and fixes and maintenance to hold together their mechanistic view of the world and of their place in it.

Those of you who are about my age may remember a cutting remark that was popular on our grade school playgrounds: "Where were you when the brains were passed out?" Well, we might say to business, "Where were you when the postmodern age began?"

The story of the twentieth century is one of qualities taking their place alongside quantities, relationships taking their place with objects, ambiguity taking its place with order. This holds across practically the entire spectrum of human intellectual development. This shift made possible the work of everyone from Einstein to Picasso, from Neils Bohr to George Balanchine, from Richard Feynman to Fats Domino. The twentieth century is when nearly all of educated civilization discovered that there was no such thing as "one best way."

But business slept through every minute of the postmodern awakening. Even as it was toppled from unassailability in science, Newtonian mechanics remained firmly lodged as the mental model of management. Jobs were divided ever more narrowly, turning workers into so many tiny objects performing mindless, repetitive tasks; the whole, after all, was always equal to the sum of its parts. We all know how history's first management consultant, Frederick Taylor, used to tell workers, "You are not supposed to think... there are other people paid for thinking around here."

Before long, the mainframe computer accelerated the centralization of information and control. Economics departments and MBA programs taught quantitative methods that treated the workplace and marketplace as clockwork: pay a seamstress another penny, and she will produce five more pieces per hour. Each $1 million in national advertising equals so many share points on the Nielsen scale. Management's job was assembling the right pieces, pointing them toward the optimum, and then making sure the system never wavered.

This stuff worked in a simple world. It worked, for instance, when there were still economies of scale to be cashed in through gargantuan size and central control. The economist R.H. Coase (who ultimately won the Nobel for this work) proposed in 1937 that the corporation existed to eliminate transaction costs that would otherwise exist between individual entrepreneurs. In a wildly hypothetical moment, Coase went on to say, "In the absence of transaction costs, there is no economic basis for the existence of the firm."

We're rapidly approaching that point.

Newtonianism worked when all the variables in a system could be controlled. But beginning in a big way in the 1960s, modern social and economic life defied all attempts at control because it was simply too complex. It was too sensitively dependent on initial conditions, as the chaostructurists say. The linear had turned nonlinear. Newtonianism worked when the principal constraint in economic society was the ability of a few producers to supply society's needs; it worked less well when the principal constraint in economic society was determining what the consumer wanted. Newtonianism worked when the principal organizing force in economic society was capital and less well when creativity took its place.

But while other domains of intellectual life were making the transition to postmodernism—while Gainsborough turned into Picasso, Freud into Maslow, and Beethoven into the Beatles—what was management doing? It was searching for the bailing wire and woodglue necessary to hold together the Newtonian paradigm. Newtonian mechanics had conditioned managements to believe that following the same set of steps would produce the identical outcome on every attempt. "Follow these steps every time, and you will get the same result." Thus, holding together Newtonian management involved a search for new steps, new methodologies, new optima, especially by consulting firms. Those methodologies that climbed past a certain point on the s-curve of diffusion became the lipstick shade of the day. And that helps explain why management is so vulnerable to fads.

So where does this leave complexity? Complexity is trendy. Complexity does seem to resonate with the times. (My wife recently spotted an ad in a fashion magazine for a new scent. It was called Chaos.) Yes, business will discover complexity. Business *is* discovering complexity. One *Wall Street Journal* columnist was so bold as to proclaim the beauty of complexity as one of the major corporate trends for 1998.

But for all those managements looking simply to apply a new layer of lipstick, I am delighted to say that complexity is likely to very quickly prove disappointing.

Complexity is a way of describing what occurs in a system. Complexity describes the world *as it is*. By its very nature complexity does not predict an outcome. Any management seeking to use complexity as a tool to obtain particular preordained results will abandon the concept very quickly. For this we should be highly grateful.

I think it is imperative that we bear in mind this fundamental, deeply rooted limitation of complexity as we begin our deliberations here. Complexity is not about adding behaviors; it is about removing them. It is not the addition of another program; instead, it signals a retreat from programs. As I've heard Ken Baskin (see Chapter 6) say, it is not about reengineering, but deengineering.

I don't mean to suggest that complexity tells us simply to step back and observe the dynamics of dissipation in organizations—to let the chips fall entirely where they may, as it were. Complexity, after all, does not necessarily require us to tolerate complication. Liberty is not licentiousness. Self-organization is not anarchy. As Kauffman and a few others have taught us, good outcomes may emerge solely through chance or solely through selection, but better outcomes emerge when these processes occur within good design principles. Complexity also begs us to think about infrastructure in our organizations—about the rates of connectedness and the design principles most apt to nudge our organizations toward the emergence of favorable outcomes.

I think we should take some encouragement from the fact that complexity thinking *is* being put to worthy use in business and other organizations right now. I'm not talking about academic exercises in game theory. Nor am I talking about the use of complexity-based modeling and synthesis tools such as genetic algorithms, as powerful as these might be. Rather, I'm saying that an intellectual orientation toward the virtues of complexity thinking is occurring at all level of scale in business organizations—including at the levels of greatest potential value, which is the human level.

I see the evidence of this practically by the week. Not long ago I walked into the office of Robert Shapiro, the chairman of Monsanto Corporation, a major chemical company. On his credenza sat a dozen copies of *Out of Control* by Kevin Kelly. Shapiro distributes the book at every chance. Can you imagine: a Fortune 100 chief executive officer giving his colleagues a book called *Out of Control?*

I saw another small piece of evidence in a tiny town called Gloucester, Ohio, in a century-old flatiron building along a lone set of railroad tracks, where the owner of a company called Frog Ranch Foods had a copy of *At Home in the Universe* sitting behind his desk.

I have a longstanding interest in Boeing Corporation, which, as many of you may know is now caught in the throes of trying to ramp up production of the most complicated product on earth—a jetliner. And Boeing has more or less acknowledged that it has surpassed the point at which it can control that complexity. As a result, one now hears wide-open discussion of biological organization metaphors around the Boeing organization these days.

I see many, many consultants and practitioners helping to foster better organizations by holding a complexity lens to the eyes of their clients—and it is such a delight to anticipate that many of them may be reading this book.

But the best evidence I see for the ripeness of these concepts is the work of owners, executives, and entrepreneurs who use complexity thinking in their organizations without realizing that there is such a thing as complexity thinking—and this, trust me, is a very large group indeed.

When historians recount this period in economic history, they will see that a new economy began to emerge in the early 1990s. I don't mean just globalization, though, of course, that's a big part of it. An extraordinary convergence of forces occurred in the early 1990s that ripened the conditions for economic emergence. One factor was the deep recession triggered by war in the Persian Gulf. This recession introduced a new concept to business and a new word to the vernacular: downsizing. This time the victims were disproportionately managers, people who had occupied precincts of ambition. Like a dandelion gone to seed, the corporate world released these energetic and well-capitalized progeny to the wind.

Just as economic pressures once created larger and larger organizations (with all the problems that accompany gargantuan size), a new set of pressures began pushing business in the opposite direction. In lobby directories and Yellow Pages, a teeming census of small companies began filling niches of ever-narrowing size. At nearly every level of scale—across product lines, industries, indeed entire nations—the small became more numerous and more specialized. In short order, our economy became more diverse—composed of a greater number of smaller agents.

Long-building demographic changes, meanwhile, worked in parallel with the economic restructuring. Baby boomers—the best-educated and most independent generation in world history, raised on Dr. Spock, demand feeding, and Jefferson Airplane—attained the ranks of middle management in great numbers. Raised to "question authority," as a popular bumper sticker once urged, the boomers continued this practice even after the authority was theirs. (As the social commentator Brent Staples has noted, "Those 20-year-olds who danced naked at Woodstock did not just leave the planet when they grew up.")

The significance of this demographic trend cannot be overstated: the agents in our economic system had become more truly autonomous agents.

Meanwhile, a nascent intellectual movement called "systems thinking" took a few modest steps toward validating the retreat from Newtonianism. Also, in 1991, new economic and cultural forces braided with technological forces through the release of Windows—a simple disk of code that endowed the kludgey personal computer with the liberating simplicity of a kitchen appliance. Just as all those downsized executives were thrown into their spare bedrooms to pioneer in the new economy, an easy-to-use tool met them there, a back-office-in-a-box as well as a medium for looking out on the rest of the world. Thus, there were not only more agents and more autonomous agents—they were now connected to one another.

Let me conclude by citing what is the more convincing display yet of the advent of a new economy and of an inchoate new paradigm in management. It is the very existence of the institution that brought many of us together: complex-M.

The complexity-in-management mail list is continually revealing episodes that enlighten our understanding of complexity in organizations. We read of real cases in real organizations. We hear from consultants, practitioners, academics, and the occasional journalist. In time we will have more news of such breakthroughs to share.

I wonder if anyone else shares my disbelief and excitement at what an extraordinary gathering this is. Think about it. In the space of 18 months or so, this group, the members of complex-M, has formed an entire microsociety linked by nothing except acquaintance with a few concepts and a self-organizing enterprise called the Internet. There are argument, debate, celebration, collaboration, exultation, and (as Stuart Kauffman might point out) ex-adaptation in this list almost every day.

It is emotional as well as intellectual. It is social as well as personal (sometimes deeply personal). Sometimes it's on-point, sometimes it's wildly off-point, but it's damn near always interesting.

When our group gathered in Toronto to first meet in person, among the other interesting things we learned was the effect of "full bandwidth" communication in a society heretofore limited by narrow bandwidth. We learned that the properties of self-organization unfold differently when people are in the same room as well as in the same mail list. The dynamics of the mail list changed as a consequence of seeing and hearing the people we had mostly been reading. We saw the proof of the modern-day verity that nobody is as smart as everybody.

This book is an outcome of that first real-time gathering of what had been a virtual society. In sharing our insights with you, the reader, I hope that we will, in some small way, advance the state of this art and the strength of this science—in a way that helps us provide theory and substance to a new way of managing that is trying very hard to take hold.

With theory and substance behind it—no, complexity is not a fad.

Chapter 4

Complexity, Computational Ability, and the Corporation of the Future

Arnold J. Wytenburg

Corporations' ability to keep pace with the changes affecting the modern business world is a reflection of their capacity to make sense of the complexity that simultaneously constitutes the environment in which they exist while defining the extent, nature, form, and behavior of their participation within that environment. This modern market environment is what the "new sciences" define as dynamic, complex, nonlinear, and self-organizing—such are the conditions under which the ways and means of leadership, governance, management, and production will be measured in the corporation of the future. To perform successfully under these circumstances, corporations must possess the ability to acquire, develop, and apply knowledge within the context of a market environment characterized by a principally different class of systemic behavior than they are accustomed to dealing with.

In the emerging future, corporations will be required to adopt a substantially more sophisticated and complete means of understanding the extent, nature, form, and behavior of their market environment at its most fundamental level. The backdrop against which this capacity must be developed requires the ability to perceive the corporation and the market environment in which it participates from a whole system perspective. When seen from a whole system perspective, corporations appear not as concrete, well-defined, structurally stable entities but, rather, as members of a dynamic, simultaneously interacting, continuously evolving system of systems.

The implications are profound: from a whole system perspective, the very notion of why, when, where, and how we draw boundaries to circumscribe corporations must be fundamentally rethought and redefined. Together, the science of complexity theory, the principles of emergent behavior, and the discipline of systems thinking can enable organizations to see and understand a corporation simultaneously as comprising systems, as being a system in its own right, and as being part of a larger system that, taken together, constitute a market environment that is inherently complex, volatile, and unpredictable. The capacity to perceive and interact with the market environment on this basis is the measure of a corporation's computational ability.

During the past decade, the subject of change has become the central theme underscoring virtually every aspect of economic endeavor. Consequently, most corporations are now well aware that an age of significant change is unfolding, that it is likely to continue to do so for some time, and that virtually every aspect of organizational activity will be impacted regardless of where it occurs or who is involved.

Failure to respond accordingly may very well result in the failure of many organizations. Few of today's corporate leaders, directors, managers, and workers can attest to any substantive grasp on the priorities effecting a meaningful response. Unfortunately, a history of past success does little more than create a false sense of security. The nature of the change occurring in today's social, cultural, political, and economic environments is fundamentally different from anything corporations have previously faced—a viable response to an unfamiliar problem is unlikely to bear a familiar earmark.

The change that is currently unfolding is a function of the exponential growth in information that marks a trend emerging at the end of the last century, gaining momentum following the World War II, and dominating social, cultural, political, and economic agendas since the early 1960s. The complexity introduced into the market environment by this growth in information density has reached the stage where traditional means of designing, managing, and operating corporations must be radically altered or, in many instances, completely redefined.

As daunting a proposal as this may seem, the task comprises an even greater challenge than is obvious at first glance: a new model for facilitating organizational success under these circumstances does not yet exist. As corporations face an unknown future, they must lay down the path in front of them as they transform their most basic notions of social, cultural, political, economic, and organizational endeavor.

INFORMATION AND THE KNOWLEDGE ERA

Twice during the past millennium, the market environment underwent substantial change. The first instance marked the transformation of a predominantly agrarian society into an industrial society. The introduction of technology led to the onset of the machine age and marked the beginning of a transition to what would eventually be called the industrial era. Land was no longer the critical factor of production: ultimately, success came to those possessing the costly technologies available only to corporations with access to financial capital. The most basic rules of organizational, economic, political, cultural, and social behavior were altered forever.

The second instance is only now beginning to emerge in its full force. The current wave of change marks an epochal transition equally as radical as what led up to the industrial era. In much the same manner that the machine age marked the start and end of a transition from an agrarian to an industrial society, the so-called information age marks just such a shift from the waning industrial era into the knowledge era of the future. Serving as a transition period between past and future, the dynamics of the information age are establishing an underlying matrix of information that simultaneously creates and describes the nature and behavior of the market environment. From this matrix emerge the attributes that will ultimately serve to characterize the extent, nature, form, and behavior of the unfolding knowledge era.

The agrarian era posed little serious demand upon humankind with respect to the accumulation and processing of information. Rather, it called for efficiency primarily regarding the utilization of land and its various constituencies. Human endeavor was fundamentally oriented around direct, tangible realities: land, crops, livestock—what you saw was what you got. The only "mysteries" that life presented were attributed to the gods of the day and, even then, tended to exhibit certain reliable characteristics—accumulated experience allowed humankind to predict with sufficient accuracy the cycles of the seasons, weather patterns, and life cycles of the crops and animals under its husbandry. Survival and success were substantially a direct product of diligence in the application of physical human effort according to the tenets of experience. Arable land was, for all intents and purposes, the most important factor of production, followed by labor as the means by which land could be leveraged. Given the relative scarcity of arable land versus the wide availability of labor, the landowner was the dominant force affecting the human condition.

The dominant proxy for understanding performance during the agrarian era was output. The degree to which production could be maximized within the context of limited access to arable land was the principal concern of agrarian society. The innate human desire for improvement focused both Landowner and Labor of the day on increasing output under these circumstances. These efforts, in turn, led to the development of tools and processes, referred to here generically as technologies, capable of improving the utility of land and increasing the reliability with which outputs could be produced under the given constraints of nature.

Under the dynamics of latter-day agrarian society, goods and services were typically traded for each other within the context of a physical marketplace on an as-needed and when-needed basis. Initially, emerging technologies were also traded within the same marketplace. Rather than trading grain for meat or labor for domicile, agrarians exchanged their goods and services for the technologies of production.

Within acceptable parameters of predictability, agrarians' land, crops, and livestock represented a distinct and tangible reality, the individual and collective value of which was easily rendered as a function of their direct and unequivocal utility in the production of food, shelter, clothing, and other principal staples. Thus, during the agrarian era, movement of these outputs became the universal proxy for simultaneously understanding the nature and dynamics of human interaction as well as the environmental extent of those interactions. Under that scenario, technology possessed little inherent value when considered in terms of its direct role in the production of outputs. Rather, technology was a production factor subordinate to land and labor, its value realizable only by virtue of the efficiencies it could facilitate in support of direct production.

However, as technologies grew in sophistication and capacity, they also became more specialized, more fragile, more stationary, more costly, and ultimately, less readily exchangeable in the then-classic sense. Many technologies came to be valued at multiples of goods and services far in excess of the immediate trading priorities of their vendors thus rendering the framework of the primary market restrictive. Trade in the technological means of production began to differentiate itself from the simple exchange of outputs by increasingly necessitating the use of an intermediary exchange mechanism that possessed an infinite shelf life and that was universally exchangeable. The parallel development of more efficient means of production and the dynamics of what became monetary exchange ultimately contributed to the development of a state where the acquisition cost of viable technologies frequently exceeded the financial capacity of labor.

With the monetization of exchange in the marketplace, the fundamental dynamics of agrarian society were altered. While production and exchange of outputs happened in real time and real space, technology transfer behaved in ways that transcended the here-and-now dynamics of that historical, premodern marketplace. The growing cost of technology placed a strain on the prevailing systems of valuation and exchange, which were based primarily on the relationships between land, labor, and the seasonal verities of nature. The need for increasing amounts of monetary wherewithal, ultimately followed by the need to amortize technology resources over periods of time that exceeded the scope of traditional agrarian cycles of production and exchange, created a new type of market dynamic. Thus emerged the concept of a fiscal life cycle and, along with it, the notion of a marketplace that was no longer dominated exclusively by the relationship between landowner and labor.

In short, the marketplace started to behave in a manner independent of the terracentric constraints that defined agrarian sociocultural and socioeconomic behavior. Rather, its dynamics began to follow a rhythm echoing the cycles of technological evolution, thereby foretelling a fundamental shift in the underlying dynamics of the human condition.

As the role and importance of technology expanded, the machine age became firmly entrenched. Subsequently, the focus of human endeavor shifted from that of pursuing access to arable land to that of acquiring the means necessary to underwrite the technologies of production. Defined by the relative scarcity of financial capital, an entirely new market began to emerge, devoted exclusively to transactions focused on optimizing the efficiency with which that financial capital was employed.

Essentially, this emerging market directed its favor to those who demonstrated the most efficient utilization of financial capital in the production of tangible outputs. In exchange, these efficient producers returned to their financiers a premium for the use of their capital. Ultimately, the nature and content of these transactions were almost exclusively monetary, deviations serving merely to mitigate uncommon risks or eventualities. This market eventually became known simply as the capital market, those individuals who traded there bearing the monikers of industrialist and capitalist.

The formalization of a viable capital market signaled the culmination of the machine age—thus was executed the final stroke marking humankind's transition from an agrarian to an industrial society. Landowner and labor were no longer the thesis and antithesis that together established the basis upon which the extent, nature, form, and structure of agrarian society had been founded. In their place were industrialists wielding powerful technologies capable of transforming input resources into output goods and services with unprecedented efficiency and capitalists providing the financial means necessary to facilitate the development, acquisition, and utilization of those technologies. Thus was born the industrial era.

The industrialization of society coupled with the effects of population growth as well as sociocultural and sociopolitical expansionism placed increasing demand on the relationships among each and every constituent of the industrial era, yet no relationship played as significant a role as that between industrialist and capitalist. The availability of financial capital had rapidly become the single most critical factor of success in the industrial era. The eclipse of the agrarian era marked the occurrence of a fundamental shift in the most basic orientation of the human agenda. In the industrial era, humankind exalted those who held sway over financial capital and rewarded them based on their ability to wield that capital in a manner that led to the highest monetary return from its deployment. One needed simply to note the movement of capital as the universal proxy for understanding the orientation, structure, and dynamics of the market environment during this era.

Together with the emergence of a capital market, the concept of the modern corporation was born to facilitate the effective and efficient performance of the relationship between industrialist and capitalist. The placement of large amounts of financial capital presented both parties with substantial risks and responsibilities. Capitalists required that industrialists' obligations to them survive any and all unforeseen or untoward circumstances. In turn, industrialists required a means by which risk could be mitigated in such a way as the potential burden was not so onerous that it may altogether discourage their participation in the market environment. Consequently, an intermediary legal fiction was created to serve as a means of simultaneously cushioning both capitalist and industrialist from potential negative consequences yet allowing each the freedom and latitude to pursue their respective undertakings in good faith: the modern Corporation was that entity.

The corporation represented an objective, contractual scenario that spelled out the nature of the intentions, rights, and obligations existing between capitalist and industrialist. Efforts at monitoring and directing the increasingly more complicated relationships among these parties created a need for corporations to document and distribute certain facts of their existence and performance.

The greater the degree of interdependency that developed among the membership of this so-called industrial economy, the greater the demand for information became. Corporations found themselves at the center of this demand, being forced to expend substantial quantities of scarce, costly capital resources in support of their information-processing capacity. The development of the modern corporation was accompanied by the need to acquire, process, administer, and report information. Within the very essence of the change that brought about the industrial era was written the signature trace of what would bring about its eclipse and, in so doing, signal the beginning of the transition to the knowledge era. Thus began a new period of transition presently referred to as the information age.

As the information age progresses, the primary content of virtually every interaction in which corporations participate has become substantially comprised or been dependent upon information in some form or other. Even traditional, tangible products as simple as bricks and mortar possess an increasingly larger and more significant information aspect. No activity within any modern corporation can be accomplished without information: information has literally become the stuff of corporate life.

In much the same way that the increasing importance of capital marked the progress of a transition from an agrarian to an industrial society, so the increasingly more critical role of information marks a paradigm shift that foreshadows the imminent arrival of a new era. The extent, nature, form, and behavior of virtually every aspect of contemporary social, cultural, political, and economic effort are rapidly and irrevocably shifting to a paradigm of human endeavor based substantially on the capacity for accessing and making sense of the increasing flood of information overtaking the modern world.

In the agrarian era, the movement of direct goods and services provided a proxy for understanding the performance of the market environment. In the industrial era, this proxy was replaced by the movement of financial capital as the universal means of understanding the dynamics of postagrarian existence. In the knowledge era, the ebb and flow of information will fill this role.

Every transaction undertaken by corporations today is reflected in the tacit and explicit "signature trace" of information that is created, consumed, modified, embodied, and eclipsed by that transaction. By considering information in abstraction—rather than by seeking to understand merely its content—by seeing it as a whole, as a system of information that simultaneously embodies both "text" and "context," it becomes possible to interpolate an understanding of the orientation, organization, and dynamics of the environment from which that information emerges. In essence, it is possible for the informational signature traces representative of the dynamics of human endeavor to serve as a substantially complete and accurate proxy of the extent, nature, form, and behavior of the postindustrial market environment of the future.

CHANGE, COMPLEXITY, AND COMPUTATIONAL ABILITY

It has been speculated that the amount of information in our world has nearly doubled over the course of the past six or seven years. In other words, since the early 1990s, we have created or discovered as many items of information as in the period from when humankind first developed consciousness until just six or seven years ago. The nature and dynamics of this phenomenon reflect themselves in the increasing pace and magnitude of change experienced throughout the market environment.

During the past 100 years, the means of widespread, low-cost transportation and communication emerged, compressing business cycles, redefining sociocultural and geopolitical boundaries, rapidly increasing the intensity of competitive interaction. Consequently, contemporary corporations have produced and accumulated more information than their predecessors could even begin to have imagined possible. The production of increasing volumes of information spawned truly monumental advances in the development of the disciplines and technologies necessary to make them manageable. But with each advance in corporations' capacity for managing information, the market environment responded by creating even more information.

From the mid-1950s to the present day, corporations have been engaged in a dramatically escalating relationship between information and technology that has supposedly rendered them more "informed" than at any other time in history. Paradoxically, however, while information continues to increase in plenitude by the microsecond, meaningful knowledge is rapidly becoming more scarce. Therein lies the root cause of so many of the difficulties that today's corporations face: they are adrift in a vast ocean of information from which they are increasingly less able to render any relevant utility.

With every change that occurs in the market environment, more and new information is created and accumulated, and more and new degrees of complexity develop. This pattern repeats itself endlessly and infinitely, building upon each prior instance of change, thereby increasing the information density of the market environment. Information, the complexity of its arrangement, the ambiguity of its meaning, and the volatility of its structure increase: corporations' capacity for coping is challenged. The ability to produce information is growing faster than the ability to employ it. In spite of the time, energy, and resources being expended in an effort to keep pace, most corporations are quickly reaching the limitations of their sense-making competencies—their computational ability.

Beginning at approximately the middle of the twentieth century, the translation of facts, data, and information into useful form became a critical component, if not the entire focus, of the efforts of an increasing percentage of corporations' workforce participants. As the information age moved into full swing, organizational functions, structures, and competencies were typically modified and enhanced to acknowledge this increasingly more critical aspect of doing business. New and more sophisticated technologies were developed in response to increased demand for information-processing capacity. Since the commercialization of the digital computer, hundreds of billions, possibly trillions of dollars have been invested in the development of corporations' capacity for processing information.

Yet, even the most heavily invested corporations can do little more than tread water while many thousands of the less fortunate drown in a sea of information. Why, in spite of the attention paid to information management and the unprecedented investment in supporting technologies, do organizations remain at the mercy of information? The problem lies not with corporations' capacity for information processing but, rather, with the extent of their ability to derive useful knowledge from information. That capacity is referred to here as a corporation's computational ability.

Make no mistake: computational ability and processing capacity are distinctly different concepts. A failure to recognize the difference has already caused the demise of many corporations over the past several decades, with more sure to follow. While complicated, expensive, and time-consuming, information processing is essentially little more than a mechanical, quantitatively oriented process that requires limited human intervention given today's advanced technologies. Computational ability, on the other hand, is inherently a function of human cognition, judgment, and choice. No machine in existence today, regardless of how sophisticated, can substantially demonstrate these essentially heuristic capacities.

The essential problem that corporations face as the knowledge era unfolds is not a processing challenge. Rather, it is an issue of their ability to transform information into knowledge. With the phenomenal growth of the information curve comes an exponential increase in the degree of complexity existing within the market environment. This, in turn, has the effect of substantially increasing the need for more computational ability. But coping with exponential growth in the complexity of the market environment was never considered a criterion upon which historical methods of organizational design, management, and operations were based.

Information is merely raw input that can become meaningful only when considered within the context of the situation or environment in which it has been gathered, created, and employed. Nevertheless, most corporations continue to mistakenly equate information-processing capacity with computational ability. When new information conflicts with traditional notions of market dynamics, particularly those built up over generations of familiar experience, these corporations are frequently stymied. Essentially, they lack the ability to garner sufficient contextual perspective necessary to render the information they are faced with into any meaningful form of knowledge or understanding.

All too often, corporations' ingrained organizational response to new perspectives is one of "creative dismissal" in favor of a familiar, traditional, and seemingly more rational perspective. Generally, such a response focuses on applying physical technologies aimed at improving corporations' capacity for capturing, storing, manipulating, and reporting information. This focus underscores the conventional mind-set: information is typically perceived as proprietary, limited in scope and utility, and inferior to other factors of production.

But implementing additional information-processing technologies or imposing greater administrative control merely serves to increase corporations' frustrations with the dynamics of change. When taken from this perspective, the contextualization of information is imposed by inwardly focused technological and organizational fiat rather than by being allowed to reveal itself based on the inherent dynamics of the market environment from which it emerges.

When change increases the information density of the market environment to a point where it exceeds a corporation's ability to transform information into usable knowledge, then a shortfall exists in that organization's computational ability. Such a corporation will inevitably find itself incapable of rendering the decisions necessary to survival and success within a dynamic and increasingly more complex market environment.

SENSE-MAKING IN A COMPLEX WORLD

As the pace of change within the market environment accelerates, assumptions with respect to one's points of reference within that environment are challenged. This is experienced firsthand through the failure of all but the most shortsighted of corporations' predictive devices. Consequently, corporations no longer have the luxury of confidence they once did with respect to interpreting, understanding, aligning with, and engaging the market environment. This uncertainty presents an unwelcome challenge—increasingly, it will threaten many corporations' very existence.

While change in the market environment may indeed be the basis on which corporations must act, it is not the cause of their problems: the real culprit is complexity. This complexity arises against a backdrop of constant change. As one aspect of the environment is eclipsed, new and potentially more attractive alternatives emerge, accompanied by more information and a consequent increase in complexity.

Unfortunately, many of today's corporations simply aren't up to the challenge: they weren't designed for the complexity, volatility, and uncertainty that characterize current market conditions, let alone for what the knowledge era promises to bring. The principles, priorities, and imperatives constituting the historical context upon which most modern-day corporations were founded simply don't reflect the realities of today's business environment. Furthermore, the new context evolving and unfolding around them defies efforts at perception and cognizance when considered from a vantage point rooted in the past—an entirely new way of seeing and understanding is needed.

The market environment can be envisioned to behave in much the same way as we understand a biological ecosystem to perform. An ecosystem evolves in response to changes in its component species as well as the relationships among these as they are formed, dissolved, and reformed over time. The interdependent mutuality of this evolutionary process is a natural and necessary consequence of the seemingly infinite number of influencing factors that prevail upon each other within an ecosystem. Thus, the inherent nature of an ecosystem is that it is simply not stable.

And therein lies the issue: the market environment within which today's corporations exist is also not stable. The contextual, functional, structural, and cultural imperatives that corporations face are continuously shifting, sometimes subtly, sometimes dramatically, occasionally disappearing altogether or being eclipsed through the emergence of new and often unexpected priorities.

Historically, corporations believed that precise, predictable, machinelike organizational structures and controls would lead to the single-mindedness of focus and behavior crucial to realizing the efficiencies demanded by the market environment of the day. Thus, at the onset of the industrial era, corporations were conceived as cause-and-effect machines, designed to leverage the deterministic nature of an essentially stable market environment to the express advantage of those "in control." Predictable behavior was the critical means of ensuring successful performance, typically achieved through the establishment of rigid hierarchies of command and control.

When the nature and behavior of an environment are predictable, decisions can be made once, then enacted repeatedly—processing capacity, substantially enabled by technology, becomes the principal lever of success under these circumstances. However, such mechanistically oriented approaches lack the ability to function in an environment that is ambiguous and uncertain—computational ability, essentially the capacity for exercising judgment and choice, becomes the critical success factor under these conditions.

If it was simply a matter of processing larger quantities of information, technological advances should save the day. The problem is not specifically one of dealing with the volume of information, but rather one of the increasing complexity brought about by its proliferation. With each additional increment in the volume of information, we experience a virtual order of magnitude growth in the complexity of the interrelationships that exist among discrete elements of information.

This presents a substantial challenge: traditional approaches to leadership, direction, control, and production emerged from a perspective that can only be described as being in polar opposition to what characterizes the contemporary market environment. That historical perspective evolved from a distinctly reductionist model of the world, depicting it as being machinelike, linear, predictable, and, consequently, controllable.

The change defining the dynamics of any market environment in transition does not progress at a constant pace, in any substantially repeatable manner, or in any deterministic direction. Rather, it manifests itself in fits and starts, the scope, scale, and timing of which provide little or no opportunity for easy understanding. When considered in this way, one can begin to conceive of the market environment as being fundamentally dynamic, complex, non-linear, and self-organizing. Under such circumstances, predictability and, hence, meaningful and readily achieved understanding are all but impossible beyond the immediate time frame when approached from a traditional perspective.

Scientific research shows that the greater the scope and scale of the range of complexity within a given environment, the more dense, diverse, and vibrant are the potential opportunities that exist within that environment. Translated into business terms: the more readily corporations can embrace the complexity of the market environment, the healthier and more productive they are likely to become. Conversely, the lesser the corporations' capacity for coping with complexity, the fewer are their opportunities for engaging in the competitive activities from which emerge thriving companies, markets, economies, cultures, and, ultimately, societies.

The highly volatile, unfamiliar, and uncertain nature of today's market environment is such that much of the knowledge critical to corporations' viability and success is best described as what contemporary cultural theorists refer to as "truth within the situation." Knowledge is a function of being able to understand both the relevant and discrete facts, data, and information *as well as* the relationships among them and the potential implications of those relationships. The greater the degree of complexity in an environment, the more dynamic and unpredictable that environment becomes. When this context is highly dynamic and, consequently, volatile and uncertain, the value of a given instance of knowledge is characterized as possessing a tightly limited scope of relevance and an extremely short shelf life.

As we approach the knowledge era, the historical paradigm which we have based much of our human and organizational capacity for absorbing and processing the vast quantities of information we create is simply not up to the task. Knowledge, rather than financial capital, is rapidly becoming the most critical factor of corporate viability: in a fast-paced world where little is stable or predictable, knowledge begets other factors of production far more readily than they can beget knowledge. Consequently, what was taken for granted only a few short decades ago—knowledge, and the means of its acquisition and leverage—is becoming the singularly most sought after and most important production factor in virtually every quarter of the market environment.

Expanding complexity within today's market environment will force corporations to recognize and respect a new and radically different reality from the one to which they have become accustomed. At a baseline level, the shift in imperatives accompanying the emergence of the knowledge era is forcing a new paradigm of corporate orientation, structure, and performance that differs radically from historical convention. This paradigm shift posits a fundamentally different set of organizing principles from those which corporations' prevailing business infrastructures are based.

KNOWLEDGE IN A POST-INDUSTRIAL ERA

Historically, boundary conditions, both internal and external to corporations, remained relatively stable for years, decades, and, in some cases, even centuries. The increasingly more volatile, unfamiliar, and uncertain nature of today's world is such that, now, these boundary conditions are in a state of continuous flux. Consequently, knowledge resources suffer an increasingly shorter shelf life, necessitating constant efforts to refresh and rejuvenate this most critical factor of sustainable corporate viability. Unfortunately, the pace, scope, and scale of the changes occurring in today's market environment render knowledge of that environment invalid at a rate that frequently exceeds corporations' ability to remain synchronously aligned.

Viable action cannot take place without a conscious or unconscious decision to act. Conscious decisions cannot be made without the presence of an understanding of the pros and cons associated with the actions being considered. Understanding is based on knowledge; thus, knowledge can be described as "the range of one's understanding": it is what one believes to be true of one's environment.

While information may be ubiquitous, constant, and frequently universal across the full breadth and depth of the market environment, knowledge embodies precisely the opposite characteristics. In one corporation, a given piece of information can be perceived as meaning "A," while in another corporation (or in the same corporation, but at a different time or place), this same information can be perceived as having meaning "B," where A and B are distinctly different and, increasingly more often, are in contradiction with each other. While A and B may both be true within the context of their respective situations, neither represents a consistent, absolute truth.

Knowledge is information that has been oriented within a framework of perception, comprehension, and application: it is a function of the environment within which it takes form, finds its meaning, and derives its utility. The more dynamic the environment, the more difficult is the process of creating knowledge; the more complex that environment, the more narrowly the resulting knowledge is applicable; the more rapidly that environment changes, the shorter-lived such knowledge becomes.

In a market environment characterized by complexity, volatility, and unpredictability, what knowledge corporations possess rapidly becomes inconsistent, unreliable, even contradictory. Corporations unable to continuously, immediately, and relentlessly reinvent their perceptions of the structure and meaning of information in the face of an ever-changing and never-certain context quickly find themselves unable to sustain a competitive profile within the market environment. Inevitably, these corporations' misalignment will lead to fragmentation, then isolation, and, ultimately, organizational failure.

The misalignment that arises as a consequence of outdated, insufficient, incomplete, or inaccurate knowledge breeds anxiety and discomfort among a corporation's leaders, directors, managers, and production workers. This, in turn, typically elicits exactly the type of organizational response that is most likely to result in corporate failure: attempting to force accumulated information into familiar, traditional perceptions of the market environment. In short, corporations generally focus on extending and reinforcing what they already know, rather than on attempting to discover what they don't know.

The alternative is to embrace misalignment as a natural consequence of change and to seek, through the processes of cognition, valuation, and information, to continuously create a ready supply of fresh knowledge and insight necessary to sustain corporate alignment within the market environment. Embracing misalignment as a systemic reality insists that corporations replace their emphasis on possessing complete, definitive knowledge with developing the capacity to create a sufficient range of understanding that is reflected as a continuously evolving "truth within the situation." In short, corporations must revise their perspectives on knowledge creation from prioritizing it as a periodic, ancillary activity to one that is intrinsic within every action they undertake.

Knowledge can be created only within the context from which it emerges—otherwise, it is merely fact, data, or information, the raw material from which knowledge may be created. Context is substantially constructed of tacit perceptions, or mental models, of reality. Consequently, the ability to create useful knowledge becomes a function of the comprehensiveness and sophistication of those mental models. Unfortunately, when corporations encounter information that cannot be readily assimilated within existing mental models, the vast majority typically fail to perceive the information at all.

For example, when a change in the market environment involves a quantitative shift, the information signaling that change generally takes the form of an imperative to adjust volumes of production. Such a change can be described as essentially linear in nature, as fitting within the boundaries of a preestablished range of understanding: a corporation already possesses a mental model within which it can recognize and cope with such change. The new information serves as input to existing formal and informal processes of learning, judging, and communicating that focus on adjusting corporate endeavor within the bounds of its prevailing contextual, functional, and structural orientation.

But not all change is as just described, and not all change is linear. More and more frequently, corporations face situations in the market environment where the nature of change is qualitatively unfamiliar. In these instances, the extent, nature, form, and behavior of the market environment are being fundamentally altered: corporations generally have no preexisting basis to facilitate recognition and thus no relevant mental model into which they can assimilate such change. Unfortunately, the signals indicating the existence of this substantially contextual change frequently go unnoticed until well after the fact of their emergence. Such a circumstance brings to mind the adage, "We don't know what we don't know."

Too often, corporations are unaware of a shift in the organizing principles of their market environment before disequilibrium has become deeply entrenched. This so-called crisis of perception renders a corporation's essential orientation out of alignment with the context of the market environment, thus placing that corporation in jeopardy of losing its competitive position to a more knowledgeable contender. To avoid being overwhelmed by the future in this way, corporations must approach the creation of knowledge from the perspective of enhancing their ability to accommodate new information more quickly, effectively, and efficiently than their competitors. In short, corporations must focus their strategies on the processes of continuous sensing, learning, and adjustment needed to ensure that their priorities, infrastructures, resource allocations, and production efforts remain aligned with the context of a market environment in flux.

Bear in mind, it isn't that corporations haven't been creating knowledge all along. The issue is that they must learn how to do so differently: they must discover how to continuously expand the extent of their knowledge rather than merely increasing the certainty and understanding of what is already known. Learning that is biased predominantly in favor of assimilation is not sufficient. The increasing frequency and magnitude of discontinuous change in today's market environment force corporations to emphasize an increasing bias in the direction of a form of learning that simultaneously incorporates sensing and adjusting.

As information assumes an increasingly larger proportion of the content of corporations' productive activity and output, the importance of possessing the most complete and up-to-date knowledge becomes the defining critical success factor. In the increasingly more complex and volatile market environment of the knowledge era, ensuring continuous and immediate access to high-quality knowledge must become the overriding concern of corporate leaders, directors, managers, and workers.

In the complex world foreshadowing the knowledge era, computational ability is rapidly becoming the single most important attribute of successful corporations. The market environment of the foreseeable future calls for the development of a portfolio of organizational competencies comprising assumptions, beliefs, and behaviors intended from the outset to leverage the continuous creation and application of high-quality knowledge.

The process of creating or developing knowledge is called learning. The process of creating a corporate knowledge base is organizational learning. Engaging the full concentration and effort of a corporation to focus on continuous, relentless creation, development, application, and renewal of its knowledge base is intrinsic learning. Intrinsic learning requires a corporation to recognize that the means of enhancing its knowledge base must literally and figuratively be embedded within every activity performed by each and every individual within that corporation.

THE POSTMODERN CORPORATION

Peter Drucker, cited as the progenitor of modern management science, draws to our attention the following question: *Does a company exist to make a profit, or does it make a profit to exist?* He asserts that a corporation must choose either one or the other, sustainability or profit, as its first priority in the service of which all subsequent decisions and actions will be taken. Based on the prevailing dynamics of the market environment, Drucker concludes that, ultimately, we do not have a choice: sustainability must be at the top of the corporate agenda. He informs us succinctly that, in his opinion, profit must invariably be considered as "part of the cost of doing business."

This would seem to be heresy for the vast majority of today's corporate leaders, directors, managers, and production workers. However, when characterizing the corporation in terms of its systemic interdependencies vis-à-vis the prevailing natural, social, cultural, political, and economic imperatives of the postindustrial market environment, we are brought to a substantially different conclusion.

Much contemporary business theory and practice are based on an assumption of systemic stability, structural linearity, and operational determinism. Under these assumptions, logic dictates that an organization participating in a capital-dominated socioeconomic system must focus on the generation of profit as its top priority. Unfortunately however, today's market environment is anything but stable, linear, or predictable. Change rather than constancy characterizes the prevailing business climate. The very existence of change requires that corporations pay attention to sustainability in addition to profit generation. The current pace of that change insists that sustainability be placed at the top of the priority list.

Continuous, sustainable viability of a corporation operating within a volatile, complex, and unpredictable market environment depends primarily on two significant criteria: first, the capacity of that corporation to establish an objective, functional alignment with the context of its environment, and, second, its innate capacity to remain sufficiently flexible to respond interactively with the dynamics of that environment.

Yet, practically every current theory, philosophy, and method of organizational design, management, and operation invests corporations with infrastructures whose various components are substantially and rigidly isolated from each other, thus rendering timely, effective, and interactive alignment virtually impossible. The vast majority of popular approaches to corporate life derive their underlying principles from classical reductionist philosophy and science. Within the informationally dense market environment of the knowledge era, designing effective corporate infrastructures will not be a matter of simply accumulating and assembling the requisite discrete elements, "summing the parts" so to speak.

In the industrial era, *efficiency in the deployment of financial capital* was the corporation's critical success factor. Traditional industrialists' and capitalists' thinking correctly focused on *minimizing* the demands upon that most scarce of resources. In the knowledge era, however, *effectiveness in the deployment of knowledge* will become the corporation's most critical criterion of performance. Paradoxically, the corporation of the future must concentrate on *maximizing* the demands upon its knowledge resources. In the knowledge era, post-capitalists and post-industrialists alike will discover that the traditional reductionist logic of history will be antithetical to sustainable corporate success.

Creating and leveraging knowledge require judgment, an innately human trait. The more informed the judgment, the more knowledgeable the choice and, ultimately, the more successful the corporation. While technology may be capable of exercising choice, it can do so only based on the choice parameters embedded within it by a human being. In other words, while a machine may execute a choice, it cannot go through the rational and emotive processes of distinguishing and selecting one course of action from all possible others in the first instance. This is far too heuristic a process for even the most advanced present-day technologies.

Technologies can act upon information only in a mechanistic sense. To incorporate a heuristic perspective on information invariably requires human judgment. Therein lies the historical basis for establishing executive and managerial control over the processes of choosing options, directing organizations, and controlling activity—if one sees the inherent purpose of a corporation as being focused on establishing tight control over resource allocations, then such a perspective will inevitably lead to a hierarchical organization.

Industrial era corporations legitimately believed that the absence of hierarchical structure and control would result in their inability to achieve the necessary efficiency that a single-mindedness of purpose and action could bring. As the industrial era progressed, and the nature of competition evolved, information became significantly more plentiful, albeit the constancy of its structure and the nature of its meaning were not affected substantially. In essence, this allowed traditional rationalizations for hierarchical structure and control to remain both viable and practical.

But corporations cannot be truly controlled: control depends on certainty, predictability at the very least. Unfortunately, rigid control structures are optimally effective only when the environment within which they operate is sufficiently stable that the organization and meaning of the information both constituting and describing that environment behave predictably throughout the relevant time frames of corporate decision-making, direction, control, and production.

When the pace of complexification outstrips a corporate infrastructure's capacity for transforming raw information into meaningful and appropriate knowledge, then a discontinuity is created in that organization's alignment with the larger market environment in which it participates. The corporation of the future must comprise an infrastructure that allows for immediate, local, subjective integration and interaction among the many and various constituencies of its market environment.

Consider for a few moments the ways and means by which most corporations were historically conceived and constructed. At the most rudimentary level, the vast majority were designed along the lines of a five-stage model: *contextualization* established the parameters of the market environment; *orientation* set the corporation's strategic priorities; *functionalization* defined the infrastructure necessary for the corporation to carry on business; *implementation* established its capacity to realize competitive levels of performance; and *production* focused the corporation's leaders, directors, managers, and workers in their efforts to carry out the day-to-day activities of producing output goods and services.

Once a given stage was complete, and its imperatives established, the corporation's focus and energy typically cascaded to executing the next stage, and so on until the organization was deemed fully operational. Ultimately, the entire process was, and continues to be, performed in a manner that results in a given corporation's primary focus resting almost exclusively on the final stage: production. As long as the context of the market environment within which such a corporation interacted remained relatively constant, that corporation could enjoy a long and healthy future.

Therein lies the rub. Such a corporation's mental models of organizational design, management, and operation become frozen in the organization's collective consciousness, are taken for granted, and, consequently, remain essentially static. Among the most open-minded corporations, an occasional reevaluation and realignment will occur, but seldom, if ever, will a corporation's position vis à vis the first principles of its orientation, function, design, and operation be reconsidered.

When the market environment entered a new period of disequilibrium marked by the onset of the information age, corporations began to experience an increasing degree of misalignment. Furthermore, as the fundamental nature of social, cultural, political, and economic endeavor begins its inevitable transition into the knowledge era, most corporations will ultimately find themselves wholly misaligned, placing them in a substantially noncompetitive state. Under these circumstances, a fundamental rethinking of the basic concepts upon which these corporations have been founded becomes essential.

Transforming information into knowledge is not a passive, discrete, or ancillary event: knowledge creation is a distinctly heuristic process that cannot be conducted separately from the context within which that knowledge derives its relevance. In effect, every action a corporation engages in must, by definition, explicitly and unequivocally recognize, respect, and incorporate the ways and means necessary to establish and capitalize upon the value of the knowledge created. Increased investment in rigid, capital-intensive infrastructures will fail to result in the materialization of relevant solutions: knowledge can be created only by people and only within the moment of its need: hence, leveraging information successfully is possible only with the explicit, continuous, voluntary participation of an organization's entire workforce.

From a human perspective, the wholesale change that marks the transition from one era to another is invariably accompanied by a dramatic reformulation of the priorities associated with virtually every aspect of social, cultural, political, and economic endeavor. Whenever the defining parameters that establish the market environment's context undergo such change, the imperatives prevailing upon the individuals and organizations constituting that environment must also be restated. Discontinuous change of the magnitude now being experienced insists corporations make precisely such a dramatic shift in the perspectives upon which they base the extent, nature, form, and behavior of their organizations.

The conjoined impact of modern transportation, communication, computerization, and globalization is greatly extending and expanding the shape, scope, and scale of the market environment. Not only is the impact of change becoming more dramatic, but it is also occurring more frequently, with greater rapidity, and with increasingly less predictability. The challenge corporations face is not one of recycling through the previously outlined stages of organizational development more rapidly, more frequently, or at all. Instead, they must develop an innate ability to exist within all stages of development simultaneously.

Such a corporation will appear not as a concrete, well-defined, structurally consistent entity but, rather, as part of a dynamic, simultaneously interacting, continuously evolving system of systems. Rather than focusing priority, effort, and resources on reaching a stable production stage, corporations and their constituencies must become comfortable with living in a state of continuous flux, where the ability to achieve and sustain alignment within the market environment becomes the earmark of a successful organization. Thus, the corporation of the future will most likely be defined as a network of simultaneously independent and interdependent collaborator agents in which each is perceived as an autonomous system within itself.

CROSSING THE INFORMATION BOUNDARY

Think back for a few moments to primary school and one of the early lessons received. For many of us, our teachers attempted to instill within us a model of systemic design and behavior that, while seemingly elegant in its simplicity, is actually profound in its error. We were asked to stand in a circle, the first person whispering a message to the person either on left or right. This person, in turn, would pass the same message along to the next person, and on until the last person passed the message back to the one who started the process. Invariably, the message had been dramatically altered from its initial form.

For reasons that seem untenable today, our teachers insisted that the flaw that created this purported distortion rested within us, that we must learn to exercise greater discipline and precision lest we destroy the integrity of the message we were meant to convey. In effect, the emphasis of importance was placed upon the informational content of the exercise—its so-called text—while the mechanisms of its conveyance were endowed with subordinate status. Content was sacred, the processes associated with it—the so-called context—wholly in its service.

Essentially, this philosophy was based on a notion that the systemic nature of our world is fundamentally linear and predictable and that unless we exert substantial amounts of control over its processes and systems, it will collapse into a state of complete, utter, and irredeemable chaos. Nothing could be further from the truth!

Think back now to that same time in our lives and remember how we actually communicated among ourselves when left to our own devices. Information was passed along to whoever was present, in whatever form it was available, in whatever state of completeness it existed, wherever the opportunity presented itself, often in group situations, and rarely, if ever, according to the strictures of a predefined, rigorous time schedule, structural protocol, or semantic frame. Each individual in receipt of information was given opportunity to explore and interpret its meaning, to augment its content, and to choose an appropriate course of action.

In short, the activities of communication, understanding, and acceptance occurred through an informal, dynamic, unpredictable, adaptive network of relationships in which every participant played an independent and yet directly interactive role. When allowed to follow a natural, unbounded course such as described, text and context merge to form a system of accomplishing meaning. Essentially, that system is information—in effect, information is no longer a thing. Instead, information becomes a process, albeit substantially heuristic in nature.

The system of information described by this latter example discovered its own natural characteristics within the situation. The outcome was frequently characterized by a richness of understanding and contextual relevance that simply couldn't have been achieved in any predictable fashion. Yet, this is precisely the type of behavior our teachers and mentors were intent upon preventing. It is also precisely the nature of the system in which corporations participate on a day-to-day basis: the market environment.

Contrary to the lessons of childhood, the system that is the market environment is not out of control. Any attempt to understand today's environment from a perspective favoring centrist, hierarchical control and linear, sequential processes will not lead to the level or degree of interaction essential to achieving sustainable alignment. Ultimately, complex systems such as the market environment can be understood and engaged only as a whole in which the processes of information comprise a critical dynamic in its performance.

At a baseline level, the system comprising the market environment is truly a weblike, complex, dynamic arrangement of constituencies, intersections, and relationships engaged in seemingly random, unpredictable, and ever-changing patterns of organization and behavior. Given that much of traditional Western pedagogy has not provided the means of understanding the world in this way, it is no surprise that we often insist it be linear, predictable, and ultimately controllable and that we subsequently persist in designing and operating corporations in accordance with this quintessentially reductionist perspective. The corporation of the future must overcome this hurdle by developing the capacity to perceive and comprehend the dynamics of the market environment in a way that allows it to engage in the processes of continual, mutual alignment critical to sustainability.

Consider as a further example the nature and behavior of an ecosystem. When observed closely over time, one discovers that the so-called boundaries serving to define the extent of the ecosystem are constantly changing. While itself comprising of myriad independent components, each a system in its own right, the ecosystem cannot and does not exist independently of the larger geological, political, social, cultural, and economic systems forming the context within which it interacts. Where the boundary of an eco-system begins and ends ultimately becomes a highly subjective issue: within a structure where everything connects to everything else, what should one consider within the system as opposed to outside it when, by definition, anything that has an impact on the system is inherently a part of it?

We face the same issue in attempting to establish the bounds of a corporation or, for that matter, the market environment in which it participates. Consequently, it is neither possible nor prac-tical to assume a fixed, objective boundary. Rather, it makes more sense to acknowledge the subjectivity of the matter and consider identifying an organizational "horizon" instead of imposing a for-mal boundary extent. By definition, horizons are relative to one's subjective viewpoint and, consequently, allow for an almost infi-nite number of "possibilities" to emerge—horizons are ultimately more respectful of the notion of a dynamic market environment.

Every organization in existence today has both formal and in-formal boundaries. Every corporation consisting of more than one person inevitably creates internal boundaries that define depart-ments, divisions, positions, responsibilities, accountabilities, and so on. Actually, one can barely imagine any organization without definite, albeit intangible, boundaries. But why, in fact, is it that these boundaries exist? Boundaries place limits, which help to con-tain risk by creating an illusion of stability. Hence, boundaries serve an extremely useful purpose—they facilitate differentiation, thereby implying certainty. In effect, a boundary sets out the extent of one's concern. But boundaries also comprise an associated, although fre-quently invisible, cost: they block our view of the context that ex-ists beyond them.

Newton's determinism presumes all things can, and should, be understood in an objective, reductionist, and mechanistic way. Cor-porate boundaries are a function of these traditional deterministic approaches to understanding and controlling the workings of the market environment. This approach, however, substantially fails to grasp the dynamic, complex, and unpredictable nature of the contemporary world, where not only is there far more at play than we can possibly know and understand, but also constituents' be-havior is highly volatile, seemingly arbitrary, and simultaneously highly independent and interdependent.

To maximize the potential of sustainable success, a corpora-tion must constantly and diligently update its perspectives of the context within which it participates. To do this requires a formal acceptance that the "system" in which it is engaged is large, com-plex, unpredictable, and constantly changing, that it is ultimately unknowable, and that it is filled with a virtually infinite degree of potential. This implies that corporations must adopt the ways and means of constantly testing and adjusting their market alignment relative to the prevailing horizon of opportunity. This nontrivial task is possible only by recognizing the nature of the corporation as a system of systems, existing within a system, the viability of the whole being significantly dependent on the heuristics of "information as process."

COMPUTATIONAL ABILITY AND SYSTEMS THINKING

No organization is a wholly self-contained entity: each and every corporation invariably participates in a broad range of social, cultural, political, and economic undertakings in conjunction with a host of other constituents that, together, constitute a market environment. This market environment provides a contextual background for the corporation, serving as a forum within which its actions can be played out. Such an environment is essentially a system by any definition.

In a system characterized as inherently dynamic, complex, nonlinear, and self-organizing, there are few, if any, absolute truths, little upon which one can base predictions, and scarce certainty that efforts at interacting within the system will bear fruit. Thus, the extent, nature, form, and behavior of such a system are innately subjective. Such a system cannot be understood using conventional approaches based on expression solely in terms of reducing that system to its component elements. While one may well develop an understanding of the parts constituting the system, one will substantially fail to form any meaningful perspective on the full spectrum of actual behavior and outcome that inevitably emerges from the interaction of those parts.

For example, biological evolution is impossible to understand in terms of how any individual species evolves or, alternatively, how an entire ecosystem evolves as a complete whole. Rather, it can be understood only when seen concurrently as a whole *and* as a collection of parts, neither of which could exist without the other. To accomplish this requires one to perceive biological evolution as a system of individual species that exist independently—each defined as an instance of "text"—and that simultaneously interact together within a shared environment—the instance of "context" that binds them—which concurrently "defines" each species and "is defined by" each one of those species.

In much the same way, it is impossible to understand a society, a market environment, or a corporation by analyzing one, several, or even all of their separate components individually or, alternatively, as a "black box" system into which one cannot peer: they can be understood only in terms of the systemic dynamics relating their components and the properties that emerge from that interaction.

During the late 1940s and throughout the 1950s, many of the abstract principles of the new sciences found practical application through the emerging field of system dynamics. What the new sciences did for our understanding of the complex dynamics of the universe, they could also do for improving our understanding of the nature of everyday life. Based on this notion, systems theorists succeeded in developing both a conceptual framework and a practical language for describing and understanding the holistic nature of our sociotechnical environment at its most fundamental level.

During the 1960s and 1970s, the principles and methods of dynamical systems theory crossed a boundary into the so-called soft disciplines of sociocultural, sociopolitical, and socioeconomic study and practice. Systems theorists, sociologists, and behaviorists were quick to confirm their hypotheses that organizations of people, regardless of their purpose or orientation, could, in fact, also be better understood as complex, dynamic systems of a holistic nature. By the late 1980s and early 1990s, these confirmations led to the evolution of an organizational discipline simply called "systems thinking."

Parallel with these developments, interdisciplinary work among the world's leading physical scientists, mathematicians, and philosophers brought forth, first, a comprehensive theory of chaos and, shortly thereafter, workable theories of complexity and emergence. Biologists, sociologists, and economists quickly grasped the value of applying these findings and theories to their respective disciplines. From these efforts evolved a perspective describing social, cultural, political, and economic systems not only as complex, dynamic, and unpredictable, but also as possessing a self-organizing, adaptive capacity.

While these hypotheses, theories, and assertions may seem somewhat abstract or academic to many in the corporate world, they have tremendous implications for developing a meaningful understanding of how corporations must behave, interact, and organize within the market environment of the future. Based on these new perspectives, virtually every principle historically held to be true with respect to the optimum design of corporations has been rendered no longer sufficiently complete or robust, demanding that they be rethought, redrafted, and rebuilt from the foundation level upward.

In the language of systems theory, the synchronized interaction of the parts optimizes the performance of the whole, while, concurrently, the optimum state of the whole facilitates the syn-chronization of the parts. According to complexity theory, the bound-ary conditions of a system are substantially a function of the per-spective one chooses to take within the moment of the need to do so. Under the rubric of the emergence hypothesis, the inherent strength and viability of a system lie within its innate capacity to exist in a state of continuous flux, moving synchronously with the ebb and flow of the competitive landscape within which it partici-pates. These assertions find themselves wholly at odds with the conventional wisdom of mechanistic determinism which posits that optimization of the whole is simply and purely a linear function of the optimization of its parts.

By discarding the latter and embracing the former, the corpora-tion of the future will become recognizable as an unending pro-gression, or thematic unfolding, along a continuum of activity that seeks to continuously adapt to the tension existing between chaos and order, thereby creating a unity of existence, all for no purpose more singular than to ensure the ongoing sustainability of itself, the market environment within which it participates, and the com-ponent elements that it comprises. The challenge this presents today's corporations is to develop the conjoined capacities of con-tinuously sensing, learning, and adjusting to the dynamics of a complex, nonlinear, self-organizing market environment. In short, this calls upon corporations to be in a state of constant change.

Most corporations respond to a change imperative by simply in-creasing or reducing the "volume" of their productive output—in es-sence, a "text-focused" response. In fact, no real change occurs to the inherent function, structure, or competencies of that corpora-tion. The challenge is met simply by a quantitative adjustment in the volume of production. A change that affects production in a strictly quantitative manner is referred to as a first-order change. A first-order change typically has a very limited span of effectiveness.

Corporations with the sensory capacity to recognize or predict the underlying patterns of change in their market environment typically respond from a deeper level. The initiatives forthcoming from these organizations are substantially more comprehensive, more timely, and more appropriate. Change takes place within these corporations' structure and competencies manifested by the redefinition, redesign, or reconstruction of one or more infrastruc-ture elements constituting their business systems. Such an effort comprises temporary suspension of a corporation's content-focused orientation to facilitate a shift in context. This type of response, resulting in both quantitative and qualitative differences in pro-ductive output, is second-order change. A second-order change circumvents the necessity of having to continually react to the same types of change events over and over again.

Few corporations existing today have developed the capacity to adopt change as a constant state of being—a state of continuous, mutually altering interplay between text and context. Such is a state of incorporating the capacity to change as an inherent element of an organization's central function or purpose. In these corporations, the market environment is recognized as being in a continuous state of flux that demands the extreme in flexibility and interactivity. Successful respondents to these conditions constantly and consistently differentiate their performance by being engaged in a permanent process of what is referred to here as third-order change.

Market leadership in the complex, fast-paced, unpredictable, and self-adaptive environment of the knowledge era will demand the capacity to be agile in the face of a constantly competitive landscape. Third-order change represents a fundamental shift in an organization's perception of its central role within its market environment: these corporations serve as avatars of a future that they actively and consciously create. The dynamics of the "text/context" interplay that define the emerging market environment demand of corporations an agility that can increasingly be realized only from within a state of third-order change. Third-order change is not about *doing* change successfully: rather, it is about *being* change successfully.

CONCLUSION

As humankind approaches the end of the millennium, the industrial era is rapidly being eclipsed by the knowledge era. In the knowledge era, strategic advantage will be gained only by those corporations that are fully, consciously, and continuously aware of, and aligned with, the fundamental dynamics forming their market environment. The movement of information will serve as the most comprehensive, most current, and most readily accessible expression of the orientation, structure, and dynamics of that environment.

The transition from the industrial to the knowledge era in which we are simultaneously observers and participants is characterized by a market environment that is highly volatile, increasingly complex, essentially unpredictable, and fundamentally self-determining. Under these conditions, computational ability, not processing capacity, as is so often assumed, becomes the basic performance imperative for the corporation of the future.

REFERENCES

Argyris, Chris. *On Organizational Learning*. Cambridge and Oxford: Blackwell, 1995, 1992.

Argyris, Chris and Donald A. Schon. *Organizational Learning II: Theory, Method, and Practice*. Reading, Mass.: 1996.

Bergquist, William. *The Postmodern Organization: Mastering the Art of Irreversible Change*. San Francisco: Jossey-Bass, 1993.

Bertalanffy, Ludwig von. *General System Theory: Foundations, Development, Applications*. Rev. ed. New York: George Braziller, 1995, 1968.

Bohm, David. *Wholeness and the Implicate Order*. London and New York: Routledge, 1995, 1980.

Capra, Fritjof. *The Turning Point: Science, Society, and the Rising Culture*. New York: Bantam Books, 1988, 1982.

Capra, Fritjof. *The Web of Life: A New Scientific Understanding of Living Systems*. New York: Anchor Books, Doubleday, 1996.

Chawla, Sarita and John Renesch, eds., *Learning Organizations: Developing Cultures for Tomorrow's Workplace*. Portland: Productivity Press, 1995.

Cohen, Jack and Ian Stewart. *The Collapse of Chaos: Discovering Simplicity in a Complex World*. New York: Viking/Penguin Group, 1994.

Darwin, Charles. *The Origin of the Species by Means of Natural Selection, or The Preservation of Favoured Races in the Struggle for Life*. New York: Penguin Books, 1976, 1859.

Dawkins, Richard. *The Selfish Gene*. New York and Oxford: Oxford University Press, 1989, 1976.

De Geus, Arie. *The Living Company: Habits for Survival in a Turbulent Business Environment*. Boston: Harvard Business School Press, 1997.

Drucker, Peter F. *Managing in Turbulent Times*. New York: Harper and Row, 1985, 1980.

Drucker, Peter F. *Post-Capitalist Society*. New York: HarperCollins, 1993.

Drucker, Peter F. *Managing in a Time of Great Change*. New York: Truman Talley Books/Dutton, 1995.

Gleick, James. *Chaos: Making a New Science*. Harmondsworth: Penguin Books, 1987.

Handy, Charles. *Beyond Certainty: The Changing Worlds of Organisations*. London: Arrow Books, 1996.

Heijden, Kees van der. *Scenarios: The Art of Strategic Conversation*. Chichester: John Wiley and Sons, 1996.

Holtzman, Steven R. *Digital Mantras: The Languages of Abstract and Virtual Worlds*. Cambridge and London: MIT Press, 1994.

Kauffman, Draper L., Jr. *Systems 1: An Introduction to Systems Thinking*. Minneapolis: Future Systems, 1980.

Kauffman, Stuart A. *The Origins of Order: Self-Organization and Selection in Evolution*. New York and Oxford: Oxford University Press, 1993.

Kauffman, Stuart. *At Home in the Universe: The Search for Laws of Self-Organization and Complexity*. New York and Oxford: Oxford University Press, 1995.

Kuhn, Thomas S. *The Structure of Scientific Revolutions*. 3rd ed. Chicago and London: University of Chicago Press, 1996, 1962.

Laszlo, Ervin. *Introduction to Systems Philosophy: Toward a New Paradigm of Contemporary Thought.* New York, Evanston, Ill., San Francisco, and London: Harper and Row, 1973, 1972.

Lewin, Roger. *Complexity: Life at the Edge of Chaos.* New York and Toronto: Macmillan/Maxwell Macmillan, 1994, 1992.

Lyotard, Jean-François. *The Postmodern Explained: Correspondence 1982–1985.* London and Minneapolis: University of Minnesota Press, 1993, 1988.

McLuhan, Marshall and Bruce R. Powers. *The Global Village: Transformations in World Life and Media in the 21st Century.* New York and Oxford: Oxford University Press, 1992, 1989.

Morecroft, John D. W. and John D. Sterman (eds.). *Modeling for Learning Organizations.* Portland, Productivity Press, 1994.

Nicolis, Gregoire and Ilya Prigogine. *Exploring Complexity: An Introduction.* New York: W. H. Freeman, 1989.

Nonaka, Ikujiro and Hirotaka Takeuchi. *The Knowledge-Creating Company: How Japanese Companies Create the Dynamics of Innovation.* New York and Oxford: Oxford University Press, 1995.

Ohmae, Kenichi. *The Borderless World: Power and Strategy in the Interlinked Economy.* New York: HarperCollins, 1991, 1990.

Penzias, Arno. *Harmony: Business, Technology and Life After Paperwork.* New York: HarperCollins, 1995.

Prigogine, Ilya and Isabelle Stengers. *Order Out of Chaos: Man's New Dialogue with Nature.* New York: Bantam Books, 1984.

Schein, Edgar H. *Organizational Culture and Leadership.* 2nd ed. San Francisco: Jossey-Bass, 1997, 1992.

Schwartz, Peter. *The Art of The Long View: Paths to Strategic Insight for Yourself and your Company.* New York: Doubleday, 1996, 1991.

Senge, Peter M. *The Fifth Discipline: The Art and Practice of the Learning Organization.* New York: Doubleday, 1990.

Sloan, Alfred P. Jr. *My Years with General Motors.* New York: Doubleday, 1990, 1963.

Stalk, George Jr. and Thomas M. Hout. *Competing Against Time: How Time-based Competition Is Reshaping Global Markets.* New York and London: The Free Press, 1990.

Stewart, Thomas A. *Intellectual Capital: The New Wealth of Organizations.* New York: Doubleday, 1997.

Teilhard de Chardin, Pierre. *The Phenomenon of Man.* London: Wm. Collins Sons, 1965, 1955.

Thurow, Lester C. *The Zero-Sum Society: Distribution and the Possibilities for Economic Change.* Harmondsworth: Penguin Books, 1984, 1980.

Varela, Francisco J., Evan Thompson and Eleanor Rosch. *The Embodied Mind: Cognitive Science and Human Experience.* Cambridge and London: MIT Press, 1996, 1991.

Wadsworth, Barry J. *Piaget's Theory of Cognitive Development: An Introduction for Students of Psychology and Education.* New York: David Mckay, 1971.

Waldrop, M. Mitchell. *Complexity: The Emerging Science at the Edge of Order and Chaos.* New York: Simon and Schuster, 1992.

Waterman, Robert H. Jr. *Adhocracy*. New York and London: W. W. Norton, 1993, 1990.

Wheatley, Margaret J. *Leadership and the New Science: Learning about Organization from an Orderly Universe*. San Francisco: Berrett-Koehler, 1992.

Wheatley, Margaret J. and Myron Kellner-Rogers. *A Simpler Way*. San Francisco: Berrett-Koehler, 1996.

Zohar, Danah. *Rewiring the Corporate Brain: Using the New Science to Rethink How We Structure and Lead Organizations*. San Francisco: Berrett-Koehler, 1997.

Part II

Strategy

The three chapters in this section examine strategy from a complexity perspective and complexity from a strategy perspective.

Steve Maguire's "Strategy as Design: A Fitness Landscape Framework" views business strategy from a strategist's perspective. Maguire takes the reader through some basic perspectives on strategy, contrasting two major schools of thought (Michael Porter's industrial organization framework and the resource-based view of the firm), and shows how a third perspective, which sees strategy as a design process, draws on the strengths of both. He then reframes the design process in terms of fitness landscapes, showing how different generic strategic problems can be viewed as different kinds of exploration of a firm's fitness landscape. The chapter has two distinct halves. The first half will be of great interest to anyone who wants an overview of the main currents of thought framing strategic management. It is easy, when talking about strategy in the abstract, to trivialize the task: frameworks, by their nature, simplify the world and create the illusion that managing is simply to do with identifying some key variables and making straightforward decisions about them. By using the example of the questions that have to be answered when designing something as simple as a chair, Maguire shows how the way different design features interact make even this an exercise in considerable complexity. By implication, strategic management problems are orders of magnitude more complex. In precisely these kinds of situation the fitness landscape has proved so powerful, and the second half of the chapter shows how the framework can be applied to a range of strategic problems. Here, the design problem is reframed as a scramble over the landscape, in search of the highest peak, representing the "most fit" (i.e., most successful) strategy.

Ken Baskin's "Markets in Phase Transition" continues this argument by describing the scramble as "a manager's nightmare." Not only is it impossible to guess what shape markets will finally take, but even the dynamics driving the turbulence remain poorly understood. Baskin goes on to argue that because markets are complex, adaptive systems, we can look at these transformations as phase transitions, that chaotic period between an old stable state and an emerging stable state. From this perspective, he suggests, we can understand the dynamics driving phase transitions in markets by comparing them with the dynamics driving phase transitions in natural ecologies. Managers can use such a model of ecologies in phase transition to understand the dynamics driving their market transformations and develop tools for making more informed decisions. By applying the principles of natural ecology phase transition, they can explore the apparently chaotic activity in their markets as part of an unfolding natural process, try out experiments in the directions their markets seem to be taking, and build on what works. Baskin is not proposing that understanding phase transitions is a prescription for success but rather suggests that such understanding can provide a competitive advantage "by focusing managers on the patterns shaping that turbulence."

Robin Wood's "The Future of Strategy: The Role of the New Sciences" rounds out this part by placing this debate in the context of strategy consulting over the past 50 years. Wood clearly believes that Baskin and Maguire are right about the importance of a new kind of understanding. He argues that what is being required of leaders and managers are innovation, flexibility, responsiveness, and change. "If there is one connecting theme unifying all of these, it is learning from complexity—understanding it, valuing it, and managing it effectively at all levels." Wood suggests that the central task of business leaders is to create and appropriate sustainable value for the stakeholders in the organization. "At the heart of this process lies the ability to learn from complexity faster and more effectively, either faster than, or at the rate of, change (if one is shaping the environment) or faster than one's competitors or substitutes (if one is adapting to the environment)." To Wood, then, complexity is the heart of the new kind of understanding of which Baskin and Maguire write. Complexity science provides managers with the opportunity to use new metaphors, frameworks, tools, and models to develop strategies and organizational designs that emphasize intelligence, learning, flexibility, creativity, and adaptiveness.

Chapter 5

Strategy as Design: A Fitness Landscape Framework

Steve Maguire

The strategy literature is diverse, fragmented, and characterized by sharply differing paradigms or "schools of thought" (Mintzberg, 1990). It has given rise to a number of different typologies and taxonomies of generic strategies (Miles and Snow, 1978; Porter, 1980; Mintzberg, 1988), organizational structures (Mintzberg, 1979), industry environments (Porter, 1980; Gilbert and Strebel, 1992), and managerial or leadership archetypes (Wissema et al., 1980; Pitcher, 1993). In addition, recurring patterns of correlation among variables that measure elements of a firm's environment, strategy, and structure—termed configurations in the organizational literature—are empirically demonstrated phenomena (Miles and Snow, 1978; Miller and Friesen, 1980; Miller and Friesen, 1984; Miller, 1986). These configurations have themselves been summarized and ordered into a number of taxonomies and typologies (Miles and Snow, 1978; Miller and Friesen, 1980; Miller and Friesen, 1984; Miller, 1986). Figure 5.1 contains a summary of this literature, showing those variables measuring organizational strategies, structures, environments, and leadership that tend to correlate in the patterns indicated.

It has been found that firms in the stable, simpler, yet competitive environments of mature industries frequently pursue strategies of conservative cost control characterized by an emphasis on production efficiency, asset intensity, and relatively little research and development (R&D) (which, when it occurs, is oriented toward developing more efficient manufacturing process technologies rather than new product technologies). The structures of these firms tend to be bureaucratic, emphasizing planning, formal controls, and

Figure 5.1
Configurations of Firm Strategy, Structure, Leadership, and
Environment

	Production	Research & Development	Marketing
GENERIC STRATEGY			
Porter's (1980) generic strategies	low cost	differentiation	differentiation
Miller's (1986) generic strategies	cost leaders (B)	innovators (A$_2$)	marketers (A$_3$), niche marketers (A$_1$)
Mintzberg's (1988) differentiation strategies	price	quality, design	image, support
STRATEGIC PRIORITIES			
Dominant dimension (from Miller, 1987)	conservative cost control	complex product innovation	marketing differtiation
production emphasis asset management innovation, R&D marketing emphasis	efficiency intensity almost none low price	flexibility parsimony very high novelty, quality	efficiency parsimony varies varies, but high advertising intensity
ENVIRONMENT			
Types (from Mintzberg, 1979; Miller, 1986, 1987)	simple and stable	complex and dynamic	moderately dynamic
technology	mass production (not very complex)	automated or custom production (very complex); sophisticated product	varies
competition	high	low	high
Stage of product life cycle (from Hofer, 1975; Miller, 1986)	maturity	emergence and growth	

Figure 5.1 (continued)

	Production	Research & Development	Marketing
STRUCTURE			
Types (from Mintzberg, 1979)	bureaucratic structure (machine bureaucracy)	organic structure (adhocracy)	combination of bureaucratic (production activities), organic (marketing activities)
key coordinating mechanism centralization formalization planning and control	standardization of work high high action planning	mutual alignment medium to low	
LEADERSHIP			
Types (from Wissema et al., 1980; Jauch and Glueck, 1990; Pitcher, 1993)	manager, bureaucrat, technocrat	entrepreneur, pioneer, artist	
attitude towards risk	risk-adverse	risk-taking	

the centralization of decision-making authority with risk-averse technocrats and managers in charge. In contrast, in emerging and growing industries where product technologies are sophisticated, and the environment is complex and dynamic, organizational structures, leadership, and strategies are different. Firms found here tend to have more organic structures that combine decentralized decision authority, less formal planning, and fewer bureaucratic controls. The risk-taking entrepreneurs or "pioneers" found leading these firms frequently implement product innovation strategies aimed at differentiation in the marketplace and characterized by a commitment of firm resources to R&D and to production facilities that employ fixed assets parsimoniously and are flexible.

Yet, despite the general acceptance of these stylized facts, no integrating theoretical framework has emerged to explain them (Miller, 1996). This chapter addresses this theoretical gap by weaving previous, disparate strands of theorizing into a conceptual synthesis built around the notion of "design."

Drawing upon diverse streams of theorizing within the organizational literature, we propose an integrated view of corporate and business strategy as "design" that poses a dual challenge to firms related to content and process. Firms are viewed as evolving solutions to large and complicated technology design problems relating to the form and functionality of both their products and their production operations. Such technological challenges can be factored into a large number of lower-level design decisions, and these are highly interdependent with each other as well as with those of other actors in the economy. The design problems of individual firms can be conceptualized as combinatorial optimization problems, with the economy viewed as a set of such problems, and fitness landscape frameworks drawn from research into complex systems are particularly useful for eventually formalizing all of this. We demonstrate how concepts and variables from strategy and organization theory can be mapped relatively neatly into such a model. This framework allows strategy to be more deeply understood by highlighting (1) the various components of generic design problems, (2) the different types of design problems that organizations construct for themselves, (3) the different approaches they adopt for solving these problems, and (4) the linkages and tendencies for coherence between (1), (2), and (3). This is demonstrated by discussing the insights of the model into such phenomena as generic strategies, configurations, and sustainable competitive advantage.

An important contribution of the proposed framework is its integrating potential, and because its main purpose is synthesis, the scope of the chapter is wide and encompasses diverse literatures addressing configurations, generic strategies, technological evolution. and industry life cycles. Such an approach is not without risk, and the reader is cautioned that the author's statements may appear overly sweeping and bold. They are to be interpreted as suggestive rather than conclusive and are made with an intent of stimulating, and not closing, debate.

STRATEGY AS DESIGN

Organizations act and, by definition, not randomly. Their actions display a consistency that, if characterized along variables that strategy researchers deem of interest, can be termed their strategy according to the most general definition offered to date: a "pattern in a stream of action" (Mintzberg, 1987; Mintzberg and Waters, 1985). Typically, organizational researchers assume that organizations have goals or objectives, frequently operationalized as profit maximization by economists or survival or fitness maximization by organizational ecologists, where fitness measures the organization's probability of survival (Rumelt, Schendel, and Teece, 1991; Hannan and Freeman, 1977). So, most basically, a firm's strategy is its patterned action aimed at fitness maximization. This is frequently decomposed into two components: corporate-level strategy and business-level strategy (Miller, 1986). Corporate strategy applies to the highest level within the firm and represents the firm's choice of markets to which it will put on offer some product. This choice of product-market domain is essentially a choice of environment (where the firm competes), as it determines the industry structure and societal trends affecting supply and demand with which the firm must contend. Business-level strategy applies to individual business units and represents how they compete within their respective industry or product-market domain (Porter, 1980). Typologies of generic business strategies include cost leadership, differentiation, and niche (Porter, 1980) as well as quality, design, support, image, and price (Mintzberg, 1988). Because comparisons to competitors are implicitly or explicitly made in attaching these strategy labels, strategy is often conceived of in terms of a position relative to existing and potential rivals (Porter, 1980; Mintzberg, 1987, 1990).

This positionist thinking is typically identified with researchers working within the industrial organization (IO) framework who take an external perspective on the firm, but it is also in evidence more recently with researchers adopting the other popular strategy framework inherited from economics, which is the resource-based view of the firm (RBVF). IO approaches the firm from the outside in, "knowing" it—identifying it and characterizing it relative to other firms—in terms of differences in products offered to markets. These product differences are, in fact, the inspiration for the various generic strategies listed in Figure 5.1. RBVF, on the other hand, approaches the firm from the inside out, "knowing" it—identifying it and characterizing it relative to other firms—in terms of differences in the resources it possesses, its capabilities, and its competences. Though debate continues about the relative merits of these two approaches, many researchers view them as complementary and are attempting syntheses (Mahoney and Pandian, 1992; Amit and Schoemaker, 1993).

In opening up firms to internal analysis, authors from different traditions employ different concepts. Consultants view firms as bundles of business processes that can be reengineered; Porter (1996) prefers to speak of firms as bundles of activities or "activity systems"; RBVF researchers refer instead to bundles of resources, competences, and capabilities (Wernerfelt, 1984; Prahalad and Hamel, 1990; Teece, Pisano, and Shuen, 1990); and evolutionary economists write of bundles of routines (Nelson and Winter, 1982).

RBVF researchers work with the most flexible concept, as the term "resource" has been said to include "all assets, capabilities, organizational processes, firm attributes, information, knowledge, etc." (Barney, 1991). Hence, processes, activities, and routines can all be considered "resources," RBVF researchers have also attempted to capture the emergent nature of certain resources by proposing a hierarchy of concepts: factors are combined into resources, which are then combined either in a simple manner into a contained resource or in a complex manner into a system resource (Black and Boal, 1994). In such a framework, system resources can contain lower-level, nested system resources, so one could conceivably refer to the firm as a whole as a single, highest-level system resource.

In this chapter we view the firm, from the inside, as a single, but complex, "activity system" (Porter, 1996) or resource. Firms represent the highest-level resource imaginable in the RBVF framework and can be unbundled or factored into a number of lower-level resources, routines, activities, processes, or, more generally, resource design decisions, depending on researchers' preferences. From the outside, we view the firm as a portfolio of products, but to simplify our analysis, we consider here only firms producing a single product for a well-defined target market. A firm's product can also be factored into a number of lower-level parts, product attributes, product features, or, more generally, product design decisions. Combining internal and external views, firms can be seen as a resource-product technology nexus. At any moment in time, they employ a particular process (i.e., production) technology to manufacture a particular product technology.

Our notion of strategy will be connected to patterns over time in the position of a firm in a space of technological possibilities for products and resources.

RECONCEPTUALIZING STRATEGY AS DESIGN

The "design" school of strategy has always sought to balance externally focused and internally focused analyses and in so doing bridges the IO and RBVF perspectives, though without their formalisms, given its preferred research methodology of case studies (Andrews, 1971; Mintzberg, 1990). Essentially, this chapter seeks to demonstrate how one might formalize the notion of business strategy as design. At the chapter's core are the "three major problems which management must continually solve: entrepreneurial, engineering and administrative problems" introduced by Miles and Snow (1978: 21). The entrepreneurial problem involves the choice of "a specific product or service and a target market or market segment." Once this choice is made, it immediately gives rise to the engineering problem, which "involves the creation of a system which puts into actual operation management's solution to the entrepreneurial problem" (Miles and Snow, 1978: 22) and implies the implementation of a "choice of technologies" for products as well for manufacturing and delivering them to customers. Once implemented, this system must be managed, giving rise to the administrative problem facing the firm, the solution of which involves a choice of organizational structure, incentives, decision-making process, and resource allocation rules.

Moving left to right across Figure 5.2, we see the reconceptualization and mapping necessary to translate this accepted organizational terminology into a fitness landscape framework. The terminology of Miles and Snow is first recast in terms of the construction and solution of a "design problem," which can then be viewed as a problem of combinatorial optimization to which formal models of fitness landscapes can be applied.

Solving the Entrepreneurial Problem: Recasting Corporate Strategy as the Identification of a "Product-Resource" Design Problem to Be Solved

Corporate strategy, the firm's choice of product-market domain, is the firm's solution to its entrepreneurial problem. To simplify our discussion, this chapter considers firms operating in a single product-market domain, which we define in terms of the customers targeted and their needs that the firm's single product or service seeks to serve. By specifying a product-market domain, a firm essentially "chooses" a technological design problem to be solved. It must design a product that meets the targeted need as well as the resource to manufacture and distribute this product. Customers' preferences, wishes, and tastes are used to evaluate the product-resource combination offered by the firm in terms of its perceived value—the maximum revenue that the firm can generate from its particular product and resource design combination—while expenses incurred in the offering of the product-resource combination to customers give rise to delivered cost (Gilbert and Strebel, 1992). Firms attempt to maximize the difference between the two. "As a result, the rules of the game may also be described as providing the highest possible perceived value to the final customer, at the lowest possible delivered cost" (Gilbert and Strebel, 1992: 84).

The design problems facing firms are complex. Our single-product-single-resource firm can be seen as a long string of interdependent product and resource design decision variables. A design process implies choices and trade-offs in desirable features that are reflected in design content. The complexity of understanding and making these trade-offs "wisely"—of optimizing the overall design—increases with the number of individual, lower-level design decisions with their becoming subject to more and more conflicting constraints. For any individual design decision, conflicting constraints arise from interdependencies with other individual design decisions on a given design evaluation criterion. If multiple evaluation criteria are used, design problem complexity is also increased.

Let's illustrate this with an example. The chair you are sitting on is the final result of a surprisingly large number of design decisions, all of which are interdependent, concerning the chair's own design along with the design of the activities performed to produce and to distribute it. This interdependence of design choices refers to the fact that the "wisdom" or "utility" of any particular individual,

Figure 5.2
Key Relationships in Mapping Organizational Reality to a Fitness Landscape Framework

Fundamental firm challenges (Miles & Snow, 1978)	ORTHODOX STRATEGY terminology	STRATEGY AS DESIGN terminology	COMBINATORIAL OPTIMIZATION terminology	FITNESS LANDSCAPE representation
Entrepreneurial	product-market domain, organizational environment	corporate strategy => design problem	combinatorial space of all conceivable resource-products	landscape of given topography and stability
Engineering	choice of resource and product technologies	business strategy content (current resource-product nexus) => design content	point occupied by firm in the space	point occupied by adaptive agent on the landscape
Administrative	organization structure, lagging and leading priorities, prevailing concept of firm strategy	business strategy process => design process	optimization approach	search (sampling) and adaptation (move) rules

lower-level design choice is contingent upon its context, which is determined by all the other lower-level design choices.

A firm's product design decisions are highly interdependent among themselves. The chair's legs, arms, back, seat, and all their subparts require decisions about size, shape, materials, relative placement in space, and so on, and the "wisdom" of any individual choice is highly contingent. For example, the "wisdom" of the lengths chosen for front legs depends on the lengths chosen for back legs. The "wisdom" of a choice of leg diameter depends on the weight to be supported, which depends on the design decisions regarding materials, shapes, thicknesses, and so on for the arms, the back, and the seat. Each individual design choice sits suspended in a web of contingencies.

A firm's product design decisions are also interdependent with its resource design decisions—with all the choices it makes regarding the activities involved in getting the chair to the customer. Obviously, the "wisdom" of choices concerning routings in the manufacturing plant, the portfolio of tools and machinery to be used, and their sequencing depends on the desired form and functionality of the end product, the materials used, their weights and strengths, and other technical considerations. A firm that selected a carpenter's workshop to produce a chair made of polyvinyl chloride (PVC) or aluminum would be very "unwise" indeed.

In addition, a firm's resource design decisions are highly interdependent among themselves. Choices made regarding operations are made in the context of other operations. This is true not only within a factory, where machine capacities and flow rates must be balanced, tolerances must be coordinated, material-handling equipment must be able to navigate around machinery, and so on, but also between different departments. So, for example, sales teams should promote orders of a "convenient" quantity, purchasing should buy raw materials of "appropriate" quality, and material-handling transactions must mesh with information systems to generate "enough" details to satisfy auditors and cost accountants.

Finally, a firm's product and resource design decisions are highly interdependent with the product and resource design decisions of other actors. The obvious relationship is with customers, where a good deal of effort goes into understanding their needs. In the case of consumer goods, products must "fit" into their lifestyles and with complementary products, and in the case of intermediate goods, products must "fit" into clients' equipment, machines, schedules, organizational routines, and so on. But other actors and stakeholders can be just as relevant.

In general, interdependencies among lower-level design decisions complicate and make more difficult the optimization of the overall design because the need to coordinate them reduces the decomposability of the problem (Simon, 1969).

In the preceding paragraphs we glossed over the evaluation of design choices by employing the notion of "wisdom" or "utility," but its apparent simplicity hides much that is interesting and relevant. The overall design of the chair you are sitting on was likely evaluated by subjecting it to numerous evaluation criteria like size, weight, comfort, style, resistance to wear and tear, ease and speed of assembly, safety, flammability, and, of course, cost. Similarly, the design of the activities used to manufacture and distribute it was also evaluated along a number of criteria, with cost again being very important but including others as well, such as worker safety, effluent toxicity, manufacturing lead time, and so on. These criteria frequently conflict. That cost conflicts with many features desired by customers and other relevant "evaluators" (e.g., regulators) is accepted wisdom (e.g., features that increase perceived value by increasing product quality and shortening delivery lead times typically increase delivered cost). That design is characterized by such trade-offs between perceived value and delivered cost is the basis of economics.

But noncost criteria can also conflict among themselves, necessitating trade-offs (e.g. features like soft, plush fabrics that increase a valued feature, on one hand, like comfort, but may decrease another valued feature, on the other hand, like resistance to wear and tear). So design is also characterized by such value-value trade-offs. All of this means that generating a single measure of "wisdom" or "utility" from the customer's perspective, which we have termed perceived value, may be difficult. In general, multiple evaluation criteria tend to render design problems more complex.

But despite its challenges, complexity may be intentionally cultivated because design complexity makes strategy relevant and rents possible. We wish to underline the importance of these interdependencies, conflicting constraints, and trade-offs for strategists. If a lower-level design decision can be optimized without reference to any context, then this means that its impact upon either delivered costs or perceived value is independent of other design decisions. The overall design can be decomposed into that decision and all the rest. The tuning of such decisions would fall under the term "operational effectiveness", not "strategy" (Porter, 1996), and could be left to—and purchased at a fair price from—functional experts. Because this design decision does not interact with others, all firms with the same target market would eventually be able to tune this design variable to its optimal value, and it would not figure into achieving sustainable competitive advantage. Strategy is most relevant when the "strategic complexity" of the problem the firm is solving is at an intermediate level because "strategy is not so much about optimizing standard problems as about finding heuristic solutions to problems that have been complicated—often deliberately—beyond the point of optimization" (Schoemaker, 1990: 1178).

Porter (1996: 64, 68) argues that "the essence of strategy is in the activities—choosing to perform activities differently or to perform different activities than rivals" and that "a sustainable strategic position requires trade-offs." It is precisely the increased complexity of design problems that increases the number of trade-offs that a firm must make, along with the difficulty of making them wisely, and therefore creates more opportunities for firms to distinguish themselves from their competitors.

In general, ceteris paribus, design problems grow more complex with increases in the following parameters: (1) number of lower-level technological design decisions, (2) number of different alternatives for each of these lower-level design decisions, (3) degree of interdependency and interactive effects between lower-level decisions upon the total design's performance against some evaluation criteria, (4) number of different evaluation criteria, constraints, goals, or dimensions along which the total design will be measured, (5) degree to which these constraints, goals, and criteria conflict, and, of course, (6) the degree to which the mapping between possible designs and perceived value or delivered costs is known or has been compressed into an accurate, solvable model or heuristic.

Solving the Engineering and Administrative Problems: Recasting Business Strategy as the Solution of a "Product-Resource" Design Problem

This terminology of "design" has many advantages. The design school of thought has a long history within the strategy discipline and occupies a special role in strategy pedagogy. In addition, there is a commonality of this literature's message with those of IO and RBVF regarding the importance to the firm of achieving uniqueness in the design that results from strategy formulation (Mintzberg, 1990). But there is yet another advantage: "design" can be both a noun and a verb. This enables it to capture the fundamental paradox of strategy: strategy is simultaneously concerned with content and process.

As a noun, design refers to business strategy content (drawing upon Mintzberg's [1987] definition of strategy as patterned firm action: the employing of particular resources to yield particular products) and hence can be seen as the firm's solution of its engineering problem—its concrete "choice of technologies" (Miles and Snow, 1978: 22) for product and resource. Firms seek to distinguish themselves from competitors in the same product-market domain by seeking out unique positions in the design space. "Different positions (with their tailored activities) require different product configurations, different equipment, different employee behaviour, different skills, and different management systems. Many trade-offs require inflexibilities in machinery, people or systems" (Porter, 1996: 69). Implementing a particular design rather than another involves trade-offs and commitment to that design over some time frame, as financial resources are converted with some degree of irreversibility into bricks and mortar to realize the engineering solution.

As a verb, design refers to the business strategy process, hence, can be seen as the firm's solution of its administrative problem, and has two components, which are termed lagging and leading. "In the ideal organization, management would be equally adept at performing two somewhat conflicting functions: it would be able to create an administrative system (structure and processes) that could smoothly direct and monitor the organization's current activities without allowing the system to become so ingrained that future innovative activities would be jeopardized" (Miles and Snow, 1978: 23). When we refer to the firm's solution of its administrative problem, we are referring to whether and how it decides whether and how its concrete operations—its current solution to its engineering problem—will evolve. This comprises the firm's administrative processes: its organizational structure, its decision making, its performance measurement systems, and so on, which determine resource allocation.

Unsurprisingly, both the strategy process and the process of design have previously been characterized in terms of processes of resource allocation (Bower, 1970; Nona and Bower, 1996; Simon, 1969). Strategy/design processes address two issues of resource allocation: (1) to the implementation of strategy/design content "chosen" and (2) to the maintenance of the strategy/design process itself. Miles and Snow's leading and lagging components can be recast in these terms. Administrative solutions with a bias toward lagging components are those that reinforce the firm's commitment to its current engineering solution and allocate resources to exploiting the firm's current position: organizational routines are documented, communicated, and enforced; depreciating production equipment is replaced with similar technology; current technologies are replicated to realize economies of scale; departing personnel are replaced with people of similar, not different, skills; details are fiddled with to increase efficiency; and others. On the other hand, instead of focusing on the high-fidelity reproduction of the firm as it currently is, administrative solutions with a bias toward the leading component of administrative activities are those that allocate resources to search for better engineering solutions—through internal reengineering or research and development or external scanning of the environment—and, if improvements are found, subsequent adaptation. In the former, the design process becomes almost "degenerate" as resources are shifted from redesign activities of search and adaptation to activities that reinforce the firm's commitment to its current product and operations technologies. The former might be characterized as favoring exploitation, with the latter characterized as favoring exploration (March, 1991).

So, firms can be seen as evolving solutions to a technological design problem that is "posed" by their corporate strategy choice of product-market domain. They are "living," self-referential processes of design constantly monitoring, evaluating, and implementing/retaining—or changing/mutating—their content.

DESIGN AS NAVIGATION OF A FITNESS LANDSCAPE

A formal model of strategy as design would necessarily emphasize the interdependencies among design variables and hence design complexity, because ultimately it must formalize a very old and useful concept in strategy: synergy. Strategy is about seeking out, creating, and attempting to understand synergies: the combining of activities (or, from other research traditions, processes, or routines, resources, or, to use our general term, resource design variables) into a whole that is more valuable than the sum of its constituent parts. "While operational effectiveness is about achieving excellence in individual activities, strategy is about combining activities" (Porter, 1996: 70).

Porter is right. Strategy is about combining activities. It is about combining particular lower-level product and resource design decisions with other particular lower-level product and resource design decisions in a manner that creates synergies, distinguishes the firm from its rivals, and generates rents. We can frame our firm's product-resource design problem as one of combinatorial optimization and then draw insights from that branch of analytical and computational mathematics.

Indeed, recently, such models have been used to characterize technological evolution (Kauffman, 1995a, b; Kauffman and Macready, 1995). These authors speak of "objects" and "parts" in their factoring of the overall technology, which suggests a bill-of-materials, but, in fact, these "objects" and "parts" need not represent physical pieces. The overall technology can be thought of in more general terms as a "design" seeking to meet some objective, while the parts can be thought of in terms of lower-level design decisions or variables. Technology is designed rather than merely assembled. We prefer this terminology of design because conceiving of strategy in these terms highlights the potentially critical role played by processes of cognition and social construction, as notions of what string of design variables constitutes various product or activity technologies, which of these are considered open to manipulation, what are the possible values or states they can take, as well as the which criteria are invoked to evaluate operations and products not necessarily "out there" to be discovered but arising out of individual insight and intuition as well as social processes of discussion, debate, argumentation, legitimation, and reality construction. This framing may perhaps facilitate the bridging of the gap between strategy researchers favoring quantitative and qualitative techniques.

Of course, in order to move toward an eventual formalization of our model mathematically, we must adopt here a more technologically deterministic stance, so for the time being, let's ignore boundary problems related to (1) marketing myopia (the "boundary" or precise definition of what constitutes the firm's "product") and (2) outsourcing, subcontracting, and vertical integration (the "boundary" of the firm or precise definition of what constitutes the firm's "resource"—the activities in the value chain are under the hierarchical authority of the firm). We assume that what constitutes the "product" as well as the "resource" for our single-product-single-resource firm is unambiguously defined so that the boundaries of the engineering problem are well specified. In addition, we assume (1) that we as researchers can agree on a factoring of the overall design problem of product and resource design into a large number of smaller design choices, subproblems, or variables arranged in a string and (2) that the choice set for each of these variables is finite. So, our single-product-single-resource firm can be seen as a long string of interdependent product and resource design decision variables.

The set of all the possible combinations of different states of these design variables gives rise to a combinatorial "design space." Imagine now that for each possible overall design—each possible point in the combinatorial space—an evaluation of "degree of fit" or "fit-ness" ("fit" being what strategists seek in the design school [Andrews, 1971]) can be assigned such that each possible technological design has some inherent fitness. Recall that for this chapter we have opted for a simple measure composed of perceived value less delivered cost. Some designs will obviously be more fit than others, and, indeed, many will be nonviable, money-losing designs (think of our carpenter making PVC or aluminum chairs). There will be at least one point in the space—an optimal product-resource design—that maximizes fitness. We assume that firms are in search of this position and that by modifying their products and resources, firms "navigate" the design space, seeking out those combinations of lower-level design decisions that map to higher perceived value and lower delivered cost.

This string of product-resource design variables, all in a particular state at any given moment, is the firm's solution to its engineering problem. It is what the firm is concretely doing at that point in time and gives rise to particular values for its product's perceived value and delivered cost. Patterns over time in the firm's solution to Miles and Snow's engineering problem—the firm's position(s) in the combinatorial space along with the perceived value and delivered cost components of fitness that are associated with this (these) position(s)—characterize, when contrasted to the position(s) of other firms, the firm's realized strategy content.

Framed in these terms, the challenge of the strategy process—the firm's solution to Miles and Snow's administrative problem—can be restated as, How should one go about optimizing this particular combinatorial problem? Recall that the firm's design process—its organizational structure, decision making, and resource allocation—determines whether and how the firm changes its implemented design content. The firm's solution to its administrative problem (its search and adaptation rules for navigating the combinatorial space) determines how it goes about solving its engineering problem (the optimization of its position in the combinatorial space).

FITNESS LANDSCAPES

Mappings of combinatorial spaces to fitness functions—giant combinatorial, lookup tables—can be converted to fitness landscape frameworks by defining the concepts of "neighbors" and "neighborhood." That is, we must define different designs as being "adjacent to" or "near to" or "far away from" others. "The landscape metaphor is unintelligible without the notion of a neighborhood. For a certain point to be a peak, all the surrounding points must yield lower profits (fitness). But precisely which points are 'surrounding,' are in the 'neighborhood,' of a putative peak?" (Kane, 1996: 3). In our framework, we can define neighbors as designs that are different from each other on only one lower-level design variable.

The mapping of Miles and Snow's fundamental problems facing management to a fitness landscape framework is now complete. The solution of the entrepreneurial problem by upper management, which is the choice of a product-market domain in which the firm will compete, establishes a technological landscape on which the firm can be seen to be seeking points with higher fitness. This landscape is the engineering problem facing the firm, and its current solution—the firm's particular choice of technologies and what it is actually doing in terms of its activities and its product on offer—places it at a particular point, with a given fitness, on the landscape. Finally, the solution of the administrative problem, which is the firm's organizational structure and resource allocation rules, can be recast in terms of search and adaptation rules that dictate if and how the landscape will be explored and navigated in search of higher fitness.

Because different search and adapt rules outperform others on different landscapes (i.e., different optimization techniques outperform others on different classes of combinatorial optimization problems), we can draw insights from our model as to which types of administrative procedures (i.e., strategy process: organizational structure, decision making, resource allocation rules, etc.) are best suited for which types of technological environments. Notice that up to this point we have not yet introduced Kauffman's N or K or built up our fitness landscape randomly. The mapping outlined in Figure 5.2 is a conceptual one and hence could be used to connect the strategy literature to various combinatorial optimization or fitness landscape models.

In this chapter, we draw upon insights from research into adaptation on rugged landscapes built up randomly. Figure 5.3 outlines how a firm's corporate strategy—its choice of product-market domain—is essentially the choice of a landscape of a given topography, stability, and novelty and how this can be captured using variables from Kauffman's NK rugged landscape model. Readers are referred to Kauffman (1995a, b) and Kauffman and Macready (1995) for an explanation of the variables in that model. Our use of the NK model is illustrative, as our purpose here is to highlight the possibility of mapping organizational reality to combinatorial optimization and fitness landscape frameworks in the hope that this may eventually facilitate the formalization of certain strands of strategy research and the building of bridges between organizational and complex systems researchers. But our arguments here are qualitative.

As has been suggested in other work addressing technological evolution (Kauffman, 1995b; Kauffman and Macready, 1995), the space of technological possibilities, if a fitness value is assigned to each point and the notion of neighbor defined, yields a fitness landscape. Figure 5.3 outlines how the technological options available to firms for meeting a customer need by producing a particular product using particular manufacturing and delivery operations, with their inherent contingencies and interdependencies, define a landscape for the firm's product-resource design. This landscape will have a given ruggedness flowing from the complexity of interdependencies among design variables as well as a given stability flowing from the coupledness of the technologies to other technologies in the economy, which may themselves be evolving. In addition, the stage of the life cycle of the product that the firm has chosen to produce can be thought of in terms of the landscape novelty or the amount of search that has already occurred on that particular landscape.

Figure 5.3
Corporate Strategy Determines the Fitness Landscape the Firm Must Navigate

(example here illustrates translation of organizational reality into variables from Kauffman's NK model)

Organizational Terminology	Rugged Landscape Terminology
PRODUCT CHARACTERISTICS	IMPACT ON LANDSCAPE
A) "Inherent" product and resource design complexity	A) Landscape topography
1) parts or variables in firm's engineering problem: few parts => many parts few alternatives per part => many	1) size [A^N] and dimensionality [$N(A - 1)$] of combinatorial search space: low N => high N low A => high A
2) interdependencies in engineering problem: none (simple, decomposable) => many (complex) single evaluation criteria => multiple criteria	2) landscape ruggedness: low K => high K low K => high K
3) interdependencies with other engineering problems in the economy: independent => many interdependencies	3) landscape coupleness: low C => high C
B) Life cycle	B) Landscape novelty
1) phase of product life cycle: introduction/growth => maturity	1) stage of adaptation process on landscape: early => late

ADAPTATION ON RUGGED FITNESS LANDSCAPES

The basic optimization technique for models of adaptation on rugged fitness landscapes, an adaptive walk, can be described in terms of a few characteristics related to its search and adaptation algorithm. Figure 5.4 summarizes these. These characteristics can be altered to generate different optimization algorithms, as suggested in the explanations in Figure 5.4. The impact of changing these characteristics can be captured in two basic elements: the quantity and quality of search and the amount of foolish adaptation, which we define as movement downhill on the landscape. There are at least two ways to achieve foolish adaptation: error-making and decentralization.

A certain amount of foolish adaptation is functional on rugged landscapes because it permits the algorithm to escape suboptimal peaks and perhaps open up a path uphill to solutions of higher fitness. Hence, one counterintuitive finding from fitness landscape research is that a strategy of logical incrementalism (Quinn, 1980) has its limits on rugged landscapes (i.e., in complex environments), as it can leave firms trapped on suboptimal peaks. This may explain why "quantum" changes in organizations are common and popular (Miller and Friesen, 1984; Tushman and Romanelli, 1985). They represent attempts by firms to change neighborhoods without traversing valleys of low fitness.

Using these two simple and coarse-grained properties of optimization techniques ("search" and "adaptation"), we have distilled some lessons from the rugged landscape literature. Admittedly, more sophisticated analyses of the performance of different optimization techniques on different landscapes are possible, but in a chapter that seeks to be suggestive, we are invoking the CLAW principle (crude look at the whole) for this first step. Optimization algorithms that differ in terms of the quantity and quality of search and the amount of foolish adaptation can be expected to perform "better" on different types of landscapes and at different stages in the optimization process in that they find fitter solutions faster. These insights are summarized in Figure 5.5.

Ceteris paribus, the returns to significant, nonlocal, unconstrained search are higher early in the optimization process. For problem solvers who begin at a point chosen at random in the space, the expected fitness of this starting point is "average." Not only do we expect that half of the possible combinations are of higher fitness, so that search should pay off, but in addition, we search far away which samples points beyond the correlation length of the landscape can turn up solutions of significantly higher fitness. Committing to a particular region of the landscape does not make

Figure 5.4 (Part 1 of 3)
Characterizing Search and Adaptation

Search:	explanation	adaptive walk	impact of changes
exploration rate	- search activity per unit time (number of sampled points per unit time)	exploration rate = 1	changes quantity of Search
exploration distance	- search distance (Hamming distance from current solution of sampled solutions)	exploration distance = 1	changes quality (locus) of Search in terms of localness
exploration direction	- search direction (variables on string that are changed to create sample solution)	exploration direction for sampling at all steps of the search = random (i.e., no map is developed that may suggest promising directions)	changes quality (locus) of Search in terms of commitment to a specific region by constraining search
Adaptation:			
adaptation rule	- rule invoked to decide if current solution will change, and if so, to what	adaptation rule is: if fitness (sample[t]) > fitness (current solution[t]), then set current solution(t+1) = sample(t), else set current solution(t+1) = current solution(t)	see "error-making rate" and "decentralization of fitness measure" below

Figure 5.4 (Part 2 of 3)

Adaptation:	explanation	adaptive walk	impact of changes
error-making rate	- rate at which adaptation rule is contravened, such that the current solution actually transitions from higher to lower fitness every now and again	error-making rate = 0 (at the level of the entire string, the fitness remains constant or increases in each time slice)	changes amount of Foolish Adaptation
decentralization of fitness measure	- level at which fitness measures are calculated for input into adaptation rule - to increase decentralization one divides the overall string into substrings, for which individual fitnesses can be calculated and attempts made to "optimize" at this new lower level of analysis - to measure decentralization, one can use the number of substrings into which the overall string is divided; hence it can vary from 1 to N (from: no decentralization with level of analysis at level of entire string,	the entire string is the level at which fitness is calculated for input into the adaptation rule, so decentralization = 1	changes amount of Foolish Adaptation

Figure 5.4 (Part 3 of 3)

Adaptation:	explanation	adaptive walk	impact of changes
	to: complete decentralizat-ion with level of analysis at individual variable/part level)		
parallelism of search	- if decentralizat-ion is > 1 (i.e., we are working with substrings rather than the entire string), then one can optimize these substrings in serial (parallelism = 0; Glauber dynamics) or in parallel (parallelism = 1)	with only one string to optimize across, the "parallelism" of the search is meaningless	

sense early in the optimization procedure when any possible map the algorithm may build up will necessarily be of poor quality given the limited sampling.

Ceteris paribus, the returns to significant, nonlocal, unconstrained search are higher on more rugged landscapes. Local search—the sampling of 1 mutant neighbors—can "trap" the problem-solver on local peaks. Map-building, commitment to particular regions, and constraining search make more sense on smoother landscapes because the low complexity will permit compression into such a map. In the limit (with $K = 0$), variables need be tuned only once.

Ceteris paribus, the returns to significant, nonlocal, and unconstrained search are higher on deforming landscapes. This is

Figure 5.5
Adaptation on Rugged Landscapes and the Characterization of
"Better" Optimization Approaches

1) How much search?		
	LESS SEARCH activity is "better" if	SIGNIFICANT SEARCH activity is "better" if
stage of optimization	late	early
landscape ruggedness	smoother	more rugged
landscape stability	stable	deforming
2) Where to search?		
	SEARCH NEARBY is "better" if	SEARCH FAR AWAY is "better" if
stage of optimization	late	early
landscape ruggedness	smoother	more rugged
landscape stability	stable	deforming
	CONSTRAINED SEARCH is "better" if	UNCONSTRAINED SEARCH is "better" if
ADAPTATION DYNAMICS (change of position on landscape) 3) Apply comprehensive test of fitness conservatively, heeding all constraints, and in error-free manner?		
	REDUCING FOOLISH ADAPTATION is "better" if	INCREASING FOOLISH ADAPTATION is "better" if
stage of optimization	late	early
landscape ruggedness	smoother	more rugged
landscape stability	stable	deforming

most easily understood by making reference to the earlier argument about the stage of the optimization process. The impact of a deformation of a landscape can be to lift the current solution to higher fitness as the landscape is raised or to sink the current solution to lower fitness as the landscape gives out underneath it. The former poses no problem, but the latter can be seen as shifting the search back to an earlier stage. Depending on the ruggedness of the landscape (K) and the coupledness of the landscape to the source of the deformation (C), the deformation of a landscape can, in the extreme, "restart" the search by randomizing a large number of fitness contributions.

The arguments are similar for foolish adaptation.

Ceteris paribus, the returns to foolish adaptation are higher early in the optimization process. This is the principle at work in simulated annealing algorithms of optimization where "temperature" is decreased over time, and the algorithm essentially becomes "risk-averse" as time passes (Carley and Svoboda, 1996). Foolish adaptation early in the optimization process gets the problem solver off suboptimal peaks, which are likely to be only of "average" fitness. Later in the search, foolish adaptation is more likely to take the problemsolver off relatively high peaks.

Ceteris paribus, the returns to foolish adaptation are higher on more rugged landscapes because this foolishness is needed to escape suboptimal peaks.

And finally, ceteris paribus, the returns to foolish adaptation are higher on deforming landscapes. Again, the impact of a landscape deformation that fitness is analogous to setting the optimization process back to an earlier stage. Depending on the ruggedness of the landscape (K) and the coupledness of the landscape to the source of the deformation (C), the deformation of a landscape can, in the extreme, "restart" the search by randomizing a large number of fitness contributions.

QUALITATIVE INSIGHTS FROM THE FITNESS LANDSCAPE FRAMEWORK

In this section, we demonstrate qualitatively how insights about adaptation on rugged landscapes are confirmed by findings in the configuration literature. Early in technological life cycles, search that is aggressive in terms of both of quantity (lots of resources devoted to it) and quality (it is nonlocal), combined with foolish adaptation (i.e., risk taking) should be rewarded. Later on, conservatism should dominate, especially if the technology is simple enough such that the landscape it gives rise to can be comprehended and mapped through navigation. For complex technologies, aggressive search and risk-taking may continue to pay off over longer time frames. This is precisely what is found in the literature, as outlined later. Figure 5.6 demonstrates how traditional organizational variables can be mapped to variables that characterize optimization approaches in the fitness landscape framework.

Our fitness landscape framework neatly captures what are generally accepted as generic or archetypal strategies in the literature, as the ideal types in different typologies and taxonomies of strategy

Figure 5.6 (Part 1 of 2)
Some Examples of the Mapping of Strategy Variables to Characteristics of Optimization Approaches

Strategy variable	Optimization approach variable	Cor-relation	Rationale
STRATEGIC PRIORITIES			
production efficiency (vs. flexibility)	Search	-	an efficiency emphasis is consistent with exploitation rather than exploration, which would be reflected by a flexibility emphaisis
asset intensity (vs. parsimony)	Search	-	fixed assets can be seen as essentially "design decisions" that have been "locked in" for the life of the asset; their presence constrains search and decreases flexibility
innovation, R&D	Search	+	obviously, R&D can be seen as search for solutions/designs of higher fitness; innovation occurs upon the acceptance of one of these discovered solutions
marketing emphasis on novelty	Search	+	marketing emphasis will correspond with the R&D emphasis

Figure 5.6 (Part 2 of 2)

Strategy variable	Optimization approach variable	Cor-relation	Rationale
STRUCTURE			
coordination via standardization (vs. mutual adjustment)	Search	-	standards for products, operations, and the execution of tasks become performance targets and discourage search; the routinization of activities, by definition, discourages search
power centralization	Foolish adaptation	-	centralization of decisions increases the likelihood that the "interests" of the entire firm and not the parochial interests of one department will be taken into account in adaptation decisions
bureaucratization & formality of administration	Search	-	formal rules, procedures, and policies eliminate search; they represent the impact of past lessons and learning on the present
planning & control	Search	-	plans become targets and discourage search, especially as they are elaborated at finer and finer levels of detail
LEADERSHIP			
Presence of risk taking entrepreneurs, pioneers, artists at apex	Foolish adaptation	+	risk taking, use of intuition, and vision reduce "rationality" of adaptation and increase probablity that every so often the firm will step "downhill"

Figure 5.7
Generic Business Strategies

	Character-defining commitment of firm resources to sustaining . . .		
	DESIGN CONTENT (exploitation)	DESIGN PROCESS (exploration)	DESIGN FITNESS (exhortation)
Khandwalla's (1981) key competitive factors	production	research & development	marketing
Porter's (1980) generic strategies	low cost	differentiation	differentiation
Miller's (1986) generic strategies	cost leaders (B)	innovators (A_2)	marketers (A_3), niche marketers (A_1)
Mintzberg's (1988) differentiation strategies	price	quality, design	image, support
Miller's (1987) dominant dimensions of strategy	conservative cost control	complex product innovation	marketing differentiation

and dimensions of strategy can be neatly matched with different elements of the design problem. These are outlined in Figure 5.7.

Khandwalla's (1981) typology of key competitive factors points to three possible strategic priorities or "character-defining commitments" (Selznick, 1957) involving different commitments of resources. Our fitness landscape framework highlights these different priorities and suggests that they represent three fundamentally different ways of competing in a technological design competition.

Character-Defining Commitment to a Design Content

Generic strategies in the first column are based on cost leadership or conservative cost control (Porter, 1980; Miller, 1987) and are frequently implemented by "defenders" (Miles and Snow, 1978). Typically, they are characterized by the absence of manipulation of product design variables. Firms adopting these strategies commit to a particular standardized design content that is mass-produced. To execute this strategy, product designs are "frozen," which stabilizes the contingencies between product and resource design variables (the "K" linkages within the NK framework). With the product design stabilized, the firm has committed to a position in the space of product designs, which means that it has committed to a particular region in the overall design space and can only then reach the fitness peaks within that region. The firm exploits the information it has gathered that has led it to this region. Once the coupling between product design variables and resource design variables is stabilized, then suddenly more long-term and irreversible investments in resource design content make sense. Subsequent investment in plant, equipment, machinery, and other fixed capital essentially "freezes" individual resource design decisions, although cost leaders may continue to channel some resources to exploration of the resource design space in hopes of discovering resource designs with lower delivered costs (i.e., production process R & D). The allocation of resources to plant and equipment means that fewer resources are available for research and development: hence, the exploration/exploitation ratio drops. As investment in fixed capital increases, exploitation displaces exploration not only by taking resources from it but also by making it more difficult to find better designs by limiting it to a particular region of the landscape. Commitment to a particular design content occurs in a self-reinforcing cycle until ultimately the firm self-designs itself into a "machine" producing unchanging products at low cost (Porter, 1980), competing along price differentiation (Mintzberg, 1988).

Firms characterized by exploitation essentially "bet" on product design stability over the lifetime of their capital investments in resources and opt for asset intensity. They are convinced that continued manipulation and tuning of product design variables will yield only marginal improvements in the perceived value component of fitness and hence only marginal movement uphill on the landscape, so they turn their attention to resource design variables and lowering the delivered cost component of fitness.

Insights from the fitness landscape model can help us understand and explain why these strategies are found in particular environments and which strategy processes (particular structural features, resource allocation priorities, and types of leadership) will correlate with them.

First, such strategic bets are more likely to pay off, if indeed, the design content that the firm freezes on is one of high fitness. Successful "freezing" is more likely to occur later in the optimization effort or, in strategy terms, later in the industry or product life cycle (which is when demand growth and industry dynamism slow, and competition intensifies). The design problem is "solved," especially the product portion of the resource-product design problem, so commitment to a particular content makes sense. This is the life cycle argument commonly seen in the Configuration literature and in contingency theories of strategy (Hofer, 1975; Mintzberg, 1979; Miller, 1986, 1987; Herbert and Deresky, 1987). Firms that freeze their product design and begin to commit to a product design content too early, before a dominant product design emerges, for example, are quickly bypassed and eliminated by more adhocratic firms that have not yet adjusted their exploration/exploitation ratios. These bets are also more likely to pay off if the product technology is a simple one, with few "parts" in its bill-of-material or few "design variables" open to manipulation (low N and low K within the NK framework). This is the complexity argument. Because smaller and smoother landscapes are easier for firms to understand and "map," the firm has a higher probability of having developed a reasonably accurate map and hence can be more assured that its search has terminated at a relatively high peak. Think of commodity products. They are commodities specifically because there is no design involved, and competition must be on the basis of cost. These bets are also more likely to pay off if the fitness landscape is stable (low C, or C-coupling to technologies evolving on slow time scales in the NK framework), such that the firm's peak does not sink due to the evolution of other technologies in the economy. This is the stability argument. Other sectors tend to "design around" these products, which are frequently nearer the extraction end of a "raw material to consumer goods" transformation process or are standardized such that they are at the core of economic webs. Commodities and intense cost competition are frequently found upstream in value chains.

If we return to Figure 5.1, we notice that the strategy process variables from the configuration literature that correlate with this strategy and these environmental characteristics are those that tend to minimize search and the likelihood of foolish adaptation. Defenders' administrative solutions—their strategy process—are a "degenerate" design process with a strong bias toward lagging priorities and against search (Miles and Snow, 1978). Obviously, search is reduced if few resources are channeled to R & D and if the goal of efficiency guides production. But search is also reduced and severely constrained by the formal bureaucratic rules and procedures that characterize machine bureaucracies. The existence of formal, documented procedures also reduces the probability of foolish adaptation, as does the tight, centralized control exhibited within such structures. The conservativeness and prudence of professional managers and bureaucrats also reduce the likelihood of risky or foolish adaptation. These firms are structured as "machine bureaucracies" and, like all machines, reflect a commitment to a particular design content.

Hence, the fitness landscape framework helps us to explain configurations in terms of a match between problem-solving approaches and design problems of a particular structure.

Character-Defining Commitment to a Design Process

Generic strategies in the second column are characterized by an ongoing manipulation of product design variables. Firms adopting these strategies never commit to a particular design content over a long time frame and can be characterized as prospectors (Miles and Snow, 1978). They continue to explore. Product designs are not "frozen," which means that the contingencies between product and resource design variables are never stabilized. This makes investment in fixed plant and equipment quite risky unless it is very, very flexible. Also, besides the risks involved, investment in exploration leaves fewer resources available for plant and equipment. Hence, it is not surprising that these firms are characterized by high asset parsimony and production flexibility (Miller, 1986). If product designs never "freeze," resource designs cannot "freeze" either. The firm never commits to a position in the space of product designs but rather commits itself to the continued exploration of the space, attempting to seek out points of higher perceived value. This leaves the entire space available for exploration, and many directions open for testing to see if they lead uphill. At all points in time, firms are producing some implemented design, so they must be at some position on the landscape. As they explore, discover, and implement designs of higher fitness, they change position on the landscape so observers who labeled strategies from the perspective of "products" would tend to label them as innovators (Miller, 1986) and their strategy as differentiation through innovation (Porter, 1980) or complex product innovation (Miller, 1987).

Mintzberg nuances these strategy labels based on the distance traveled across the landscape to get to the design of higher fitness which indicates how the firms were exploring. If firms search relatively locally, this gives rise to Mintzberg's quality differentiation strategy, that "has to do with features of the product that make it better—not fundamentally different, just better" (Mintzberg, 1988).

On the other hand, if they explore far away from the current design, then if they discover a more fit design, this would be labeled a design differentiation strategy because they would introduce "something that is truly different, that breaks away from the 'dominant design' if there is one to provide new features" (Mintzberg, 1988).

These firms essentially "bet" against product design stability over the lifetime of possible capital investments, opting for asset parsimony. They are convinced that continued tuning of product design variables will indeed yield significant improvements in fitness and take the firm uphill on the landscape. This is the bet that they make, which is that their current position on the landscape combined with their search algorithm will find fitter points faster than their rivals. If they are competing with another firm that has frozen its design, they bet that they can climb the perceived value component of fitness faster than their rival can descend the delivered cost component. Because they never "freeze" the product design, they never commence the spiral toward mechanization and machineness. Investment in machines and formal procedures would be investments "wasted" on stabilizing a way of doing things the firm is convinced will not stand the test of time. Because exploration continues to pay off, exploitation does not displace it.

Betting against a particular product design content is more likely to pay off in particular environments, and, once again, our fitness landscape model helps to explain this, with life cycle and complexity arguments that are basically the inverse of those discussed for commitment to a product design. Hence, early in the life cycle of a technology, one expects to see firms thriving with innovative differentiation strategies. Notice that this means that over an industry life cycle we can expect one type of archetypal strategy transition, from innovation to low cost, and this is confirmed in the literature (see, e.g., Miller and Friesen's [1984] maturation transition). Adhocratic prospectors also thrive in industries characterized by very complicated and complex products and on shifting landscapes. Evidence for this complexity argument is abundant, though authors use different terms, like "complex," "sophisticated," and "multiple technologies" (see Miles and Snow, 1978; Mintzberg, 1979; Miller, 1986; Hambrick, 1983a, b). Because product designs in these industries keep changing, the environment is dynamic and uncertain. Continued increases in fitness, through either increased perceived value or decreased delivered cost, keep demand growing and environmental munificence high.

Here again, insights from the fitness landscape model accurately predict the types of strategy processes that should thrive in these environments: firms with administrative solutions (i.e., design processes) with a bias toward leading priorities (Miles and

Snow, 1978), those that favor significant, nonlocal, and uncon-strained search, and those that encourage some foolish adapta-tion. The former is favored by high R&D budgets along with the less rigid and more informal controls of organic structures. The "intu-ition" or "vision" or "irrationality" of pioneering entrepreneurs may be what is needed to help the firm to foolishly adapt, that is, to take risks and to act in defiance of available, accurate information that indicates that an action will take the firm downhill in fitness, at least in the short term. Decentralization also encourages foolish adaptation. This constant redesign of themselves—the evolving nature of their products and implemented activities—has led au-thors to describe such firms as organic.

Character-Defining Commitment to Maintaining Design Fitness

This last way of competing in a design competition is a bit dif-ferent from the previous two. Up until now in this chapter we have assumed that landscapes are a given and that they come with the choice of a product-market domain. This determinism is likely a good assumption if customers' "perceived value" measures of prod-uct design fitness have a basis in objective reality—if it really is a concrete product "technology" that the firm is designing for a par-ticular product-market domain. For products that have a signifi-cant value component that is socially constructed, like certain con-sumer goods that are linked to social status or serve as a form of social signaling, then perhaps this is not the case. This last ge-neric strategy in our model addresses those cases where fitness functions are more malleable.

Marketing differentiation strategies are implemented by mar-keters who attempt to manipulate the perceived value contribution to the fitness function via discursive interventions in the realm of ideas, which changes the preferences used in the calculus of cus-tomers (i.e., manipulation or maintenance of the fitness function via advertising and marketing such that its peaks lie atop the firm's design). Generally, they do not make significant physical changes to resource or product design. With this strategy, attempts are made to shift the global maximum on the perceived value function such that it maps to the firm's current position in design space. Such strate-gies are characterized by high advertising intensity (Miller, 1987).

Mintzberg (1988) nuances this and identifies image differen-tiation strategies along with support differentiation strategies. The former is what is meant by other authors when they speak of mar-keting differentiation. The latter is also an attempt to manipulate the perceived value contribution to the fitness function, but in-stead of using discursive interventions in the realm of ideas to change the preferences used in the calculus of customers, these firms attempt to change customers' calculus "objectively" by introducing complementary products and services that materially change the costs and benefits invoked in the choices made by customers. Essentially, these firms identify certain other goods and services to which their original product's fitness is coupled (via C connections in the NK framework), enter those product-market domains, then jointly design the pair of goods. We might expect to see image differentiation more frequently in consumer goods markets and support differentiation more frequently with intermediate goods, if we assume that firms are less prone to image-driven consumption than are individual consumers.

In both of these instances, resources are channeled neither to exploitation nor to exploration, but to making both of these irrelevant. Firms "bet" that the perceived value component of fitness is pliable enough to be shifted such that regions of high fitness sit atop their current implemented design or such that regions of low fitness sit atop their competitors' implemented designs. They channel resources into constructing and/or manipulating and/or maintaining the landscape itself. We have playfully labeled this strategy as one favoring exhortation, as firms exhort and exclaim the merits of the particular product design content that they have on offer.

SUSTAINABLE COMPETITIVE ADVANTAGE

The fitness landscape framework can also be used to shed light on the question of sustainable competitive advantage. Certainly, as the complexity of the firm's design problem grows, more opportunities for rent generation are created (Schoemaker, 1990), and this can be examined in terms of the design metaphor and the fitness landscape framework. Complexity can be increased by (1) increasing the number of design variables (N), (2) increasing the number of alternatives per design variable (A), (3) the interdependencies among design variables on relative evaluation criteria (K), and (4) the number of distinct evaluation criteria that eventually get collapsed into "perceived value less delivered cost," especially if these conflict (K). Not only do an increased number of possible designs increase the opportunity for differentiation, but the framework also suggests more promising bases for differentiation. Evaluation criteria should be identified that, when met, put the firm far away from current designs, preferably in a region of design space not fully understood.

Take quality, for instance. For durable differentiation, quality should not be one feature that can be merely "added on" to a product.

It should be a feature that, if it is to be achieved and maintained, changes the context of all the other design decisions, so it puts the quality leader "far away" from the cost leaders in design space. This is because the interaction of quality with many product and process design variables may increase inimitability due to causal ambiguity (Rumelt, 1984; Reed and DeFillippi, 1990; Barney, 1991), and the localization of the quality leader "far away" from other firms may make rivals' inertial constraints more binding because getting to a position in space near the quality leader requires "quantum change" of many variables at once (Tushman and Romanelli, 1985). As an example of this, take a new entrant that revolutionized the fresh mushroom market of Quebec in the 1980s—a product considered more or less as a commodity, with competition on price—by emphasizing quality. Achieving mushroom quality meant redesign of the entire value chain, placing this firm on a peak "far away" from industry incumbents. Comparing this company to incumbents, it can be seen that it completely redesigned the fresh mushroom value chain, introducing new technologies for climate-controlled cultivation, nonseasonal, year-round production, new, permeable plastic packaging, frequent delivery by refrigerated trucks directly to customers (bypassing wholesalers), and even education of its customers by a trained sales team. Its packaging was imitable in a rather short time frame, but all the other changes took some time before competitors could match it. It placed itself far away in product-resource design space, on a peak of high fitness.

Another example might be the Body Shop, with its promotion of "green" cosmetic and beauty products—the manufacture of which would be next to impossible for larger, traditional health and beauty products suppliers, who would have to change everything, from their "unnatural" ingredients, to their "polluting" suppliers, to their "unethical" testing methods, to their "excessive" packaging, and to their "sexist" advertising. This firm was able to carve out a significant niche for itself in what was a rather stable and mature market, but to do so it had to break with "industry formulas" and redesign the entire value chain.

Hence, our framework suggests that a nuancing of RBVF wisdom is possible, where three types of isolating mechanisms can be imagined: "simple barriers," "complex barriers," and "long distances." For the first, firms may be faced with different product and resource technological options due to unique, simple resources—like patents or trademarks or mineral rights to higher-quality land, for instance—that others understand but cannot duplicate for some reason because they are legally not allowed to visit that region of the design space. They may be nearby in the design space and understand the landscape, but they face a barrier. The second, "complex" barriers, are those that are emergent from the combining of simple resources by the firm, making opaque the link between resources and superior rents such that inimitability stems from causal ambiguity of the mapping of individual product-resource design decisions and fitness. Attempts at imitation are likely to fail because the imitating firm must ensure that it is observing and mimicking all the relevant product-resource design variables, which is made more difficult as contingencies, conflicting constraints, and design complexity increase. Finally, for barriers of "long distances," the combining of resources into a particular activity system (Porter, 1996)—a particular product-resource design, in our terminology—may put the firm so far away in design space that its competitors cannot achieve the same position due to resistance to such significant change. The original complexity of the design problem facing the firm makes this possible, yielding peaks of high fitness in disparate regions of the landscape. Research into technological change suggests that new entrants into industries are more likely to seek out and discover peaks "far away," as they are not constrained—as are incumbents—to local search around a current design content to which some commitment has been made (Tushman and Anderson, 1986; Anderson and Tushman, 1990).

Our framework also suggests the importance of monitoring the different components of generic design problems that give rise to landscape topography and stability. Technical advances in other industries to which the firm's technology is linked (via C connections in the NK framework) along with new conceptions or social constructions of the design problem of the focal industry have the potential to alter competition and the relative survivability of adhocracies versus machine bureaucracies. For example, environmental and occupational health and safety legislation can be seen as adding constraints to firms' product-resource design problems. New environmental regulation that can be met by the mere addition of end-of-pipe technology will be much more easily dealt with by machinelike firms than regulations that imply more fundamental and systemic change of extraction, transformation, and distribution processes. The latter would favor the more adhocratic and less mechanistic firms in that industry or at least trigger a loosening of organizational structure and an increase in search activity.

Perceived design constraints might be removed as well, opening up new regions of the design space previously considered impossible or off-limits. This is what the strategy literature that emphasizes "thinking out of the box" and "challenging assumptions" is aimed at—uncovering what has previously been treated as a fixed parameter, then treating it like a tunable variable. Set-up times come to mind, when North American manufacturers and inventory control managers who were taught Japanese JIT techniques realized that lot size did not have to be calculated as a dependent variable but could be set at a low value as the independent variable and then turned their attention to "redesigning" their set-up and reordering activities.

CONCLUSION

Our discussion of the insights of the design metaphor and the fitness landscape framework is meant to be suggestive rather than conclusive. Drawing upon diverse streams of theorizing within the organizational literature, this chapter proposed an integrated view of corporate and business strategy as "design" that poses a dual challenge to firms related to content and process.

Firms have been viewed as evolving solutions to large and complicated design problems, and it was argued that the construction then solution of this problem by the firm are the essence of strategy. This overall design problem involves a large number of lower-level design decisions concerning the firm's product and its operations that are highly interdependent with each other as well as with those of other actors in the economy. These interdependencies led us to propose that the design problems that individual firms are solving be viewed as combinatorial optimization problems and that the economy be viewed as a set of such problems. This allowed us to move toward formalization of this view of strategy using fitness landscape models and, in particular, Kauffman's NK rugged landscape model.

We have made a special effort to connect and anchor the proposed model in existing streams of strategy research. At some points this was, admittedly, a stretch, but an acceptable one for a chapter meant to be suggestive rather than conclusive. Conceptually, the language of design resonates in strategy and connects to many other strands of theorizing, including that of technological evolution and the strategy process. Perhaps it can serve in some small way as a tool of synthesis and integration. Continued work by researchers of complex systems, more computationally minded organizational theorists, and strategy researchers who are following the development of research into complex systems is needed. Such a collaboration may help the field of strategy to formalize and to distill its many insights into the working of the complex, adaptive systems that are firms and the economy.

REFERENCES

Amit, R. and Schoemaker P. "Strategic Assets and Organizational Rent." *Strategic Management Journal*, Vol. 14, 1993, 43–46.

Anderson P. and Tushman, M. "Technological Discontinuities and Dominant Designs: A Cyclical Model of Technological Change." *Administrative Science Quarterly*, Vol. 35, 1990, 604–633.

Andrews, K. R. *The Concept of Corporate Strategy*, Homewood, IL: Dow Jones-Irwin, 1971.

Barney, J. B. "Firm Resources and Sustained Competitive Advantage." *Journal of Management*, Vol. 17, No. 1, 1991, 99–120.

Black, J. A. and Boal, K. B. "Strategic Resources: Traits, Configurations and Paths to Sustainable Competitive Advantage." *Strategic Management Journal*, Vol. 15, 1994, 131–148.

Bower, J. L. *Managing the Resource Allocation Process*. Boston: Harvard University, 1970.

Carley, K. and Svoboda "Modeling Organizational Adaptation as a Simulated Annealing Process." *Sociological Methods and Research*, Vol. 25, No. 1, 1996, 138–168.

Gilbert, X. and Strebel, P. "Developing Competitive Advantage." In *The Strategy Process*, edited by H. Mintzberg, H. and J. B. Quinn, Englewood Cliffs, NJ: Prentice-Hall, 1992, 82–93.

Hambrick, D. C. "An Empirical Typology of Mature Industrial-Product Environments." *Academy of Management Journal*, Vol. 26, No. 2, 1983a, 213–230.

Hambrick, D. C. "High Profit Strategies in Mature Capital Goods Industries; A Contingency Approach." *Academy Of Management Journal*, Vol. 26, No. 4, 1983b, 687–707.

Hannan, M. T. and Freeman, J. "The Population Ecology of Organizations." *American Journal of Sociology*, Vol. 82, 1977, 929–964.

Herbert, T. T. and Deresky, H. "Generic Strategies: An Empirical Investigation of Typology Validity and Strategy Content." *Strategic Management Journal*, Vol. 8, 1987, 135–147.

Hofer, C. W. "Toward a Contingency Theory of Business Strategy." *Academy of Management Journal*, Vol. 18, 1975, 784–810.

Jauch, L. R. and Glueck, W. F. *Management Stratégique Et Politique Générale*. Montréal: McGraw-Hill, 1990.

Kane, D. "Local Hillclimbing on an Economic Landscape." Santa Fe Institute Working Paper, 96-08-065, 1996.

Kauffman, S. A. *At Home in the Universe: the Search for Laws of Self-Organization and Complexity*, New York: Oxford University Press, 1995a.

Kauffman S. A. "Escaping the Red Queen Effect." *The McKinsey Quarterly*, No. 1, 1995b, 119–129.

Kauffman, S. A. and Macready, W. "Technological Evolution and Adaptive Organizations." *Complexity*, Vol. 1, No. 2, 1995, 26–43.

Khandwalla, P. N. "Properties of Competing Organizations." In *Handbook of Organizational Designs*, edited by P. C. Nystrom and W. H. Starbuck. New York: Oxford University Press, 1981, 409–432.

Mahoney, J. and Pandian, J. R. "The Resource-Based View within the Conversation of Strategic Management." *Strategic Management Journal*, Vol. 13, 1992, 363–380.

March, J. G. "Exploration and Exploitation in Organizational Learning." *Organization Science*, Special Issue, Vol. 2, No. 1, 1991, 71–87.

Miles, R. E. and Snow, C. C. *Organizational Strategy, Structure, and Process.* New York: McGraw-Hill, 1978.

Miller, D. "Configurations of Strategy and Structure: Toward a Synthesis." *Strategic Management Journal*, Vol. 7, 1986, 233–249.

Miller, D. "The Structural and Environmental Correlates of Business Strategy." *Strategic Management Journal*, Vol. 8, 1987, 55–76.

Miller, D. "Configurations Revisited." *Strategic Management Journal*, Vol. 17, 1996, 505–512.

Miller, D. and Friesen, P. "Momentum and Revolution in Organizational Adaptation", *Academy Of Management Journal*, Vol. 23, 1980, 867–892.

Miller, D. and Friesen, P. *Organizations: A Quantum View.* Englewood Cliffs, NJ: Prentice-Hall, 1984.

Mintzberg, H. *The Structuring of Organizations*, Englewood Cliffs, NJ: Prentice-Hall, 1979.

Mintzberg, H. "The Strategy Concept: 5 P's for Strategy." *California Management Review*, Vol. 30, No. 1, 1987, 11–24.

Mintzberg, H. "Generic Strategies: Towards a Comprehensive Framework." In *Advances in Strategic Management*, Vol. 5. Greenwich, CT: Jai Press, 1988, 1–67.

Mintzberg, H. "Strategy Formation Schools of Thought." In *Perspectives on Strategic Management*, edited by J. W. Fredrickson. New York: Harper and Row, 1990, 105–235.

Mintzberg, H. and Waters, J. "Of Strategies, Deliberate and Emergent." *Strategic Management Journal*, Vol. 6, 1985, 257–272.

Nelson, R. R. and Winter, S. G. *An Evolutionary Theory of Economic Change.* Cambridge: Harvard University Press, 1982.

Nona, T. and Bower, J. L. "Strategy Making as Iterated Processes of Resource Allocation." *Strategic Management Journal*, Vol. 17, 1996, 159–192.

Pitcher, P. "L'artiste, L'artisan Et Le Technocrate." *Gestion—Revue Internationale De Gestion*, Vol. 8, No. 2, 1993, 23–29.

Porter, M. E. *Competitive Strategy,* New York: Free Press, 1980.

Porter, M. E. "What Is Strategy?" *Harvard Business Review* (November-December 1996), 61–78.

Prahalad, C. K. and Hamel, K. "The Core Competence of the Corporation." *Harvard Business Review*, (May-June 1990), 79–91.

Quinn, J. B. *Strategies for Change: Logical Incrementalism.* Homewood, IL: Irwin, 1980.

Reed, R. and DeFillippi, R. J. "Causal Ambiguity, Barriers to Imitation and Sustainable Competitive Advantage." *Academy of Management Review*, Vol. 15, No. 1, 1990, 88–102.

Rumelt, R. P. "Toward a Strategic Theory of the Firm." In *Competitive Strategic Management*, edited by R. Lamb, Englewood Cliffs, NJ: Prentice-Hall, 1984, 556–570.

Rumelt, R. P., Schendel, D. and Teece, D. "Strategic Management and Economics." *Strategic Management Journal*, Vol. 12, 1991, 5–29.

Schoemaker, P. J. "Strategy, Complexity and Economic Rent." *Management Science*, Vol. 35, 1990, 1178–1192.

Selznik, P. *Leadership in Administration.* Evanston, IL: Row, Peterson, 1957.

Simon, H. A. *The Sciences of the Artificial*, Cambridge: MIT Press, 1969.

Teece, D. J., Pisano, G. and Shuen, A. "Firm Capabilities, Resources, and the Concept of Strategy." Ccc Working Paper 90-8, University of California at Berkeley Centre for Research in Management, 1990.

Tushman, M. L. and Anderson, P. "Technological Discontinuities and Organizational Environments." *Administrative Science Quarterly*, Vol. 31, 1986, 439–465.

Tushman, M. L. and Romanelli, E. "Organizational Evolutiuon: A Metamorphosis Model of Convergence and Reorientation." *Administrative Science Quarterly*, Vol. 31, 1985, 439–465.

Wernerfelt, B. "A Resource-Based View of the Firm." *Strategic Management Journal*, Vol. 5, 1984, 171–180.

Wissema J. G. "Strategic Management Archetypes." *Strategic Management Journal*, Vol. 1, No. 1, 1980, 37–48.

Chapter 6

Markets in Phase Transition

Ken Baskin

Health care, banking/finance, telecommunications—these are markets that should strike fear into the heart of every manager. Because these markets are transforming themselves, the business pages tell an almost-daily story of the mergers and acquisitions that might reshape them. Will Citibank and Traveler's Group join to dominate financial markets? Or will their merger produce an unwieldy behemoth? What will happen when Columbia/HCA, once the bellwether of managed care, sheds a third of its hospitals? Will the combined MCI and WorldCom finally reduce AT&T to just another long-distance carrier? Beyond all this Merger and Aquisition activity, these markets are being bombarded not just by new products but by entirely new ways of serving customers. What will happen when Motorola's Iridium enables telecom customers to communicate via satellite from any part of the globe to any other? Or when the Internet makes cheap investment available to anyone with a computer?

This is a manager's nightmare. Not only is it impossible to guess what shape these markets will finally take, but even the dynamics driving this turbulence remain poorly understood, because no one has ever documented the process.

What we do know is that markets are complex, adaptive systems (CASs)—systems whose behavior emerges from the interaction of many independent units. For that reason, we can look at these transformative markets as CASs in phase transition, that chaotic period between an old stable state (the industrial age, in this case) and an emerging stable state (what Kevin Kelly calls "neobiological civilization"). That, in turn, leads us to a question,

Can we understand the dynamics driving phase transition in a CAS we don't understand (markets) by comparing them with the dynamics driving phase transition in a CAS we do understand (natural ecologies)?

More specifically, evolutionary biologists have extensively studied the phase transitions when major disruptions in natural ecologies force them to re-form. What can we learn about what's happening in transformational markets, such as health care, by comparing them to phase transitions in the evolution of natural ecologies? In making this comparison, I believe we can develop some basic thought tools for managers operating even in the most turbulent of markets.

Before we do, it's important to remember that, while both markets and natural ecologies are CASs, they have enormous differences. Consider the dimension of time. Tyrannosaurus rex dominated its ecologies for about 20 million years; General Motors dominated its markets for about 40 years. It takes 10–30 million years to re-form an ecology; it takes 20–40 years to re-form a market. So the time equivalence is on the order of magnitude of a million geological years to every market year.

In addition, our DNA, the code that enables us to evolve, is built into our cells' molecular structure. Organizational DNA, on the other hand, is purely intellectual and, as such, simpler to change.

All the same, the similarities are striking. For example, ecologies re-form after major disruptions in two ways. First, after a mass extinction, entire ecologies are wiped out, and life's interconnections must re-create themselves from scratch. That's what happened 65 million years ago, when a comet apparently destroyed ecologies across the planet, killing off the dinosaurs. Second, a shift at one "feeding level" of a mature ecology can transform its basic nature. We'll examine this type of disruption by looking at how a change in the body type of plant-eating dinosaurs transformed ecologies 140 million years ago.

Like natural ecologies, markets can form either way. Personal computer (PC) markets, for example, formed from scratch. There was no PC infrastructure, and the people who used mainframes or minicomputers weren't initially interested in PCs. On the other hand, the markets in phase transition we're talking about, such as health care, were already mature when market disruptions forced them to transform.

HIGH-BROWSERS AND LOW-BROWSERS, BIRDS AND BEES

When we walk through a forest on a spring day or run through a city park, the natural world we see, hear, and smell is very different from what it once was. The ecological mix we're used to developed followed a shift in the body type of plant-eating dinosaurs about 140 million years ago. Those dinosaurs evolved from "high-browsers," like the brontosaurus, which grazed on leaves high on trees, to "low-browsers," like "duck-billed" dinosaurs, which ate much closer to the ground. Until that time, plant life could grow slowly. Conifers, a dominant form of plant life, were generally safe until they matured and grew high enough for high-browsers to graze on their leaves. Their relatively few seeds were also safe.

However, the low-browsing dinosaurs could eat their conelike seeds and graze on young trees, making it difficult for them to mature and reproduce. As Robert Bakker (1986) noted in *The Dinosaur Heresies*, plant life had to adapt to this new reality or face extinction. Life's answer to this challenge appears to have been the first flowering plants, which developed at about this time. Flowering plants grow quickly and spread many seeds. They were the perfect adaptation to this change in the ecology.

In turn, the spread of flowering plants appears to have enabled insects to become abundant, as they are today. In addition, birds evolved from dinosaurs at roughly this time. It may be mere coincidence that birds evolved relatively soon, in geological terms, after flowering plants. Still, the appearance of flowering plants altered the world for birds and insects, both of which became highly dependent on flowers. Taken together, these changes transformed ecologies across the planet and created the natural world we know today.

This progression of evolutionary developments—low-browsing, plant-eating dinosaurs, flowering plants, new types of insects, birds—illustrates the way one change in a highly interdependent natural ecology begins a ripple of adaptations that can travel through the entire system. Three principles stand out in this process:

1. Punctuated Equilibrium. Long periods of relative stability are punctuated by periods of enormous change, phase transitions. In this case, the change in plant-eating dinosaur physiology set off an ecological phase transition.
2. Different Rules. After the events that cause these changes, species find themselves subject to "different rules" for survival. Life will experiment to find what kinds of living things thrive within these different rules. Those that can adapt, like flowering plants and insects, thrive; those that can't become extinct. Over 3.5 billion years of life, 99.9 percent of all species that once lived on Earth have become extinct.
3. Succession. Evolutionary shifts stabilize by what we can call "feeding levels"—classes of living things defined by their common dependence for food on other feeding levels—as changes at any level destabilize other levels dependent on it. Once plant-eating dinosaurs became

low-browsers, plant life had to evolve. Once plant life evolved flowering plants, insects could evolve. A stable population of flowering plants
and insects could support the evolution of birds. New forms, at different feeding levels, may evolve simultaneously. But no feeding level
can become stable or abundant until the feeding level it's dependent
on has achieved sufficient stability.

What happens, then, if we examine a market in transition, health
care, for example, according to these principles?

PUNCTUATING HEALTH CARE EQUILIBRIUM

Back in the 1950s, when I was growing up, the equilibrium in
health care markets rested on an illness model. People sought their
doctor's help when they were sick. The doctor was then responsible
for "healing" them. Health care tended to be highly personal, and
the health care delivery feeding level, including hospitals and doctors' offices, was central. Patients had free choice of physicians,
and the best doctors nurtured close relationships with patients.
Physicians were paid for the services they rendered, sometimes
through health insurance but more often from the patient's pocket.

Two social phenomena punctuated this equilibrium. First, federal government spending, mostly through Medicare, gave "free"
coverage to the growing population of senior citizens, who use
more health care services per capita than any other demographic
sector. As a result, the demand for medical services exploded.
Mostly as a result of Medicare, federal government spending sky-
rocketed from $3 billion in 1960 to $196 billion in 1990 and $328
billion in 1995.

In addition, a series of social problems—from substance abuse to
violence, from pollution to teenage pregnancy—further drove up the
cost of health care through the 1970s and 1980s. In many cases, the
people whose health was damaged were uninsured. So their costs
were absorbed by those who were insured or could pay out of their
own pockets. The end result: as a percentage of gross domestic product, health care in America nearly tripled, from about 5 percent in
1960 to above 13 percent in the mid-1990s.

DIFFERENT RULES

At first, the key different rule of health care markets seemed
to be that cost now counted. Until the early 1990s, the dominant
method on the payment feeding level (insurance companies, pushed
by the companies that most often paid them, and federal government) was pay-for-service, in which physicians and hospitals were

paid per service rendered. This method offered no incentive for restraining costs. As the price of insurance premiums rose at two or three times inflation through the late 1980s and early 1990s, large corporations, which footed much of the insurance bill, demanded significant change. Executives at GM even began talking about what had been unthinkable—nationalized health care.

To meet this challenge, the insurance feeding level of the market ecology evolved managed care. The idea was that health maintenance organizations (HMOs) could combine the payment and health care delivery feeding levels by collecting a fixed sum for each member. Members could then see a doctor whenever they wanted, either for nothing or a small copayment. Theoretically, when they started becoming popular in the 1970s, HMOs were an attempt to shift toward prevention and a wellness model of health care. Providers would work with members to help them take responsibility for their own health, rather than seeing them only when they were sick.

With the run-up in insurance costs by the early 1990s, managed care refocused on reducing costs. The profits of HMOs and the hospitals they worked with absolutely depended on their ability to restrain costs. So HMOs began doing things like using nurse practitioners to work with members in cases where physicians weren't absolutely necessary. As one HMO executive was quoted in the *Wall Street Journal* (June 18, 1997), "We see people as numbers, not patients. It's easier to make a decision. Just like Ford, we're a mass-production medical assembly line, and there is no room for the human equation in our bottom line. Profits are king."

As more patients joined HMOs through the 1990s, doctors found fewer independent patients and contracted with HMOs in larger numbers. To profit from this growing demand, for-profit hospitals began buying others to create hospital chains, such as Humana or Columbia/HCA, focusing all their hospitals on reducing costs. Even not-for-profit hospitals were merging so they could reduce overlapping services and overhead costs. Chains of HMOs had become the dominant force controlling both the insurance and the delivery feeding level of the health care market ecology, and cost-cutting was their focus. As the HMO executive's quote suggests, the decision-making power often tipped to insurers, and cases where patients were deformed or even died because their doctors' recommendations were overturned as too costly appeared in the media more and more often.

Managed care's single-minded focus on cost reduction, however, overlooks a second different rule. Theoretically, as we move from the mechanical model of the industrial age to the more organic model of a neobiological age, maintaining strong relationships with other parties in any market should become critical. After all, machines exist to generate products; living things exist by nurturing mutually beneficial relationships. More practically, as long as a market remains in phase transition, businesses in it will be rapidly coevolving—that is, in changing to meet shifts caused by other market members, they are, in turn, further shifting the market so that others must change. Creating a strong network of relationships enables any business to identify and react to the process of coevolution more quickly. That's part of the reason IBM and Apple lost leadership in PC markets to Microsoft and Intel. IBM and Apple thought they only needed to produce boxes (generate products) for desktops. Microsoft and Intel realized that they needed not merely to produce operating systems and microchips, respectively, but also to manage relationships (creating mutually beneficial relationships in their market ecologies) with computer and part makers, software writers, distributors, and customers.

Like IBM and Apple, managed care has focused on generating a product, low-cost health care. Yet, in almost everything they've done, managed health care firms have excited anger and antagonism, rather than relationships they can build on. These companies have pursued the bottom line so aggressively that they've alienated nearly everyone in their market ecologies, as we can see in state legislatures' limiting their power or federal government investigations into their operations. Patients often feel they're getting insufficient treatment; doctors are alienated at the loss of the autonomy they believe they need to be effective healers; and nurses are more and more overworked, as their numbers are reduced to cut costs. Only employers who were mostly concerned with costs, anyway, seem happy with much of managed care.

If the comparison between phase transitions in markets and natural ecologies is valid, we can expect a more relationship-oriented model of health care to emerge.

SUCCESSION

So far we've looked at how events on the payment feeding level of health care (insurance companies) have forced changes on the delivery level. Developments on other feeding levels are also adding to the turbulence of this phase transition. At the pharmaceuticals level, drug makers feel pressured to lower costs. So we've seen merger activity, with Merck & Co. buying the distribution company Medco, Glaxo purchasing Wellcome, and SmithKline Beecham casting around for a merger partner, first American Home Products, then Glaxo Wellcome. In addition, we've gotten media stories about insurance companies' exclusively using large pharmacy chains, that negotiated special deals with drug makers. In Philadelphia, local pharmacies brought a court case for discrimination against those drug companies. It may have to go to the U.S. Supreme Court before it's settled. Similarly, in summer 1997, some insurers started cutting compensation to the point that some pharmacies insist they'll be losing money on every sale. With a relationship-based approach, insurance companies and drug makers might, instead, work with pharmacies to reduce costs so that all parties prospered.

Other feeding levels offer rich opportunities as we move to a lower-cost, relationship-based, wellness model of health care. Consider another level dependent on the delivery level, medical technology. As computers become more and more widespread, the market for devices that can diagnose patients from their homes will open up. What would happen if researchers developed a device dental patients could place in their mouths, that would examine for cavities, gum problems, and other disease and send the diagnosis to the dentist's office? What if it could also use sound waves to clean patients' teeth? What if a simple device could monitor critical signs for patients with high blood pressure or diabetes? Might such devices be able both to cut costs, as patients no longer needed to visit the doctor as much, and to improve health, as the simplicity of such procedures made periodical examinations easier and, therefore, more likely to occur? The possibilities are limited mostly by our imaginations.

As long as the rate of change continues at its current high level on any of these feeding levels, the health care market is likely to remain in phase transition. Nonetheless, by studying the way phase transition works in natural ecologies, managers can begin to develop some thought tools with which they can make more effective decisions.

TOOLS FOR MANAGERS

How, for example, can managers use this model to create an alternative to managed care for reducing costs? There are two ways to reduce costs. A mechanical model suggests that managers must control the organization to drive down costs. The organic alternative to control is evolution. From this model, managers can ask what they must do to encourage their hospitals to evolve ways to meet their market ecology's different rule of cost-consciousness. At VHA, Inc., an organization that networks not-for-profit hospitals, members have joined in an effort to use complexity science to encourage just this sort of self-organizing behavior. Two examples of what they've been able to do follow.

At Muhlenberg Regional Medical Center, the vice president for patient care, Mary Anne Keyes, used Gareth Morgan's ideas about minspecs—freeing people to solve problems limited only by the most essential restrictions—to redesign admissions. With the old process, patients might take as long as six hours before they got to their rooms. Finding a way to speed admissions was important because patients did better if they got antibiotics within an hour of admission. In addition, everyone disliked the existing process. Patients hated all the waiting. Doctors often had to run to the hospital, while their offices were packed with other patients, and fill out a lot of time-consuming paperwork. Staff members also disliked the repeated visits they had to make to get all the needed tests completed.

So Keyes brought together a group of doctors and nurses interested in streamlining the process. She gave them one minspec: that all the admissions work be done within an hour of the patient's coming into the hospital, without reducing the quality of care. Freed from other constraints, the group decided to staff admissions with additional nurses who gave newly admitted patients concentrated attention to ensure they got all their initial tests completed within an hour.

Express Admissions, as it became known, produced a series of benefits. Patients were now getting to their rooms within an hour and getting treatment faster. Satisfaction levels increased for doctors and staff, as well as for patients. Because the doctors and nurses self-organized a solution to a problem that bothered everyone, rather than having management impose one, it became an attractor, rather than a point of resistance for change in the hospital's culture. People across the hospital began coming to the group asking for help solving problems, and its culture began to shift in the direction of increased self-organization.

At the Washington Hospital Center in Washington, D.C., Dr. Mark Smith, chairman of the Department of Emergency Medicine, improved efficiency of the Emergency Room (ER) through a series of efforts to make it more self-organizing. In one initiative, he helped reduce the cycle time for receiving lab test results for ER patients. When Smith arrived, the process could take as long as two hours, because it had become so cumbersome. Once the physician decided on a test, a clerk had to enter the request into the hospital's order entry system; the specimen had to be taken and sent to the lab via pneumatic tube or courier; the specimen had to be passed from the lab accession station to the stat lab; and finally, results had to be returned to the physician. By that time, the process had been in seven pairs of hands.

Instead, in a joint effort with the Department of Pathology, Smith had a point-of-service lab set up in the middle of the ER. Now, physicians could request tests by handing a request directly to a lab technician, who drew blood from the patient, processed the sample, and handed the result back to the physician. The cycle time had been cut to less than five minutes. In a few cases, this time reduction got critical information to physicians quickly enough to improve clinical outcomes significantly. In all cases, the new system reduced the time patients had to spend in the ER, eliminated unnecessary work, and cut overall costs.

These are only two of many such efforts that the VHA initiative alone has made possible. The key is that, in freeing people within an organization to adapt to the demands of their market ecologies in a self-organizing manner, health care managers can develop highly effective ways of reducing costs while actually improving the quality of care.

BUILDING RELATIONSHIPS

A second intellectual tool concerns the implications of the shift from a product- to a relationship-oriented market. With the old, mechanical view, people saw society's institutions as separate, temporary stops in their life journeys. We're born into families, generally supported by a church, temple, or mosque within a community. From there, we move through education and then on either to higher education or the work world. The work world could include education, business, the church, health care, sports and entertainment, or government. At any stage in our lives, we might take advantage of any of these institutions. But we thought of them as largely separate. So we went to the doctor or a hospital when we became sick to receive the product of health care.

Today's social problems, such as violence and substance addiction, have so complicated the job of health care providers that it seems absurd to talk about the high costs of emergency rooms, for example, without talking about the underlying social problems. Yet, to make connections between the social problems and their cost to the health care system, we need to view society as an organically interconnected system, with all its institutions interlocked.

An ecological perspective suggests exactly that. For example, bringing up healthy, happy children requires the active cooperation of family, church, education, health care, and social service agencies. When we look at society this way, we see not separate institutions but interlocked, interdependent institutions that can succeed only if they work together. With this view, health care is not merely the job of doctors and nurses in offices, hospitals, and clinics. Nor are patients passive objects to be "cured" or "healed." Rather, an organic model suggests that people are autonomous and, therefore, must be responsible for their own health. The job of health care providers, then, is to help people understand that responsibility and, when necessary, to help them heal themselves.

For people to accept this responsibility, however, the whole community must become involved with health care. After all, many health care problems are largely a question of personal choices. For example, tobacco, diet/activity, alcohol, firearms, and sexual behavior are among the leading causes of death in the United States. These are problems that health care providers can't address by themselves. They need to work with community leaders and educators to build community values that support healthy lifestyles and with social service providers and local government to reduce the social tensions that drive people to unhealthy choices. As a result, the preferred organic solution to these problems would integrate all these members of the community.

That, in fact, is what's happening in a movement toward community-based health care, all around the country. The Champlain Initiative in Chittenden County, Vermont; the Healthcare Forum, a national resource and education organization; the Community Health Improvement Network of VHA—all are working to create partnerships between health care facilities and the widest variety of community institutions.

THE CAMDEN COLLABORATIVE

One of the most interesting of these experiments—the kind of experiment we'd expect to proliferate in phase transition—is the Camden Health Improvement Learning Collaborative in New Jersey. This collaborative began in 1994 as a project using total quality management tools to improve community health, under the leadership of Our Lady of Lourdes Medical Center. Camden, New Jersey, is a troubled city. Nearly 50 percent of the population is under 25, and more than 60 percent of its children live below the poverty line. Syphilis and gonorrhea rates are six times higher than New Jersey state averages; other health statistics are equally dismal. Yet, its 85,000 people don't take advantage of the three health care facilities that serve them.

Initially, representatives from five community organizations— Our Lady of Lourdes, the Camden City Board of Education, the diocese of Camden, the University of Medicine and Dentistry of New Jersey–School of Osteopathic Medicine, and the Area Health and Education Center—met monthly to discuss how to deliver health care to two communities in Camden. Their early talk focused on putting a primary health care center in each of those communities. But community representatives said they really needed help organizing the community so that people would be willing to take advantage of new sources of health care. So the collaborative hired a community health organizer for each community.

For more than three years, the collaborative supported this basic work in preparing the communities. It's now beginning to show results. Where community members used to be wary of each other and of health care providers, trust is growing. Where health care providers in different facilities thought only in terms of competition, they now cooperate, applying for grants together.

By October 1997, the collaborative had grown to 12 organizations, including the Camden Police Department and West Jersey Hospital, a longtime competitor with Our Lady of Lourdes. The collaborative is now ready to begin setting up a "Neighborhood Living Room" in each community. These facilities will be places where neighborhood people can get access to health care but also learn about health issues and resources. One day a week, there might be a free clinic; on another day, there might be a doctor available. A neighborhood host or hostess will staff the facility, and people in the community will be invited to make themselves comfortable. A social worker will be available for counseling, referral, and case management. Each community will use the building as it sees fit, to hold adult education classes, for example, or after-school programs.

A theory of market ecologies suggests that managers who want to create a strong position in any market in phase transition need to conduct experiments in relationship-building, like the Camden collaborative. The very meaning of health care seems to be evolving, and experiments like this one in Camden may provide a more accurate picture of the future of health care delivery than the HMOs that currently dominate it.

Health care organizations can also explore more specific partnerships within the community. One technique they may want to use is 3M's Integrated Solutions program, which enables 3M to understand customers' operations so thoroughly that the company can make significant contributions to those customers' efforts to cut costs and improve processes. In so doing, 3M evolves from being a supplier to becoming a partner. Similarly, health care organizations can ask questions that move them toward partnering with other institutions. What are potential customers' central problems? A manufacturer of specialty chemicals, for instance, might be interested in employee safety or potential problems with new manufacturing processes. A school system might want to find more effective ways to communicate the dangers of smoking and drug addiction. Social service agencies might want to explore better ways to reduce teen pregnancies.

Beyond this, it's possible to map market relationships so health care organizations or those in other market ecologies can understand where they need to cooperate and where to compete. These "ecographs," examined in my book *Corporate DNA*, offer a visual representation organizations can use to begin exploring which feeding levels they're strongest on, whether they want a dominant or niche position, and how they can leverage their positions on one feeding level to another.

These thought tools—focusing on self-organization within organizations and on relationships in markets—are only two that managers can develop from an ecology model of markets. But just these two suggest how powerful this model can be for explaining the apparent chaos of phase transition and even for predicting general directions in which markets in phase transition are likely to move.

A GENERAL THEORY OF MARKETS IN PHASE TRANSITION?

At this point, we need to ask whether the pattern of phase transition in health care parallels those in markets such as telecommunications or banking/finance. The answer seems to be yes. As the rush to merge financial institutions in April 1998 reminded us, the first step in market phase transition seems to be agglomeration. Mergers between giants such as Citibank and Travelers Group, BankAmerica and NationsBank, and Banc One and First Chicago seemed to race each other for media attention. Like the growth of managed care giants, Columbia/HCA or Humana in the middle 1990s, or the joining of telecommunications giants—Bell Atlantic and NYNEX, for example, or U.S. West and Continental Cablevision in 1996, then MCI and WorldCom in 1997—the financial services mergers we noted reflect the mechanical belief that growth is simply about getting bigger.

The central question—one that these merging companies appear to overlook—is whether today's rapidly shifting markets can be better served by extremely large organizations, with all their resources, or by more agile, entrepreneurial local networks. The ecological model we've explored points to the agile networks. Already, we've seen the advantages of the alliances developed in community-based health care over cost-focused managed health care. Similarly, credit unions are presenting such a threat to larger banks that the issue of exactly whom credit unions can serve has become an issue in both federal courts and Congress. We can't know what direction the banking/financial market will take until it's fully competitive. But the dynamics of phase transition suggest that long-term success in this market will go to those organizations that build networks whose members create mutually supportive success.

As a result, managers can use this model of market ecologies in phase transition to understand the dynamics driving their market transformations and develop tools for making more informed decisions. By applying the principles of natural ecology phase transition, especially different rules and succession, they can explore the apparently chaotic activity in their markets as part of an unfolding natural process, try out experiments in the directions their markets seem to be taking, and build on what works. As we can see in health care, understanding phase transition may not be a prescription for success in these highly turbulent markets. But it can provide a competitive advantage by focusing managers on the patterns shaping that turbulence.

REFERENCES

Bakker, Robert T. *The Dinosaur Heresies: New Theories Unlocking the Mystery of the Dinosaurs and Their Extinction.* New York: William Morrow, 1986.

Baskin, Ken. *Corporate DNA: Learning from Life.* Boston, Mass.: Butterworth-Heinemann, 1998.

Gould, Stephen Jay. "The Panda's Thumb of Technology" *Bully for Brontosaurus: Reflections in Natural History.* New York: W. W. Norton, 1991.

Leakey, Richard and Roger Lewin. *The Sixth Extinction: Patterns of Life and the Future of Humankind.* New York: Doubleday, 1995.

Smith, Mark. Interview with Ken Baskin and Gareth Morgan. March 31, 1998.

Ward, Peter. *The End of Evolution: A Journey in Search of Clues to the Third Mass Extinction Facing Planet Earth.* New York: Bantam Books, 1994.

Chapter 7

The Future of Strategy: The Role of the New Sciences

Robin Wood

At the edge of the twenty-first century we stand before a discontinuity of unprecedented magnitude. The rate of change in many parts of the world appears to be accelerating. Yet, we find people and institutions across all walks of life struggling to cope with the scale of change and the rapidly changing nature of the assumptions we are able to rely upon in our daily affairs. Although human longevity may be increasing, we find the longevity of our collective arrangements such as governments, political institutions, and commercial enterprises decreasing. How can leaders and policymakers design and enable our institutions to be more robust, sustainable, and beneficial for all their stakeholders?

The futurists Watts and Wacker have described this situation as the "500 year delta": the end of the 500-year age of reason is upon us, while the age of possibility is just being born. While we were able to explain our world and make progress based on linear cause-and-effect models during the age of reason, the complexity of the resultant technical infrastructure and social arrangements does not yield to mechanistic thinking. We need new ways of thinking and understanding to enter the age of possibility, which is why the new sciences offer us such a rich seam of new insights. As the durability of our assumptions decreases, so, in order to thrive and survive, does the need for learning and intelligence increase. This need for greater learning and intelligence is manifested in several ways:

- As individuals, we sense the need to do things in less time, under more stressful conditions than we have ever experienced.

- As groups and teams, we find the diversity of our makeup and the potential for conflict in our functioning increasing.
- As organizations, we struggle to create coherent and compelling working environments and corporate visions that draw upon the full richness of our corporate inheritance and human potential.
- As social and national institutions, we are faced with challenges of unprecedented complexity that require solutions that are often simply beyond the scope of our current structures and ways of doing things.

The breakthroughs in classical science that followed the publication of Newton's *Principia* in 1686 catalyzed a series of technological advances that spawned the Industrial Revolution. Such advances also led to unprecedented social, economic, and political change, while providing an intellectual framework for economic theory and inspiration for early management theorists. Though classical theory has served us well in its time, the science of complexity is creating a new understanding of the world and of social and economic systems that highlights the deficiencies of the linear and simplistic classical theories.

Complexity science is one of the major scientific breakthroughs of the twentieth century, providing managers with the opportunity to use new metaphors, frameworks, tools, and models to develop strategies and organizational designs that emphasize intelligence, learning, flexibility, creativity, and adaptiveness. It can be defined as follows:

Complex systems research (or "complexity science") is the study of the properties, behavior and evolution of complex biological, computational, technological, and economic systems. (What we will refer to hereafter as "complex adaptive systems"). It builds on the mathematics of chaos and catastrophe theory that describe nonlinear systems and integrates findings from evolution and cognitive science that describe the emergence of life and intelligence. Complexity is not a single discipline but a process that represents the sharing of ideas, method and experiences across a number of fields. The resulting synthesis has generated a powerful set of theories, tools and models that can provide important insights into the complex realities of organizational development, business strategy and economic change.[1]

Recent research suggests that complexity, life, and intelligence arise at the boundary between order and chaos, where complex systems are both stable enough to store information yet evanescent enough to transmit it and hence be spontaneous, adaptive, and alive. Complex, adaptive systems (CASs) grow complex structures and environments that are adaptable, resilient, and capable of generating perpetual novelty. They do, however, often lack efficiency, predictability, controllability, and immediacy. At their best, complex, adaptive systems

- are self-generating and self-organizing
- thrive on individual choice and spontaneous creativity
- are robust, capable of stability and also self-renewal
- are capable of developing and displaying intelligence

In this chapter we explore how the principles of the new sciences (which we refer to in shorthand as "complexity science" or "complexity thinking") can help leaders in both corporations and institutions of governance and policy making understand and address the challenge of change and adaptation.

The central task of business leaders is to create and appropriate sustainable value for the stakeholders in the organization. At the heart of this process lies the ability to learn from complexity faster and more effectively, either faster than, or at the rate of, change (if one is shaping the environment) or faster than one's competitors or substitutes (if one is adapting to the environment). Or one may be able to shape one's environment such that the rate of change is slowed to a manageable level, which itself requires learning.

The core task for leaders of government and our other key social institutions is to provide the environment in which and processes by which the members of such institutions can shape the priorities of the institution in a democratic way, for their collective benefit. At the heart of this task lie the ability to sense, shape, and facilitate the collective agenda and the processes of collective learning that underpin this.

The single biggest missed opportunity for policymakers and leaders of for-profit and nonprofit organizations is the failure to capitalize on the collective genius of the people in their organizations and communities. In the business community, this is recognized by top stock market analysts when they rank quality of strategy, quality of people, and quality of management among the top five determinants of share price out of a list of 50 items. Yet the focus in most management teams appears to be on the nonessential budgets, financials, and nonintellectual capital in the business.

In the nonprofit and government sectors, there is a genuine sense of frustration and disillusionment among the members (whether "residents," "voters," or "patients") in the ability of such institutions to change and adapt to their needs, while they see growing evidence of such flexibility in commercial organizations around them. Management teams in such institutions often find themselves operating under hostile conditions where it is very difficult to catalyze beneficial change.

What is being required of leaders and managers at all levels across all our institutions are innovation, flexibility, responsiveness, and change. If there is one connecting theme unifying all of these, it is learning from complexity—understanding it, valuing it, and managing it effectively at all levels. The process and importance of learning from complexity need to be better understood by every individual. In parallel, the critical differentiator for organizations is the ability of senior management to harness all the relevant knowledge and experience in their organization so that they can shape, adapt to, or reserve the right to play in their particular area of the business landscape of the future.

The same principle applies at community, national, and international levels—a supportive climate for, and effectiveness in learning from, complexity together provide the source of continued progress. Every person, team, and organization both survives and progresses through the ability to internalize and act upon this fundamental insight.

THE BUSINESS FOSSIL RECORD

What evidence is there to support our contention that evolution is accelerating, particularly in the realm of business? Let us start with the growth rates of Fortune 1000 companies over a five-year period. These statistics demonstrate that a majority of the largest companies in the world are growing at or below 10 percent per annum—there are a small minority of highfliers growing at 20 percent or more per annum and a fairly long tail of companies declining between 10–40 percent per annum. It is clear that a significant proportion of these companies may not be around in the next five-year period. That is sobering for companies of this size, just as is the statistic that only about 10 percent of the companies quoted on Wall Street in 1945 were still listed in 1995. The statistics also show that the average company lives for only around 40 to 50 years,[2] and that a full third of the Fortune 500 companies listed in 1970 had vanished by 1983. In fact, the average life expectancy of all companies, regardless of size in Japan and much of Europe, is no more than 12.5 years. We also know that more than 60–70 percent of start-ups fail within their first five years.

Further evidence of the growth and decline of firms and industries is exhibited in Figure 7.1, which demonstrates how, as industries and firms mature, they move from the value inflow to the value outflow stage. Figure 7.1 also illustrates, however, how some firms in the same industry can be at different stages in this process of maturation, either through the rejuvenation of a mature

Figure 7.1
Value Migration

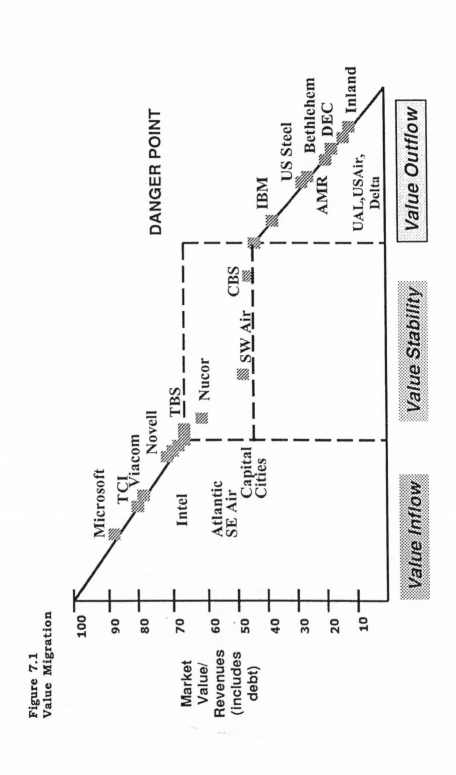

business (such as the specialist steel company Nucor, when compared with U.S. Steel and Bethlehem Steel) or through the development of a fast-growing new market (such as Microsoft and Novell in the value inflow stage versus the fate of IBM and DEC in the value outflow stage).

If left to their own devices, however, it appears that firms and industries generally flow from the top left of this diagram to the bottom right, as the evolutionary process unfolds. The speed at which industries and firms are moving from value inflow to value outflow has accelerated markedly in the past 50 years, according to recent research.[3]

ACCELERATING EVOLUTIONARY WAVES—DRIVERS OF INNOVATION

In order to understand and survive in the growing complexity and turbulence around us in the political, economic, social, and technological fields, it is useful to appreciate the evolutionary trajectory driving innovation. There are seven broad stages of human evolution. At each stage, a particular set of knowledge breakthroughs and innovations drives the economic engine of the most advanced areas of the global economy, forming the platform upon which the next wave of breakthroughs can develop. These "seven stages of mankind" are set out in Figure 7.2, and each stage forms the basis for an economic "long wave."[4]

Stage 1—The Language Breakthrough: 40,000 B.C. Homo sapiens sapiens emerged from the mists of evolutionary time approximately 120,000 years ago somewhere in the Afar triangle in what is now East Africa. This "wise ape" was a toolmaker and user and soon spread across the Eurasian landmass, colonizing new habitats and evolving new technologies as he went. Our ancestors were also highly social, egalitarian creatures whose social structures we can still observe in the last few tribes of Bushmen in the Kalahari Desert. By 40,000 B.C. these hunter-gatherers had evolved a functional language that facilitated their ability to develop strategies for hunting, domesticating animals, and "doing business."

Stage 2—The Agricultural Revolution: 5,000 B.C. to A.D. 1500. Gradually, this nomadic lifestyle settled down in some places to exploit the new agricultural technologies that had emerged from innovations in animal husbandry and crop growing. It is possible to still see this kind of totally agricultural economy in some developing countries, where oxen and wooden plows count as advanced technology. We relied on nature to act as our "factory," replicating plants and animals on a scale that enabled us to accumulate surpluses and trade

Figure 7.2
The Seven Ages of Mankind

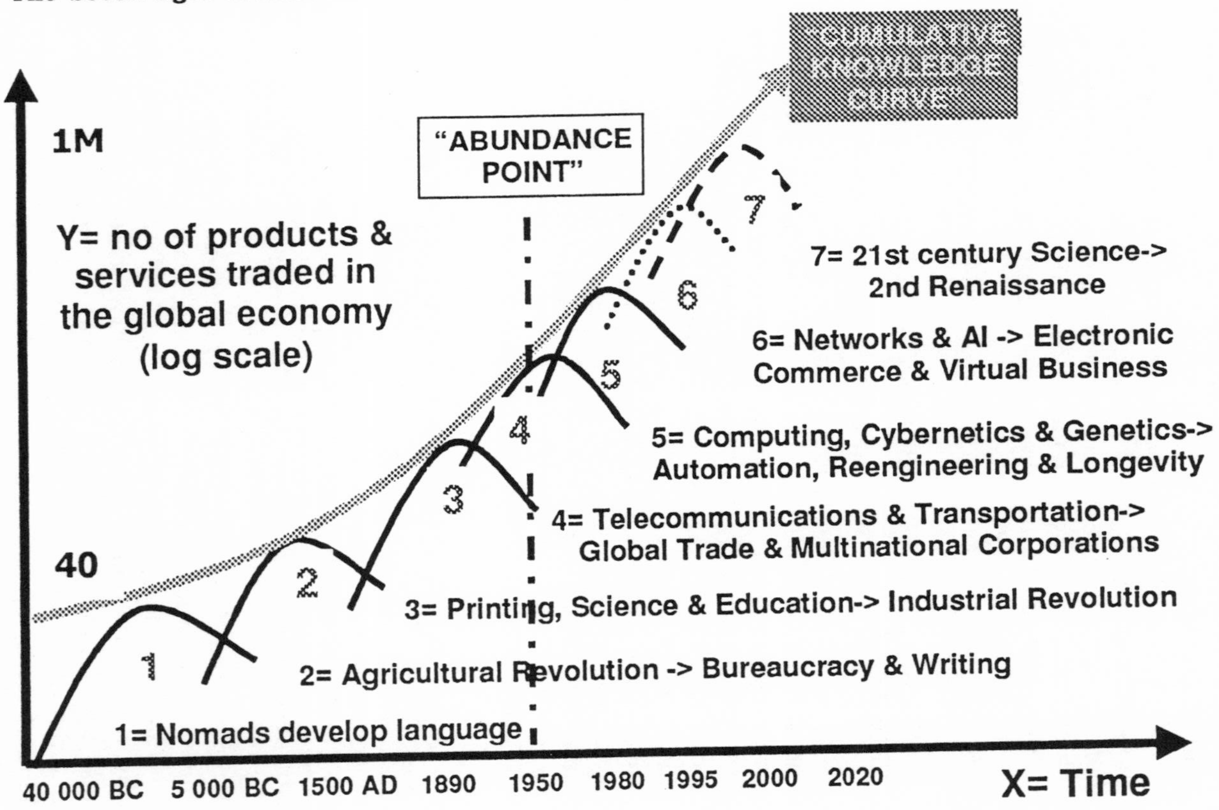

1M

Y= no of products &
services traded in
the global economy
(log scale)

40

"ABUNDANCE
POINT"

CUMULATIVE
KNOWLEDGE
CURVE

7= 21st century Science->
2nd Renaissance

6= Networks & AI -> Electronic
Commerce & Virtual Business

5= Computing, Cybernetics & Genetics->
Automation, Reengineering & Longevity

4= Telecommunications & Transportation->
Global Trade & Multinational Corporations

3= Printing, Science & Education-> Industrial Revolution

2= Agricultural Revolution -> Bureaucracy & Writing

1= Nomads develop language

40 000 BC   5 000 BC   1500 AD   1890   1950   1980   1995   2000   2020

X= Time

extensively across the known world. Writing emerged, and hierarchical structures of organization enabled specialization to occur. The codification of knowledge this enabled created a clerical elite, which dominated the allocation of resources, together with the dominant male oligopolies that characterized early tribes.

Stage 3—The Industrial Revolution: A.D. 1500 to 1850. The clerical elite gradually spread the ability to codify and transmit knowledge across generations. Once the concept of formal education had started, it was only a matter of time before the printing press revolutionized our ability to access new knowledge, without having to literally "reinvent the wheel" every time. This led to an explosion of new knowledge, culminating in the Renaissance and the Enlightenment. Once science and scientific thinking became respectable, the 500-year age of reason could begin. Now we could methodically invent new technologies that could replicate themselves and other technologies, products, and services. This led to the explosion of new species of technologies never seen before and to advances in medicine, the social sciences, and commerce. The world suddenly became dramatically more complex and divided into the industrial haves and have-nots, just as information technology is doing today. Some of the technologies that emerged during this period include printing, coal mining, canals, textiles, and wrought iron. The age of reason believed in itself and in progress—given the right starting point, we could do anything. The linear thinking and technologies produced during this age, however, had some real limitations, and political and economic governance mechanisms evolved to deal with the complex problems of urbanization and modernization. Many of our modern-day organizational structures are still largely designed around these principles and are equally out of date.

Stage 4—The Transport Revolution: 1850 to 1940. By the late 1800s it was becoming possible to transport both atoms and electrons around the globe increasingly rapidly. Advances in shipping and roads led to global trading empires based on colonial patterns of dominance, while, using telegraphs, "wireless," and the telephone, we could communicate across the planet. While still available only to an elite, these technologies would transform our ability to coordinate trade and organize manufacture. The advances in chemistry, physics, and related fields of engineering in this era led to the emergence of the steam power, gas lighting, smelting, steel, petroleum, automobile, aircraft, and chemical industries.

Automobiles, railways, and airplanes now enabled rapid transport to ship people and goods around the planet, and the roots of the telecommunications industry enabled us to talk to each other across vast distances. New organizational forms emerged to cope with the complexity and speed of such technologies and the associated social infrastructures they enabled. Modern cities and sky-scrapers evolved out of these forces, and the seeds of the next wave were born.

Stage 5—The Computational and Electrochemical Revolution: 1940 to 1975. The speed of industrial and transport technologies required much more sophisticated ways of managing technology, organizations, and governments. Catalyzed by the challenges of guiding missiles during World War II, electronic computing was born. Some 15 years later, DNA was discovered, leading us to understand that the origins of life were indeed based on chemical grammar. The growth of the modern economy was largely driven by the automobile, electrical, aviation, chemical, consumer goods, synthetic fiber, pharmaceuticals, radio, and television industries. Organizations began to harness these new technologies, although their basic design did not change radically—traditional ways of doing things were simply speeded up. The emergence of computing and genetics laid the foundations for the late twentieth-century boom in these new fields.

Stage 6—The Network Revolution: 1975 to 2000. The convergence of computing, telecommunications, and media gave birth first to corporate and government networks and then to the Internet. A whole new wave of technology stocks were now in vogue, especially biotechnology, software, entertainment, and information providers. The network revolution enabled electronic commerce to be born and gave billions of people around the planet the opportunity to communicate at virtually no cost with each other and suppliers of goods and services. Breakthroughs in biotechnology and the biological sciences, together with 100,000-fold plus increases in computing power, led to a new wave of scientific innovation in physics, chemistry, biology, and the social sciences. The new "macroscope" of computing enabled us to model complex systems in great detail for the first time. We began to see that there were some fundamental principles emerging about the way in which life, social systems, and business are born, coevolve, mature, and die. These principles form the foundation of the next wave of economic growth, the second renaissance.

Stage 7—The Second Renaissance: 2000 to ? Breakthroughs in complexity science, quantum physics, chaology and fractal geometry, biology and genetics, neural nets and advanced computing and networking are being applied to expand our understanding of the economic and social webs in which we find ourselves operating. We are discovering that the "laws" of equilibrium economics are more the exception rather than the rule and that competitive strategy does not tell us much about business success. Rising productivity in manufacturing and service industries driven by these technologies, together with rising employment and lower inflation in most developed economies, continues to surprise politicians and economists of the old school. Global trade is now over 12 percent of global gross domestic product and rising, and the dominant issues on the agenda are no longer war and peace, famine and disease, but education, learning, and local quality of life issues. New forms of art and culture flourish just as they did in the first renaissance, particularly popular forms of self-expression and communication.

In the second renaissance we find policymakers and executives undergoing a transformation in their perceptions about what it means to lead and manage. A number of fundamental assumptions are being challenged, including:

- Equilibrium is assumed to be the norm, and the strategists' job is to find ways of maintaining corporate equilibrium through planning approaches and systems—even when we know that organizations and markets are complex, adaptive systems operating far from equilibrium.
- Predictability and control—we work in areas and ways in which we can attempt to predict the future and control most of the aspects of our destiny. We may even know what we don't know, but what kills businesses is what we don't know we don't know. How do we deal with uncertainty?
- Choice and intentionality—we assume that with enough information and a rational planning process we can make logical choices and deliver on the intentions we set ourselves. Our plans and budgets have a bad habit of coming unstuck with monotonous regularity. What does strategic choice mean in a complex, uncertain, far-from-equilibrium, fractal world?
- Best way of doing things—we believe that there are recipes that will guarantee success, if we can just find them and make them stick. We use these recipes as alibis when things go wrong and then reach out for the next fad. Surely there must be a way to escape this vicious circle of "initiativitis."

At the core of complexity-based strategy lie the art and science of economic webs, understood through the laws of complex, adaptive systems theory. An economic web is actually a set of firms acting as nodes in a network, interconnected by a web of relationships, contracts, and transactions across which flow resources and information. Such webs are often referred to as a "business ecosystem." Economic webs lie at the heart of business evolution, for the coevolution of the players, relationship, and resources in an economic web drives innovation and thereby evolution.

Strategy can be viewed as both an object and a process. "Strategy as object" usually defines a sequence of moves or a "play" in a specific situation and is of a lower order than strategy as a process of conscious evolution. As an object, we can recognize a strategy when we see it, usually in retrospect for example, "Alfred Sloan's strategy of decentralization and divisionalization for GM was superior to Ford's strategy of centralized bureaucracy." We can also select a specific strategy as one we believe will deliver a particular payoff, for example, "If we buy competitor X, that will give us a entrée into market Y, which will finally make dimension Z profitable."

So how can we think differently and learn to cocreate desirable futures for ourselves and our organizations under these conditions? Leaders and managers need to learn how social and business evolution works, in order to make a difference.

Some interesting examples of the very different perspective that complexity thinking provides on business success and failure are captured in a series of "laws" coined by the author Kevin Kelly.

1. *Distribute being:* distribute intelligence and resources outward in any CAS to the parts, providing redundancy in functionality and resources. Ensure that the parts are, however, designed to be complementary, to ensure their collaboration. The challenge is to ensure effective integration within a complex system of many parts, where that integration is embodied in the "genetic code" of the parts. Apple Computer grew successfully in this mode during the 1980s through its principle of "Apple genes" in the Apple family of companies.[5]

2. *Control from the bottom up:* let the parts of the CAS coordinate their own control systems rather than imposing them from the "top." VISA is a successful network of banks offering the VISA card around the world. The network operates around some basic standards for issuing cards and processing transactions. The members of VISA agree to a code of practice that ensures that fraud is minimized and that good service to customers is guaranteed. Although there is a VISA head office, the system works only due to the "bottom-up" control exercised by its members.

3. *Cultivate increasing returns:* increase the leverage of small actions that have large cumulative effects as they amplify their power through feedback processes. This is often done through a "win-win" action, for example, Netscape originally distributed its first version of Netscape Navigator software for free over the Internet and within months had over 90 percent market share of the browser market. It was then able to sell much more server software to companies that wanted a presence on the Net.

4. *Grow by chunking:* chunk multiple, simple components/layers into more complex systems, using very simple rules, much as DNA uses four building blocks to create a large number of proteins and cell types. McDonalds grew in this way during its first three decades, where the core design invented by the McDonald brothers in San Bernardino, California, was replicated first across the United States and then around the world one chunk at a time. Each new outlet provided new lessons and challenges that were incorporated into the learning process to improve subsequent outlets.[6]

5. *Maximize the fringes:* encourage diversity, eccentricity, and instability at the fringe of a system, thereby increasing resilience through perpetual innovation. 3M's Post-it note story[7] is a classic example of how the "skunk-works" principle in 3M's laboratories enabled a failed "sticky" glue formula to be reinvented as the weak adhesive on the back of Post-it notes by Art Fry, the lab technician involved. Skunkworks are projects at the fringes of 3M where inventors and technicians are encouraged to work on their own agenda some 10–15 percent of the time.

6. *Honor your errors:* use errors as key signals for new learning that needs to take place in a system, rather than responding by attempting to shift blame. It is a little-known fact that the complaints department in most organizations is the source of many potential improvements and innovations—if only complaints were treated as opportunities for learning in more organizations. Nordstrom takes this to its extreme when it tells employees that the only company rule is "that there are no rules." Delighting the customer is the number one priority in Nordstrom, and employees are empowered to do just about anything to do this, particularly when a customer complains, or there is some sort of internal problem.

7. *Pursue no optima:* have multiple goals: in constantly shifting strategic landscapes (otherwise known as "fitness landscapes" or "knowledge landscapes"), optima are very expensive to pursue, as they not only take major investment to achieve but also rigidify an organization into an overspecialized position that makes change and adaptation very difficult. The concept of a portfolio is one way of hedging against uncertainty—whether the portfolio contains markets, products/services, goals, shares, or people. It also positions the organization to pursue opportunities in "adjacent possible" terrains accessible to it by virtue of the flexibility inherent in having multiple goals.

8. *Seek persistent disequilibrium:* encourage change and learning in an organization through disequilibrium. This is a recurring theme in much of Tom Peter's work, from *In Search of Excellence* to liberation management, which revolves around *Thriving on Chaos,* the title of his second book. Disequilibrium enables an organization to move very quickly from one position to another, in much the same way as sprinters are poised at the starting blocks prior to a race rather than lying flat on their backs or standing at attention (i.e., at equilibrium)! All living systems operate at the "edge of chaos," which is very far from equilibrium. Equilibrium is the state of inanimate objects, that is, dead things. For example, the human body reaches equilibrium upon death, but while it is alive, it relies on chains of catalytic reactions that are prevented from causing chaos within the body by regulatory functions at many levels.[8]

9. *Change changes itself:* the dynamics of change ensure that living systems are continually undergoing change at one or more levels. Because successful species and individuals are regularly initiating, responding to, adapting to, and changing as a result of changes in themselves and their environment, the process of life itself can be seen as fluid and highly unstable. Learning organizations[9] recognize the

ninth law by institutionalizing the change process into the genetic code of their processes and systems. This reemphasizes the point made by Senge that the fifth discipline (systems thinking) is essential to deal with all the complex feedback in living systems, particularly organizations. If change changes itself, then we must be capable of understanding the consequences of change, and design our organizations and business ecosystems accordingly.

THE DEATH OF "OLD STRATEGY" AND THE EMERGENCE OF THE "NEW STRATEGY"

Over the past decade, "old strategy" has died, and "new strategy" has been born. What is "new strategy," and what is its future? The purpose of this part of the chapter is to sketch an artist's impression of where strategy is going and why the future of your business, job, and career depends on your knowing where it's headed.

Let's start with "old strategy." The crisis of "old strategy" began when Jack Welch threw out the strategic planners at GE in the early 1980s, and Tom Peters and Bob Waterman imported "culture" and "a bias for action" into the managerial vocabulary. Henry Mintzberg had long proclaimed that the strategic planning emperor had no clothes. The fall of the oxymoron called strategic planning also coincided neatly with the death throes of fourth-wave industries and the creative destruction unleashed in all of our mature economic structures.

Meanwhile, a major shift took place in the managerial zeitgeist. A new generation of savvy, wired baby boomers moved into the executive suites and began to transform the hierarchical, bureaucratic structures they inherited. From the mid-1980s onward, the vertical, pyramid organization was to become a lethal legacy, not the safe haven of lifetime employment it had once promised to become.

A decade of focusing on the core business and core competencies followed, leaving us with much leaner, fitter organizations capable of competing in global markets awash with tantalizing new opportunities and unprecedented competitive threats. The speed with which deregulation, privatization, downsizing, delayering, and reengineering swept the planet between the mid-1980s and early 1990s hammered the final nails in the coffin of "old strategy," which was to prove useful only in the slower and more predictable world of the first three postwar decades.

SOWING THE SEEDS OF "NEW STRATEGY"

While "old strategy" was being dragged into the old-age home, the seeds of "new strategy" were being sown. Pierre Wack, the head of planning, and the committee of managing directors at Shell began experimenting with scenarios in the early 1970s, telling us that even if we could not predict the future, we could at least learn from uncertainty. Then, in the mid-1980s, Hamel and Prahalad were starting their work on core competencies, strategy as stretch and corporate reinvention. While Michael Porter was putting the finishing touches to his various opuses on competitive strategy based in classic industrial economics, the resource-based strategy thinkers such as Hannan and Freeman and Snow and White were beginning to explore the implications of ecology and natural selection for populations of organizations.

The euphemistically named "right-sizing," quality, and reengineering bandwagons dominated many executive agendas during the early 1990s. In 1994, however, when Hamel and Prahalad published *Competing for the Future* at much the same time that Peter Schwartz's *The Art of the Long View* hit the bookshelves, it became clear that "new strategy" was being born.

During this period, groundbreaking work was taking place at the Santa Fe Institute led by Stuart Kauffman, John Holland, and Brian Arthur. They began to sketch the outlines of a new science that would transform the way in which we think about ourselves, our organizations, and our economies. Building on the work of early pioneers in the fields of chaos, complexity, artificial life, evolutionary biology, and the new economics, teams at Santa Fe argued and modeled their way to a new understanding of what it means to "do strategy" in complex, living, evolving systems.

Two further landmark events completed the sowing of the seeds: in 1996 Jim Moore's *The Death of Competition* and Adrian Zlywotzky's *Value Migration* laid firmer foundations for our understanding of the forces of coevolution in economic webs and the practical implications of this for business strategy and design in the field. Now new strategy could start sprouting out of the rich soil of research and insights generated by these pioneers.

NEW STRATEGY SPROUTS GREEN SHOOTS

What do these developments mean for you, your business, and the economy? New strategy may be the most powerful unifying concept yet to emerge in the worlds of business, management, and organizations, and those who grasp it have the opportunity to build fortunes and make differences in the world that previous generations of managers and strategists would find startling, for new strategy goes to the heart of the process of value creation, underpinned by scientific and creative endeavors that are only just beginning to gather momentum. It also tells us much about what it means to be human.

The heart of the story begins with the speed at which the global economy and technology are now coevolving. As Stan Davis and Chris Myers point out in *Blur,* and Kevin Kelly and his kin make clear in *Wired,* the global economy is moving at a faster pace than ever before in history. Trying to keep ahead or even apace is proving increasingly difficult for executives, consumers, technologists, politicians, and strategists. The complexity of the global economy is now increasing at an exponential rate, driven by the positive feedback loop between knowledge breakthroughs, technology waves, and organizational evolution. The smarter that organizations, people, and societies become, the faster they develop and demand complex new combinations of products, services and infrastructures. For example, our cave-dwelling ancestors could trade in no more than 20–40 commodities in 40,000 B.C. Today we grapple with nearly 1 million tradable products and services in the global economy, and

Table 7.1
Adaptive and Non-Adaptive Incumbents versus Rule Breakers

Rule Breaker	Adaptive Incumbent/s	Nonadaptive Incumbents
Direct Line Insurance	Norwich Union	Traditional Insurance Brokers
Amgen	Glaxo Wellcome, Smith Kline Beecham	
Nintendo	Sony	Philips
Amazon Books	Barnes & Noble	Traditional bookstores
Canon		Xerox
Netscape	Microsoft	Novell
Virgin Airlines	British Airways	Air France, U. S. Air
Japanese, Swatch & Electric Cars	Ford, Chrysler	General Motors
Compaq	Hewlett Packard	IBM, DEC, NCR
Category Killer Retailers, e.g., Toys-r-Us, Benetton	Wal-Mart	K-Mart, Sears Roebuck

the number is rising exponentially as you read this sentence. That is not to mention the variety and range of products and services within those 1 million categories, which provides us with uncountable infinities of choices and demands.

In order to deal with the complexity and dynamism in this global, instant, electronic knowledge economy, new strategy has emerged around four core building blocks. New strategy is essentially

1. A strategic conversation between a community of stakeholders about the future of their community and their joint enterprise. Strategic conversation is embodied and given voice through strategic dialogue.
2. A future navigating process within the enterprise that ensures that the organization has a robust strategic direction capable of learning from uncertainty and dealing with the unexpected.
3. An approach to business design enabling the enterprise and its management to explore and find the profit zones in its value network and protect those profits in a sustainable way.
4. A way of developing the coherence between a business design and an organization's capability to deliver the value implicit in that design, together with the capacity for self-renewal.

To get to grips with these elements of the new strategy, we need grounding in the dynamics and principles of social and business evolution.

SOCIAL AND BUSINESS EVOLUTION

The rapid evolution of the world around us has been the subject of media comment since the publication of *Future Shock* in 1973. An industry of writers about change has surfaced,[10] while management gurus such as Tom Peters declare, "We are quite simply in the midst of the most violent and profound economic change in at least the last 150 years... the technological revolution... is the most profound in well over 200 years."

This rapid change has now led to the situation that some industries are facing product and model changes anywhere between three months (the PC business) to two years (automobiles and aircraft). Service companies may have only a matter of weeks or months to innovate in response to emerging customer needs, supplier changes, or competitor moves. In Table 7.1 we can see a list of "rule breakers," new entrants who have changed the shape and structure of the industry they were in. Although not all rule breakers survive, they have the effect of shaking up an industry and changing the rules of the competitive game. Some incumbents manage to be adaptive and innovate around the new entrants, while others lose market share and fail to adapt. It is estimated that over 70 percent of major new entrants into markets come from outside the traditional industry boundaries.

There is now growing evidence to suggest that the parallels between how rule breakers create or enter a market and how the incumbents respond have remarkably similar dynamics to the way in which new species create a new niche or invade an existing one in nature. In other words, the principles of natural evolution can now be seen to apply in the social as well as the biological field, though with some important modifications.

Given the evolutionary story we have just unfolded, it is clear that the way we make a living, what constitutes a business or a government, and how we run them have changed quite dramatically over the past few millennia. There is some evidence to suggest that the way in which this change happens, however, may have some common themes:

The Power Law. The process of evolution tends to produce many small extinctions and changes and a few large ones, this is called the power law and applies to both the birth and death rates of businesses as well as the changes that take place inside them. This is also known in some quarters as the principle of punctuated equilibrium.

The Law of Selection/Substitution. Sometimes species and business designs simply die out due to their inability to respond to the changing environment around them. At other times, extinction is a result of new species, tribes, cultures, languages, and business designs invading the niches of others in a characteristic way. The substitution of one species (or business design) for another is also a form of natural selection.

The Law of Complementarity and Innovation. New species, tribes, cultures, languages, and business designs emerge spontaneously from rich, "supracritical" environments where interesting combinations of things tend to combine and recombine into novel forms and styles. The most successful combinations evolve into future generations, and the less successful are demoted or disappear.

The Law of Self-Organization. For a complex system to emerge at the boundary between order and chaos, at a physical level, there must be

- a suitable number of basic elements in the system that are
- capable of being connected to each other in
- somewhere between two to five ways so that
- flexible emergent structures form that are
- capable of changing and evolving.

BUSINESS ECOSYSTEMS: NETWORKS OF RELATIONSHIPS ENABLING VALUE CREATION

In order to enhance the way in which executives, managers, and leaders of all kinds facilitate the value creation process using the principles of business evolution, it is useful to think of two broad domains of activity occurring within and around a firm: (1) the external domain—this describes the world of possibilities external to a firm, over which it has little or no control. Within this world there are stable elements (some of which may be predetermined), trends, and uncertainties. (2) the internal domain—this describes the world of capabilities within a firm, which are a function of decisions and commitments by the firm, over which the firm has total, or at least some degree of, control or influence.

The External Domain—Landscapes of Possibility

The domain external to a firm can be usefully divided into four of subdomains, in which the lower levels are contained within the higher levels. At the highest level, we have:

The business environment, which is a set of political, economic, social and technological actors and forces that are largely outside the control and influence of a business and that can potentially impact the business both positively and negatively. At the next level we have:

A business ecosystem, which is a community of organizations and stakeholders ("players") operating within a particular business environment that collaborate and compete in an economic web of relationships. This web of relationships coevolves through time subject to the general forces in the business environment and the specific moves made by the web of players. At the next level we have:

Strategic landscapes, which are the locations in a business ecosystem in which competition and collaboration take place between players according to the rules of the game they are playing. The players and the landscapes coevolve depending on the nature of their interactions and outcomes. At the next level we have:

Scenarios, which are different possible future configurations of the business ecosystem, each of which has different implications for the design, operation, and management of a business. Scenarios can also describe how the specific strategic landscapes for a product/process/infrastructure play out under different rules of the game.

The external domain comprises a land of possibility for the firm. Such possibilities can be both positive (e.g., new business opportunities) as well as negative (e.g., competitor entry into a firm's most profitable market). In the language of complexity, this land of possibility can sometimes go "supracritical," where small changes in initial conditions at the microscale lead to large effects at the macroscale in the business environment. This kind of chain reaction can be the result of for example:

Figure 7.3
External and Internal Domains in and around a Firm

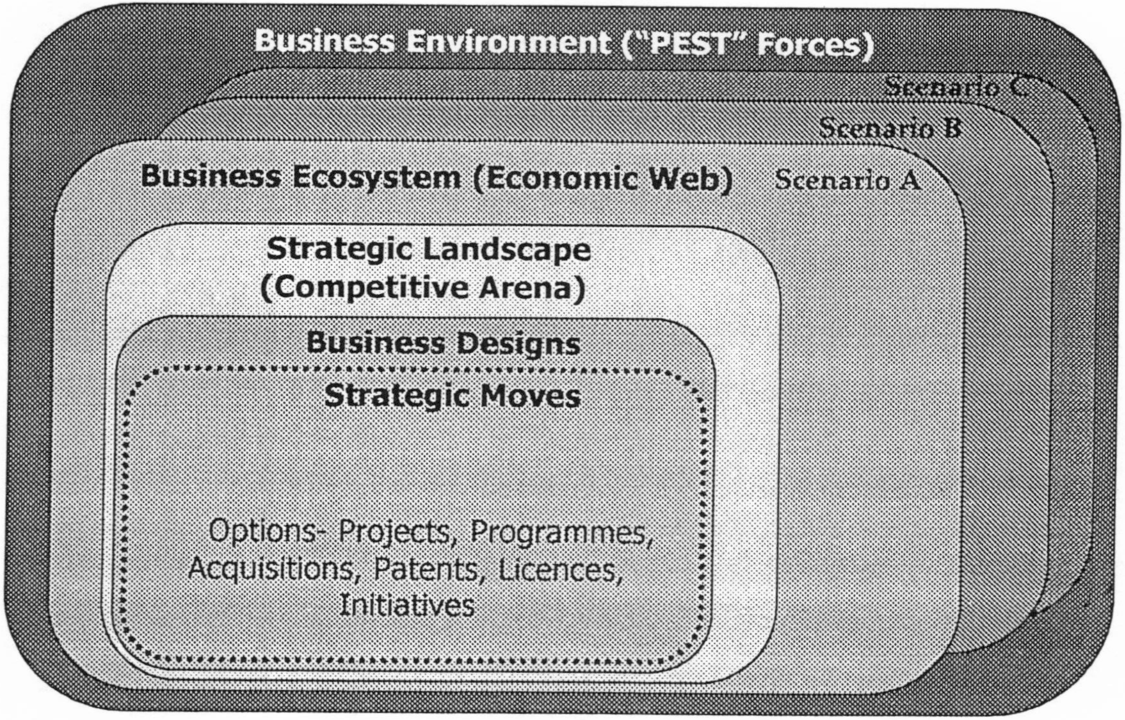

Business Environment ("PEST" Forces)

Scenario C
Scenario B
Scenario A

Business Ecosystem (Economic Web)

Strategic Landscape
(Competitive Arena)

Business Designs

Strategic Moves

Options- Projects, Programmes,
Acquisitions, Patents, Licences,
Initiatives

1. Microeconomic events, such as product and standard lock-ins, which lead to increasing returns and high barriers to entry, as in the case of VHS in video players and Microsoft Windows operating systems for personal computers.
2. Macroeconomic events, such as the collapse of the Korean economy through the collapse of the key *chaebols*, leading to a major economic downturn in Asia during 1997.
3. Political events, such as the election of the Labor Party to power in Britain in 1997 and the election of the Democrats to power in the United States in 1992, leading to major restructuring of the economic and social landscapes in both countries.

The Internal Domain-Capability Space

The domain internal to a firm can be usefully divided into four subdomains, in which the lower levels are contained within the higher levels. At the highest level, we have:

Business designs, which describe different possible configurations of a business idea and how that idea adds value and is embodied through the application of distinctive capabilities to relevant markets to create sustainable competitive advantage. Like species in natural ecosystems, business designs have fitness and sustainability functions that can be improved in a number of ways, through more appropriate strategic moves being made on the strategic landscape and a broader range of robust and complementary options being available to the firm from which to make strategic moves. At the next level we have:

Strategic moves which are groups of activities (such as projects, programs, acquisitions, licenses, patents) intended to improve the strategic position of a business/product/technology on a specific landscape. Such moves can improve the fitness and sustainability of the firm if they are informed by a broad range of strategic choices. At the next level we have:

Options, which are alternative strategic moves that might be made depending on which scenario (pure or hybrid) we believe we are operating in. Options link into real/financial options methods plus economic and shareholder value-added measures, as each option can be compared with other options and the status quo without the option. At the next level we have:

Human activities and business processes, which are the primary building blocks of the capability of a firm. Without such activities and processes, business designs, strategic moves, and options would be hollow blueprints or recipes, rather than embodied value-adding systems.

Within the internal domain we have the worlds of management and organizations, where the familiar events and rituals of work are played out against the backdrop of the external domain (or "outside world," as it is often called in firms and institutions). We need to explore some of the dynamics of the entrepreneurial process, which appears to drive much of business evolution and the gales of "creative destruction" noted by Schumpeter earlier this century.

ENTREPRENEURIAL STRATEGY FORMATION AND EVOLUTION

At least three primary entrepreneurial and leadership processes that help explain how entrepreneurial value creation happens in the world of complex social systems:

1. Reconfiguration of combinations of building blocks (practices/technologies/designs) at many levels, including functionality, competencies, values, capabilities, infrastructure, processes, and systems.
2. Cross-appropriation of practices/technologies/designs that work in other worlds or subworlds.
3. Articulation—solidarity, community, and emergence of shared identity in a shared disclosive space.

Reconfiguration, cross-appropriation, and articulation are enacted within the external and internal domains of an organization or institution. Each of these domains is located at a specific point on the map of socially constructed reality in a society, which point is different for each organization or institution.

Business designs and customer value propositions are situated in particular styles of practice within these different, socially constructed realities. The usefulness of the activities of reconfiguration, cross-appropriation, and articulation lies in their ability to define how customer value propositions evolve within the web of cultural practices and norms that underlie the purpose and practice of businesses and institutions in postmodern societies.

Scenarios are particularly powerful ways of producing different narratives set in the future, which enable historical disclosure to occur, that is, they make visible the anomalies and taken-for-granted conditions prevailing in the rich tapestry of societies. By forcing us to confront the hidden assumptions underlying our current practices and styles of life and business, scenarios generate a radically different kind of thinking and valuing that help shape the future. Thus, future navigation processes provide a powerful way of questioning and reexamining the assumptions inherent in our current business designs and ways of doing things, or our "style."

The style of businesses and business designs is generated by the attractors that both conserve and develop new practices in us. Style is the ground of meaning in human activity because it opens a disclosive space in a consensual domain in which

- actions are coordinated through self-organization
- the meaning of things, events, and people emerges, and
- archetypal patterns are formed that can be transferred from situation to situation, that is, generalized.

Our subdivided attractor neural networks enable style to emerge and evolve in the disclosive space, which is any organized set of practices for dealing with oneself, other people, and things. Disclosive spaces are organized inside us as worlds that enable us to engage with interrelated pieces of equipment for specific purposes from which our identities emerge. For example, surgeons or carpenters are defined by their tools, practices, and purposes. So, too, are all aspects of purposive human activity defined by, and defining of, the worlds we construct through our engagement in those activities.

Activities involve the training of feed forward neural networks at the level of perceptive (sensorium or "input") and motor (motorium or "output") systems. Cognitive processors and processes become aware of anomalies between the input and output systems in these feed forward networks and attribute meaning and make appropriate responses to these anomalies, whether they be breakdowns, surprises, opportunities, or threats. This happens largely at the sub- and preconscious levels, except when the specialized processors that have been trained to deal with such situations cannot cope and recruit each other to generate a conscious field or disclosive space in the mind in order to interpret and act on what is happening.

At the level of socially constructed reality, disclosive spaces become shared worlds that emerge from webs of practices and meanings. In turn, subworlds form within homogeneous worlds, and local worlds emerge from the interaction between different worlds. Organizations and business ecosystems are such worlds, and industries define the split between types of equipment, the nature of the purposes to which it is put, and the identities and roles of the actors who are constructing those worlds.

In a self-organizing universe it is not therefore surprising that new patterns are continually emerging and that such patterns combine and recombine to form new patterns through natural, social, and technical processes. There is a great deal of uncertainty and complexity inherent in the way in which such patterns emerge, develop, stabilize and decay. Subdivided attractor networks imprint experience and evolve in ways that are related to the correlations between the elements of those experiences. The functionality of vision, language, smell, and taste, for example, derives from the existence of separate functional, specialized processor units in different parts of the brain collaborating with each other through internodal networks.

The activity of a social network operates in much the same way. Different functional patterns evolve to become correlated in different ways and emerge as crafts, guilds, industries, and business ecosystems, all with their characteristic styles. As these patterns of industrial, commercial, trading, and political activities become more densely interconnected, so they coevolve in surprising ways. Such processes of coevolution depend on the capacity of the neural and social networks to learn, by changing

- the nature of the nodes in the network
- the number of nodes in the network
- the pattern of connections between the nodes in the network
- the strength of the connections between the nodes in the network

Complex, adaptive systems need to learn most rapidly in the disclosive space generated by the intersection of worlds. If the complex, adaptive system is too ordered due to its attraction to a period or oscillating attractor, then it will fail to engage with other actors and worlds and learn in such a disclosive space. Equally, if the complex, adaptive system has become defensive, fatigued, or disoriented due to excessive stress, anxiety, or excitement caused by turbulence, then the neural nets will be too thrown into deeply chaotic dynamics to perceive or interpret patterns and therefore learn.

HUMAN AND SOCIAL COGNITION AS HISTORY-MAKING

We need to find and occupy disclosive spaces in which we can be aware of our role in two kinds of narrative formation (or history making): customary disclosure (seen in a business context as "traditional value creation") and historical disclosure (seen in a business context as "entrepreneurial value creation"). Both modernism and postmodernism disclose different ways of being and practices that emphasize customary and historical disclosure, respectively. Modernism and postmodernism are dialectically opposed, being different states or modes. Our subdivided neural attractor networks can occupy either the "certain" state of modernism or the "uncertain" state of postmodernism, depending on the situation at hand.

Customary disclosure occurs where we evolve a set of practices that embrace stability as the supreme good. Modernists see incremental progress in our practices as the goal, generating order and certainty through lawlike features and reductive explanations derived from detached observations of systems where we distance ourselves from the phenomenon observed. Theories and models derived from the metaphors and practices of modernism dominate most of the management textbooks. Scientific management, time-

and-motion studies, operations research, systems analysis, cybernetics, total quality management, software engineering, business process reengineering, and work-flow systems design all embrace this logical, analytical, deductive, process-based approach to change.

Postmodernists embrace change as the supreme good and recognize the chaos, complexity, and uncertainty of social, technical, and organizational life. Historical disclosure emerges from ways of seeing oneself and the world anew regularly and as a matter of course. The ontological skill of disclosing new ways of being enables one to reexamine old experiences from new perspectives. Thus, postmodernism provides us with a way of being alive to the anomalies, paradoxes, and dilemmas inherent in daily life, without trying to find "solutions" or final answers to everything.

Postmodern management involves (following Baxter, 1996)

- recognizing the endlessly deferred meaning of things, concepts, and people
- understanding that process generates structure
- the questioning of the privileging of one thing or system over another, for example, nations, cultures, top management versus workers
- avoidance of conceptual closure through the continual application of reflexivity
- the continual interplay between opposites as figure and ground in an undecidable exchange of attributes
- an appreciation of the supplementarity of meanings between opposites
- acknowledgment of the replacement by the factual of representational, that is, that personally and socially constructed realities are encodings and decodings of the meaning of things, events, and processes

A postmodern analysis is a pragmatic, action-oriented approach intent on enriching an organization's understanding of itself and its actions. Deconstruction begins with a reflexive debate about the privileged existence of a dominant paradigm or dominant coalition. When the debate about a concept's worth dies, so, too, does the potential to motivate social action. Such self-reflection and resultant change, generates stress as much as relieves stress, however, and potentially evoke clashes between worldviews. Let us look a little more carefully at how we can deconstruct our world(s) a little more effectively and how this generates greater value.

We need to explore how each of these activities relates to the broader business and environment in which value-creating processes are embedded. The key difference between these means of historical disclosure and customary disclosure is Kauffman's idea of "combinatorials of strings," or the recombination of chunks of old practices and technologies with new or emerging practices and technologies:

Traditional value creation—value-creation within traditional social processes. Here an enterprise seeks to be better at doing traditional things, through continual improvement in its core business. No new social practices (or new markets) need to come into being in order to enable the enterprise to flourish—it is feeding off an existing pool of demand and competing with a known array of suppliers who compete on resources and costs.

Entrepreneurial value creation: value-creation through new technologies and social processes. Here an entrepreneur seeks to change the habits of entire industries and societies through a series of innovations that require new ways of seeing oneself and the world. New forms of value are created out of a patchwork assembled for traditional technological and social process, with a totally different value equation thatis much greater than the sum of its parts. The Model T, personal computer, disposable razor, the Bessemer process are but a few examples of thousands of technological and social breakthroughs that have taken place over the past few hundred years. This form of value creation has a much higher risk/reward profile and is responsible for the massive changes we have experienced in the global economy since the agricultural revolution and the Industrial Revolution began. This is also the place where the greatest value gains are made and where new industries and ways are being shaped.

In traditional value creation, the focus is on "doing things right," on improvement, and on defending an existing infrastructure, set of resources, and ways of doing things. Traditional value creation occurs most frequently during the mature stages of the life cycle of a product, ecosystem, or economy. Although traditional value creation is unglamorous, it performs a vital economic function: allocating scarce resources efficiently and improving the utilization of those resources. Organizations driven by traditional value creation are usually pyramid-shaped hierarchies. Through downsizing and de-ayering these hierarchies may have been flattened and made more efficient, but they are hierarchies, nonetheless. At their most efficient, such organizations become "machine bureaucracies," which are also highly rigid and inflexible.

Organizations and individuals using entrepreneurial value creation, however, focus on "doing the right thing." For them, doing things in the traditional way is not good enough. Entrepreneurial organizations and individuals perceive anomalies in themselves and their environment that provoke them to innovate new ways of doing things that are reflected in new techniques, products, and services. The key to this form of value creation is the ability to "reperceive," or to see in new ways the world(s) around us and in us.

Entrepreneurial value creation occurs most frequently during the pioneering and renewal phases of the life cycle of a product/service/industry or business ecosystem. The function performed by entrepreneurial value creation is to transform the lives of individuals, organizations, and societies, even though the entrepreneur's motives may simply be a better mousetrap or a bigger profit (as Adam Smith noted when describing the action of the "invisible hand" in the *Wealth of Nations*).

Organizations that pursue entrepreneurial value creation come in a wide variety of shapes and sizes, like networks, "pizza," and horizontal, process-based structures. The keys to success in entrepreneurial value creation lie in both b*usiness idea and design*—having a more imaginative understanding of the anomalies in one's world and marketplaces—and o*rganizational capability*—developing an entrepreneurial vision and insights into an organizational form that is capable of realizing the vision.

WHAT IS VALUE, AND WHERE DOES IT COME FROM?

This is the basic question, which both the economists and accountants have tended to duck by saying, "Value is what somebody is prepared to pay for something," which leads into a circular argument without actually answering the question. Value was being created long before money and even barter were ever dreamed of. In its most fundamental sense, value is a property of cognitive and social processes. Homo sapiens recognizes value in very different ways than do the 10 million other species in the animal kingdom, as only Homo sapiens can construct personal and social realities through cognitive and social processes using language and symbol systems.

In other words, value lies in what is in our heads and hearts and in the relationships between us. "Things" are not valuable in themselves—only when we attribute value to them do they become valuable. "Things" also have value only within a context, which is created by cognitive and social processes.

Given our industrial age obsession with things and objects, it is no wonder executives are having difficulty trying to understand the implications of the knowledge age for the creation of sustainable value. This is like trying to understand quantum mechanics using Newton's *Principia* or trying to come to grips with relativity using pre-Copernican mathematics—it just does not work.

Let us start with our traditional understanding of corporate success, as put forward by John Kay and Gary Hamel. Kay's basic theory is that when what organizations are good at (their distinctive capabilities) is applied to markets that appreciate what they are good at (relevant markets), then competitive advantage results for that organization. This then leads to the ability to reinvest in what one is good at, and so on ad infinitum, yielding corporate success. This tends to explain traditional value creation well.

Hamel's basic approach centers around three key concepts: competing for the future, core competencies, and stretch. Hamel states that organizations must focus on competing for the future, as once their competitors do this (and this is happening increasingly across all industries), they find and create new products, services, and markets for survival. Competing for the future requires that organizations understand very clearly what things they need to be good at, that is, their core competencies.

They then need to stretch themselves to develop the company's resources needed to compete for the future. This approach explains entrepreneurial value creation well, although neither Kay nor Hamel is able to tell us either where distinctive capabilities and core competencies are formed and how they evolve or how enterprises discern "relevant markets" or the "markets of the future."

What organizational arrangements are required to compete for the future or achieve organizational success? Much of the management literature has similar difficulty explaining the new knowledge age economy using modernist science and metaphors. The new sciences, which include the cognitive and complexity sciences, enable us to explain cognitive and social processes in providing the key to understanding sustainable value creation.

So far we have made three key observations about value:

1. The source of value lies in human heads, hearts, and relationships.
2. Value is created within a context, which is the product of cognitive and social processes.
3. Products and services are not intrinsically valuable—it is only when we attribute value to them do they bear value.

The source of value is people, their relationships and emergent roles and identities. Value is generated, perceived, and consumed by people and does not exist in the absence of people. One person can create, perceive, and consume value and is able to prioritize between different kinds of value for different needs and wants in different situations. A "Robinson Crusoe" economy of one person is, however, rather limiting and technically impossible. Nonetheless, it illustrates the point that value is originally a function of our cognitive processes, which determine how we perceive, understand, and interact with our world.

When two or more people interact, we find social processes and relationships coming into being. Value then becomes determined not only by cognitive processes but also through social processes. The roles and identities we assume in our social world are strong influences on the ways in which we create, perceive, and consume value. Such roles and identities are defined by

- the equipment and resources we have on hand and are familiar with,
- the purposes and tasks we seek to accomplish,
- the knowledge we are capable of bringing to bear in specific situations, and
- the relationships and situations we are in (our "context").
- Such roles and identities creating or consuming value in particular relationships and situations require us to disclose and examine the context we are in and its origins.

Value is created within a context, which is a product of cognitive and social processes. Value is an attribute of things, people, events, processes and outcomes in a particular situation. The specific context within which value is attributed emerges from

- the actors in a situation and
- their interests, combined with
- their worldviews plus
- personalities and roles, as well as
- the collective context in which they are "thrown" together and
- the processes from which that collective context emerged.

Such processes can be understood as dynamical systems, which manifest themselves as one or more of

1. complex materials (from the global oceanic and climatic systems, to clay minerals, to proteins, to neural networks)
2. complex organisms (from cells, to living organisms, to human beings)
3. complex biological ecosystems (from biomes such as rain forests and savannahs, to the biosphere)
4. complex social systems (from couples, through families and groups, to military, corporate, not-for-profit, and governmental institutions, to supranational and international organizations such as the United Nations)

Complex social systems comprise both personally and socially constructed realities that are continually self-organizing, renewing, and transforming themselves. The mutability of value is a reflection of the web of relationships being woven between and by these realities as they experience the world and each other.

This, then, leads us to the conclusion that *"things and processes are not intrinsically valuable."* Only when we attribute value through a role or identity within or outside a relationship, does value come into existence. We can illustrate some of these principles in action by looking at the concepts of stocks and flows (things and processes that economists and accountants are very comfortable measuring and counting). Stocks are things (and, increasingly, include information), that sit in warehouses and storerooms and stockyards all around the economic world. Assets such as buildings, plant and equipment, money, technology, and infrastructure populate the surface of our planet. Accountants and economists attribute value to such assets by reference to their cost of purchase, price of sale, or some valuation determined by reference to assets of a similar kind.

As any liquidator or receiver knows, however, the value of these stocks or things and information is totally dependent on the context the organization finds itself in. As a "going concern" (i.e., able to trade profitably with a positive net asset value), the value of the assets is worth considerably more than they are when an organization gets into trouble. "Fire sales" of stocks and assets often result in the realization of less than 10–20 percent of the "going concern" value of an asset.

Equally, auctioneers of fine art and antiques know how rapidly their stock can appreciate or depreciate in value, depending on the context they are in—in a deep recession, fine art is often worth somewhere between 20 percent and 50 percent of its value in an economic boom. Both examples illustrate the context dependence of value—but in terms of sustainable value creation, assets/stocks are only evidence that a value-creating process once happened or is about to happen—without such value creation processes the "things" are without value.

What creates, perceives, or consumes value is a "flow." "Flow" is shorthand for the processes that take place in dynamical human activity systems, that is, people working and playing alone or interacting with each other. Value, like energy and power, flows along the paths of least resistance through human activity systems. This is where the new sciences are particularly valuable in explaining the creation and distribution of value.

STRATEGY AS LEARNING FROM COMPLEXITY

The impact of all of this is a world of growing complexity that behaves turbulently and feels highly uncertain. In addition to economic uncertainties, we face increasingly complex political uncertainties around the future of the nation-state and the explosion in the number of nation-states (over 200 at the last count[11]) and around the social divisions and inequalities of wealth distribution generated by rapid economic growth and technological change.

The net result of evolution is usually an increase in complexity, and we can see the results of this graphically illustrated all around us. There has been exponential growth in infrastructure technologies, which, in turn, has led the world to become more of a global village than McLuhan could have imagined. In turn, the greater interdependence this has created has increased the sensitivity and instability of the global political, economic and financial systems as well as impacted our biosphere. This increasing complexity and rising rate of change have raised the level of uncertainty we all face on a daily basis.

What does this mean for us as human beings and as business executives, consultants, and researchers/teachers? The first implication is that we can rely on fewer assumptions about how the world works, what our role in it is, and how we should be organizing, managing, and leading our businesses. As illustrated in Figure 7.4, the rate of change in our assumptions has increased dramatically, leading to a lower durability of those assumptions over the past few centuries. This "half-life" of assumptions means that we are all experiencing a level of cognitive confusion and dissonance, which we handle in different ways. We experience this as the "turbulence zone," where much of what is happening is hard to understand or does not make sense—hence Toffler's term "future shock."

The need for intelligence and learning rises dramatically in order to survive in this kind of environment. In order to survive as an autonomous system, such learning must enable an organization to comprehend and respond to or anticipate the changes going on around it, so that it makes the appropriate moves in its business environment. This can happen only if the effective complexity of the organization is equal to, or greater than, the complexity of its environment.[12]

There are at least two kinds of learning that can enable an organization to make more appropriate moves: (1) single-loop learning (or "doing things right"), where we improve our current operations and activities without questioning the basic assumptions behind what we are doing, (2) double-loop learning (or "doing the right things"), where we question the assumptions behind what we are doing and perhaps decide to do different things and/or do what we are doing in a fundamentally different way. This kind of learning enables adaptation and preadaptation.

In chaotic and turbulent environments, it is crucial for double-loop learning to be effective in an organization, as the failure of this kind of learning is usually the cause of business failure. In addition, we need to be able to think differently and learn faster to make both single- and double-loop learning work well.

So what does this mean for how executives and those working in the worlds of business and organizations should be learning and what they should be learning? The items on the agenda of many of the leading companies in the world, as well as Organization for Economic Cooperation and Development (OECD) governments, are apparent. The fruits of this learning enable knowledge workers to

Figure 7.4
Degree of Order in the Business Environment

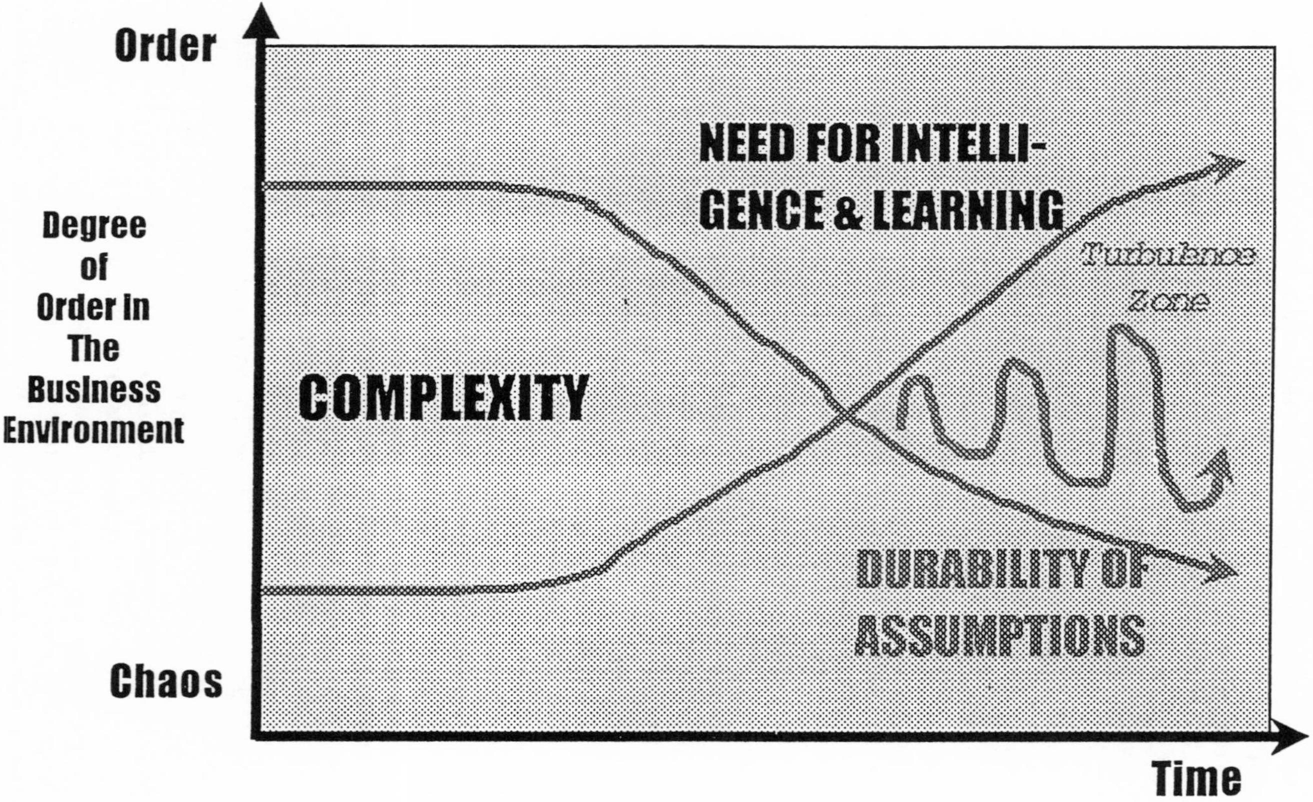

add more value and design and lead organizations that in turn add more value in a sustainable way in the global economy. Such fruits grow on the branches of particular kinds of knowledge that are enabling the value-adding and entrepreneurial processes to work better in those organizations that are applying them.

THE EVOLUTION OF COLLECTIVE INTELLIGENCE

Organizations and the business ecosystems in which they live are complex, adaptive systems. As a result, the basic rules that apply to complex, adaptive systems apply to organizations, but in a rather special way. When we describe the operation of learning in the mind of an individual, we are able to point specifically to the networks of neurons in the brain and body making new connections and changing the strengths of older connections as the learning process unfolds. In an organization, however, it is networks of relationships that learn. These relationships can be human or artificial, but they all rely on symbol systems such as language to establish relationships and communicate with each other. Thus, unlike networks in living organisms or other complex, adaptive systems, an organization does not rely on physical contact to establish relationships and communicate. People in organizations are able to establish contact and communicate remotely as well as locally, using a variety of communications and collaborative technologies. Whatever the nature of such contact and communication, however, language of one sort or another is essential for the establishment of such contact and communication.

People and organizations are conscious systems, capable of learning through feedback and experimentation, with a desire to see their work create enduring results. In other words, the behavior of people exhibits values by which what they are doing in organizations can be judged. People are generally not evolutionary automatons, blind or indifferent to the outcomes of their work. Unconscious, complex, adaptive systems are, however, by their very nature, uncaring about the outcomes of the forces at work. People at work are generally conscious (though there is the odd dreamer or sleeper!) and care about their work and its results. They not only want and need some degree of control of their work but also expect the impact of their work to make a difference to the world outside work.

All people and organizations exhibit some form of intelligence, which enables them to exert a degree of control in their own lives through learning. They can distinguish between desirable and undesirable outcomes and plan to influence events toward the future state that suits them best. This intelligence distinguishes

Homo sapiens from the other 10 million species on Earth and makes the intelligent organization a possibility.

Networks of complex, adaptive systems generate greater uncertainty and many more novel stimuli, which have to be handled by both individuals and organizations. Intelligence has evolved to handle complexity and uncertainty through more rapid and appropriate responses to situations and through increased learning and new behaviors that are more effective. If a system exhibits the capacity to alter its behavior as a result of experience (i.e., "learn"), it must be classified as intelligent. Intelligent behavior can be recognized as having one or more of the following attributes:

- experiential intelligence: the ability to take part in, and comprehend, an experience so that it can be understood during or after the experience.
- situational intelligence: encouraging behavior that is appropriate to a situation and conducive to the continued well-being of the actor(s) in that situation.
- reflective intelligence: capable of reflecting on experience and learning from that experience so as to improve the repertoire of behaviors that can be called upon in different situations.
- creative intelligence: capable of creating new and different creations out of the old and familiar materials that surround the creator(s), whether these be products, scientific theories, works of art or social institutions such as organizations.

How do organizations become intelligent? We know that individuals acquire intelligence through continual learning, at many different levels:

Structure: our biological inheritance. The biological structure of intelligence depends on the interaction of an individual's genetic makeup with the environment and the personality and habits that this interaction produces. Each individual's mind and body provides relatively hard-wired (and often very different) reaction times, inspection times, and "average evoked potential,"[13] which measures the work rate of the brain as evidenced by electromagnetic brain patterns. Intelligence is evident in individuals with fast reaction and inspection times and in the complexity of the brain waves generated when facing a complex pattern or task, intelligent individuals fire fewer neurons when facing familiar stimuli and fire more neurons with more complex brain waves when facing novel stimuli.

Content: what we are good at and think about: the 10 domains of intelligence. Building on Gardner's[14] theory of multiple, distinct intelligences, we can distinguish between 10 discrete intelligences: factual, analytical, physical, musical, spatial, logical, linguistic, practical, mathematical, intrapersonal, interpersonal, and kinesthetic. Each of these intelligences can exist without the others,

both physically and functionally, though they are mutually supportive in most instances.

*Process: how we think and act: the several stages of intelligent
thought and action.* One can describe a "top-down" way of being intelligent, where an individual goes through stages such as goal
formation, research, strategizing, tactics, creativity, and implementation,[15] which does in some formal cases describe how people reach
decisions and act upon them. In most cases, it appears that people
use several different cognitive faculties[16] in combination: perception, creativity, analysis, systemic thinking, future thinking, constraint thinking, and decision thinking.

Organizations are capable of developing and exhibiting collective
intelligence to handle the increasing complexity and uncertainty in
our world. The structure, content, and process of this intelligence
operate across a network of relationships rather than a network of
neurons, with individuals, groups, and teams playing different roles
in the development of this institutional intelligence. The work being
done in developing "learning organizations"[17] has begun to open up
this complex frontier, but we are still a long way from having a useful
model of how organizational intelligence develops and operates.

STRATEGIC DIALOGUE

Strategic dialogue is the medium in which strategic conversations flow and collective intelligence can be developed. Without dialogue, strategic conversations tend to be shallow and may not connect into a coherent pattern. Such a dialogue comprises a large
number of conversations taking place within the network of relationships in and around an organization. Within this network of
conversations collective strategic learning takes place.

The first principle of strategic management is that in our rapidly changing and complex world, the future is not knowable, and
prediction cannot be the source of success. Instead, the source of
success at any given moment is alignment with the landscape, ecology, or culture in which the organization is situated. Such alignment is gained through the process of strategic dialogue, which both
harnesses and generates individual and organizational learning.

The way to build future success is to design oneself through
strategic dialogue to be maximally effective in three areas:

1. adapting to current circumstances
2. influencing the circumstances one finds oneself in
3. increasing ability and flexibility in order to achieve the previous two
   goals more effectively in a wider range of circumstances

To the extent that individuals, groups, organizations, and the business ecosystems in which they operate are capable of learning through conscious reflection and through the exchange of knowledge/information via language or representational systems, they can

- change conditioned behavioral routines to be more adaptive
- generate and evaluate a wider range of hypotheses about the future
- select appropriate mind-tools and environments to enhance their learning, thinking and implementation capability, thereby improving their chances of doing successfully[18]

Effective strategic management should therefore enable an organization to create a desirable, sustainable future within its business ecosystem,[19] using the full range of technologies available to it to change, generate new hypotheses about the future, and select those tools and environments that can enhance its capability to learn faster than its competitors. This requires that the learning process be made as conscious as possible and that collective learning be accelerated to this end. The ability to develop effective strategic management relies on the integration of thinking, action, and planning, through the development of scenarios for the future and strategic options that can be tested against such scenarios. This process is known as strategic dialogue.

Arie de Geus (ex-head of planning at Shell) provides an excellent description of how Shell developed its scenario process in "Planning as Learning," the title of his article in the *Harvard Business Review*.[20] In so doing, he describes Shell's successful response to Standard Oil's market tactics earlier this century and then says:

Outcomes like these, don't happen automatically. On the contrary, they depend on the ability of a company's senior managers to absorb what is going on in the business environment and to act on that information with appropriate business moves. In other words, they depend upon learning, or, more precisely, institutional learning, which is the process whereby management teams change their shared mental models of their company, their markets, and their competitors.

In a nutshell, de Geus concluded, "The only sustainable competitive advantage may be the ability to learn faster than your competitors." Cees van der Heijden, a colleague of Arie's, further described the elements of strategic conversation in 1996 in "Scenario Planning—the Art of Strategic Conversation."

As stated by de Geus, learning is the key competence required by any organization that wants to survive and thrive. Strategic learning focuses on the helicopter view of how organizations adapt to a changing world and create their own futures. The four elements that need to be balanced to achieve strategic learning are

- the past, which needs to be interpreted and understood in the context of today;
- the future, which needs to be created from desirable elements of the past together with new elements;
- the external environment (the "outside"), which needs to be viewed as a source of possibilities (both good and bad); and
- the internal environment of the organization (the "inside"), which must change to accommodate and seize possibilities of varying kinds.

In many organizations, the pressure of events generated by the operations of the organization crowds out the opportunity to learn and develop. Rapid change of any sort (e.g., skyrocketing growth, serious shocks, or serious decline) will make it difficult for the firm to get ahead of its own operational necessities and think strategically about the future. Then, when the environment changes, the organization is unprepared for such change and begins to evidence signs of stress and potential failure to cope.

This is why it is so important for all organizations to maintain the space to keep organizational learning alive, as this competence is the key to sustainable success in a rapidly changing and increasingly complex world.

The extent to which an organization can be seen to learn is thus a function of the extent to which networks of relationships can be said to be gaining new knowledge, framing and reframing shared mental models, and applying such knowledge and models to make better strategic and operational moves. Such learning could be both (1) subconscious and (2) conscoius. It could be subconscious—below the threshold of conscious awareness, in which case the organizational learning process is operating as a form of imprinting or conditioning. Such organizational reflexes are largely built into the corporate culture and into its day-to-day routines. As a result, such learning accumulates unexamined assumptions that often result in the organization's failing to adapt or innovate. Second, such learning could be conscious—here the team/group/organization becomes self-aware and aware of the relationship between the team/group/organization and its environment. Where there is awareness of the learning process ("metalearning") and what is being learned, it is then possible to direct the organization's attention to those trends and possibilities in itself and its environment that require consideration and, in some cases, a response.

Unfortunately, far too many organizations operate at the level of subconscious learning. They are thus incapable of directing their collective attention to strategic possibilities and vital turning points in themselves and their environment and therefore fail to develop an appropriate strategic intent to pull them forward into the future before their competitors. Some of the key attributes of strategic dialogue include

- strategic dialogue is pervasive, spreading its tentacles throughout an organization and its network of stakeholders, suppliers, and customers.
- strategic dialogue is inclusive, ranging across young and old, top management and new joiners, majority and minority groups, and young turks/old guard.
- strategic dialogue is embodied in the fabric of the organization, not simply "in the air" in conversation. It affects real decisions about the key elements of the business.

Some of the key outcomes of strategic dialogue include

- collective learning in the organization, which can be sensed and measured in the new competencies and capabilities that the organization demonstrates in its marketplace
- coherence in the strategic moves made by an organization and in the strategy-making process itself. Shared meaning between the different players in the dialogue enables things to happen quickly and coherently.
- commitment of those involved implementing the strategy results from their involvement in making the strategy. The processes of making and implementing strategy become very closely intertwined, if not indistinguishable.

Strategic learning and dialogue must become the driving forces of strategic management, as they are the key enablers of real-time, on-line learning in an organization, enabling executives to adapt their mental models to the changes in the world around them. Such adaptation assists executives in making more appropriate and timely business moves, faster than their competitors.

Strategic dialogue also provides the process through which innovation can be generated, thereby providing the platform upon which a desirable future for the organization can be created. Such a future inevitably draws its robustness and resilience from the competitive advantage provided by the unique value proposition and business design of an organization.

Where the strategic dialogue generates possibilities, the business change process provides the capabilities required to deliver on those possibilities, which become part of an organization's strategic direction. The strategic and change dialogues should be aligned to stimulate and guide transformation in the most effective manner possible.

All of this implies that a radically different strategic management process is needed to take organizations forward into the twenty first century from that prevailing in most executive suites today. The core of such a process is the use of scenarios to sensitize executives to the implications of multiple possible futures for their business and to stimulate the strategic thinking required to provide the organization with the options it needs to become flexible and more intelligent.

THE FUTURE NAVIGATION PROCESS

The most important aspect of the future is that we cannot predict it. While some elements of the future may be largely predetermined (such as the number of people over 50 in 2020), at the other extreme we find aspects of the future that are unknowable. This unknowability is caused by the uncertainty inherent in living and social systems.

Uncertainties that could have a major impact on our organization are known as critical uncertainties. Critical uncertainties are key elements in building scenarios to navigate the future and enable us to understand how the future might unfold into different kinds of scenarios. The technology that enables us to do this is at the heart of the future navigation process.

Anticipation is the key to generating the lead time required to create a desirable future for an organization. A business strategy for a specific future is not required or possible, as this would imply the ability to predict the future—what is needed is a requisite variety of options centered around the core theme for the business, which can then be played out as appropriate under the different possible future realities that can be anticipated.

Effective future navigation processes are wired, interactive, and multisensory. Because the future navigation process is embedded within the strategic dialogue in an organization, the faster information can be shared and knowledge created in the strategy process, the faster the organization can learn. There is definitely little room in the future navigation process for top-down, imposed, strategic decision making, as this kills the motivation to learn, share information, and cocreate new knowledge.

Creativity and entrepreneurship are key components of the future navigation process, as the ability to spot value-creating opportunities for the organization is key to making the process a success.

The future navigation process is knowledge building—the collective learning of those involved in strategic diagnosis, strategy development, and execution needs to be embodied in a knowledge base that forms the reference point and log book for strategic decisions and changes in course.

BUSINESS DESIGN

Business design is the means by which the insights into value creation gained in the future navigation process are translated into a capacity for action. Business design requires either an intuitive or an explicit understanding of the network of relationships in which a business idea or concept resides and how the embodiment of such an idea might beneficially influence that network. In order to do this explicitly, we need to draw on some of the logic inherent in the principles of the new sciences, particularly those contained in work in the areas of business ecosystems and fitness landscapes.

A good strategy describes how, over time, an organization will develop the requisite capabilities to enable it to capture those possibilities available to it in the future. A vision for an organization describing what the desirable future state of its business ecosystem is and what the organization will become is essential in order to provide a foundation for organizational foresight.

Possibilities. Such a vision is replete with a variety of possible, relevant business ideas for the future, which require different arrangements of the business ecosystem components and the organization's value chain. Such potential "business designs" provide multiple options for the organization, available to it in order to succeed in whichever future the organization finds itself. One of the components of a good business idea is the foreknowledge of one or more potential distinctive capabilities. There is thus an interaction between the thinking that takes place about possibilities and the process of bringing into being the competencies and resources from which the capabilities required to realize the vision are built.

Capabilities. Depending on which capabilities are required to be distinctive in deploying a specific business design, a variety of configurations of business processes is required so as to structure an appropriate value chain for a specific future. Such processes draw upon the core competencies of the organization, which, in turn, harness the core resources available to the organization. Different business designs and strategic options require different sets of competencies and resources.

The ability to turn good business ideas into value-added for customers and wealth for stakeholders relies on the generation and alignment of possibilities and capabilities. This is one of the major functions of the strategic dialogue process. The development of a compelling vision requires visionary leadership, which is capable of

- developing effective new strategies
- influencing those with the resources and power to act to support the new strategies
- building an organization and culture that embed the new strategies in the organization

CONCLUSION: THE FUTURE OF STRATEGY

Complexity science provides an explanation of why the strategic management practices of major corporations will need to change radically in order to cope with the pace of change in the twenty first century. Anticipation, flexibility, and intelligence are the key characteristics required in organizations able to master their destiny in such a complex, fast-moving world. The nature of organizations is changing dramatically as a result, from the modern vertical structure to the postmodern collaborative, network-based structure, providing a healthy balance between control and learning, hierarchies and networks. Such a design facilitates the emergence of intelligence in an organization.

Complexity-based strategy defines a powerful, innovative way of reinventing the strategy process in an organization in order to enable it to shape the way in which new wealth is created in its marketplace. The result is a more entrepreneurial, intelligent organization capable of creating innovative value propositions and applying them in relevant markets through a set of distinctive capabilities on a sustainable, self-renewing basis.

Organizations are complex, adaptive systems comprising physical, cognitive, and socially constructed realities. Such systems coproduce each other and coevolve with their environment. In many organizations such processes of coproduction and coevolution are unconscious, driven by incoherent political, economic, social, or technological forces in the organization and its environment. Under such conditions organizational success or failure is a function of a random walk, and outcomes are unpredictable and difficult to influence.

The purpose of business strategy is to influence the course of business evolution positively in favor of the organization on behalf of which such strategy is being formulated and enacted. In order to have a beneficial influence on the longevity of an organization, business strategy must be conscious, coherent, communicable, and intelligent. To meet such criteria the strategy process needs to enable an organization to

1. *Focus and Sense*—Define the organization and the context in which it is operating with some precision.

2. *Anticipate*—Anticipate the ways in which the organization's context might change and how the organization might respond to those changes.

3. *Influence*—Develop ways in which the organization might change its context in order to improve its own sustainability.

4. *Scan*—Continually scan its environment in order to maintain an accurate view of

- itself in relationship to its context and whether its strategy is working
- the effectiveness of the moves and changes the organization is making in enacting its strategy

5. *Act*—Motivate intelligent action at the right time in the right place in accordance with the themes of the strategy.

6. *Learn*—Promote learning coherent itself and the context of the strategy.

NOTES

1. Definition courtesy of Alex Trisoglio in his paper to the LSE Strategy Seminar, January 25, 1995, entitled "Managing Complexity."

2. See Arie de Geus, *The Living Company* (London: Nicholas Brealey, 1997).

3. Adrian Zlywotzky, *Value Migration* (Boston: Harvard Business School Press, 1996).

4. Mandel and Kondratieff have documented those technology long waves occurring since 1792. See Mike Davidson, *The Transformation of Management* (Woburn, Mass.: Butterworth-Heinemann, 1996).

5. See John Sculley, *Odyssey: Pepsi to Apple* (New York: Fontana 1987).

6. See John F. Love, *McDonalds—Behind the Arches* (New York: Bantam Books, 1995).

7. First told in Tom Peters, and Robert Waterman *In Search of Excellence* (New York: Harper and Row, 1982).

8. John J. Medina, *The Clock of Ages: Why We Age—How We Age—Winding Back the Clock* (New York: Cambridge University Press, 1996).

9. Peter Senge, *The Fifth Discipline* (New York: Doubleday Currency, 1991).

10. For example, the work of John Naisbitt, *Megatrends, Megatrends 2000,* and *Global Paradox;* Alvin Toffler, *Future Shock, Third Wave, Powershift;* Ian Mitroff, *The Challenge of the 21st Century;* and John Petersen, *The Road to 2015.*

11. Although only 171 of them have a population over 1 million or gross domestic product (GDP) of over $1 billion, the littlest ones can be a real source of instability.

12. Ross Ashby referred to this as the principle of requisite variety in cybernetics, and complexity science now articulates why this is so and how this principle works in practice.

13. Pierce J. Howard, *The Owners Manual for the Brain* (New York: Leornian Press, 1994). H. Gardner, *Frames of Mind: The Theory of Multiple Intelligences* (New York: Basic Books, 1983).

14. H. Gardner, *Frames of Mind: The Theory of Multiple Intelligences* (New York: Basic Books, 1983).

15. R. J. Sternberg, *The Triarchic Mind: A New Theory of Human Intelligence* (New York Viking, 1988).

16. R. L. Wood, "The Role of the Seven Cognitive Faculties in the Development of Effective Directors" unpublished research paper for the Institute of Directors, London, 1994.

17. Peter Senge, *The Fifth Discipline: The Art and Practice of the Learning Organisation* (New York: Doubleday Currency, 1990).

18. Daniel C. Dennett as quoted in John Brockman, *The Third Culture: Beyond the Scientific Revolution* (New York: Simon and Schuster, 1996).

19. A business ecosystem is defined as a coevolving economic community supported by a foundation of interacting organizations and business processes, producing goods and services of value to customers.

20. "Planning as Learning" is the most reprinted article of all time from the *Harvard Business Review.*

Part III

Creativity and Communication

The four chapters in this section look at the intersection of complexity, creativity, and communication. The chapters seek to ask and answer, What is it about the complexity perspective that alters the way we both approach problems and see and communicate about the world?

If Price picks up on the notion of using the words "at the edge of chaos" in his "Images or Reality? Metaphors, Memes, and Management." Price suggests that complexity theory has contributed greatly to what now seems to be an emerging "organic" paradigm; that is challenging the traditional, mechanistic view of organizations. He then argues the need to balance self-organization with selection, in reaching that new paradigm. Price bases his argument on the notion of memes—ideas that function much like genes in a gene pool. Thus, "the edge of chaos" is but one example of a meme's orginating in complexity theory. Price argues that memetic patterns underpin strategy. Rather than considering strategies as memes, he interprets them as expressions of the underlying mental models of the organization. Price sees rules as an expression of memetic patterns and views the economy as a selective competition between rules and technologies. To Price, memetics provides a unifying proposition for other proposals concerning economic and social systems evolving as a result of selective competition between habits and routines, technologies, rules, paradigms, or strategies. Each of these thoughts or ideas can be seen as a different expression of an organization's memetic pattern. Memetics offers a link between the numerous metaphors of organizations as evolving systems and the evidence for socially constructed realities defined in the corporate world as "mental models" or organizational paradigms and, in the educational world, as meaning spaces or barriers to learning. In the propagation of memes from mind to mind and then in the link from memes and mental models to unwritten rules and strategies, Price argues, we see the operation of the memetic replication cycle.

From this perspective the new understanding for which the authors in Part II argue so strongly becomes a meme in and of itself, replicating and creating a new reality. Here lies the connection between the creativity of ogilvie and McDaniel and the strategy discussions that preceded.

Pekka Aula picks up on this discussion of memes by examining the characteristics of communication that must ensue for them to propagate. In "Chaos, Communication, and Cultural Change: Beyond the Management of Organization" Aula argues that the management of organizational change and of the organization itself is closely interconnected with the management of a given organization's communication systems and cultures. He contrasts the traditional model—"built on the assumption that people seek order, security, and certainty, at least in the workplace situation. They are motivated by clear tasks and goals, by reviews of performance against goals, and by rewards tied to goal achievement" with a chaos- and complexity-driven perspective—models that "usually recognize that people are complex and that personal goals can and do conflict with each other. People have aspirations outside the organization, as well as aspirations within it, that have little to do with the work itself. But all these are obstacles to the achievement of the organization's goals." Communication among members of an organization is viewed very differently between these two perspectives. If the memes of which Price writes are to be successful, they require a breeding ground that is more accepting of the second perspective rather than the first. An organization has not one but several complex subcultures, which stay alive in different communication arenas and whose dominance and effects upon the organization fluctuate over time and place. The role of communication is to create the conditions that favor the emergence of a culture that will nurture the desired change. Notions of organizational change, management, and communication that are founded on principles of chaos place certain conditions upon traditional management's ability to carry out changes based on strict plans. Linear ways to change are not effective enough in a nonlinear world.

Harold E. Klein in his "The Architecture of Strategic Thought: A Neuronal Network Approach" writes about causal maps as a strategic thinking and communication tool. Complexity, by definition, is hard to make sense of, and it is a truism that strategic decisions are as complex as they come. It should come as no surprise, then, that scholars of strategic management have been interested for some years in the ways managers make sense of their business environments and frame the problems they address. One of the most widely used methodologies is cognitive mapping, which comes in many varieties but usually takes the form of some kind of causal diagram: a visual representation of the factors that the subject thinks are at work and of the way each factor affects the others.

Klein addresses a problem that anyone who has worked with causal maps knows only too well: how hard it can be to find a starting point for making sense of the message they contain. The strength of these maps—that they show in compact form how everything links with everything else—is also their weakness, because it is not easy to figure out the answer to the question: Given where we are now, what would happen if we did this or that? Typically, causal maps consist of closed loops, and these questions can be answered only if valid ways can be found of cutting the loop to give a sense of a starting and an ending point.

Drawing on recent work in neuroscience that is beginning to uncover the structure of thought processes, Klein describes a modified form of cognitive mapping ("normative cognitive maps") that gives a clearer sense of the direction of causality between organizational and environmental variables. By uncovering the way these variables cluster into groups that have more connections within the group than between groups, the technique produces maps that, the author argues, overcome many of the closed-cycle problems of conventional cognitive maps.

Adam J. Koch returns this discussion to its commonsense roots in his "Strategic Management System Enhancement and the Concept of Strong Influence Strings." Koch argues that the purpose of strategic management is to help formulate, implement, and evaluate cross-functional decisions in such a way as to assist the organization in achieving its long-term objectives. To better understand the nature of the "memes" (as Price would call them) or of the "communicative environment" (as Aula would call it), Koch introduces the notion of strong influence strings. Strong influences are defined as systemic influences that have the capacity to significantly alter the responsiveness, effectiveness, and efficiency parameters of the strategic management system. Koch argues that the two weakest points of current strategic management theory appear to be its apparent failure to express all major influences on strategic management systems in logical sequences, and its failure to produce operational definitions of strategic management (system) performance. His discussion of the dimensions of strategic management performance and the subsequent presentation of several examples of strong influence strings is aimed at practical results: the examination of strategic management mechanisms and guidance for their enhancement.

Chapter 8

Images or Reality? Metaphors, Memes, and Management

If Price

Complexity, in both the wider sense of the term and, more specifically, the Santa Fe sense of complex adaptive systems (CAS), has contributed strongly to a wider appreciation of the "organic" model of an organization. Whereas an evolutionary perspective can certainly be found in "precomplexity" thinking on organizations, on strategy, on institutions, on economics, and on learning, it still rests, with a few notable exceptions, on evolution as a metaphor, or model, for socioeconomic organizations, rather than an assertion of a different scientific paradigm. Complexity theory has, however, contributed greatly to what now seems to be an emerging "organic" paradigm that is challenging the traditional mechanistic view of organizations. This chapter argues the need to balance self-organization with selection, in reaching that new paradigm.

Where the organic metaphors ends and the paradigm begins in organizational theory is itself open to debate. One might, for example (Morgan, 1986), widen the organic metaphor to embrace MacGregor's (e.g., 1954) theory Y as an alternative to the more mechanistic theory X. Somewhat more restricted are those who use "living organization" as a metaphor, which recognizes organizations as human communities, or collections of individual, sentient beings (e.g., Kofman and Senge, 1993; De Geus, 1997). The passage from metaphor to paradigm begins with those who argue for rules (Hayek, cited by Hodgson, 1993), habits and routines (Nelson and Winter, 1982), paradigms (Hull, 1988), technologies (Rothschild, 1992), or processes and systems (Baskin, 1998) as the equivalent of organizational DNA. The comparison is offered less as a metaphor and more as an assertion of a scientific truth or hypothesis concerning organizations. Finally, at the hard end of the "pre-complexity" spectrum of views, Lloyd (1990) declares that "it is time to see companies as an intelligent, alien species—the first we humans have met." As he puts it, "this is not just a metaphor" (216). Rothschild (1992) is similarly assertive on behalf of technology rather than strategy as the equivalent of DNA.

By widening the appreciation of the parallels between organizations and organisms, CAS theory could be said to supplant the debate as to whether organizations are "alive." Both share the property of maintaining, over time, some form of complicated order. I have argued (Price, 1994, 1995; Price and Shaw, 1996, 1998; Price and Kennie, 1997) that both are examples of Dawkins' (1976) proposition that such order is a general phenomenon of a selective competition between replicators, schemata with the property of reproducing themselves, via the complex structures that they enable. Rather than reduce the debate to strategy (or the assumptions behind it) versus technology, versus paradigms, versus language and rules, it seems more profitable to treat each as an expression of a memome or memetic pattern, a coadapted and complicated system of memes, Dawkins' (1976) viruses of the mind.

Selection between replicators distinguishes, I suggest, autopoietic, or self-maintaining, complex systems from those that merely self-organize. The paradox produced is a tendency for CASs to stop adapting, a bias to periods of stability interspersed by shorter intervals of generativity that emerges as a rhythm of evolution at many time scales (Price and Kennie, 1997). Indeed, if Smolin (1997) is correct in suggesting universes involved in a selection process between competing physical constants, the time scales may even include the astronomical.

Price and Shaw (1998) explore the concepts of memetic patterns at individual, interpersonal, organizational, and interorganizational levels operating as agents of stability, enabling organizational existence by generating shared norms but also limiting that performance through preservation of a limiting status quo. Stasis suits the "selfish" meme. A synthesis of memetic selection and self-organization can explain several aspects of change, learning, and organizational design. This chapter explores the memetic hypothesis in more depth, testing against it many other "images of organization", notably those summarized by Morgan (1986) but including others informed by an evolutionary epistemology. It concludes with a brief examination of the complexity "meme."

COMPLEX MEMETIC SYSTEMS: THE LITERALIST VIEW

Price and Shaw (1998) offer a fuller overview of the inherently multidisciplinary Complex Memetic Systems (CMS) hypothesis. Its key propositions can be stated as:

Nonlinear, or partially deterministic, self-organization—a property inherent in many natural systems—arises from some critical density of interconnectivity and the presence in the system of schemata, rules governing the interaction of the systems agents. It is revealed by a power law relationship between magnitude and frequency.

Within the set of self-organizing systems is a subset that also shows the property of self-maintenance (broadly, autopoiesis); hence, for example, over time the magnitude of extinction events in the geological record departs from a power law relationship. Kauffman's (1993) interpretation of Raup's (1986) extinction data fits the postuniformitarian view of the stratigraphic record (Ager, 1973) and the punctuationist, or none steady-rate, interpretation of speciation events over geological time (Eldredge and Gould, 1979). A similar punctuated dynamic may be observed in the history, or evolution, of social systems at many scales (e.g., Gersick, 1991; Tylecote, 1993; Hodgson, 1993; Price and Evans, 1993).

Within the biological domain the schemata are encoded as genes, complicated systems of information with the ability to specify structures that will, in turn, create copies of themselves. Granting the selfish gene as "a metaphor for a system of interconnected genes of almost indescribable complexity" (Dawkins, 1976), granting the operation of genes as a complex feedback systems involving their immediate and wider environment and granting that selection for reproductive continuity operates on vehicles (individual organisms) rather than directly on genes or genomes, the assertion made here is that there is no satisfactory alternative to "Darwin's Dangerous Idea" (see Dennet, 1995) as the origin of order. Complexity theory, I suggest, enriches, rather than replaces, the basic tenet of natural selection as the source of biological, small "c", complexity.

Evolving biological systems have an inherent tendency to seek an evolutionary stable strategy (ESS), which is stable until perturbed by an evolutionary crisis. Price and Kennie (1997) have suggested four classes of such events (Figure 8.1) and explored potential analogues on the strategic rather than the stratigraphic time scale.

The tendency to self-maintenance, departure from edge-of-chaos, self-organized criticality, is, if this view is correct, an inherent property of systems in which "selfish replicators" seek the stability of an ESS. The universe as a whole may even be self-maintaining on a larger scale and involved in a selective competition with rival universes (Smolin, 1997). Be that as it may, it generates a context in which self-organization occurs. Matter is not evenly distributed. Within that large-scale system, on one planet at least, a self-maintaining biological system began to evolve once physical self-organization stumbled on molecular structures capable of transmitting sufficient information to replicate. Some 3.5 billion years later that evolving biological system stumbled on a change in biological capability, the human brain and vocal system. Evolution switched gears and generated the second major class of CASs, cultural systems, showing the same properties of complex order, relationships, evolution, hierarchy, and strategies that anticipate the future (Holland cited by Waldrop, 1992) and the same punctuated dynamic (Gersick 1991; Price and Evans, 1993), albeit at a vastly accelerated time-scale.

While memetic evolution is, at least in theory if less often in practice, Lamarckian rather than Darwinian, and while it is far more susceptible to intermixing, at least by vertebrate standards (Wilkins, 1998), it nonetheless works by the same basic principle of selection between alternative, self-replicating schemata, operating via the structures that they create. Complicated genetic "patterns" code for organisms. Complicated memetic patterns enable organisations. From the gene's or meme's metaphorical perspective the organism or organization is a vehicle for genetic or

Figure 8.1
Classification of "Extinction Events" in Evolving Complex Systems

	Internally sourced events	*Externally triggered events*
Environmental Changes (abiotic)	System-induced crisis: Extinction caused by changes to external environments coupled to the evolving system, e.g., atmospheric/ climatic changes due to the evolving biosphere	Externally induced crisis: Extinction caused by physical factors external to the system, e.g., end cretaceous asteroid impact
New "competitors" within an ecosystem (biotic)	Evolution of the fitter: Extinctions/ evolutionary radiations caused purely by the development of new biological capability, e.g., Cambrian explosion following evolution of multicelled organic capability	Arrival of the fitter: Extinction due to biological competition but "new competitors" introduced due to external causes, e.g., Invasion of North American fauna/ flora into South America

Source: Adapted from Price and Kennie, 1997.

memetic replication. Memes have simply traded replicative fidelity for speed of adaptation and left genes far behind in the complexity of order they can sustain and the speed with which they can evolve.

Memes, under the original Dawkins definition of "the new replicators in the soup of Human Culture," are units of cultural transmission propagated from brain to brain. As Dawkins (1976) puts it, "When you plant a fertile meme in my mind you literally parasitize my brain, turning it into a vehicle for the meme's propagation in just the way that a virus may parasitize the genetic mechanism of a host cell." Price and Shaw (1998) envisage co-adapted, complex sets of memes integrated into memomes, or "patterns" a blend of mental models / paradigms, belief systems / values, and technologies out of which stem the perceptual biases, unwritten rules, and shared presumptions that enable an organization to function. Transmitted largely through language and also cultural artifacts, operating through unwritten, but shared, social codes, memes are suggested as enabling, but also limiting, organizations. They give rise to structures, including resistance to change, that operate in manners that enhance the pattern's chance of perpetuating itself.

Hence, it is hypothesized, memetic patterns underpin strategy. Rather than strategies being selected for in a marketplace (Henderson, 1989) or being considered memes / stremes in their own right (Lloyd, 1990), the CMS hypothesis interprets strategies, implicit or explicit, as expressions of the underlying mental models of the organization a view paralleling, for example, Mintzberg and Waters' (1994) view of strategy as "a pattern in a stream of decisions" (see also Stacey, 1993). Following Scott-Morgan's (1994) demonstration of unwritten rules as a pragmatic expression of organizational culture and Hull's (1988) observation as to how the codes and structures of science can be derived as a natural consequence of a selection competition between paradigms, the CMS hypothesis would see "rules" as an expression of memetic patterns. Memetics can thus embrace the school of economics that views the economy as a selective competition between either rules or technologies (see Hodgson, 1993; Tylecote, 1993). It also explains such phenomena as organizational innovation in peripheral isolates (Price and Evans, 1993), barriers to organizational and individual learning (Price, 1994; 1995; Price and Shaw, 1998), and the epidemiology of business fads (Price and Shaw, 1996). Here, however, my concern is to examine other areas of organizational theory and test them against a CMS perspective.

NEW LIGHT ON OLD IMAGES

The starting point must be Morgan's (1986) superb review of the different images current in organizational theory. He traces eight:

- Organizations as machines
- Organizations as organisms
- Organizations as brains
- Organizations as cultures
- Organizations as political systems
- Organizations as psychic prisons
- Organizations as flux and transformation
- Organizations as instruments of domination

Any organization may be thought of as existing because, collectively, it can fulfill some economic and social purpose that those within it cannot fulfill on their own. For an organization to exist, there must be some form of cooperation or coordination arrived at by some mix of control and "voluntary" collaboration. One can think of a spectrum from the slave ship: an extreme form of subjugation of many, to direction of one overseer, to full partnership. Cast in biological terms, it is a spectrum from a parasitic to a symbiotic relationship. If one presumes a meme's success to equate with minds infected or at least dedicated to replication of the meme, then militaristic control structures, ideally coupled with religious belief structures, have a long history in human affairs as memetically stable systems. The new technological memes, which fueled the rise of modern manufacturing, found a happy coexistence with older patterns of control. After all, those in a position to benefit took their managerial models from the Prussian military tradition (Johnson and Kaplan, 1987). If one takes Taylorism as the first managerial fad of the century, it is possible to see, in its spread, the same epidemiology as is found in other fad memes. Early applications need to deliver genuine results, but later ones come to support a self-perpetuating paradigmatic structure (see Price and Shaw, 1996).

It is hardly surprising that the older "partnership" form of organization, derived from medieval traders who shared the risk of voyages of merchant adventure, survived in professions and creative areas. Enforced control becomes less and less enabling, the more that the organizational result depends on individual, or pooled, knowledge. Equally, the demise of the mechanistic meme can be seen as correlated with the rise of economic climates in which information, knowledge, and service become bigger drivers of business success than muscle power, resources, or capital. As many studies of modern organizations have shown, the traditional, hierarchical, mechanistic organisation is failing to survive in numerous areas of organisational activity, even if the memes at its heart seek their replication where they can. By way of example it can be argued that mechanistic memes are currently prospering in many areas of the U.K. public sector, a by-product of "managerialist" structures imported from an older school of commercial management.

One paradox of the biological domain is that reciprocal altruism, the symbiotic collaboration of separate components and their genes, is a basis of multicelled life. Axelrod's (1984) experiments in the evolution of collaboration (see Lloyd, 1990; Price and Shaw, 1998) offer a likely explanation. There is a "positive sum" win-win in evolving a multi-celled capability. The resultant organisms can adapt to a wider variety of ecologic niches. In the parallel view of organizations as adapted to certain niches that one can find the origins of the organic metaphor. Morgan offers a good review of early theory. Much that was in 1986, and is more so now, central to the theory of managing in turbulent and changing times can, for Morgan, be considered as a biological view of an organization. The benefits of this metaphor are, for him, that

- it emphasizes a need to understand the organization in relation to its environment
- it emphasizes the "needs" that must be met for the organization to survive
- it focuses attention on the need for balance between the interdependent internal processes of an organization
- it alerts the fact that there is no "one best way" of designing an organization
- it alerts the need for innovation
- it focuses on the relationships between organizations

Its limitations are suggested as

- focusing too much on the concrete—organizations are also socially constructed phenomena
- assuming more "functional unity" than exists in many organizations; that is, whereas all the component parts of a biological body have to interact to preserve the whole, organizations can be subjected to "schism and conflict"
- risking becoming an ideology; a legitimization of assumptions that people are resources to be developed rather than human beings who are encouraged to shape their own futures or that social Darwinism is taken as natural law, legitimating what many would see as the socially deleterious side effects of free market competition and denying human influence and choice over what their world might be
- undervaluing the power of organizations and their members to choose their own future

Let us examine those limitations. A CMS perspective would interpret socially constructed phenomena as, themselves, being emergent, self-organizing, memetic effects. Culture, dominant patterns of language and thinking, may be interpreted as one of the highest levels of memetic pattern. To argue that, because an organization is socially constructed, it is not "alive" or at least not part of the same general class of complex systems as are organisms, is potentially to give too great an emphasis to social construction as an intentional, rather than an emergent, process. If any socially constructed phenomenon, such as a company or organization, is considered a product or reflection of prevailing memetic patterns—if, in short, not only do we shape our contexts, but our contexts shape us—then social construction becomes a phenomenon of memetic emergence.

To deny a biological or CMS perspective on the grounds of lack of functional unity is to place an undue emphasis on the term "company" or "organization." A company is, after all, only a legally conceived boundary drawn to include or exclude particular economic and social transactions. Many companies are indeed realms of competing, or at least imperfectly collaborating, parts, which merely states that they are more like a miniature ecosystem than a single organism. Many "companies"—in the sense of legal entities—are uneasy alliances of different "companies," in the sense of groups with common purposes, each seeking to perpetuate the interests of their own memome. A company where the unwritten reality is several component parts pursuing their own strategy and agenda is, from another perspective, not a company but an uneasy alliance. Accept each grouping in such a situation as a separate "company" and the limitation disappears. It is no more than a construct of the perceptual distinction normally granted to the word "company."

The last two limitations are more profound. There are, indeed, real dangers in a simplistic interpretation of nature and an appeal to laws of nature to justify particular social behaviors. This chapter does not aim at perpetuating a defense of a perceived natural order. Rather, it seeks to alert to the threat, to human intention and purpose, of memes acting as if in their own interest and, by so doing, inhibiting human choice and intention. Social Darwinism is a mental construction that thrives on memes of control and ownership. Values and "humanity" are, I firmly hope, easier to promote the more we understand the processes that produce our organizations, their functionality, and their dysfunctionality. Memes enable, and if not recognized as such, also limit. Human choice and intention can be increased by recognizing that memetic limits exist until they are appreciated as such. When they are, perhaps, we are better able to escape, or at least suspend, "the tyranny of the selfish replicators" (Dawkins, 1976).

Some ways in which those limits manifest themselves are exposed by Morgan's exploration of his other metaphors of the organization. Organizations as brains, not just organizations with brains (the boss) but organizations as brains with the intelligent capacity dispersed throughout—is a metaphor Morgan employs to question, ahead of the notion becoming popular, whether it is possible to design organizations with a capacity not just to process information but also to learn so as to

- encourage openness and reflectivity that accepts error and uncertainty in a complex environment
- encourage exploration of different viewpoints
- avoid limiting inquiry by the overuse of goals and objectives
- create structures that encourage the preceding

He suggests a parallel between the metaphor of the brain and "the more holistic and conceptual" Japanese approach to management with a lesson to be extracted in terms of a surplus of functionality and requisite variety. The brain works because of the surplus connectivity between its cells. Ultimately, therefore, Morgan sees the brain as a metaphor for organizational self-organization. In this there appears no conflict with the CMS. Just as the interconnected neuronal pathways of the brain are postulated to be the living space of memes at the individual level, so certain memes may pervade the interconnections of a company. If memes convert brains to minds (Dennet, 1991, 1995), then converting a disparate collection of people into an intelligent, or learning, organization is a function of a shared memetic pattern.

The idea of organizations as cultures introduces organizations as mirrors of the national culture that spawned them and as cultural phenomena in their own right, shaped by their own value systems and rituals, rules, and reasoning. Compare, for example, Whittington (1993) for a discussion of the influence of culture on strategy. In this sense of the word "culture," to consider an organization as a product of its culture is to consider it a creature of what the CMS hypothesis would term its wider memomes, the tradition of which it is part. Viewing organizations as memetic systems does not distinguish between different forms of organization.

Organizations as political systems explores how the realities of power and the negotiation between different groups of vested interests play out in an organizational context, a conflict that can be viewed as born out of a perceived dilemma between competition and collaboration. What sources of power are deployed, how, and by whom? What different games do people choose to play to manipulate power and conflict? The question then arises as to the intentionality or otherwise behind such interactions. What is frequently interpreted as organizational politics may, from a meme's perspective, be seen as a survival competition between different memomes. The political system is the, or a, memetic selection ground.

Organizations as psychic prisons argues that human beings can get trapped in "webs of their own creation" framed by their mental models of the world and by the underpinning psychological influences on their members' behavior. Again there is a wealth of evidence, and again Morgan's summary heralds greater attention to the limiting power of mental models in subsequent work, notably, of course, Senge (1990). Central to the CMS hypothesis is the proposition that memes seek to parasitize human brains, enabling minds but also tending to confine those minds as vehicles for replication of the same set of memes. Psychic prisoning may equally be seen as memetic parasitism. From a selfish meme's perspective it is superbly logical.

Organization as flux and transformation argues that organizations have an inherent danger of focusing inward on themselves and their reaction to their environment without recognizing the systemic interactions they have with that environment. In developing the argument, Morgan explicitly draws on concepts of biological systems as being ultimately closed, concerned only with reproducing themselves. He chooses the metaphor to include reference to, for example, Heraclitus, Bohm, Maturana, Varela, and Prigogine. In one sense perhaps this chapter, more than any other, encapsulates what has come to be seen as complexity (*sensu lato*). Contradiction and symbiosis, opposition and interdependence, yin and yang, or the dynamic of opposites, such as capital and labor are inherent in his Morgan's discussion.

Perhaps the biggest contradiction is the one noted in the introduction, the property of all CASs to tend toward order and away from pure self-organization. It seems that appreciating schemata as replicators, and hence appreciating both the interplay and the tension between selection and self-organization offer the best explanation yet conceived for the origin of this dichotomy.

Finally, organizations as instruments of domination starts with the premise that our organizations are killing us, subordinating and homogenizing those who work in them, at least until they are no longer needed, and slowly poisoning our environment, both physical and social. Roughly half of the top 100 "economies:" of the world measured by gross national product (GNP) or annual sales are corporations. Do they become "immortal institutions" conditioning those who serve them? Again, from a CMS perspective one might say that this is precisely what memes "seek" (and the intentionality is metaphorical) to achieve. If one regards an organization as a vehicle created by memes to enable their own replication, one arrives at exactly this point. Organizations are more like Lloyd's (1990) "alien species" programmed to act as if they had their own agenda.

One may thus see any of Morgan's images as an aspect of the organization as a CMS. To argue that the organization is any one of these images is dangerous and is likely to reflect the established patterns of the observer. The anthropologist will see an organization as culture, the psychologist as psychic prison, the engineer as machine, the sociologist as perhaps a political system or a tension of opposed interests, and the environmentalist as an instrument of domination. We all, after all, frame the world in our own isms and isms may be no more than another form of organization created to perpetuate its own paradigm. What matters more, in practice, is the pattern that happens to frame action and performance in a particular company.

In John Locke's words "the ideas and images in men's minds are the invisible powers that constantly govern them." Whatever those ideas and images when creating a company, once created, the entity called "company" in turn, plants ideas and images (and much more besides) into men's and women's minds. Those people may then be stuck in, and with, patterns that no longer serve an original human purpose. Most organizational theorists, whatever the metaphor they follow, operate from an implicit assumption that organizations are, at least in their origin, matters of human creation. Do they remain that way?

Perhaps we gain a deeper appreciation and more control when we realize that, once born, organizations take on a life of their own. Seeing an organization as an entity seeking to preserve its own mental replicator, its pattern, one can see it as simultaneously brain, culture, political system, psychic prison, flux, and alien instrument of domination. Whether we call such a company a living entity, or restrict "life" to the genetic domain is less important than recognizing companies for what they are, creatures of, and re-creators of, their memetic patterns. Unless we recognise them as such, paradoxically, we do not free ourselves of their psychic domination and create a truly living, human enterprise.

IMAGE OR REALITY?

We may see, then, in the proposition that CASs are systems constructed and maintained by active replicators, schemata that enable forms of organization which result in copies of those same schemata, a hypothesis capable of explaining a comprehensive range of different views or images of the reality of social organizations. Is this just another image, or does the CMS hypothesis grant us the basis of an actual science of organization?

Contrast the development of understanding of conventional, biological evolution. Darwin's theory arose out of years of detailed field observations of speciation, notably, of course, in the Galapagos Archipelago, but included reference fields as diverse as Malthusian economics and pigeon breeding. Though disputed by many, often on what one could term memetic grounds, it remains to all intents and purposes unassailable as a basic building block of biology. Even complexity theory has so far only been able to enhance natural selection as an explanation for the origin of biological order. Yet acceptance of Darwin's propositions depended, in large part, on the rediscovery in the early years of this century of Mendel's genetics as a unit of inheritance whose operation was subsequently proved as the molecular structure of DNA was unraveled. Is memetics yet capable of offering a similar, process-based, explanation of the evidence of organizational evolution? If not, what will it take to either develop organizational memetics from a hypothesis to a theory or refute it as no more than another metaphor?

WHAT DOES MEMETICS POTENTIALLY EXPLAIN

As well as the propositions considered before, the following can be claimed for the CMS hypothesis:

- It seems to provide a unifying proposition for other proposals concerning economic and social systems evolving as a result of selective competition between habits and routines (Nelson and Winter, 1982), technologies (Rothschild, 1992), "rules," paradigms (Hull, 1988), or strategies (Henderson, 1989; In the propagation of memes from mind to mind, then the link from memes / mental models to unwritten rules and strategies, we see the operation of the memetic replication cycle.
- It offers a link between the numerous metaphors of organizations as evolving systems and the evidence for socially constructed realities defined in the corporate world as "mental models" or organizational paradigms, and in the educational world as meaning spaces or barriers to learning (Argyris, 1991).
- It offers an explanation for the comparable dynamics, with time, of biological and economic evolution and for the process of innovation/speciation in peripheral isolates (Price, 1994, 1995).
- It offers an explanation of the power of complex mixtures of values, visions, identity, and language to act as "attractors" around which various forms of organization emerge.

- It is supported by the epidemiology of mental infection, whether by advertising or mass hysteria (Brodie, 1995) or by the rise of business fads (Price and Shaw, 1996). In this context it is interesting to speculate on the rise of the complexity meme. As demonstrated in the Toronto conference "complexity," even when restricted to "complexity and management," has become a broad church in which individual participants are more concerned to assert their interpretation (propagate their memes) than inquire. Complexity thus risks following the route of so many business fads/memes that, as they succeed, enable a self-maintaining structure of vested interests from consultants, academics, and journals. Price and Shaw (1996) take business process re-engineering (BPR) as their example, and while it might be easy for many attracted to complexity and a holistic perspective to accept BPR as a malignant virus, it may be harder to see "complexity" in the same light.
- It provides a theoretical framework for various lines of research that indicate the importance of language to maintaining particular forms of organizational reality (Winograd and Flores, 1987; Mingers, 1994). Several authors, for example, have demonstrated the emergence of patterns of linguistic coherence in the archives of various Internet mail groups. On the widest scale one can envisage human cultural evolution as largely a product of differences encoded in language, faith, and technology.
- It provides a theoretical framework for other evolutionary approaches to the understanding of change in organizations, notably Institutional Theory and other models of emergent socioeconomic systems (Allen, 1994).

So, is memetics a metaphor or a hypothesis? At one level the question is not important. Whether taken as metaphor or reality, the perspective can enable a depersonalized discussion of limits to change and adaptability. At another level the emergent research agenda in organizational memetics offers the prospect of a revolution in organizational science as profound as Mendelian genetics was for biology. Independent tests are beginning to emerge; hence discourse analysis applied to organizations offers the potential of calibrating various strands of meme transmission, the beginning, in effect, of the process equivalent to genome mapping. A separate and prospectively equally powerful insight is opened by organizational cladistics, where McCarthy et al. (1997) have recently demonstrated the feasibility of constructing rigorous cladistic trees, showing the descent by branching of manufacturing technologies. As with biological clades these must pass the test of consensus and peer review. In biological instance the cladistic approach to classification—that is, the phylogenetic classification of organisms in ways that demonstrate descent from common ancestors, rather than necessary similarity of form—has come to be confirmed by modern studies of DNA and particularly by the emerging field of genetic paleontology or geobiochemistry (Briggs, personal communication).

REFERENCES

Ager, D. V. (1973). *The Nature of the Stratigraphical Record.* New York: Macmillan.

Allen, P. M. (1994). "Coherence, Chaos and Evolution in the Social Context." *Futures,* Vol. 26, 583–597.

Argyris, C. (1991). "Teaching Smart People How to Learn." *Harvard Business Review* (May–June), 99–109.

Arthur, W. B. (1994). "Positive Feedback's in the Economy." *McKinsey Quarterly Journal,* Vol. 1, 81–95.

Axelrod, R. (1984). *The Evolution of Cooperation.* New York: Basic Books

Baskin, K. (1998). *Corporate DNA: Learning from Life.* Woburn, Mass.: Butterworth-Heinemann

Brodie, R. (1995). *Virus of the Mind: The New Science of the Meme.* New York: Integral Press.

Dawkins, R. (1976). *The Selfish Gene.* New York: Oxford University Press.

De Geus, A. (1997). *The Living Company: Growth, Learning and Longevity in Business,* Cambridge, Mass.: Harvard Business School Press.

Dennet, D. C. (1991). *Consciousness Explained.* Boston: Little, Brown.

Dennet, D. C. (1995). *Darwin's Dangerous Idea: Evolution and the Meanings of Life.* New York: Penguin Press.

Gersick, C. J. (1991). "Punctuated Equilibria as a Model for Organisational Change." *Academy of Management Review,* Vol. 16, No. 1, 10–23.

Henderson, B. D. (1989). "The Origin of Strategy." *Harvard Business Review* (Nov.–Dec.), 139–143.

Hodgson, G. M. (1993). *Economics and Evolution: Bringing Life Back into Economics.* New York: Polity Press.

Hull, D. (1988). *Science as a Process.* Chicago: University of Chicago Press.

Hurst, D. (1995). *Crisis and Renewal: Meeting the Challenge of Organizational Change.* Cambridge, Mass.: Harvard Business School Press.

Johnson, H. and Kaplan, R. S. (1987). *Relevance Lost: The Rise and Fall of Management Accounting.* Cambridge, Mass.: Harvard University Press.

Kauffman, S. A. (1993). *The Origins of Order: Self Organization and Selection in Evolution.* New York: Oxford University Press.

Kauffman, S. A. (1995). *At Home in the Universe: The Search for the Laws of Complexity.* New York: Oxford University Press.

Kofman, F. and Senge, P. M. (1993). "Communities of Commitment: The Heart of Learning Organizations." *Organisational Dynamics,* Vol. 22, No. 2, 5–23.

Lloyd, T. (1990). *The Nice Company.* New York: Bloomsbury.

Lynch, A. (1996). *Thought Contagion: How Belief Spreads through Society.* New York: Basic Books.

McCarthy, I., Lessure M., Ridgway K., and Fieller M. (1997). Building a Manufacturing Cladogram. *International Journal of Technology Management,* Vol. 1, No. 3, 269–286.

MacGregor, A. H. (1954). *Motivation and Personality.* New York: Harper and Row.

Mingers, J. (1994). *Self-Producing Systems: Implications and Applications of Autopoiesis.* New York: Plenum Press.

Mintzberg, H. and Waters, J. A. (1994). "Of Strategies, Deliberate and Emergent." In H. Tsoukas (ed.), *New Thinking in Organizational Behaviour*. Woburn, Mass.: Butterworth Heinemann.

Morgan, G. (1986). *Images of Organization*. San Francisco: Sage.

Nelson, R. R. and Winter, S. G. (1982). *An Evolutionary Theory of Economic Change*. Cambridge, Mass.: Harvard University Press.

Price, I. (1994). "The Genetics of the Learning Organisation." In P. DePotter and T. L. Campbell (eds.), *Proceedings of the First Conference of the European Consortium for the Learning Organisation*. London: Gower.

Price, I. (1995). "Organisational Memetics?: Organisational Learning as a Selection Process." *Management Learning*, 299–318.

Price, I. and Evans, L. (1993). "Punctuated Equilibrium: An Organic Metaphor for the Learning Organisation." *European Forum for Management Development Quarterly Review*, Vol. 93, No. 1, 33–35.

Price, I. and Shaw, R. (1996). "Parrots, Patterns and Performance [The Learning Organisation Meme: Emergence of a New Management Replicator.]" In T. L. Campbell (ed.), *Proceedings of the Third Conference of the European Consortium for the Learning Organisation*. Copenhagen.

Price, I. and Shaw, R. (1998). *Shifting the Patterns: The New Science of Organisational Memetics*. New York: Management Books 2000.

Price, I. and Kennie, T. R. M. (1997). "Punctuated Strategic Equilibrium and Some Leadership Challenges for University 2000." Second International Dynamics of Strategy Conference, SEMS, Guildford.

Raup, D. (1986). *Extinction: Bad Genes or Bad Luck?* New York: Oxford University Press.

Rothschild, M. (1992), *Bionomics: The Inevitability of Capitalism*. Futura.

Scott-Morgan, P. (1994). *The Unwritten Rules of the Game*. New York: McGraw-Hill.

Senge, P. M. (1990). *The Fifth Discipline. The Art and Practice of the Learning Organisation*. New York: Doubleday.

Smolin, L. (1997). *The Life of the Cosmos*. New York: Oxford University Press.

Stacey, R. D. (1993). "Strategy as Order Emerging from Chaos." *Long Range Planning*, Vol. 26, 10–17.

Tylecote, A. (1993). *The Long Wave*. New York: Routledge.

Waldrop, M. M. (1992). *Complexity: The Emerging Science at the Edge of Order and Chaos*. New York: Simon and Schuster.

Whittington, R. (1993). *What Is Strategy and Does IT Matter?* New York: Routledge.

Wilkins, J. S. (1998). "What's in a Meme." *Journal of Memetics*, Vol. 2. Online: http://www.cpm.mmu.ac.uk/jom-emit/1997/wilkinsjs.html

Winograd, T. and Flores, F. (1987). *Understanding Computers and Cognition: A New Foundation for Design*. Reading, Mass.: Addison-Wesley Longman.

Chapter 9

Chaos, Communication, and Cultural Change: Beyond the Management of Organization

Pekka Aula

The management of organizational change is closely interconnected with the management of a given organization's communication systems and cultures. The basis of this chapter is the observation that the traditional management models are usually not sufficiently able to picture, explain, or predict organizational behavior in the case of organizational change. It can be argued that the reasons for this insufficiency arise from the inherent complexity of the organizational culture structures and the communication systems.

The purpose of the chapter is to consider the possibilities of chaos-theoretical modeling of organizational management. Furthermore, I attempt to clarify whether chaos models can describe and explain properties of organization management that traditional management models have not been able to take into account.

ORGANIZATIONAL DESIGNS

According to traditional notions of organization management, organizations should be rational systems in which members operate as logically, efficiently, and predictably as possible. The organization's behavior should be goal-oriented, and the only way to achieve goals is by planning, organizing, and controlling. The traditional paradigm points out that each organization has an optimum *modus operandi* that can be found through rational analysis. One of the fundamental assumptions of the traditional models is that an organization consists of a group of people who share a common purpose.

A clear boundary line separates the organization from the environment within which it operates—the markets, the society, the national and international political systems, as well as the physical environment. The environment is changing. But it is one of the basic assumptions upon which the whole edifice of the rational model is built, that such change is largely predictable, at least in a statistical or probabilistic sense. (Stacey, 1991: 107)

Any traditional model is built on the assumption that people seek order, security, and certainty, at least in the workplace situation. They are motivated by clear tasks and goals, by reviews of performance against goals, and by rewards tied to goal achievement. Models usually recognize that people are complex and that personal goals can and do conflict with each other. People have aspirations outside the organization, as well as aspirations within it, that have little to do with the work itself. But all these are obstacles to the achievement of the organization's goals. The obstacles are to be removed by rules and procedures that motivate, build teams, inspire loyalty, select, train, develop and reward people, promote common beliefs and missions, and in general bring about harmony (Stacy, 1991: 112–113).

TRADITIONAL APPROACH

Contemporary notions of organizational behavior and communication have been dominated by the paradigms of traditional organization science and the positivistic sociology. In relation to everyday management these implicit notions are important because they are the roads and landscapes of mental maps that managers are using when they make decisions and act as leaders. Social systems, like organizations, are born and maintained through plans, choices, and actions of the system's members, and mental maps direct these processes.

An illustrative example of traditional organization design is undoubtedly Weberian bureaucracy (see Weber, 1947). Although we have come a long way from the Weberian era, the big picture is still, in many cases, the same. Modern organizations are often designed according to a mechanistic view of how everything works. At present, many organizations are managed by scattering them into separate components, certain managerial causes are supposed to follow certain reasons, the environment is considered to be predictable and stable, and enormous efforts are made to find ways to observe the organizational universe objectively. Even though the world is nonlinear by nature, organizational models and designs try to conceptualize it as linear realities. The machinery imagery

of spheres was seized upon by organizations in a desire to emphasize structures and parts. Responsibilities have been organized into
functions. People have been organized into roles. Page after page of
organizational charts depicts the workings of the machine
(Wheatley, 1992: 6). When considering the domain of organizational
research, the positivistic heritage is visible, especially in many
quantitative methods and methodological tools.

CHAOS AS AN ALTERNATIVE

As we know, chaos models are not based on one single explana-
tory chaos theory but instead on a group of theories affected by
different phenomena and models that were developed and presented
independently in different scientific fields. In chaos models one
finds several abstract structures that are of special significance in
the modeling of organizational change and organizational communication processes and systems. In my work I have stressed especially a sensitive dependency on initial conditions (i.e., the butterfly effect), and the concepts attractor and bifurcation.

The concept of chaos itself has several meanings. Although
chaos is commonly understood to mean disorder and confusion,
the academic meaning is somewhat different. Each discipline sets
the limits of its conception of chaos. However, in the broadest, academic sense of the word, chaos refers to the complex behavior of a
system that has the appearance of randomness but is nevertheless governed by its deterministic properties. Chaotic behavior is
something that is not random but appears to be so. Chaos does not
overrule determinism; the chaos is deterministic. Thus, it is significant that the academic or scientific meaning of chaos is distinct from its everyday usage.

The myth of the tornado caused by the flap of a butterfly's
wing is known far and wide, and its telling has spread beyond
the boundaries of the academic world. The concept of the butterfly effect refers to the property of a nonlinear system, according
to which a small change in the condition of the system at a certain moment can lead to large changes in the future. The butterfly effect is a basic property of the system that we can define
as its extremely sensitive dependence on initial conditions or
initial value sensitivity.

An attractor is a state into which a system settles. An attractor
is a set of values in the phase space to which a system migrates
over time. An attractor can be a single, fixed point, a collection of
points regularly visited, a loop, a complex orbit, or an infinite
number of points. A so-called strange attractor is an important

sign of chaos, but strange attractors and chaotic attractors are not synonymous.

Bifurcation means the condition or behavior of a system as it divides or branches out suddenly into two different or merging partial behaviors. Consecutive bifurcations form a development chain (i.e., a bifurcation tree) that can lead the system to chaos. A known development stage of a system is that one sequence and one bifurcation point represent the state of noncontinuity of a system's development. The first bifurcation is the first sign of chaos, from which a threat of potential chaotic development leading to a system's breakdown can be determined. If we cannot control the bifurcation process, we cannot control chaos.

Such properties of chaotic systems as dynamics, nonlinearity, sensitivity to changes, and unpredictability are all vital for an organization's strategies and effective planning and, above all, for the organization's management. Thus, we have reason to ponder which conditions of an organization can be put on a level with a potentially chaotically behaving system. We can identify certain features that all chaotic systems, have in common: (1) chaos appears in nonlinear, dynamic systems and (2) chaos appears in systems that are recursive, that is characterized by cycles in which a system's output at a given moment is used in the input of the following moment.

CHAOS AND ORGANIZATION

Seeing the primary characteristics of these features is easy, for example, in contemporary companies and other organizations and in their operational environments. Recursiveness plays a large role in the operational functions of an organization. Prepared plans are based, as a rule, on the previous period's achievements, and attempts are made to learn from the past. In practice nearly all learning methods arise from functions that the members of the organization try to improve. According to Giddens (1984: 2):

Human social activities, like some self-reproducing items in nature, are recursive. That is to say, they are not brought into being by social actors but are continually recreated by them via the very means whereby they express themselves as actors. In and through their activities agents reproduce the conditions that make these activities possible.

Sudden, irregular, and unforeseeable changes in the functioning of an organization can include, for example, the failure of operational plans, the interruption of production, a surprising strike, internal conflicts, and so on. Companies constantly interact with other actors in society such as customers, public, government, economic institutions and so on. Increasing structural instabilities, the loss of control, or the absence of resources caused by environmental turbulence can cause a critical state or condition for the organization that can be comparable to the bifurcation point of the chaotic system. If the change cannot be controlled, the organization's instability may begin to increase cumulatively toward chaos; actions taken within the organization can surpass the next effective operational level, causing again a new wave of change.

The sensitivity on initial conditions partly explains why an organization can fall into fateful difficulties or dire straits because of seemingly slight changes or minor incidents. The development of change includes breaks in the social consensus and changes in cultural values whose social consequences cannot be predicted. Minor incidents become major crises when changes turn into bifurcation points of social values, and sometimes the final outcome of the cumulative process of expanding changes leads to the breakdown of the company.

Not all crises lead the organization to collapse, but every crisis is an organizational bifurcation point that somehow changes the nature of the organization. A crisis becomes truly significant for the organization history when it permanently alters the organization's operations and culture. Other incidents are meaningless occurrences that leave their marks on the organization but do not cause fatal changes (Pauchant and Mitroff, 1992).

The point is that significant changes do not occur by chance but are the consequences of processes inherent in the organization. Some organizations carry change in their genes, which means that they naturally contain errors, bugs, faults, and other elements that accumulate and gain strength, giving rise to crises regardless of outside factors. Once the processes of change have begun, organizational attractors resist future interventions from outside the process because chaotic systems are inherently reflective. Such systems follow a logic of change of their own. While the inherent instability makes the change inevitable, external factors have only a minor chance of successfully altering the timing or direction of the change process.

In order to understand the significance of chaos theory for organizational management, the organization should be considered as a complex, dynamic, and nonlinear system. With these assumptions in mind, the organization can be examined as a system that is exposed to chaotic phenomena at all times.

ORGANIZATIONAL COMMUNICATION—FROM *COMMUNICATIO* TO *COMMUNICARE*

If organizations are complex systems and are able to behave chaotically, what, then, is the role of organizational communication in handling this complexity, and how is organizational communication linked to organizational change and its management?

Among the different fields of organizational communication we can find processes that are exposed to a sensitive dependency on initial conditions. Construction of communication relations, spreading of unofficial information, changes in public opinion, adoption of innovations, and so on are in their many forms and in their unexplainability and complexity comparable, for example, to the unpredictability of the weather system. Organization's communication events can be presented as periodic systems in which the output of the last event is the input of the following. Small and seemingly insignificant changes on the communication microlevel can grow in strength, which affects the macrolevel organization. It is important that anysystem, which is susceptible to the aforementioned butterfly effect, can in a short space of time change its nature unpredictably. In particular, there is reason to emphasize that chaoticness is an inherent property of a system. Although in reality the causes of chaotic behavior are usually changing conditions in the environment, chaos does not necessarily come from external factors, whose effects are often impossible to differentiate from internal chaos factors.

TWO PARADIGMS—TWO OUTCOMES

There are, broadly speaking, two types of paradigm of human communication. The first sees communication as a mechanistic process, and the second sees it as a negotiation and exchange of meaning (see O'Sullivan et al., 1994; Fiske, 1990). Traditional management models contain a process notion of human communication. Process models of organizational communication have their roots in information theory.

The mathematical theory of communication of Shannon and Weaver (1949) is an early attempt to extend the applicability of information theory into human communication, and it has been one of the most important and authoritative in the development of later communication process models and theories. It models communication on a process in which a source encodes and then transmits a message along a channel. The message is received and decoded at its destination, upon which it produces an effect. Regardless of the model's omissions and deficiencies in relation to human communication, it has remained as perhaps the longest-lasting description of the communication process (Bowman and Targowski, 1987: 25).

The theory has had notable contributions to the study of communications, including the measurement of the quantity of information by bits and the understanding of entropy as applied to communication. However, the model is, by nature, a reductionistic, sender-centered model and a straight derivative of the linear main paradigm of Western human communication: A→B = X, or, in other words A communicates something to B, with X resulting. Shannon and Weaver's theory is associated with the balancing and strengthening of a system's structure. Only one direction is possible, which is toward balance. Similarly, new information is also in the first place centred on the strengthening of already existing information structures. The amount of information is taken as given; due to inevitable disturbances it can only diminish (Jantsch, 1980: 51). Communication process models are linear and predictable, and they are more rational than a human being and can be considered part of the framework of positivistic thinking. Residual values, stochastic errors or human factors are abstract explanations of deviations from the linear model, and most often they seem to be the receiver's mistake.

The visual presentations of the communication process models define the matter. They are, more often than not, on the box-and-arrow level and cannot be used to quantify the processes they portray. Causality appears in the boxes' order and in the direction of the arrows; nonlinear factors are framed within the disturbance or noise box.

Influence of the traditional view to the underlying characteristics, which, in turn, guides the designs of organizational communication, is described in Figure 9.1. The outermost circle is the level of communication, then comes the organization level, and the innermost circle demonstrates traditional view's four main aspects. The center is labeled Newtonian to illustrate the implicit origin of the described notions.

An alternative view of communication concentrates on the relationship between fundamental components necessary for meaning to emerge. Messages, people as members of cultures, and reality interact so as to produce meaning. Accordingly, human communication can be defined as a process through which people, acting together, create, sustain, and manage meanings through the use of verbal and nonverbal signs and symbols within a particular context. As we can see, this definition combines elements from both views. It accepts that communication is a process, but the outcome is not the transmission of messages but production of meaning.

Figure 9.1
The Influence of the "Newtonian Core" on the Organization and Communication Designs

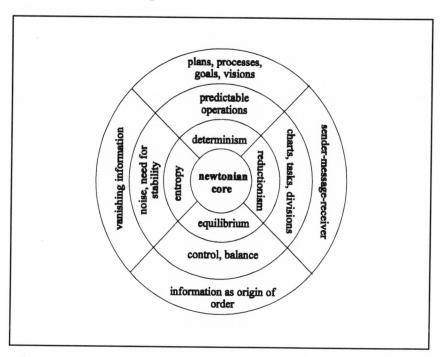

When communication takes place in an organization, the definition has to be modified a little. Organizational communication differs from general notions of communication in terms of the complexity of the context and people dimensions. Organizational relationships are both like and unlike any other interpersonal relationships. We communicate with people at work because we like them and because our tasks require us to do so. Thus, our relationships at work have both an interpersonal and an organizational dimension (Conrad, 1994: 4). Actually, this view of communication is a descendant of the original meaning of the word "communication," which comes from Latin words *communicare*, meaning doing together, and *communis*, meaning community.

As mentioned before, according to the traditional conception, an organization is a consciously coordinated social unit composed of two or more people that functions on a relatively continuous basis to achieve a common goal or set of goals. However, this is a very restrictive and functionalistic way of looking at organizations. An alternative way is to consider the organization as a set of irrational cultures (instead of rational functions) that are connected, revealed, and maintained through organizational communication. Hence, organizations are changed not by changing their functions but by changing the structure of their cultures.[1]

THE DUAL FUNCTION OF ORGANIZATIONAL COMMUNICATION

Communication as a substructure of an organization can be an effective tool for management in the safeguarding of correct choices and the realization of favorable outcomes. When undergoing change, the management of the organization tries to reduce instabilities at the critical period (i.e., bifurcation point) with the help of communication. In connection with every realized choice the organization moves toward a new point of communication space along the path it has created.

However, since communication as a system is dependent and can, in fact, be itself unbalanced or chaotic, it is clear that not just any communication clearly produces order or integration. Communication can be regarded as a qualitatively bistructural system in which one part directs the organization's development toward

Figure 9.2
Dissipative and Integrative Communication

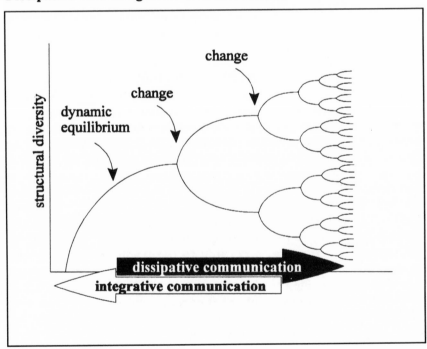

order, and the other toward growing disorder (Aula, 1996). By their qualitative properties these two structural functions of organizational communication can be called integrative communication and dissipative communication. (See Figure 9.2.)

Integrative communication and dissipative communication together form the dual function of organizational communication. Effective integrative communication would therefore be the instrument by which the organization can react successfully to pressure for change from the environment. On the other hand, dissipative communication works in reverse, and in the case of bifurcation the organization's choices become more difficult. Dissipative communication can even become damaging and direct the organization in the wrong direction. Thus, it can be claimed that every communication act realized within an organization is bipartite by its nature and that communication can simultaneously carry out two different functions.

Every communicative event, despite its original meaning or appearance, is simultaneously both integrative and dissipative. At the optimum level, an organization's communication would be directed so that the communication's integrative properties would be maximized and its dissipative properties minimised. On the other hand, existing structures and functions can be broken with controlled dissipative communication and channeled in the desired development. It is worth noticing that order is not self-evidently beneficial and disorder noxious to the organization. Table 9.1 describes qualitative properties of the dual function.

Dissipative communication is effective when an organization is in a crisis, and problem solving needs innovation and creativity. Integrative communication is productive when the crisis is over, and the organization needs control and planning. Dissipative communication is indirect and dialogical and allows communicative partners to present alternative views and interpretations. It permits new intellectual structures to emerge. Dissipative communication tends to show, rather than tell, how things are.

Table 9.1
The Dual Function and Its Qualitative Properties

integrative communication	*dissipative communication*
literal	metaphoric
reactive	proactive
intentional	spontaneous
controlled	impulsive
monophonic	polyphonic
monologue	dialogue

Integrative communication presents the content directly, logically, and efficiently and creates feelings of continuity and consciousness of control. Integrative communication is a monologic process in which a sender communicates to a receiver, instead of involving true interactive participation. Integrative communication is systematic and structurally conservative. It is more telling than showing. Dissipative communication is suitable for unique tasks that presuppose imagination and integrative communication when tasks are continuous and routine.

CULTURAL DIVERSITY OF ORGANIZATIONS

In the center of organizations are always human beings who, through their actions, influence the ways in which organizations ultimately operate in relation to themselves and their respective environments. Human beings interact through communication, and human communication is present everywhere in an organization: exchanges of texts, new media, technology, everyday meetings, unofficial networks and so on. Communication is an essential condition to any organization, and organizational cultures are products of communication.

This reciprocal relationship means that organizational cultures and communication systems are not two separate parts of the organization. The link between them can be found in Anthony Giddens' concept of the duality of structure (Giddens, 1984:25):

Structure, as recursively organized sets of rules and resources, is out of time and space, save in its instantiations and co-ordination as memory traces, and is marked by an absence of the subject. The social systems in which structure is recursively implicated, on the contrary, comprise the situated activities of human agents, reproduced across time and space.... Critical to the idea of structuration is the theorem of the duality of structure.... The constitution of agents and structures are not two independently given sets of phenomena, a dualism, but represent a duality. According to the notion of the duality of structure, the structural properties of social systems are both medium and outcome of the practices they recursively organize. Structure is not external to individuals.

Communicative processes simultaneously reveal organizational cultures and support them (Conrad, 1994: 293–294). Under its explicit, visible culture an organization has not one but several implicit, invisible subcultures. Each subculture is characterized by the nature of its communicative nature or the dominating part of the communication dual function. These invisible cultures form an implicit culture structure of the organization.

The role of communication increases in the case of management of organizational change because it is the connecting element between explicit and implicit cultures. The success of effective communication and use of the quality of the dual function is a presupposition for successful organizational change. By means of integrative communication the change processes can be guided in the desired direction of organized transformation. On the other hand, dissipative communication can further the emergence of new structures through "order by disorder."

Some researchers are of the opinion that chaos is indeed the origin of innovations, creativity, and new forms. New structures cannot emerge without breaking down the old constructions. In the same way the destruction of existing organizational and cultural structures opens up a period for disorder and confusion during which new ideas and values are free to emerge. Otherwise, distinct parts of the organization are able to communicate and cooperate in order to achieve a new consensus and to make new decisions through nonlinear processes that are spontaneous and self-organizing.

According to a common wisdom of organizational research, an organization needs a consistent organizational culture to be able to have cooperation between its members and to operate effectively. It is believed that the existence of shared cultural meanings, values, and norms forms a basis for favorable circumstances for trust and safety that, in turn, unite members behind an organization and its mission, vision, and goals. Strong cultural unity gives birth to feelings of approval and acceptance in an atmosphere where both individual benefits and contributions become identical with those of the organization. The argument often is that an organization needs a consistent culture in particular to cope with the future. However, in a dynamic environment where futures are made of multiple, constantly changing agendas of totalities, monolithic management easily fails to generate creativity, without which an organization will be unable to react fast enough (Caulkin, 1995: 32–36). Instead of being driven by one culture, an organization needs diversity of beliefs, meanings, and values to break existing ways of doing things.

THE COMMUNICATION ARENA AND THE DIVERSITY OF CULTURES

Communication is not simply a process of exchanging information with one another, although information exchange is an important part of communicating. It is a process through which we make sense out of our experiences, a complex system through which we create and share meanings (Conrad, 1994: 8). In other words, communication involves the interaction of information, knowledge, emotions, ideas, opinions, worldviews and so on. Organizational surroundings where this interaction takes place can be called communication arenas, and each arena has its explicit and implicit cultures.[2] Explicit cultures express the organization's visible characteristics, and usually remain stable over the long run. On the other hand, implicit cultures imply individual invisible values and meanings and can vary considerably between ordered and disordered designs. In brief, communication arenas are built on the diversity of cultures. In the widest sense the communication arena can comprise the entire organization when the culture structure of the arena forms the total culture of organization.

Table 9.2, describing communication in an arena's culture structure, has four interconnected fields: the struggle of cultures, the monolithic culture, the vacuum of cultures, and the anarchistic culture. On one hand, two of these cultural forms can be considered disadvantageous for the arena to operate successfully. Struggle of cultures is characterized by mixed communication climate together with disorder, uncertainty, and noisiness. There is too much communication around, and co-operation is very hard. Vacuum of cultures is the opposite of the struggle of cultures. An arena has, in practice, no active communication whatsoever, and the arena's heartbeats are very slow.

On the other hand, anarchistic culture is characterized by openness and multiplicity, and its communication is highly dissipative. Monolithic culture is closed and monotonous, and communication within is purely integrative. Sometimes the dominance of monolithic culture provides the most advantageous atmosphere for an organization to survive, and sometimes an organization needs anarchistic values to cope with environmental or internal changes.

Table 9.2
Diversity of Organizational Cultures

explicit visible culture	
implicit invisible cultures	
anarchist culture low integrative communication high dissipative communication	struggle of cultures high integrative communication high dissipative communication
vacuum of cultures low integrative communication low dissipative communication	monolithic culture high integrative communication low dissipative communication

An arena's evolution is dependent on the relationship between the cultures and the dual function of communication. The type of the culture that gets the dominant position directs the development or evolution the arena. However, the diversity of cultures is not an intrinsic value.

THE WHEEL OF CHANGE MODEL

The communication arena consists of dynamic and nonlinear culture structures that are in a recursive, interactional relationship with each other. An examination of the communication arena's evolution reveals stable stages and bifurcation points. The changes of the stable periods are, to a certain degree, predictable, whereas this is impossible at the bifurcation points. The inherent nature and sensitivity of the arena's evolution mean that communication's different qualitative properties can function as triggers for the emergence of different cultural designs.

What matters are the composition of the communication dual function at the beginning of the arena's evolution and the structure's utilization during development and especially at the bifurcation points. The intervention of integrative communication at the bifurcation point of the development can lead to monolithic culture structure. Correspondingly, the usage of dissipative communication can shift the evolution in the direction of an anarchistic culture.

Figure 9.3 describes the dynamic structure of organization's communication arena. An arena's communicative interactions between cultures and evolution of different cultural structure involves (1) histories of both past communications and earlier culture structures, (2) elements of present communication and structure and (3) expectations about future interactions and state of the arena. Lines between different forms of communication structures, and between communication and culture structures represent these complex relationships and interactions. Thus, instead of just connecting symbols, lines can be considered as two-headed arrows representing interdependencies and interactions. The model indicates that because communication influences the way an arena operates and is simultaneously influenced by the arena's culture structure, neither arena, cultures, nor communication can be understood in isolation from one another.

An organization is a merger of different cultures that can be separated into visible, explicit cultures and invisible, implicit cultures. Usually, an organization has, or it strives to achieve, one consistent visible, but also unified invisible, culture. This view is

Figure 9.3
The Wheel of Change Model of the Structure of Organization's
Communication Arena

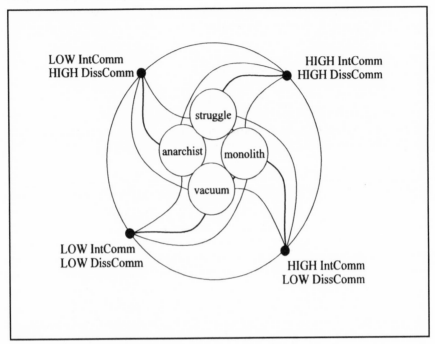

close to Schein's (1985) idea of organization culture structure, according to which culture can be divided into two levels. The visible level is composed of organizational artifacts, such as buildings, machinery, sounds, stories. The other level consists of the fundamental assumptions that establish the common unconscious memory of the organization members. The visible level is ultimately the reflection of the invisible.

The role of communication is to create the conditions that favor the emergence of a culture that will nurture the desired change. Because implicit subcultures are the source of visible organizational behavior, the organization has to manage communication in such a way that the proper dominant subculture can arise. Once a certain culture (e.g., an anarchistic culture) has emerged and become dominant, it will follow its unique attractor with consequences that are difficult to alter. An organization has not one but several complex subcultures that stay alive in different communication arenas and whose dominance and effects upon organization fluctuate over time and place. As a consequence of the complexity and sensitivity of the individual arena's culture structures, the absolute uniformity of the organization's implicit cultures is impossible.

CHANGING ORGANIZATION—CHANGING CULTURE STRUCTURE

If an organization's operative functions are considered to be a part of its visible culture structure, it can be said that the fundamental purpose of organizational change is to transform the explicit organization culture. If the organization does not "need" a profound change in implicit cultures, the change operations are directed to the explicit culture. Hence, the implicit culture structure is subordinate to the explicit culture. We have to keep in mind that implicit cultures do not produce or manufacture anything—the culture as such is not able to work, discharge, strike, and so on.

Traditionally, organizational change has been directed to either visible or invisible cultures. The common view has been that while the visible culture is easier to change, the transformation of the invisible culture is more permanent. Nevertheless, since the organization does not have a single implicit culture, an organizational change cannot perform a transition from culture A to culture B. In the case of an explicit culture this transformation can be possible.

Transformations in the relationships between implicit cultures are the predecessor and not the consequence of organizational changes. The management of organizational change is closely interconnected with the management of a given organization's communication systems and cultures, but communication cannot linearly cause such changes to take place. Thus, transforming the organization's complex culture structure through communication is a fundamental part of the management of any organizational change.

The processes of change proceed not linearly but nonlinearly, which, taking a sensitivity on initial conditions into account, means that the outcome of change is difficult, if not impossible, to predict. Successful organizational change occurs the same way that a seed of California giant redwood needs only the right circumstances—suitable soil, humidity, sunlight, and so on—to grow up to a huge, beautiful tree. Like the redwood seed, the organization inherently carries the embryo of change in itself. Changing the organization is far from moving railway carriages from the depot to the station with the help of a strong locomotive. Notions of organizational change, management, and communication that are founded on principles of chaos place certain conditions upon traditional management's ability to carry out changes based on strict plans. Linear ways to change are not effective enough in a nonlinear world.

NOTES

1. This notion of organizational cultures consider cultures as something organizations *are* instead of as something organizations *have*. See more about this distinction in Conrad (1994: 8–33).

2. The concept of an arena is borrowed from Stacey (1991), even though he uses it in a different manner.

REFERENCES

Aula, P. (1996). "Chaos and the Double Function of Communication." In W. Sulis and A. Combs (Eds.), *Nonlinear Dynamics in Human Behavior.* London: World Scientific.

Bowman, J. P. and Targowski, A. S. (1987), "Modelling the Communication Process: The Map Is Not the Territory." *The Journal of Business Communication*, Vol. 24, No. 4, 21–34.

Caulkin, S. (1995). "Chaos Inc." *Across the Board*, Vol. 32, 32–36.

Conrad, C. (1994). *Strategic Organizational Communication; Toward the Twenty-First Century.* New York: Harcourt, Brace College.

Fiske, J. (1990). *Introduction to Communication Studies.* London: Routledge.

Giddens, A. (1984). *The Constitution of Society.* Berkeley: University of California Press.

Jantsch, E. (1980). *The Self-Organizing Universe; Scientific and Human Implications of the Emerging Paradigm of Evolution.* New York: Pergamon Press.

O'Sullivan, T., Hartley, J., Saunders, D., Montgomery, M., and Fiske, J. (1994). *Key Concepts in Communication and Cultural Studies.* London: Routledge.

Pauchant, T. C. and Mitroff, I. I. (1992). *Transforming the Crisis-Prone Organization: Preventing Individual, Organizational, and Environmental Tragedies.* San Francisco: Jossey-Bass.

Schein, E. (1985). *Organizational Culture and Leadership.* San Francisco: Jossey-Bass.

Shannon, C. and Weaver, W. (1949). *The Mathematical Theory of Communication.* Urbana: University of Illinois Press.

Stacey, R. D. (1991). *The Chaos Frontier; Creative Strategic Control for Business.* Wiltshire: Butterworth-Heinemann.

Weber, M. (1947). *The Theory of Social and Economic Organization.* New York: Free Press.

Wheatley, M. (1992). *Leadership and the New Science; Learning about Organization from an Orderly Universe.* San Francisco: Berrett-Koehler.

Chapter 10

The Architecture of Strategic Thought: A Neuronal Network Approach

Harold E. Klein

The dissolution of industry boundaries, the globalization of business, and the ever-changing interconnectedness effected through extensive multilateral relationships among nations, multinationals, and even industries themselves have focused attention on management *processes* for coping with change. Experience over the last two decades has led to the realization that formal strategic planning models and techniques have not provided the decision-making vehicles for strategic development in actual corporate practice (see Mintzberg, 1994). Portfolio management techniques, virtually synonymous with strategic planning for almost three decades and still an unsupplanted mainstay of strategic management teaching in business schools, years ago had been pronounced passé by one of the field's icons (Michael Porter). There is the growing acceptance that especially in times of dramatic change "strategy" *does not* result from the application of some analytical routine and, that it *does* result from a complex amalgam of inputs, considerations, and analyses implicitly (more likely than explicitly) evaluated in a difficult-to-discern mental process—in other words, strategic thinking!

There currently are a number of books in print either with the title "Strategic Thinking" or with that as the book's main subject.[1] Strategic thinking focuses on the cognitive processes involved in reaching strategic decisions (Hendry, Johnson, and Newton, 1993). If there is one technique that has surfaced as an aid or facilitator of strategic thinking, it is "cognitive mapping."

Cognitive (or causal) mapping representation has shown itself to be a useful tool for capturing the complex dynamics inherent in a strategic decision; to date it has been used, perhaps, more for management cognition research purposes than as an applied strategic planning tool. However, notwithstanding its application, there is recognition that a cognitive map is not a "model of cognition" (Eden et al., 1992). These cognitive maps are inconsistent to varying degrees with what is known now about how the human mind generates "thoughts" (or goes about making strategic choices)—how the brain organizes, stores, retrieves, and structures information and how it uses information to decide.

In the following section, the implications of current cognitive mapping representations as a management tool are suggested, along with limitations. Next, some reasonably well agreed upon thinking and research results about how the human mind functions within the brain at the neuronal level are presented that have relevance for the design of cognitive process representation. An architecture of strategic thought based on these notions is presented, followed by a different kind of cognitive map representation, defined here as a *normative cognitive map*. These maps differ from conventional cognitive maps in at least one significant way: the revelatory power inherent in the map representation itself. The process whereby these latter maps are created has been embedded in a strategic planning process and applied in several large corporation contexts.[2] An example of the normative cognitive maps that resulted from one recent comprehensive corporate planning exercise is presented along with a discussion of its unique advantages in actual strategic planning contexts.

REPRESENTATION AND STRUCTURE OF COGNITIVE MAPS

Cognitive maps have been widely employed as the representation medium to capture the results of strategic thinking; mapping systems also have been applied in strategy formation situations to assist managers in coping with complexity and facilitating the strategy formation process itself (cf. Warren, 1995). Causal maps and influence diagrams tend to be the most widely used, certainly within the strategic management context, from among the several discernible types of "cognitive maps" (Huff, 1990). The mapping results themselves are "nonprescriptive" (Eden, 1989); the value of these maps to the viewer hereto mainly has been inferential. That is, it is through an *inspection* of the output map that the observer derives insight or other benefit. The map reader must bring to the table a knowledge base about the problem and some anticipated questions for which answers are to be found by an inspection of the map. The map itself holds no revelations for the uninitiated.

From a neuroscience perspective, these types of maps would be termed "high-level," in the sense that the map content consists of the final results of the cognitive process, the end of the line.[3] Almost invariably, the purpose for creating the map in the first place is to capture some complicated dynamic, where a visual representation is most communicative. Fiol and Huff (1992) identified four types of "managerial maps" in common use. From a representational standpoint, two of the four that happen to be the most frequently encountered are quite similar, characterized by spatially separated nodes with connections among them; another is a factor loading, star diagram while the fourth is an organizational hierarchy structure, similar to a top-down decision tree. Clearly, the term "map" currently is applied loosely, virtually to any diagrammatic representation of a set of data.

Most causal mapping results look more or less the same, notwithstanding how these are derived: a series of interconnecting nodes, where the meaning of the spatial position of any one node in relation to the others is not easily discernible.[4]

The specification of a relationship between any two nodes may range from a simple indication that the two are in some way related/linked to a sign of directionality/causality and/or intensity of impact and/or probability of occurrence. Here the resulting map should yield further insights beyond that obtainable from inspecting/analyzing the data set piecemeal. Alternatively, the causal map may be created after the fact, as a documentation of some preceding analysis or investigation.

The intent may be to get an overall idea of the complex dynamics within an organization—a holistic view—or to make a comparison, say, with another map of the same system where a factor or condition has been changed (cf. Warren, 1995). The purpose might be to identify the specific chain of events/conditions/factors impacting a strategic decision (i.e., what are the contents of a back trace from node X?); in yet others, to identify the specific sequence of intermediate decisions that must be made starting from a given data input prefacing some final outcome (i.e., What nodes come between nodes a and q?). In any of these applications, the internal structure of the map is not a critical issue, so long as the integrity of the internodal linkages is maintained.

The starting point for a mapping exercise, in most cases, is a data set indicating some extent of connection between two or more nodes. Entry data may be in qualitative or quantitative format. If the latter, the most common means of capturing node-to-node relationships is through a node identity matrix where cell intersections provide the specification of the relationship (e.g., a plus or minus sign or a numerical value, say, -10 to +10).

Any complicated, multinode relationship, of course, can then be broken down into a series of bimodal linkages. The relationship A→B→C can be expressed as A→B and B→C. However, once the data are captured within the identity matrix format, all semblance of the original three-node relationship is lost (i.e., reductionism in action). It should be noted that anytime a complex, multivariate relationship is reinterpreted into a series of pairwise linkages, the richness of the original argument is dissipated. It is impossible to re-create this richer relationship from a completed data set within an identity matrix itself. One would need to go back to the raw data, scanning each and every identified nodal relationship for its original intent.

This problem is overcome, to an extent, using qualitative and symbolic representation of multinodal relationships. Here, a verbal description of a node (it can be anything: a factor, a variable, an event, a concept) is symbolically linked to another one. The linkage symbol also can represent anything desired. Axelrod (1976) employed six types of linkages, actually all only variants on positive, negative, or neutral effect. Huff (1990) added two new linkage relationships to those of Axelrod that negated or affirmed that two nodes (or "concepts") were "equivalent" (i.e., equal or the same).[5] Axelrod hand-drew his influence diagrams (or causal maps), as it appears does Huff. Positioning of the various elements or nodes is not an important consideration except to enhance clarity of presentation and understandability.

Eden (1989) has developed a software-based procedure originally called COPE, now Decision Explorer, that does essentially the same thing with more presentation and structure options but a more limited repertoire of linkage possibilities. The user may indicate either a positive or a negative relationship between only two nodes (as opposed to the six used by Axelrod and eight used by Huff). The program automatically draws an influence diagram based on inputted positively or negatively linked "concepts"; the program is quite user-friendly.[6]

Eden anticipates a major problem in the prospective utility of a causal map: what to do when there are a large number of interrelated nodes, say, 50 or perhaps 100. The COPE program can partition the resulting causal map into two or more groups or clusters, thus creating multiple maps. The COPE program appears to have an algorithm for minimizing linkage crossovers among nodes, enhancing the readability of the map output.

The layout of the COPE program causal maps, as well as for those cited before, aims for clarity and understanding of interrelationships. However, the positioning of individual nodes and their special relation to other nodes do not appear to have much specific meaning. Generally, there is a sense that the node relationships in the upper part of the map take place before those below (or in some, moving from left to right). This, however, is not always the case.

The position of any node in relation to others using hand-mapping or such influence-diagram-generating programs such as COPE is not based on any input data that include any temporal or directional information.[7] Since the resulting diagram captures feedback loops, it is hard to infer where the system starts and where it ends (i.e., the outputs of interest).[8]

Eden (1992) identifies two structural properties of a cause map: hierarchy and linkage. However, this feature is not easily discernible in many of his complex maps with feedback loops. Eden proposes a recoding of the data that results in a unidirectional flow of linkages among the map nodes—ergo, "hierarchy."[9]

Fahey and Narayanen (1989) appeared to have followed much the same procedure in their Zenith study. In their reconfigured map, however, hierarchy in node sequencing is not clearly evident, nor can any temporal dimension be reasonably inferred (at least, with any one string of connections). The aim of their "reconstruction" was to reduce complexity so as to facilitate analysis.

As mentioned before, one weakness of causal maps is their lack of any temporal dimension. Of course, the sequence of occurrence of any node in relation to any other linked node, at least, is obvious from the directionality of the link itself. This probably is good enough for the previously described, inferential uses of causal maps. However, feedback loops confound any meaningful observation of directionality. In automatic mapping programs, the presence of a loop between two nodes is likely to cause the two to be drawn closer together, possibly distorting the map structure (see notes 6, 7). These map characteristics may not be particularly worrisome to the map reader if the aim simply is one of understanding some complex, interconnected, multinodal system. If, however, the reader wants to gain some assistance in deciding, say, what to do next, the map contents are of little help.

A word needs to be added about input data format for causal map construction. The ultimate configuration of any map is wholly constrained by the amount of information contained within the entry data. The entry data formats currently used (and as described earlier) are the heart of the problem; these are, at the same time, the attributes most attractive to researchers—mainly, the free form and flexibility to enter any kind of datum in any which way, shape, or form (whether it be a concept, an organizational attribute, an event, etc.) and in any order. Thus, while "causality" might be captured through the directionality of a linkage, there is no sense from *within the map itself* as to which node is the one of real interest to the observer, the thing that might be of most interest to the practitioner (e.g., What are the dynamics deriving the rapid decline of my market? or "What are the organizational influences leading our design group to such poor performance?"). That is what the map reader must bring to the interpretation task. It is the most serious limitation on the utility of causal maps as currently constituted: lack of any normative or prescriptive power (i.e., the derivation of specific desired information and/or decisions directly from map output).

Finally, causal maps of the type just discussed should not be construed as representations of actual cognitive processes (i.e., what takes place within the mind that reveals actual thought); rather, these are the *results* of higher-level cognitive processes as construed by the mapmaker. Indeed, researchers in the field make no such claim and recognize the distinction (Eden, 1992). This dichotomy also extends to cognitive mapping procedures, which, in practice, are quite different from what is now believed to occur in the human mind to reach comparable results. Some of these ideas and research findings on mind/brain functions are discussed later.

STRUCTURE OF CONSCIOUSNESS, MEMORY, AND THOUGHT—SOME KEY CONCEPTS

Any "thought," however simple it appears, is highly complex, even more so for a "strategic thought." The reason is that thought does not spring from "nothingness." No thought "pops into your head," as the expression goes. Its origins were there all the time. The thought may have "popped out" because of some associations or connections that were finally made within the brain among existing ideas or thoughts that may have lain dormant in memory for days, months, or even years. Perhaps, a visual stimulus, something seen or read, triggered (i.e. connected with one or more of these now suddenly remembered ideas that resulted in the "pop." It is an example of what humans do very well, and other animals do not.[10] That "pop" is an act of human consciousness. Thus, thought, memory, and consciousness are inexorably linked.

A *strategic* thought must be very complex indeed. Any strategy concept, notwithstanding whether it be broad or narrow, contains elements of objectives to be achieved (implicitly or explicitly), resources to be used, and actions to be taken employing these resources (Andrews, 1987). Furthermore, strategic choice is influenced, if not predominantly determined, by assumptions (thoughts) about external conditions, current and prospective, within which the strategy has to be implemented. More often than not, the perceived opportunity or threat provides the outside trigger for strategy formation (or reformation). But it also is the input to the strategy formation process about which the least is known—especially in times of major structural change. In such circumstances the mind of the strategist gets its toughest workout.

Only within the last 10 years or so has what goes on in the "mind" or "consciousness" (the two are treated interchangeably here) been the subject of serious systematic investigation. Largely, research on brain activity and the central nervous system (CNS) has dealt with physical (i.e., measurable) phenomena, trying to understand what is happening inside the brain under a variety of conditions/stimuli, given subjects (human and animal) presenting a range of physical, behavioral, and mental states (naturally occurring or purposefully induced) (Cohen, Renshaw, and Yurgelun-Todd, 1995). However, understanding how thoughts, emotions, or feelings emerge from neurological activity taking place in the brain remains an elusive goal (Albert, 1997; Block, 1996). The recent, widespread availability of new technology, notably, functional magnetic resonance imaging (FMRI) and positron emission tomography (PET) scanning, has rekindled interest in exploring the mind-brain nexus (Buchsbaum, 1995; Barinaga, 1997). To a greater extent than ever before, brain activity at about the neural network level can be observed and measured more or less concurrently with subject behavior. The "elusive" part is the translation of neurological activity into thought or conscious activity. While heretofore there has been no universal agreement as to whether this connection can be made (Crick, 1994), the pace of research is resolving this issue (Rugg, 1998).[11] Also, some quite comprehensive models (and "near models") have been put forth providing alternative explanations of this phenomenon (Dudai, 1989).

There are some reasonably well agreed upon notions about how cognitive functions are enacted at the neuronal net-level that are common to these efforts. These principles have formed the basis of most neural network models (Parks and Prueitt, 1993; Changuex and Dehaene, 1989).[12] There is good reason to assume that the functional processes that take place in brain activity can provide a model for how to organize and present information so that it is most effectively employed in higher-level conscious activity (such as the strategic choice situation) (Wickelgren, 1997).

Memory—the key component of all thought—is not independent of purpose. A number of different types of memory exist to handle different classes of information: short-term or long-term, visual or verbal, activity or category, past or current or prospective experience (Andreasen et al., 1995), to name the major ones. Any one item surfaced from memory is the result of neural activity in a number of scattered areas of the brain.

While there are approximate regions within the brain where certain types of information appear to be located, the retrieval of that same information under different circumstances initiates different patterns of neuronal activity (Woolf, 1996). Even a small change in the retrieval act may manifest itself in this manner. A recent report in the scientific journal *Nature*, for example, relates how different parts of the brain process verbs, depending simply on whether the verbs are regular or irregular (Gee, 1997). A tense change alone would likely have the same effect, since different neural circuits are involved in processing past and prospective experience (Andreasen et al., 1995). When the same visual experience is remembered in one case or forgotten in another, the activation patterns in those sections of the brain involved in memory encoding differ significantly (Brewer et al., 1998; Wagner et al., 1998).

Hence, memory is not static; it cannot be found in one specific place. It simply does not exist without some relation to a *stimulus*,[13] a trigger—the same goes for any thought, even a strategic thought. Thus, any thought is a complex pattern of activity within and among neuronal cells (i.e., neural network) that may reorganize itself, to a greater or lesser extent, as a result of the slightest variation in the stimulus that triggered the thought in the first place (Xing and Gerstein, 1996) (e.g., thinking about the same subject as a prospective experience as opposed to a past happening).

Modifications in the neural network representing some thought can even occur within the network itself due to the interactions of the neuronal cells that constitute it. Neurons that appear to have some affinity for other ones nearby link up; one of these cells can excite the other, chemically and/or electrically (Woolf, 1996). In this dynamic, known as the *Hebb effect*, one or both of these cells may exhibit internal change that, in turn, may induce the same effect in other connected cells in the network. In this way, properties of the whole network are modified—a process labeled with the evocative term *plasticity* (Jeffrey and Reid, 1997). In the last few years, especially due to the widespread use and availability of advanced medical imaging systems, thousands of studies have been performed examining neural network plasticity in humans and a variety of other living things. Plasticity appears to take place throughout the CNS (Donoghue, 1995). Neuronal activity resulting from reconfigured networks may well account for that "pop," that "it just occurred to me" experience.

Closely interacting neurons within a network constitute "orientation columns," *pairwise connections* of neurons (Das and Gilbert, 1995; Edwards and Wakefield, 1992). Somehow, these complex cells find each other. Each cell is adjacent to as many as 10,000 other cells.[14] It is estimated that there are 10^{12} neuronal cells (or "neurons") in the human brain and 10^{15} connections[15] (Calvin, 1997), or, on average, about 1,000 connection possibilities for each neuron. Hence, any one cell does not have to physically move in order to make a connection—or to change its connection configuration—with thousands of other like cells.

The essential neuronal architecture of a cognitive activity has been mapped out and can be reconstructed from brain imaging outputs. No individual neuron appears to operate wholly independently (Illing, 1996). Rather, neurons that are commonly excited tend to cluster together. These clusters are interconnected ("horizontal" or "lateral connectivity"). This *connectivity* may come about through a common stimulus or a connection established from one neuronal network cluster directly to another (Jeffery and Reid, 1997). A change in connective patterns can occur among clusters as plasticity takes place within one cluster (Huntley, 1997). Hence, in any particular excitation, there is an assembly of neural network clusters (or "groups") (Singer, 1995).

Commonly oriented neurons, neuron groups and group assemblies fire (i.e., electrically excite) *unidirectionally* (McGuire et al., 1991; Janig and McLachlan, 1992). Feedback (in the sense of an ordered response), indeed, does takes place within the CNS, but it is effected along different pathways in separate, often very different neuronal assemblies. These latter neural networks also operate in a unidirectional manner, just in reverse.

The issue of just where exactly the boundary of a neural group assembly—or if it even has one—has not been resolved, although its approximate position may be inferred by drop-off in measurable values of brain activity as distance increases from its center. As new stimuli are received, these boundary areas shift as neural networks reconfigure themselves in response (i.e., plasticity and connectivity in action) (Illing, 1996).

What do these *clusters* (Sporns, 1994; Jeffery and Reid, 1997) and assemblages of clusters (i.e., *neuronal group architecture*)—which may well be the neurological essence of thought—look like? One "proposal" by Nobel Laureate Gerald M. Edelman (1992) depicts conceptually the composition and architecture of neuronal groups. He identifies five archetypes of connectivity found within and among such groups and their relation to "extrinsic inputs" (outside stimuli). Any or all may be found in one localized area. The size of individual groups will differ considerably, depending on location and function, ranging from 50 to 10,000 neurons in each group. Once again, note that connections among groups are far fewer than connectivity among neurons within any one group.

A thought, then, is and is the result of a synthesis of associations (as is a "strategy"), triggered by some implicit and/or explicit stimuli. In its turn, a thought begets other thoughts—where the former becomes the stimulus for the latter.[16] So any thought (read, strategic thought) is difficult to define (or map) comprehensively: how far in the string of associations leading to the core thought is it necessary to go before irrelevance sets in? How often is a realized thought articulated incompletely, in that the stimuli or "extrinsic input" that ultimately prodded that thought into consciousness remains unstated?[17]

What then is a useful structure (or "architecture") for a strategic thought, one that provokes yet further thinking? How best to depict this thinking so that the representation reveals more than the individual components of thought, but of some whole conception, a comprehensive thought?

THE SPECIAL CASE OF THE STRATEGICALLY RELEVANT ENVIRONMENT

A process has been developed for encouraging (indeed, almost compelling) management confrontation with structurally changing (often distasteful) prospective environments. Such environments are analytically untreatable and, indeed, the subject of many cognitive mapping exercises. Hence, the renewed interest in "strategic thinking."

Barr, Stimpert, and Huff (1992) noted the importance of managers' "mental models" of their changing environment. They suggested that managers confronting such conditions (1) pay attention to environmental change, (2) be responsive to external stimuli, and (3) attempt to link perceived threats with organization responses ("solutions"). They further noted that underpinning these tasks are "managerial beliefs about causality." An appropriate strategic response to dramatic environmental change cannot be attempted without having a reasonably clear idea (or set of assumptions) about *what* aspects of the environment ("problems") have relevance for *which* strategic decision(s) ("solutions").

Increasingly, cognitive maps are used to reveal the interrelationships among internal decisions and external happenings (cf. Warren, 1995). However, no structural distinctions appear to be made between internal and external nodes; nor does the literature recognize the importance of making this dichotomy. Yet the entire map representation is predetermined by this orientation. For it is not possible for a map to encourage some structural inference regarding the impact of the external environment on internal organizational matter without any distinction being made between the two types of variables in the input data to map construction.

The development of a normative cognitive mapping approach has been a major part of a more comprehensive process for performing the environmental scanning task in a manner that facilitates strategic choice. The process has been employed in several major corporate planning exercises. Most recently, a demonstration project was conducted at one of the largest electric utility corporations in the United States.[18] Some outputs of that effort are presented here.

The mapping approach emulates the essential features of neuronal activity elaborated earlier: stimulus-response link, unidirectionality, clustering, plasticity, connectivity, and neural group architecture.

THE STRUCTURE OF MAPPING INPUTS

The basic input is a unidirectional, response-to-stimulus relationship. More accurately, the stimulus is more of a "trigger"—in this case, strategic decision issues ("solutions," to use Fiol and Huff's term). It takes the form of a verbal contingency statement incorporating some environmental dynamic that has relevance for one or more strategic decision issues confronting the company. Any such statement is reducible to the following form:

E1, E2 : E3 : E4 / C1, C2,

where E1 represents some environmental factor (event, trend, variable, statement, etc.);

C1 represents a strategic decision issue; and
[,] = "and"   [:] = "impacts"   [/] = "has relevance for"

Thus, the preceding notational statement reads:

Environmental factors E1 and E2 impact E3, which impacts E4, which has relevance for strategic decision issues C1 and C2.

E1, E2, and E3 are indirectly relevant. E4 has direct relevance for C1 and C2.

There is no limit to the number of contingency statements that may be admitted, or to the number of environmental factors or strategic decision issues. In the electric utility application, the key, relevant, environmental dynamics were contained in about 50 such contingency statements, comprising 64 environmental factors and 35 corporate decision issues. Samples of the actual verbal contingency statements used along with their respective notational format are provided in Figure 10.1. The statement list in notational format is the input to the normative cognitive map creation.

PAIRING, CLUSTERING, AND PARTITIONING ENVIRONMENTAL FACTORS AND STRATEGIC DECISION ISSUES

A heuristic program processes these inputs. Essentially, the program reorders and partitions into clusters/sets strategic decision issues that are commonly affected by closely interacting clusters/sets of environmental factors. Concurrently, the program generates reordered, partitioned sets of the closely interacting environmental factors. The result is presented as a partitioned environmental factor/strategic decision issue matrix.

REPRESENTATION AS A NEURONAL NETWORK-TYPE STRUCTURE

The matrix output yields E x C subsets of the partitioned E set with strongest implications for the commonly affected C subset. In the electric utility application, there were five such subsets or groups. These subset data are used to select out those contingency statements that reflect the identified E-C links. Each of the five subsets of contingency statements (environmental dynamics only) was inputted to a mapping program that produced the final causal maps.

Each map was drawn automatically based on the environment dynamics found in the subset contingency statements (E factor interrelationships found on the left side of the "/").[19] The Es (the last ones before the "/") that directly had relevance for one or more Cs in each of the contingency states were located. The strategic decisions (Cs) for which the Es "have relevance for" were placed adjacent, thus establishing a de facto temporal dimension (moving in time from left to right).

CONNECTIVITY AND PLASTICITY

The heuristic algorithms employed aim to minimize intergroup connectivity of E factors, similarly with the C decision issues. Within a single set, connections among E factors tend to be maximized. While it is theoretically possible for there to be no connec-

Figure 10.1
Examples of Linkage Statements of Environmental Dynamics and Strategic Decision Issues

1. Increasing concern about the environment (E 14.01, E 14.02) will lead to stricter air quality standards (E24.03), which increases R&D expenditures on electric technology applications and a breakthrough in battery technology (E10.01) for electric vehicles. This impacts corporate decisions relative to systems for delivery of electric power to electric vehicles (C6.01).

   E 14.01, E 14.02, E14.03: E10.01 / C 6.01

2. Consumer awareness of the need for a secure (non-fossil fuel) energy supply (E 13.04) leads to a demand for electric vehicles (E 6.08), which, in turn, leads to breakthroughs in battery technology (E10.01). This impacts corporate decisions relative to utility delivery systems for battery charging (C 6.01).

   E 13.04: E 6.08: E 10.01 / C 6.01

3. The existence of a market for electric vehicles (E6.08) impacts corporate decisions relative to target marketing (transportation market) (C2.04) and marketing and promotion of new end uses (C 2.08).

   E 6.08 / C 2.04, C 2.08

4. Consumers' concern for energy security (E 13.04) leads to increased demand for small on-site generating units (E2.07) and photoboltaic charging systems (E 2.06), which results in an increase in non-central station-generated electricity (E 2.01). This impacts corporate decisions relative to generation ownership mix (C 1.03), generating capacity requirements.

   E 13.04: E 2.07, E 2.06: E 2.01 / C 1.03, C 3.09

5. Improved storage battery technology (E 10 01) leads to an increase in the number of electric vehicles (E 6.08) and an increased demand for electricity (E 5.02). This impacts corporate decisions relative to generating capacity requirements (C 3.09).

6. An increased demand for electricity (E 5.02) leads to an increase in on-site generation (E 2.07) and photovoltaic generation (E 2.06), which impacts corporate decisions relative to the mix of products/services to be sold (i.e., bundled electric service versus backup power and on-site generation repair and maintenance) (C 2.03), target markets for new sales (transportation) (C 2.04), and participation in on-site generation (C 2.01).

tivity between groups (i.e., subsets), it is highly unlikely. One or more environmental factors more important (i.e., impacting on other E factors, with relevance for a C factor) to one particular group is bound to be interdependent with an environmental factor and/or have relevance for a C in another group.

The entire group network and individual group/sets can exhibit plasticity. An alteration in the measure used to determine the extent to which any two Cs, say, are "commonly affected" by an E factor will change the resulting solution. A change in one contingency statement alone can alter the variable configuration of one or more sets and, hence, the group. Certainly, the internal organization of any one group would be changed. The maps reflect the reality of a rapidly changing world and provide the means to track the ongoing plasticity and ever-increasing interconnectedness of the environment with the organization and, within the organization, among strategic decision issues.

WHY THESE MAPS ARE CALLED "NORMATIVE COGNITIVE MAPS"

Within the comprehensive planning process in which the map-generating process takes place, the maps serve only as an intermediate output. Their ultimate use is as a blueprint for the construction of relevant environmental path scenarios, providing the context for strategic decisions. However, the maps themselves reveal the answers to some rather practical, but strategically important, questions confronting the strategic manager:

Which strategic decision issues must be coordinated? Clearly, the answer is those decision issues that are commonly affected by the same environmental forces. The C decision issues are placed directly adjacent to the relevant E factors in the diagram so that these can easily be seen. Furthermore, the spread of the C clusters and their individual compositions can all be seen essentially concurrently.

What is the sequence in which strategic issues should be addressed? That is determined simply by the location of the C issues on the map. Those that are expected to be impacted earliest by environmental forces need to be addressed first (the results of the utility application were not time-scaled, although this is possible). The unidirectional nature of the map makes the sequencing obvious.

Where can we take action to proactively influence the prospective environment? The most likely places are those intermediate E points where we are compelled to take earliest C action (the same ones as immediately preceding). Since these maps are de facto path scenario structures, these reveal the intermediate environmental events, forces, and conditions that precede some ultimate future state (being here the most extreme right-hand E factor). The rightmost E factors, at the end of a chain of Es, are the ones with direct relevance for the identified strategic decisions (Cs). As shown, some of the E factors appear to have *both* direct *and* indirect relevance, but for different Cs. Strategic decisions taken at such points have the most likelihood of impacting (altering) the relevant E factor. If the latter is itself also an intermediate (i.e., indirect) factor that impacts on yet another E in its altered state, the state of this dependent E will be altered as well. Hence, the organization "shapes the environment" through its own decisions.[20]

SOME CONCLUSIONS

Structure and form do matter! It is from this particular representation that the revelatory qualities emerge. The data essentially are the same as would be used to produce a conventional causal map that is wholly nonprescriptive. However, the normative result cannot even be contemplated without a rigor and prescribed structure superimposed on the input data, but where essence/ meaning of such data is not changed in the slightest. Directionality also is important, if only to convey a temporal dimension and some notion of sequence.

Among researchers in this area there appears to be a strongly held belief in the virtues of a looped system, especially where there is an organizational decision issue that is impacted by some environmental force. Unless a feedback loop is indicated back from the former to the latter, the implication is left that the organization is not sufficiently proactive, that it is only on the receiving end of external forces. Perhaps from the viewpoint of the researcher (or even a manager) who simply is trying to better understand the complexities of a situation, such maps are meaningful. But if the purpose of creating the map is to assist and promote decision making on the part of the manager, looped maps are less than enlightening. Where every node is eventually connected to every other one, it is difficult to isolate the relevant set of issues (nodes) that need to be addressed; only their sequential relationships are evident.

There is no basis to assert that the causal map of relevant environmental dynamics as shown in the listing above is a true representation of the mind at work. But the process whereby the maps are created does appear to mimic reasonably accepted tenets of neuronal network behavior and architecture. These causal maps isolate relevant environmental dynamics for specific strategic decision issues in an unmistakable fashion. There is little room for different interpretations of map implications for the questions posed earlier. The maps encourage a confrontation with what may be an uncomfortable prospective future and indicate intervention points for a proactive organizational response. In doing so, it is hoped that it better provides that juxtaposition of events, conditions, and states with relevance for strategic decisions to engender that "pop" in the mind of the manager—which really is from where strategy springs.

NOTES

1. A search of the Amazon Books Web site (September 1998) using the key words "strategic thinking" yielded 52 books in print on the subject, 34 of which had "strategic thinking" or a variant in the book title.

2. No extended discussion is intended here of the entire process, rather the focus is on the attributes of cognitive mapping approach employed and the resulting maps.

3. From a neurocognitive perspective, the "lowest-level" map might lay out neuronal cell molecular architecture. One schematic suggests levels of organization of the nervous system beginning with the latter, followed by (2) synapse, (3) neuron, (4) neuronal network, (5) internetwork architecture (my term), (6) systems, and (7) central nervous system (CNS) at the highest level (Llinas and Churchland, 1992). Primary cognitive functions (e.g., seeing, hearing) are enacted at the systems level, while complex cognitive activity, such as thought, takes place at the central nervous system (CNS) level, primarily within the brain.

4. The various multiple criteria decision methods technically produce causal maps in the general form of a decision tree. This hierarchical structure defines distinct node levels that have predecessor/successor significance. The essential structure is predetermined (in effect, hardwired). Usually, depending on the particular method, within any one node level, there are no internode connections; also, there are no interdependencies among branches (or "children") of different nodes.

5. The larger the repertoire of linkage symbols used, the more difficult to fathom the causal map. It also makes any systematic (i.e., computer) processing very difficult.

6. The COPE cognitive mapping system is particularly discussed as it is most likely the most advanced system of its kind.

7. The problem is further exacerbated in the case of influence diagrams where feedback loops are allowed, even encouraged. When such a loop is introduced diagrammatically, it virtually forces a distortion in the visual diagram, much in the way that a rubber band held taut between two points is distorted when pulled from some point in between the two ends.

8. The notion of a feedback system inherently encourages a holistic way of thinking, where everything somehow is connected to everything else sooner or later through intermediate nodal connections. Forrester's industrial dy-

namics methodology produced such maps and was used in the much maligned Club of Rome Project (Meadows et al., 1972; Cole et al., 1973).

9. Guidelines for creating cognitive maps with decision explorer proposed more recently by its developers appear to emphasize "structure" a bit more. The aim should be to "build up the hierarchy." To this end, it is proposed that the types of "concepts" be distinguished: goals, strategic directions, and potential options. The goals should be shown at the top of the hierarchy (Ackerman, Eden, and Cropper, 1995).

10. Some animals are capable of this kind of thinking but on a much more limited basis.

11. Those who are optimistic about this matter tend to have the most faith in the ultimate success of artificial intelligence efforts to replicate higher-level human brain activity.

12. Artificial intelligence (AI) efforts have been influenced by this knowledge; most AI modeling has focused on applying neural network theory to engines replicating lower-level cognitive activity (e.g., pattern recognition, audio signal processing, etc.), rather than attempting to simulate the much more complex activity of thought generation. However, functional characteristics of the building blocks of thought—neural networks—operate in much the same manner throughout the CNS.

13. These key attributes of neuronal systems that characterize the normative cognitive mapping process described are highlighted in *italics*.

14. "Adjacent" in the sense that an extension of the cell can make contact with another one.

15. Actually, "synapses," where two neuronal cells come close together, separated by a gap, and thereby exert influence on each other's electrical activity.

16. Conceptually, these midlevel neurological dynamics seem well understood. The devil is in the details: how does this brain activity actually get translated into thought? Edelman (1992), among a number of others, thinks that he is on the right track to an answer—and he has some solid support (Sacks, 1994). This issue is well beyond the scope of this chapter.

17. Andrews' concept of strategy as stated is just that: it is confined to the strategy itself (objectives, strategies, policies, etc.), not the assumptions about the environment that surely shaped the strategy content (i.e., the extrinsic input) in the first place.

18. This project was supported by a grant from the Electric Power Research Institute, Palo Alto, California.

19. Primavera Project Management software was used to draw the diagram.

20. Finally, a feedback loop enters the system.

REFERENCES

Ackerman, F., Eden, C., and Cropper, S. (1995). *Getting Started with Cognitive Mapping*. Web site: http://www.banxia.co.uk

Albert, M. (1997). "The Science of the Mind." *Science*, Vol. 275, No. 5306, 1547.

Andreasen, N. C. (1997). "Linking Mind and Brain in the Study of Mental Illnesses: A Project for a Scientific Psychopathology." *Science*, Vol. 275, No. 5306, 1586–1593.

Andreasen, N., et al. (1995). "Remembering the Past: Two Facets of Episodic Memory Explored with Position Emission Tomography." *American Journal of Psychiatry*, Vol. 152, No. 11, 1576–1585.

Andrews, K. R. (1987). *The Concept of Corporate Strategy.* New York: John Wiley and Sons.

Axelrod, R. M. (1976). *The Structure of Decision.* Princeton, N.J.: Princeton University Press.

Barinaga, M. (1997). "New Imaging Methods Provide a Better View into the Brain." *Science*, Vol. 276, 1974–1976.

Barr, P., Stimpert, J. L., and Huff, A. (1992), "Cognitive Change, Strategic Action, and Organizational Renewal." *Strategic Management Journal*, Vol. 13, 15–36.

Block, Ned. (1996). "How Can We Find the Neural Correlate of Consciousness?" *Trends in Neuroscience*, Vol. 19, 456–459.

Brewer, J. B., et al. (1998). "Making Memories: Brain Activity That Predicts How Well Visual Experience Will Be Remembered." *Science*, Vol. 281, No. 5380, 1185–1187.

Buchsbaum, M. S. (1995). "Charting the Circuits." *Nature*, Vol. 378, 128–129.

Calvin, W. H. (1997). "Competing for Consciousness: A Darwinian Mechanism at an Appropriate Level of Explanation." Draft for *Journal of Consciousness Studies*, Vol. 4.

Changeux, J. P., and Dehaene, S. (1989). "Neuronal Models of Cognitive Functions." *Cognition*, Vol. 33, Nos. 1–2, 63–109.

Checkland, P. (1989). "An Application of Soft Systems Methodology." In *Rational Analysis for a Problematic World*, edited by J. Rosenhead. New York: John Wiley and Sons.

Cohen, B. M., Renshaw, P. F., and Yurgelun-Todd, D. (1995). "Imaging the Mind: Magnetic Resonance Spectroscopy and Functional Brain Imaging." *American Journal of Psychiatry*, Vol. 152, No. 5, 655–658.

Cole, S. D., et al. (1973). *Models of Doom: A Critique of the Limits of Growth.* New York: Universe Press.

Corbetta, M., et al. (1993). "A PET Study of Visuospatial Attention." *Journal of Neuroscience*, Vol. 13, No. 3, 1202–1226.

Crick, F. (1994). *The Astonishing Hypothesis.* New York: Charles Scribner and Sons.

Donoghue, J. P. (1995). "Plasticity of Adult Sensorimotor Representations." *Current Opinion in Neurobiology*, Dec. 5 (6): 749–754.

Dudai, T. (1989). *The Neurobiology of Memory.* New York: Oxford University Press.

Edelman, G. M. (1992). *Bright Air, Brilliant Fire: On the Matter of the Mind.* New York: Basic Books.

Eden, C. (1989). "Using Cognitive Mapping for Strategic Options Development and Analysis (SODA)." In *Rational Analysis for a Problematic World*, edited by J. Rosenhead. New York: John Wiley and Sons.

Eden, C., et al. (1992). "The Analysis of Causal Maps." *Journal of Management Studies*, Vol. 29, No. 3, 309–323.

Edwards, B. W., and Wakefield, G. H. (1992). "An Efficient Method for Detecting Connectivity in Neural Ensembles." *Journal of Neuroscience Methods*, Vol. 45, Nos. 1–2, 1–14.

Fahey, F., and Narayanen, V. K. (1989). "Linking Changes in Revealed Causal Maps and Environmental Change: An Empirical Study." *Journal of Management Studies*, Vol. 26, 361–378.

Fiol, C. M., and Huff, A. S. (1992). "Maps for Managers: Where Are We? Where Do We Go from Here?" *Journal of Management Studies*, Vol. 29, 267–285. Copyright © 1992 by Blackwell Publishers Ltd.

Gee, H. (1997). "Brain: Remembrance of Tenses Past." *Nature*, Vol. 389, No. 6650, 452.

Hendry, J., Johnson, G. with Newton, J. (Eds.). (1993). *Strategic Thinking.* New York: John Wiley and Sons.

Huff, A. S. (1990). *Mapping Strategic Thought.* New York: John Wiley and Sons.

Huntley, G. W. (1997). "Correlation between Patterns of Horizontal Connectivity and the Extent of Short-Term Representational Plasticity in Rat Motor Cortex." *Cerebral Cortex*, Vol. 7, No. 2, 143–156.

Illing, R. B. 1996). "The Mosaic Architecture of the Superior Colliculus." *Progressive Brain Research*, Vol. 112, 17–34.

Janig, W., and. McLachlan, E. M. (1992). "Characteristics of Function-Specific Pathways in the Sympathetic Nervous System." *Trends in Neurosciences*, Vol. 15, No. 12, 475–481.

Jeffery, K. J., and. Reid, I. (1997). "Modifiable Neuronal Connections: An Overview for Psychiatrists." *American Journal of Psychiatry*, Vol. 154, No. 2, 156–164.

Llinas, R., and Churchland, P. S. (1992). *The Mind-Brain Continuum.* Cambridge, Mass.: MIT Press.

McGuire, B. A., et al. (1991). "Targets of Horizontal Connections in Macaque Primary Visual Cortex." *The Journal of Comparative Neurology,* Vol. 305, 370–392.

Meadows, D. H., et al., (1972). *The Limits to Growth.* New York: Universe Books.

Mintzberg, H. (1994). *The Rise and Fall of Strategic Planning.* Upper Saddle River, N.J.: Prentice-Hall.

Parks, R. W. and Prueitt, P. S. (1993). "Methodological and Theoretical Issues in Neural Network Models of Frontal Cognitive Functions." *International Journal of Neuroscience*, Vol. 72, No. 3–4, 209–233.

Rugg, M. D., "Memories Are Made of This." *Science*, Vol. 281, No. 5380, 1151–1152.

Sacks, O. (1994). "A New Vision of the Mind." *International Review of Neurobiology,* Vol. 37, 347–368.

Singer, Wolf. (1995). "Development and Plasticity of Cortical Processing Architectures." *Science*, Vol. 270, No. 5237, 758–764.

Sporns, O. (1994). "Selectionist and Instructionist Ideas in Neuroscience." *International Review of Neurobiology*, Vol. 37, 3–26.

Wagner, A. D., et al. (1998). "Building Memories: Remembering and Forgetting of Verbal Experiences as Predicted by Brain Activity." *Science*, Vol. 281, No. 5380, 1188–1191.

Warren, K. (1995). "Exploring Competitive Futures Using Cognitive Mapping." *Long Range Planning*, Vol. 28, No. 5, 10–21.

Wickelgren, I. (1997). "Getting a Grasp on Working Memory." *Science*, Vol. 275, No. 5306, 1580–1582.

Woolf, N. J. (1996). "Global and Serial Neurons Form a Hierarchically Arranged Interface Proposed to Underlie Memory and Cognition." *Neuroscience*, Vol. 74, No. 3, 625–651.

Xing, J. and Gerstein, G. L. (1996). "Networks with Lateral Connectivity. III. Plasticity and Reorganization of Somatosensory Cortex." *Journal of Neurophysiology*, Vol. 75, No. 1, 217–232.

Chapter 11

Strategic Management System Enhancement and the Concept of Strong Influence Strings

Adam J. Koch

Recent years have seen a dramatic growth of interest within the strategic management discipline in knowledge management (Argyris, 1977; Barney, 1986; Cyert and March, 1992; Hahn, 1991; McKiernan, 1996; Senge, 1990) and competence based strategy (Barney, 1997; Hamel and Prahalad, 1994; McKiernan, 1996; Prahalad and Hamel, 1990; Sanchez, Heene, and Thomas, 1996; Stalk, 1988). Commonalities in logic and approach between the total quality management and strategic management have been explored (Stahl and Grigsby, 1997). Continuing transformation of the global business environment has brought about increased business risks and success requirements.

Calls for integration of strategic management thought and practice have been a result of maturing theoretical and practical reflection. One of the integration models developed by Cravens et al. (1997) lists five strategic management domains: development of market-driven culture and learning process, determination of the value proposition, selection of the strategy for competing on capabilities, making relationship strategy decisions, and implementation of necessary organizational change. Strategic management performance depends on continuous goal searching, improvement, coordination and adaptation occurring in all these areas. This improvement and adaptation are achieved through the strategic management process.

Whenever any significant changes to company strategic intent, corporate culture, company market definition, product-mix, or any part of its management system are introduced, strategic management process shows itself at work. Volatile and/or very competi-

tive business environments may encourage or indeed require, continuous improvement of the individual stages of strategic management process: strategy formulation, implementation, and evaluation and control.

In this chapter, the relationship between strategic management
process and strategic management system needs to be established.
A brief literature review (Barney, 1997; Bourgeois, 1996; David, 1997;
Heene and Sanchez, 1997; Miller and Dess, 1996; Mintzberg, Quinn
and Voyer, 1995; Pearce and Robinson, 1997; Thompson and
Strickland, 1998) suggests that the strategic management process
constitutes the dynamic framework of the strategic management
system, which, apart from the former, includes also

- organization's own and accessible resources (intangible assets: capabilities, knowledge, reputation, property rights, relationships, and tangible assets),
- behavior and decision rules, and
- communication.

Discussion in this chapter of strategic management as a function and as a process and of the relationships between these and
the strategic planning process will serve to build a holistic model of
strategic management. The purpose of strategic management system enhancement has been to increase, in an efficient fashion,
company strategic response capacity (Bourgeois, 1996; Hamel and
Prahalad, 1994; Hahn, 1991; Mintzberg, Quinn, and Voyer, 1995;
Stahl and Grigsby, 1997) and its capacity to attain and sustain its
global competitiveness. This chapter posits that enhancement of
strategic management system in present-day business environments must involve improvement of this system's responsiveness,
effectiveness and efficiency. It also suggests a number of relevant
operational variables by which to measure progress of an organization along these three crucial dimensions.

STRATEGIC MANAGEMENT ENHANCEMENT CRITERIA

When selecting strategic management enhancement criteria,
one should ensure that

- reliable measures or tests can be used with regard to each proposed
  criterion and that
- all selected criteria taken together are capable of covering all conceivable
  strategic management enhancement situations and objectives, in other
  words, that they have adequate content validity (Gay and Diehl, 1992).

The three criteria of responsiveness, effectiveness, and efficiency proposed in this chapter appear to meet the preceding requirements, in that they cover

- an organization's demonstrated capacity to react to environment changes, including the promptness of reaction and response frequency;
- its capacity to choose appropriate strategic objectives;
- its capacity to formulate and implement strategies effectively;
- its capacity to achieve its objectives and develop its resources in accordance with the changing environment demands;
- its capacity to achieve its objectives and develop its resources so as to maintain sufficient flexibility; and
- its capacity to do all the preceding within reasonable cost limits.

Responsiveness in strategic management is defined here as the organization's capacity to receive and make sense of signals from its environment and subsequently to modify its strategic intent and means of achieving its strategic objectives accordingly. Responsiveness is not the same as an organization's capacity to promptly react to new market situations. The latter includes also policy and behavioral aspects of strategic management.

Promptness of the organization's reaction to the environment change may determine whether objectives will be achieved (and strategies developed and implemented) within the time available to the company: as such, responsiveness is a crucial strategic management system characteristic. It is a wider concept than adaptability in that it encompasses both adaptation to environment changes generated outside the organization and active modification of its environment by an organization seeking to improve its chances of realizing its strategic intent. While the latter phenomenon may be less common, it should by no means be marginalized.

In keeping with the proposed logic, an organization's strategic management has been effective when

- the organization has demonstrated a superior capacity to ensure good dynamic match between its own and accessible, current, and future resources and market opportunities or, alternatively,
- it has shown a sustained capacity to produce successful competitive strategies.

The first alternative is appropriate for periods of substantial change in the organization's environment, the latter, for periods of environment stability.

Both the deliberate realization of intended strategies and cases of strategies that were actually realized, though they had not been intended (Mintzberg, 1994), lend themselves to the effectiveness measurement. Effectiveness, similarly to efficiency, can be measured meaningfully only in the strategy implementation stage. Pertinent questions to be used in this kind of investigation are: What competitive objectives/strategies have been selected? How good is the match between resources and opportunities they produce? Are they narrowing the targeted competitive gaps or developing competitive advantages in agreement with the organization's strategic intent?

Superior efficiency in strategic management demonstrates itself through smaller resource requirements in achieving objectives than

• either anticipated by the organization itself or
• required by its competitors in a similar situation (determined by appropriate parameters of external and internal environment, positional strengths and weaknesses, and strategic objectives).

Efficiency examination would involve questions such as: How can this objective be achieved? At what cost? How soon? In all but very munificent business environments, economical use of resources is a paramount strategic management requirement.

A specific category, efficiency of the strategic change process, has a particular place in this discussion because of this chapter's objectives. Deep systemic change involves

• questioning and replacing rules and policies that have governed strategic management activities of the company in question,
• revision of values and norms,
• abandonment of some common wisdom, and
• modification of management style and practices.

In the period of its radical punctuated change, strategic management system's efficiency and effectiveness may suffer, due to the vast learning and adaptation effort involved in such an instance at all organization levels.

Two necessary conditions need to be fulfilled for the strategic management system's enhancement to be successful. First, no such enhancement will occur until an organization becomes capable of double-loop learning (Argyris, 1977), which involves questioning and adjusting the underlying policies and objectives that shape the way in which organizations operate. Further, strategic management system change must follow a certain logical sequence for it to surpass an appropriate threshold efficiency. This logic of change may be fully defined only after all critical relationships and strong influences within that system have been recognized.

STRATEGIC MANAGEMENT SYSTEM

Contemporary views on strategic management (Barney, 1997; Bourgeois, 1996; David, 1997; Mintzberg, Quinn, and Voyer, 1995; Pearce and Robinson, 1997; Stahl and Grigsby, 1997; Thompson and Strickland, 1998) suggest that the dominant contemporary view emphasizes the cross-functional character of the process and encompasses formulation, implementation, and evaluation of strategies to achieve the organization's objectives. Yet, some approaches seem to restrict the province of strategic management to the task of strategic intent formulation (the hierarchical definition quoted by Barney), or to the executive activities aimed to influence the overall direction of the corporation (Bourgeois, 1996). Only the logic inherent in the former perspective is compatible with the logic of holistic strategic management framework relied upon in this chapter.

Strategic management decisions are usually future-oriented, concerned with both efficiency and effectiveness. They have multifunctional and multibusiness consequences, require broad consideration of the firm's external and internal environment, and affect the firm's long-term prosperity (David, 1997; Miller and Dess, 1996; Pearce and Robinson, 1997). Three paramount responsibilities of strategic management appear to be

- sustaining/increasing the organization's capacity to respond to substantial environmental change through its early anticipation, corresponding modifications of organization's stock of own and accessible resources, and their apt coordination,
- ensuring good, dynamic match between its own and accessible, current, and future resources and market opportunities, and
- bringing about a sufficiently efficient use by the organization of its own as well as accessible resources over a long period of time.

The first of these focuses on signal reception and reaction capacity of the company. The second has to do with ongoing resource development effort and the objective of ensuring sufficient strategic flexibility of the company. Efforts undertaken in discharging the latter responsibility may foster a proactive strategic orientation.

All strategic management activities would appear to be conceived and undertaken with intention to discharge these three major responsibilities.

The purpose of strategic management is to help formulate, implement and evaluate cross-functional decisions in such a way as to assist the organization in achieving its long-term objectives. The strategic management process is seen as "an objective, logical and systematic approach for making major decisions in an organization" (David, 1997:6) in which both analysis and intuition have a role to play. Another accepted perspective (Pearce and Robinson, 1997) emphasizes information flows through interrelated stages of analysis. The last view implies

- the interconnectedness of all process components;
- the sequential character of strategy formulation and implementation;
- the necessity of an ongoing feedback to assess the success of strategies as they get implemented; and
- the need to regard strategic management as a dynamic system (components of the process are constantly evolving; formal planning must "freeze" them to achieve its aims).

Strategic management is not a monomodal activity. It has three distinct activity modes: rational planning, incrementalism, and organizational learning (Miller and Dess, 1996). The greatest contribution of rational planning comes from "facilitating communication about strategic issues and achieving integration across organizational levels and functional specialties" (1996:26). The incrementalist perspective depicts business as "constantly readjusting their strategies as they are overtaken by developments that are outside management's ability to predict or control" (30). The organizational learning perspective (Mintzberg, 1994; Quinn, 1989; Schon, 1993; Senge, 1990) suggests that managers can make incremental adjustments to rational plans with the hope of moving an organization toward their goals by way of numerous small steps of progress rather than a few major strides.

CONSTRUCTING HOLISTIC MODEL OF STRATEGIC MANAGEMENT

Design of strategic management systems is believed to be influenced (David, 1997; Miles, Coleman, and Creed, 1995) by a number of factors: organization, size, management styles, complexity of environment, complexity of production processes, nature of problems experienced by the organization and the purpose of planning system. The holistic model of strategic management system developed in this chapter will have to encompass them all.

The need for proper contextualization of the strategic management theory and an increased reliance on contingency theory has been argued by many (e.g,. Barney, 1997; Mintzberg, 1994). Further progress of this theory is largely contingent, believes Mintzberg, (1996), on acknowledging the necessity of always making an explicit reference to a certain "organizational configuration." Mintzberg (1989a, b) proposes seven such configurations—entrepreneurial, machine, professional, diversified, innovative, missionary, and political—and suggests that a thorough study of all these categories explains much of what a strategic management researcher may observe.

The holistic model offered in this chapter integrates existing strategic management perspectives with the purpose of eliminating all blind spots inherent in each one of these and improving content and construct validity of the corresponding theory. This chapter draws upon

- the currently dominant logic and structure of strategic planning,
- the Sanchez-Heene model of company as an open system (Heene and Sanchez, 1996),
- the logic and scope of total quality management (Stahl and Grigsby, 1997), and
- McKinsey's 7S model (Waterman, 1982)

A popular view of structure of strategic planning is presented in Figure 11.1. It is based on the well-recognized commonalities of the relevant views (e.g., Assael, 1985; Bourgeois, 1996; Ch'ng, 1993; Cohen, 1991; Cravens, 1994; David, 1997; Jain, 1990; McDonald, 1995; Mintzberg, 1994; Miller and Dess, 1996; Pearce and Robinson, 1997; Thompson and Strickland, 1998).

The strategic planning model just presented is unidirectional and contains no information loops. In reality, multiple loops caused by inputs' updates, verifications of assumptions, modifications of strategic alternatives, and corrections of various decisions are very much part of this process (Senge, 1990).

To develop a holistic model of strategic management system, a systems perspective on the firm is required that would integrate into a single dynamic framework several dimensions of firm behavior and business environments (Sanchez, Heene, and Thomas, 1996). Their model of Company as an Open System is founded on that perspective. Their model joins the dimension of managerial cognition, that Sanchez and Heene consider critically important, with uncertainty, causal ambiguity, and strategic flexibility. Its dynamic character is underscored by the model's feedback mechanisms, which are responsible for the control of some internal and external environment conditions, change of strategic direction, and adaptation to environment changes.

As already mentioned, ensuring good dynamic match between its own and accessible, current, and future resources and market opportunities is of particular importance in strategic management. The McKinsey and Company framework—shared values, structure, systems, style, staff, skills, and strategy—is often used when examining the compatibility of company's culture, resources, strat-

Figure 11.1
Critical Requirements of Strategic Management Improvement

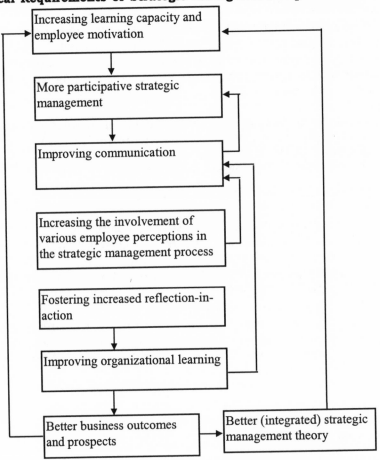

egy, organization, and management systems with changes in its competitive position and capacities it wishes to implement. Elements of that framework are included in the holistic model of strategic management proposed later in this chapter.

When integrating partial models, appropriate integration precepts are needed. In this case, a simple strategy model will help explain the logic of integration. This basic strategy model serves here as a platform on which to integrate both the structural and dynamic aspects of partial models. It forms a platform on which to include all external and internal environment factors that could be posited to be capable of influencing the company's strategic performance.

The holistic model of strategic management developed in this chapter is compatible with the competence-based strategy paradigm (Hamel and Prahalad, 1994, Sanchez, Heene, and Thomas, 1996), very useful in some business environment circumstances: interindustry competition, increased penetration of new markets by outsiders or "coopetition," that is, cooperation and competition combined (Dowling et al., 1996).

By integrating two of the partial models—strategic planning model (SPM) and company—as an open system model, a holistic model of the strategic management system (SMS) emerges. It encompasses all stages and components of the strategic planning process and, at the same time, includes all main categories of factors influencing the strategic management process. SMS does not presume any particular level of formalization of the strategic planning process. It can accommodate all three relevant activity modes of formal planning, learning and incrementalism (Dess and Miller, 1996; Quinn, 1989) and includes all crucial behavioral aspects associated with strategic management.

Associated communication flows are represented in SMS only symbolically, by way of reference to the strategic planning sequence and the elements of Sanchez-Heene model. Basic tangible (material resources, business forms, and organization configurations) and nontangible elements (competencies, capabilities and skills, perceptions of competencies, capabilities and skills, perceptions of business environment, leadership style, knowledge, and organizational principles) proposed to affect strategic management forms as well as its responsiveness, efficiency, and effectiveness are included there.

In constructing a strategic management enhancement framework, borrowings from total quality management (TQM) may prove quite useful. Elements of TQM logic, such as customer orientation, focus on business processes, customer and supplier partnerships, prevention-better-than-cure approach, zero-defect/error objective, high employee involvement and participation and striving for continuous improvement (Robinson and Pearce, 1997), play prominent roles in the proposed development.

It has been shown that SMS covers both the formal and behavioral aspects of strategic management. As its representation of the logic and structure of strategic management systems and of the strategic management process is fuller than that of any conventional "partial" model, its content validity can be argued as superior.

STRATEGIC MANAGEMENT SYSTEM ENHANCEMENT

Any strategic management system enhancement involves improvement of one or more of the following attributes: responsiveness, effectiveness, and efficiency. It is posited that strategic management responsiveness is influenced by the following major factors (Anderson and Paine, 1975; Porter,1980):

- organization's capacity to receive and make sense of signals from its environment;
- organization's ability to process these signals and reach decisions within the allowable time limit (the limit itself influenced by the volatility of the environment as well as company strategic position and objectives, in other words, the stretch required); and
- the intensity of adaptation to environment and, on the other hand, of environment change induced by the company.

Strategic management effectiveness is largely influenced by (Argyris, 1977; Lewis, 1987; Senge, 1990):

- the quality of the organizational learning;
- involvement, or otherwise, of multiple perspectives and employees' strategic management participation levels;
- the amount and reliability of information used in the strategic management process;
- appropriateness of analytical tools usage throughout the process; and
- impediments to information flow inside the organization.

Strategic management efficiency is strongly influenced by the following factors (Mintzberg, 1989; Senge, 1990):

- the organizational maturity (e.g., sophistication and suitability of management systems and individual procedures employed);
- competence of individual employees;
- their levels of motivation; and
- their prescience (in particular, employees' general ability to anticipate accurately enough the outcomes of strategies with regard to which they have no relevant experience).

Next, a basic strategic management improvement logic founded on the same premises is proposed. The proposed logic of strategic management improvement can be explicated by following the sequence of Figure 11.1. Perhaps the most natural starting-point for any strategic system improvement is forming a work environment in which learning capacity of individuals can grow substantially and their work motivation is very strong. Without improving individuals' learning capacity and increasing their motivation few such efforts become successes (David, 1997; Hamel and Prahalad, 1994; Senge, 1990). For employees' knowledge, competence, and skills to be utilized as proposed, people must be properly motivated, believe in their capacity to favorably influence the future of their company, and benefit from it, materially and otherwise. When it coin-

cides with a nonauthoritarian management style, stronger motivation is likely to increase strategic management participation
considerably.

Advances of computer technology in business management have
had far-reaching consequences for the ways strategic decisions
may be prepared and taken these days. Drastic reduction of the
role of middle management, on one hand, and increasing knowledge and decision-making capacity of employees in nonmanage-
rial positions on the other, more strongly than ever before stress
the need to increase employee participation in strategic management (Hamel and Prahalad, 1994; Senge, 1990). Without tapping
this huge potential appropriately, many companies may never rise
above mediocrity in the medium term and would put themselves in
danger of obliteration in the long term.

No outstanding strategic management performance is achiev-
able these days without superior quality of communication (Hay
and Williamson, 1997). What is the essential mechanism of communication improvement in strategic management system enhancement? Once the benefits of strategic management participation become obvious to the individuals involved, a substantial
further improvement of intracompany, or internal, communication
is likely to ensue. It will then be reinforced by the involvement of
employee perceptions of the company external and internal environments, which would augment stocks of knowledge, competence,
capabilities, and skills accessible to the company.

Level of employee participation and the range of perceptions
involved are positively correlated with the validity and reliability of
prediction in strategic management (Anderson and Paine, 1975;
Glaister and Thwaites, 1993; Senge, 1990). New perceptions and
knowledge will challenge the existing ones and produce, in time,
improved, more reliable bases on which judgments and strategic
decisions can be made. Superior quality of strategic management
communication within the organization reduces the chances for
strategy failure.

Involving multiple perception in the strategic management process is posited to have a strong positive influence on the reliability
of information and the quality of the strategic management decision-making processes (David, 1997; Koch and Hubbard, forthcoming; Heene and Sanchez, 1997). In rapidly growing industries undergoing substantial transformation, such as telecommunications
or computer software, companies that make best advantage of employees' knowledge, competence, and a high level of employee strategic management participation are likely to produce superior strategic management performance, particularly in volatile and/or very
competitive business environments.

Extra time that may be expended by such companies on

- extra data collection effort,
- more thorough strategic options examination,
- comprehensive internal communication, and
- gaining employee understanding of, and support for, the strategy to be realized

is often recovered with a vengeance through faster strategy implementation (Kono, 1992).

Wide employee participation in the strategic management process advances reflection-in-action and improves their understanding of strategic thinking and processes. Increased strategic management participation will require employees to provide new kinds of information and assume new strategic decision making-related roles. To meet the related, new systemic requirements, employees will need to reflect-in-action much more (Schon, 1993); this increased, ongoing reflection will help verify their views and upgrade their skills. It will also enrich the intracompany communication, develop the organizational knowledge basis and strengthen the organizational learning capacity (D'hanis and Perneel, 1997).

More reflection-in-action is a prerequisite for faster individual and organizational learning (Schon, 1993). Without the interpersonal skills, individual learning is fundamentally adaptive, not generative (Senge, 1990). Learning's pace may be slowed down by such circumstances as, for example:

- an extremely fast pace of business environment change (leading to paralysis by confusion),
- the amount of time needed to collect and process sufficient amounts of data on the outcomes of actions in significantly changed circumstances (after a major discontinuity), and
- any barriers to sharing reflection-in-action.

More reflection-in-action facilitates organizational learning and improves long-term business outcomes. Continuous programmed improvement of business performance helps develop better understanding of how to design and implement systemic change and presents academics with a superior opportunity to study the factors that affect company performance.

Companies that seek to achieve a wide employee participation in strategic management give their employees the best chances of self-development and have better than average chance of attracting best people (Hamel and Prahalad, 1994). By encouraging their employees to be always critical of the current situation and strive for excellence, Motorola management make it possible for its organizational learning to occur at a faster pace than in most other companies. Work attitudes and strategic management contributions induced by these systemic arrangements have been found capable of improving company strategic performance considerably.

In a rapidly transforming environment, it is the companies that learn faster that adapt better (Hamel and Prahalad, 1994). Not only do they generate stronger competitive strategies, but they also implement and modify their strategies more efficiently and effectively than most.

On the basis of the discussion so far, it appears that the critically important means of strategic management system enhancement would be

- employee information access;
- employee motivation levels;
- employee strategic management participation;
- intra- and interorganizational communication; and
- organizational learning capacity.

As with any very complex system, the sequence of steps taken in strategic management system enhancement is of critical significance. By its nature, improvement of such complex systems occurs mostly by relatively small increments (Senge, 1990).

MEASURING STRATEGIC MANAGEMENT SYSTEM ENHANCEMENT

Strategic management system enhancement measures should be selected with a view to ensuring appropriate level of content validity (they need to cover the areas of responsiveness, effectiveness, and efficiency) and reliability. Availability of suitable information to utilize in these measurements or feasibility concerns in general should also be taken into account. Specific requirements of systemic change measurement (multiple criteria, time delay, contextualization, etc.) are another thing to consider. The list of candidates for measurement could well be extended by adding strategic flexibility, environment match, resource growth and access, coordination, particular resource use efficiency, and so on.

Responsiveness in strategic management could be measured by, for example:

- the amount of strategy modifications over a period of time;
- amount of strategy modifications over a period of time, compared with competitors;
- time it takes the organization to respond to a certain category of signal;

- number of environment signals over a certain period left without response; and
- number of signals overlooked by the company over a period of time, compared with its competitors.

Strategic management effectiveness can be compared between companies by, for example:

- looking into their market share trends;
- examining market penetration;
- investigating customer loyalty levels and changes thereto;
- studying product's quality perceptions; and
- examining specific customer value-for-money ratios.

Relative, rather than absolute, measures of strategic management effectiveness are recommended to make the measurement more reliable.

Strategic management efficiency can be measured in a number of ways. This author suggests that the following measures be adopted in this respect:

- amount of particular resource(s) the organization requires to achieve a strategic objective;
- amount of particular resource(s) the organization requires to achieve a strategic objective, compared to the amount that was anticipated;
- decrease in the amount of resources required to achieve an objective (shows the effectiveness of organizational learning).

Effective organizational learning is very likely to lead to improved strategic management responsiveness, efficiency, and effectiveness (Senge, 1990).

Since the aspects of strategic management systems to be measured are extremely complex, as are the constructs in use, none of the measures may have sufficient diagnostic accuracy (Schwenk, 1984). To increase this accuracy, it would be better for any such measures to be used in conjunction, rather than separately. None of them should be regarded as a substitute for any other. Rather, all of them should be deemed complementary one to another.

WHAT IS "STRONG INFLUENCE STRING"?

To examine the logic of any complex system is an extremely difficult task. The immense variety of elements that make up such systems and relationships between them erects tremendous cognitive barriers and slows down, if not stops altogether, effective induction-based intellectual processes (Schwenk, 1984).

Each of the schools of thinking on strategy formation (Mintzberg, 1994) has developed a confined spectrum of analysis that excludes many factors considered capable of influencing the strategic management process.

A conscious incremental approach (Quinn, 1989:48) helps management actors

- "cope with both the cognitive and process limits on each major decision,
- build the logical and analytical framework that these decisions require and
- create the personal and organizational awareness, understanding, acceptance and commitment needed to implement strategies efficiently."

Enhancement of any complex system necessitates, however, a sufficiently comprehensive and detailed grasp of the system's mechanisms. How can one overcome the formidable obstacles posed by the perceived complexity of the strategic management systems? What methods would be effective in reducing this complexity and thus be able to open new opportunities to investigate various mechanisms and relationships inside these systems?

Review of the strategic management literature (e.g., Mintzberg, Quinn, and Voyer, 1995; McKiernan, 1996) suggests that the two weakest parts of the current theory are:

- its apparent failure to express all major influences on strategic management systems in logical sequences and
- its failure to produce operational definitions of strategic management (system) performance.

Each partial theory of strategic management offers an inventory of factors it considers relevant because of its spectrum of analysis and a limited description of the influence these factors have on strategic management performance. Senge (1990) argues that lasting, significant improvements in the performance of organizations will increasingly depend on their tireless pursuit of leverage through implementation of systems thinking, personal mastery, mental models, building shared vision, and team learning. He builds a holistic logic and encourages seeing the interrelationships between factors rather than linear cause-effect chains and looking into processes of change rather than taking snapshots.

To reliably inform strategic management theory and practice, an overview is needed of the literature and a suitably conceived inquiry should be conducted into the relationships between all major categories of factors believed to strongly influence the strategic management performance and that performance. Such an inquiry should produce "patterns where others see only events and forces to react to" (Senge, 1990:126) and the much needed capacity to see both "forest and trees." To that aim intuition and reason need to be deployed in an integrated fashion (Mintzberg,1996b; Senge, 1990).

Once the dimensions of strategic management enhancement have been defined, and strategic management relationships examined, formulating hypotheses of strong interrelationships between strategic management variables becomes a feasible task. With critical requirements of strategic management improvement serving as the organizing logic, one can use induction to construct the model of strategic management enhancement. Its elements will be the proposed sequences, or strings, representing some critical aspects of strategic management enhancement. The construction of such a model would offer an ample opportunity for incremental learning for all strategic management participants.

The sequential explication of interrelationships between groups of factors shown to play a role in strategic management enhancement would

- help reduce the perceived complexity of the strategic management system (Schwenk, 1984),
- provide a new, consistent logic for the relevant inquiry, and
- facilitate the relevant inquiry through enabling the use of methods and tools of inquiry new to the discipline of strategic management.

Success of the proposed approach is contingent on the discipline's capacity to define a sufficient, possibly full list of sequences with which to represent the entire mechanism of strategic management enhancement. We assume that there is such a universally applicable mechanism. It follows from this assumption that at least some of the interrelationships observed in the studies of the strategic management systems' performance would work in all contexts in much the same way. Of the same view is Senge (1990), who believes that finding a universal interpretation for many such interrelationships should be possible, as "not all is unique in management."

The operational definitions of strategic management system enhancement offered earlier in this chapter found a basis on which to propose a related theory development: the strong influence string (SIS) construct. Strong influences are defined here as systemic influences that have the capacity to significantly alter the responsiveness, effectiveness and efficiency parameters of the strategic management system. Responsiveness, effectiveness, and efficiency will be referred to as aspects of strategic system enhancement.

SISs would arrange specific influences on strategic management systems sequentially, each of them relating to some aspects and mechanisms of the systemic enhancement. Some of them might have similar, significant impacts on various structural and performance characteristics of strategic planning systems irrespective of the context. These would be universally applicable. The significance of other SISs might depend on the context. A contextualized analysis focusing on individual aspects of strategic management enhancement responsiveness and efficiency improvement would help reveal whether this particular characteristic had significance.

In presenting interrelationships in a sequential form, any suggestion of linear cause-effect relationships between single factors should be avoided (Senge, 1990). Relationships represented by SISs are likely to be far more complex than this. Indeed, one can anticipate

- a multilevel interdependence of variables that ultimately influence an organization's strategic management performance and
- a great variety of possible relationships between individual factors, as well as between any one of them and the strategic management performance there.

The list of these relationships would include causal (one or more factors required), reinforcing, attenuating, neutral, and excluding forms of relationships. Study of the influences of each such category on the three dimensions of strategy system enhancement—responsiveness, effectiveness and efficiency—would most certainly produce some interesting observations on which to develop both theory and practice of strategic management.

Some elements of SISs would be outside an organization's control; some others, within it. Further, some influences would require much less time to influence the strategic management system performance than some others. This amount of time and the extent of feasible control would often depend on business context and would bear practical implications for strategic management system enhancement. Analysis of SISs is likely to reveal strong potential leverages between the relevant groups of factors.

SOME PROPOSED STRONG INFLUENCE STRINGS

The hypothesized influences (see Figure 11.2) correspond with the holistic model of strategic management and relate factors representing four broad categories (organization's external environment; organizational attributes, capabilities and resources; interpersonal factors and intrapersonal factors; see Koch and Hubbard, forthcoming) to various strategic management tasks.

Figure 11.2

"Strong Influences" in Strategic Management

1. External Environment ⇒ Strategic Orientation ⇒ Perceptions Of External Environment ⇒ Evaluation Of Internal Resources ⇒ Organization Configurations ⇒ Corporate Objectives ⇒ Strategy Formulation ⇒ Business Forms ⇒ Strategy Implementation ⇒ Strategy Control ⇒ Strategic Logic ⇒ Organizational Principles

2. Perceptions of Environment ⇒ Evaluation of Internal Resources

3. Organization Configurations ⇒ Perceptions of External Environment & Evaluation of Internal Resources

4. Cognitive Style ⇒ Decision Making Behavior ⇒ Strategy Formulation ⇒ Strategy Implementation

5. Leadership Style ⇒ Internal Communication Barriers

6. Communication Filters ⇒ Cognitive Biases

Examination of various strains of contemporary theory and of individual experiences and perceptions is certain to produce some more hypotheses of strong influence strings in strategic management. The role of subconscious, or tacit, knowledge as well as metacognition in defining these relationships would be quite significant. SISs proposed by this author serve to illustrate the construct discussed here. Brief comments concerning their role are made below.

Commencing from the definition of environment category, string 1 (Figure 11.2) essentially reflects the core logic of the strategic management process of the "fit" type (Hamel and Prahalad, 1989). However, if string 2 is attached to string 1 in parallel by doubling its twin element there, the original string converts into one that represents the "stretch" strategic management process. Multiple environment perceptions are more likely than a single one to lead to a number of alternative deployment options for company knowledge, resources and capabilities being contemplated, the corresponding competence gaps being examined, and appropriate "stretch" strategies being developed and implemented.

The relationship between management level and function, on the one side, and the group and individual perceptions of both external environment and the company resources on the other, is represented by string 3. It shows that many various perceptions of environment and internal resources are the rule rather than exception (Glaister and Thwaites, 1993). This has some very important implications for the organizational and individual learning

(Senge, 1990) and for strategic system performance. String 4 demonstrates the dependence of strategy selection on decision-making behavior, which, in turn, is influenced by the cognitive styles of participants in the strategic management processes (Barnes, 1984; Mintzberg, 1996b; Schwenk, 1984).

String 5 relates to the way leadership styles may contribute to the formation of various internal communication barriers, through encouraging/inhibiting open communication and verifying/distorting information (Lewis, 1987; Stohl, 1995; Wofford et al., 1987). The role of communication filters in creating cognitive biases with the company employees is addressed by string 6 (Barnes, 1984). Those filters are a particular feature of the corporate management culture and of management styles represented by individuals. Sometimes, a communication filter will be a by-product of a certain strategic vision or of the relative positions of individual management functions within the company.

The preceding strong influence strings are believed to work much the same in most contexts but may need to be modified to reflect an organization's context. Definition of other SISs and empirical verification of them all are likely to enhance strategic management theory and practice.

CONCLUSION

Strategic management theory has been developing so far in the form of partial theories. This has made the examination of the entirety of influence that various factors have on the structure, forms, responsiveness, effectiveness, and efficiency of strategic management systems very difficult. Some recent contributions, such as the theory of learning organizations and the paradigm of competence-based competition, form a basis on which a holistic approach to strategic management can be adopted. This chapter looks for a new tool of strategic management inquiry, a tool that would fit the holistic logic.

Strategic management system enhancement is proposed here to have three dimensions: responsiveness, effectiveness, and efficiency. A number of relevant operational variables by which to measure progress of an organization along these three dimensions are suggested. The importance of double-loop learning for the enhancement of strategic management systems is raised, and the recommendation is made that strategic management system changes be based on the proposed logic. For this logic to be fully defined, all critical relationships and strong influences within that system would ultimately need to be uncovered.

The holistic model of the strategic management system (SMS) proposed in this chapter integrates two partial models. The purpose of this integration is to encompass all stages and components of the strategic planning process and to include all main categories of factors known to influence the strategic management process. SMS covers both the formal and behavioral aspects of strategic management and thus it represents the logic and structure of strategic management systems and of the strategic management process more truly than the conventional "partial" models.

Two weakest points of the current strategic management theory appear to be its apparent failure to express all major influences on strategic management systems in logical sequences and its failure to produce operational definitions of strategic management system performance. To address this relative weakness, the strong influence string construct is introduced. The discussion of three dimensions of strategic management performance and the subsequent presentation of several examples of strong influence strings have two practical purposes: to facilitate the examination of strategic management mechanisms and relationships and to guide in the enhancement of strategic management systems.

Strong influence strings offer a different format of inquiry into the mechanisms of strategic management system improvement. They would facilitate intellectual processes leading to the formulation of relevant hypotheses and will amplify the researcher's or manager's cognitive capacity. As an analytical tool of considerable versatility, they would help embrace strategic management mechanisms better, enhance the three critical performance parameters of strategic management systems, and produce new competitive advantages.

REFERENCES

Anderson, C. R. and Paine, F. T. (1975). "Managerial Perceptions and Strategic Behavior." *Academy of Management Journal*, Vol. 18, 811–823.

Argyris, Chris (1977). "Double Loop Learning in Organizations." *Harvard Business Review* (September–October), 115–125.

Assael, Henry (1985). *Marketing Management: Strategy and Action*. Boston: Kent Publishing.

Barnes, J. H. (1984). "Cognitive Biases and Their Impact on Strategic Planning." *Strategic Management Journal*, Vol. 5, 129–137.

Barney, Jay B. (1986). "Organizational Culture: Can It Be a Source of Sustained Competitive Advantage?" *Academy of Management Review* (July), 656.

Barney, Jay B. (1997). *Gaining and Sustaining Competitive Advantage*. Reading, Mass.: Addison-Wesley Longman.

Bourgeois, L. J., III (1996). *Strategic Management: From Concept to Implementation.* Fort Worth, Tex.: The Dryden Press.

Bowman, C. and Asch, D. (1987). *Strategic Management.* London: Macmillan Education.

Ch'ng, David. (1993). "MOSAIC mac-b: A Comprehensive Framework for Marketing Planning." *Asia-Australia Marketing Journal,* Vol. 1, No. 1, 9–18.

Cohen, William A. (1991). *The Practice of Marketing Management.* 2d ed. Singapore: Macmillan.

Cravens, David W. (1994). *Strategic Marketing.* 4th ed. Ridge, Ill.: Irwin Burr.

Cravens, David W., Greenley, Gordon, Piercy, Nigel F., and Slater, Stanley. (1997). "Integrating Contemporary Strategic Management Perspectives." *Long Range Planning,* Vol. 30, No. 4, 493–506.

Cyert, R. and March, J. (1992). *A Behavioral Theory of the Firm,* 2d ed., Englewood Cliffs, N.J.: Prentice-Hall.

David, Fred R. (1997). *Strategic Management.* 6th ed., Upper Saddle River, N.J.: Prentice-Hall.

D'hanis, Wanda and Pernell, Luc. (1997). "Reflection as a Building Block for Strategic Thinking and the Development of an Organizational Philosophy." In Aime Heene and Ron Sanchez (Eds.), *Competence-Based Strategic Management.* Chichester: John Wiley and Sons, 313–330.

Dixit, A. and Nalebuff, B. (1991). *Thinking Strategically.* New York: Norton.

Dowling, Michael J., Roering, William D., Carlin, Barbara A., and Wisnieski, Joette. (1996). "Multifaceted Relationships Under Coopetition: Description and Theory." *Journal of Management Inquiry,* Vol. 5, No. 2 (June), 155–167.

Gay, L. R. and Diehl, P. L. (1992). *Research Methods for Business and Management.* Singapore: Macmillan.

Glaister, Keith and Thwaites, Des. (1993). "Managerial Perception and Organizational Strategy." *Journal of General Management,* Vol. 13, No. 4, 15–33.

Hahn, D. (1991). "Strategic Management—Tasks and Challenges in the 1990s." *Long Range Planning* (February), 26–39.

Hamel, Gary and Prahalad, C. K. (1989). "Strategic Intent." *Harvard Business Review,* Vol. 67, No. 3, 63–76.

Hamel, Gary and Prahalad, C. K. (1994). *Competing for the Future.* Boston: Harvard Business School Press.

Hay, Michael and Williamson, Peter (1997). "Good Strategy: The View from Below." *Long Range Planning,* Vol. 30, No. 5, 651–664.

Heene, Aime and Sanchez, Ron. (1996). "A Systems View of the Firm in Competence-Based Competition." In Ron Sanchez, Aime Heene, and Howard Thomas (Eds.) *Dynamics of Competence-Based Competition: Theory and Practice in the New Strategic Management.* New York: Pergamon Press, 39–62.

Heene, Aime and Sanchez, Ron. (Eds.). (1997). *Competence-Based Strategic Management.* Chichester: John Wiley and Sons.

Hofer, C. W. and Schendel, Dan E. (1978). *Strategy Formulation: Analytical Concepts.* St. Paul, Minn.: West.

Ireland, R. D., Hitt, M. A., Bettis, R. A., and Auld De Porras, D. (1987). "Strategy Formulation Processes: Differences in Perceptions of Strength and Weaknesses Indicators and Environmental Uncertainty by Managerial Level." *Strategic Management Journal*, Vol. 8, 469–485.

Isenberg, D. J. (1984). "How Senior Managers Think." *Harvard Business Review*, Vol. 6, No. 84, 80–90.

Jain, Subhash C. (1990). *Marketing Planning and Strategy*. Cincinnati: South-Western.

Koch, Adam and Hubbard, Graham. (forthcoming). "Towards an Integrated Theory of Strategic Management."

Kono, Toyohiro (Ed.), (1992). *Strategic Management in Japanese Companies*. Oxford: Pergamon Press.

Lewis, P. V. (1987). *Organizational Communication: The Essence of Effective Management*. 3d ed. New York: John Wiley and Sons.

McDonald, Malcolm. (1995). *Marketing Plans. How to Prepare Them: How to Use Them*. 3d ed. Oxford: Butterworth Heinemann.

McKiernan, Peter (Ed.), (1996). *Historical Evolution of Strategic Management*. Hanover, NH: Dartmouth.

Miles, Raymond, Coleman, Henry J., and Creed, W. E. Dougles. (1995). "Key to Success in Corporate Redesign." *California Management Review*, Vol. 37, No. 3 (Spring), 128.

Miller, Alex and Dess, Gregory G. (1996). *Strategic Management*. 2d ed. New York: McGraw-Hill.

Milliken, F. J., and J. T. Lant. (1991). "The Effect of an Organizations Recent Performance History on Strategic Persistence and Change: The Role of Managerial Interpretations." In J. Dutton, A. Huff, and P. Shrivastava (Eds.), *Advances in Strategic Management*, Vol. 7, Greenwich, Conn.: JAI Press, 125–152.

Mintzberg, Henry. (1989). *Mintzberg on Management: Inside Our Strange World of Organizations*. Free Press.

Mintzberg, Henry (1996a). "Five Ps for Strategy." In Henry Mintzberg and James Brian Quinn (Eds.), *The Strategy Process, Concepts, Contexts, Cases*, 3d ed. Englewood Cliffs, N.J.: Prentice-Hall, 10–17.

Mintzberg, Henry (1996b). "The Manager's Job." In Henry Mintzberg and Quinn, James Brian (Eds.), *The Strategy Process, Concepts, Contexts, Cases*, 3d ed. Englewood Cliffs, N.J.: Prentice-Hall, 19–34.

Mintzberg, Henry, Quinn, James Brian, and Voyer, John (Eds.). (1995). *The Strategy Process*. Englewood Cliffs: N.J.: Prentice-Hall.

Pearce, John A., II and Robinson, Richard B., Jr. (1997). *Strategic Management. Formulation, Implementation, and Control*. 6th Ed. Chicago: Irwin.

Porter, Michael E. (1980). *Competitive Strategy: Techniques for Analyzing Industries and Competitors*. New York: Free Press.

Prahalad, C. K. and Hamel, Gary. (1990). "The Core Competence of the Corporation." *Harvard Business Review* (May–June), 79–91.

Quinn, Brian J. (1989). "Strategic Change: Logical Incrementalism." *Sloan Management Review* (Summer), 45–60.

Quinn, Brian J. (1996). "Strategies for Change." In Henry Mintzberg and James Brian Quinn (Eds.), *The Strategy Process, Concepts, Contexts, Cases*, 3d ed. Englewood Cliffs, N.J.: Prentice-Hall, 3–10.

Rajagopalan, Nandini and Spreitzer, Gretchen M. (1996). "Toward a Theory of Strategic Change: A Multi-Lens Perspective and Integrative Framework", *Academy of Management Review*, Vol. 22, No.1, 48–79.

Rumelt, R. P., Schendel, Dan and Teece, David J. (1991). "Strategic Management and Economics," *Strategic Management Journal*, Vol. 12, 5–29.

Sanchez, Ron, Heene, Aimee and Thomas, Howard (Eds.). (1996). *The Dynamics of Competence-Based Competition: Theory and Practice in the New Strategic Management.* New York: Pergamon Press.

Schon, D. A. (1993). *The Reflective Practitioner—How Professionals Think in Action.* New York: Basic Books.

Schwenk, C. R. (1984). "Cognitive Simplification Processes in Strategic Decision-Making." *Strategic Management Journal*, Vol. 5, 111–128.

Senge, Peter M. (1990). *The Fifth Discipline: The Art and Practice of the Learning Organization.* New York: Doubleday.

Simon, H. A. (1986). "The Information Processing Explanation of Gestalt Phenomena." *Computers in Human Behaviour*, Vol. 2, No. 4, 241–255.

Soelberg, P. (1972). "Unprogrammed Decision Making." Reprinted in J. H. Turner, A. C. Filley and R. J. House, *Studies in Managerial Process and Organizational Behaviour.* Glenview, Ill.: Scott, Foresman and Co.

Stahl, Michael J. and Grigsby, David W. (1997). *Strategic Management: Total Quality and Global Competition.* Oxford: Blackwell.

Stalk, G. (1988). "Time—The Next Source of Competitive Advantage." *Harvard Business Review* (July–August), 41–53.

Stohl, Cynthia. (1995). *Organizational Communication: Connectedness in Action.* Thousand Oaks, Calif.: Sage.

Thompson, Arthur A., Jr. and Strickland, A. J., III (1998). *Strategic Management: Concepts and Cases.* Boston: McGraw-Hill.

Waterman, R. H., Jr. (1982). "The Seven Elements of Strategic Fit." *Journal of Business Strategy*, Vol. 2, No. 3, 69–73.

Wofford, Jerry, Gerloff, Edwin and Cummins, Robert C. (1977). *Organizational Communication: The Keystone to Managerial Effectiveness.* Tokyo: McGraw-Hill.

Part IV

Applications

Chapters 12 through 19 examine how complexity-influenced theories of management can actually affect day-to-day management practice. The domains examined range from telecommunications to windmills to Soviet power politics. The lessons drawn, however, are applicable day to day to most of us as managers.

Janet Bardyn and Donna Fitzgerald's "Chaos Theory and Project Management: A Perspective on Managing the Complex Project" opens the Part. It is becoming increasingly common for the future to be called into question of both organizations as they now typically exist and the employment contract defining membership of organizations. Many writers take it almost for granted that the project-based organization will take over as the new form: comparatively loose arrangements of people who work together for as long as the project requires it, then move to the next project. That may or may not be, but this chapter implicitly makes the point that projects are no panacea for management problems. A large project—and the subject of this chapter is certainly one of these—represents a major managerial challenge.

The chapter describes the ideas behind the approach that a major U.S. telecommunications firm, NYNEX, took when it tackled a records information system design project. The central concept is one of accepting that projects of this kind are complex systems that respond in unexpected ways, rather than assuming that they are not and being unprepared for the unexpected. The design principles involved establishing an initial area of order, creating a learning environment to maximize the use of change, borrowing ideas from the telecommunications business itself when designing project management information channels, and accepting that the system itself must continue to evolve over the life of the project. This subject does not lend itself to easy solutions, and the authors do not pretend to offer any: a large project is a form of temporary organization, which, if anything, increases the difficulties associated with managing it.

A large telecommunications project also forms the setting for the next chapter. Among the many challenges to the hegemony of the organization, the interorganizational network regularly appears. Mark W. McElroy in "Complexity, IT, and the Interprise" argues that the conventional form of business, commonly known as the *enterprise,* is slowly giving way to the emergence of a new model, referred to as the *interprise.* This chapter discusses the role information technology will play in the life of these interprises (inter-enterprises). Many themes are covered, including the role of the customer in the business loop, rather than as the end of a chain, and the ubiquitous learning organization. The chapter's basic point is summed up in the aphorism: "in the *old* world of the enterprise, one used to say, 'the network is the computer'; in the *new* world, the *interprise* has become the company, and the extranet [a network spanning the member organizations of the interprise] is its computer." The interprise, which is an opportunistic collection of individuals and/or businesses working together in a collaborative manner, routinely exemplifies the new business paradigm of *co-opetition* and *mass customization* (i.e., the antitheses of traditional *competition* and *mass production*). McElroy describes the salient characteristics of the interprise, including its customer orientation, its roots in the study of organizational agility, its groundbreaking focus on demand chains, and its fundamental definition as a collection of processes. All of these features combine to suggest a radically different view on how best to apply information technology (IT) in the new context of the interprise.

McElroy characterizes the interprise as a dynamical system that exhibits the kind of unstable behavior found in other complex, nonlinear systems. He draws an analogy between the interprise and an organism by revealing the behavior of both in reciprocal terms, suggesting a new paradigm on how best to organize business assets in markets that behave more like ecosystems than rule-bound regimes. The role of IT is seen as crucial: as interprises form, IT managers have to redirect their efforts to developing systems that are no longer exclusively organizationally based. IT, rather than responding to the new strategies, should be leading them; knowledge management moves to center stage. The second part of the chapter delves into the implications of this point and draws on the writings of authors such as Prigogine, Capra, Maturana and Varela, and Wheatley to illuminate the issues that emerge.

Mark White's "Adaptive Corporations" changes the setting to smaller, more organic corporate forms. White draws on illustrations of highly innovative companies such as 3M and Hewlett-Packard and Holland's concept of classifier systems: all rules serve as hypotheses, more or less confirmed, rather than as incontrovertible facts. White draws the distinction between what he calls the common and Roman law approaches to rules: Roman law forbids everything unless expressly allowed, while common law does the opposite. Nonadaptive corporations, he argues, typically follow the precepts of Roman law, effectively stifling new ideas. Their command-and-control systems were fine during a time of slow technological change, but now that this condition no longer holds, corporations must become adaptive, calling for a focus on the ideas that White puts forward.

Joel A. C. Baum and Brian S. Silverman's "Complexity in the Dynamics of Organizational Founding and Failure" is a serious look at how complexity theory can help explain the history of a significant business concept: the success of start-up firms. By comparison with many other chapters in this book, this offering is much more analytical. Foundings and failures of companies have long been a subject of interest to scholars of organizations and business strategy. Baum and Silverman are interested in the possibility that competitive interorganizational systems display the kind of complex behavior that might place them at the edge of chaos. Too much interdependence might lead to systems that are so closely interlinked that they become unstable; if too independent, they lose the ability to influence each other. Returning to first principles, the authors explain the differences between orderly, chaotic, and random behavior and the attractors characteristic of each. Next, they address the problem. If one has a time series of data describing the behavior of a system over time, how can one tell whether the system is behaving in an orderly, a chaotic, or a random manner? They describe some of the tools available to distinguish between these different cases. Finally, the authors use these tools on data sets from a number of studies of foundings and failures in different industries and show that in at least some there is good evidence of chaotic behavior.

Glenda H. Eoyang and Thomas H. Berkas offer some explanation of this phenomenon in their "Evaluating Performance in a Complex, Adaptive System (CAS)." Complex adaptive systems (CASs), by definition, do not behave in straightforward, linear ways. The significance of this less-than-profound observation becomes apparent when the CAS in question is an organization, and the issue of evaluation moves to center stage. This chapter traces through the nature of this connection, by reviewing the features of complexity that make evaluation a problem. CASs, the authors argue, are dynamic, massively entangled, scale-independent, transformative, and emergent. So, for example, the dynamic nature of these systems means that "the whole concept of projected and predictable outcomes is an artificial construct when evaluating performance.... An evaluator may be able to frame expectations, but the self-organizing nature of the system may result in completely different outcomes from those expected." The chapter draws together many themes from organizational and systems thinking and puts them together into a package of ideas for evaluating organizational processes using the language of CAS. A variety of tools is recommended, including causal diagrams, iterative redesign, feedback, and time series analysis. The chapter finishes by returning to the lesson of the Hawthorne studies (or the Heisenberg principle, if it comes to that) with the reminder that the evaluator is not an objective and uninvolved instrument but an agent of change. The more complex, nonlinear, and unpredictable the system, the more relevance this observation takes on.

Ted Fuller's chapter, "Complexity Metaphors and the Process of Small Business Foresighting," opposes this approach. Fuller draws on the work of a future studies research team at Durham University Business School. He describes the application of complexity metaphors to a process of illuminating alternative futures of small business in the U.K. Fuller argues that the enterprise of complexity theory is to attempt to simplify, rather than complicate. Essentially, complexity theory is a study of order, not of chaos. Futures studies is a study of order or, more properly, of alternative "orders" that may exist or may be understood to exist beyond the present time. A major contributor to our ordering of the world is metaphor. "Metaphors—are one of the few tools to create compact descriptions of complex phenomena" (Weick, 1995). Fuller's chapter describes how the framework for "scenarios" was created from complexity metaphors. Through the lens of complexity theory it explores relationships between small firms and their environment.

Robert M. Cutler's "Gorbachev as CEO Roadkill" may be the most controversial chapter in this collection. The political disintegration of the USSR can be regarded as a failure by the Soviet system to adapt successfully to demands from increasingly complex international and domestic environments. As such, there is direct relevance to the situation encountered by managers in complex bureaucracies today. Cutler argues that the Soviet system imploded and collapsed due to accumulated structural inertia, under the force of being required to deal with too much cognitive change and consequent organizational chaos too fast. This collapse holds lessons for the modern North American corporation. Most prominent among these lessons are strategies for dealing with the tension of stress and its duration. With this in mind, it is easy for an organizational observer to find analogies between the Gorbachev era of Soviet politics, on one hand, and, on the other hand IBM's failure to exploit the personal computer, American auto manufacturers' inability to deal with changing markets, Apple's failure to develop its market niche, Microsoft's initial response to the Internet, and even the quick demise of "New Coke." All such analogies are based on the presence of cognitive dissonance between different organizational levels: what management understands as "fact" may mean little to the folk in the field, and vice versa. Cutler's chapter is a worthwhile excursion to the boundaries of politics and business with fascinating lessons and analogies to be drawn from both.

In Chapter 19, "The Emergence of Technological Fields" by Raghu Garud, Peter Karnøe, and E. Andres Garcia, poses and answers the question, How do agents constituting a technological field navigate the complex landscapes that they confront? Complexity is a key facet of many dynamic phenomena, including the emergence of technological fields. Actors engaged in the development of technological fields deal with complexity by adopting different approaches based on their institutionalized ways of thinking and doing. Given complexity—indeed, because of it—it is very likely that agents will adopt different approaches to guide their choices and behaviors based on beliefs of what is and what is not possible. These approaches can have dramatically different consequences as initial choices become amplified through learning processes that generate knowledge in a recursive manner. Consequently, complexity is as much about how we deal with nature as it is about nature itself. The authors explore these issues through a comparative study of the development of wind turbine fields in Denmark and in the United States—not as controversial as Soviet foreign policy, perhaps, but a case-based perspective with which to end our observations.

Chapter 20 provides the reader with a look at ideas occurring in the complexity and management arena between the times these papers were prepared and the publication date of this book.

REFERENCE

Weick, K. (1995). *Sensemaking in Organizations*. Thousand Oaks, CA: Sage Publications.

Chapter 12

Chaos Theory and Project Management: A Perspective on Managing the Complex Project

Janet Bardyn and Donna Fitzgerald

Complexity theory, second-order cybernetics, nonlinearity, and chaos theory are all terms that attempt to describe the non-Newtonian fact that things are messy around the edges and that the "messiness" tends not only to disrupt the linearity of a system but, over time, through the result of both negative and positive feedback, actually causes the system to change or adapt.

What do these theories mean to us as project managers? Dave Olsen in his 1993 book *Exploiting Chaos: Cashing in on the Realities of Software Development* describes our current situation as one of existing within a structure that includes a number of paradigms. Our first paradigm, the one most of us confront on a daily basis, is "Murphy was right." We live with the disaster of the week and spend our time madly scurrying around putting out fires. The area of orderly space in this paradigm is small, and the disorderly space is large. Our second paradigm is that of Newtonian physics, or what for project managers approximates the Holy Grail. This paradigm tells us that the world is really an orderly place and if we just had better tools and better resources, we could virtually eliminate the chaos, or disorderly feedback, that we live with on a normal basis. According to this view of things, the area of orderly space is large, and the area of surrounding disorganization is small. Our third paradigm is that of complexity theory itself, which tells us that we are not crazy and that the reason Murphy was right is that "projects" are nonlinear complex systems that respond to different rules from those we were led to believe. By recognizing this fact as *reality* (i.e. inherent in the very nature of the process) rather than as something we are cursed with because we have not done a better job of planning or execution, our paradigm will shift, and we will work with, rather than against, the nonlinearity of the project management process.

COMPLEXITY THEORY AND THE REAL WORLD: AN OVERVIEW OF THE ECRIS PROJECT

It is our intention in this chapter to ground the theories we're exploring in a real-world example, so the following is some historical background on our "test" project.

The Engineering Construction Records Information System (ECRIS) was designed to support the work management aspects of outside plant engineering and construction within one of the regional Bell operating companies (RBOC) by increasing the flow of jobs between accounting, engineering, and construction, thereby reducing nonproductive time spent doing manual activities such as maintaining job logs, juggling schedules, preparing daily forms, and recycling work through engineering.

A project team was created to build a wide area network across the Northeast region, deploy over 1,000 personal computers, install or configure over 100 file servers and 20 data base servers, convert a million records into ECRIS, and train over 1500 users, all within a nine-month period. The customers of this system were engineers, control managers, and clerical, accounting, and staff personnel. They are grouped into multidiscipline design build teams and dispersed through 82 locations in the Northeast corridor from Presque Isle, Maine, down to lower Manhattan, New York. The goal of the ECRIS project team was not only to deploy the software but to support the transformation of these 82 centers from stand-alone, nonstandard business units into a highly productive group that would use state-of-the-art tools to respond quickly and efficiently to rapid market changes. (See Figure 12.1.)

The project team was organized into two major categories: dedicated and matrix support personnel. The dedicated team comprised a centralized support center that included system developers, business subject matter experts, two program managers, and a project director. In addition to the support center there were seven field implementation teams deploying ECRIS. The field implementation teams consisted of a project manager, business subject matter experts, system engineers, and human resource trainers. The client services team was matrixed to the project director and provided the procurement services of hardware and software and coordinated the equipment installation.

Figure 12.1
ECRIS Production Network

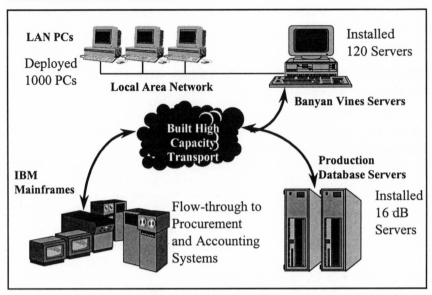

A key ingredient in the ECRIS deployment plan was that the four initial project managers helped create the project work breakdown structure (WBS). Two plans were developed for management: deploy ECRIS in 9 months with six implementation teams or 12 months with four teams. Of course, management picked the more aggressive schedule, and the ECRIS project became the showcase re-engineering deliverable for that year. The project comprised four major undertakings: building the wide area network, converting existing records into ECRIS, training and support of the users during the conversion transition period, and ensuring the ECRIS product met the customer requirements. ECRIS was considered a high-risk project, and we found out later that management had privately given us only a 20% chance to succeed. Since our own assessment of our odds of success wasn't that much higher, we quickly decided we were going to have to take a nonstandard approach to this project in order to achieve success. We chose to adopt a nonlinear paradigm.

THREE ELEMENTS FOR MANAGING IN A NONLINEAR OR CHAOTIC WORLD

The mechanistic and deterministic Newtonian world view—emphasizing stability, order, uniformity, equilibrium, and linear relationships

between or within closed systems—is being replaced by a new paradigm. This new paradigm is more in line with today's accelerated social change, and stresses disorder, instability, diversity, disequilibrium, non-linear relationships between open systems, morphogenesis and temporality. What is reassuring in this novel and therefore risky field of research is that there seems to be indeed a convergence of paradigms: all the blind men seem to have their hands on the same elephant.
　　　　　—Felix Geyer (1994), "The Challenge of Sociocybernetics"

Once we've accepted the concept of nonlinearity how do we go about applying it to our day-to-day task as project managers? Scheduling the event in our WBS—"apply nonlinear problem solving"— somehow seems to miss the point. What we've chosen to concentrate on for the purposes of this chapter are three underlying elements or concepts that we feel maximize the potential for success in a project. For the sake of convenience we've numbered these elements, but that implies a linearity that doesn't exist. These elements, like everything else we'll be discussing, are decidedly nonlinear, nonsequential, and iterative.

Element 1: Establish an Initial Area of Order

Weather prediction is absolutely impossible. The reason is that the behavior of the system is sensitively dependent on initial conditions. If I have a weather system that I start up with a certain temperature and a certain wind speed and a certain humidity—and if I then repeat it with almost the same temperature, wind, and humidity—the second system will not behave the same. It'll wander off and rapidly will become very different from the first. Thunderstorms instead of sunshine. That's non-linear dynamics. They are sensitive to initial condition: tiny differences become amplified. The shorthand is the "butterfly effect." A butterfly flaps its wings in Peking, and weather in New York is different.
　　　　　—Ian Malcom, *The Chaos Page*

Fundamental to chaos theory is the phenomenon of sensitive dependence on initial conditions, commonly referred to as the Butterfly Effect.

This quote is something of a mantra within the complexity theory community, and, based on our experience, it should become the same thing in the project management community. We've all had drilled into our heads the importance of a well-defined requirements document, the need to know we've got the right sponsorship for the project at the start to carry it through the rough spots, and so on. But this knowledge comes to us through the doctrine of observed best practices within an assumed linear system. Within a linear paradigm things can be fixed along the way (though conventional wisdom acknowledges the increasing cost of fixing a problem later in the project). A nonlinear paradigm tells us that because of the "sensitive dependency on initial conditions," no two projects will *ever* be the same. There will always be differences and unexpected/unforeseen occurrences that will happen on any project. What we're interested in is the size of the perturbation that will occur as a result of the initial conditions.

Anything that can go wrong will, and even if nothing can go wrong, something still will.

—Murphy's Law

Complexity theory offers us a theoretical underpinning for what we see on a daily basis, but does it offer us anything more concrete than that? We feel that it does. Despite the best practice disciplines we mentioned before, we believe that there is often an implicit assumption in conventional project management, that a project starts on firm ground at its inception and then begins to deteriorate from there. Based on our experience, both individually and on the ECRIS project, a more typical starting point for most projects is an environment that is highly disordered. Using the model of a nonlinear system as our starting point two methods can be used to establish order in any project: negative feedback (which we hereafter refer to as control) and positive feedback (which we call change).

Establishing order through applying control. Returning once again to our real-world example with the ECRIS project, we chose to establish an initial area of order before the project began by applying control. Based on sample data from the field, we determined a year prior to the ECRIS implementation that the quality of records we were intending to convert upon deployment was very bad. A four-person task force was then chartered to work with the individual field offices and corporate accounting to reconcile and complete as many open jobs as possible prior to system implementation. This ensured that we would be able to set a target for accuracy for the records we were converting (less than 3% fallout rate) and know that we had a chance of reaching that goal in the narrow window of time we allotted to each site.

There are a number of factors to take note of in the preceeding example. The first is that we had the opportunity to acknowledge the disorder and fix it early. We've seen other examples that drive the point home in their failure to establish an initial area of order. One of us had a client who requested help in implementing a mail package on 25,000 desktops worldwide in a nine-month period—an extremely ambitious schedule, but one that might be possible if everything worked like clockwork. Unfortunately, in an evaluation of their "initial conditions" it turned out that only 10% of the exchange servers (the platform to support the mail package) had been installed and that over 55% of the company was still running Windows 3.1 (the new software required either Windows 95 or NT as a base platform). Also, there were three independent project teams, each chartered with solving one piece of the puzzle. Two additional factors also contributed to the initial instability. The version of the back-office software they were implementing at the time wasn't a seasoned product and had a tendency to fail at inopportune times. Second, the company had a deeply ingrained culture that simply prevented anything from getting done quickly.

The point of this example is that it clearly paints the picture of how "tiny differences" (quoting our Lorenzian weather model) can vastly affect the final outcome. Unstable software, three separate implementation projects, and a culture that attempted to moderate the impact of change by doing things slowly certainly guaranteed that the company would get some result, but the only certainty was that the result wouldn't be an "on time, on budget" project. Any project can fix one or two problems, but in the situation we encountered, the initial conditions were too unstable to ever allow for success.

So as not to end on a negative note, using the premise of establishing an initial area of order, there are some solutions to the problems we articulated in this example. The first and most obvious is to combine the operating system upgrade with mail package upgrade and schedule them in sequence directly behind the hardware/server upgrades. This has the advantage of defining a stable hardware/mail server environment as being the initial area of order, which then reduces the variables for the rest of the project by combining two implementations into one.

Establishing order by allowing change. The second method of establishing order at the outset of the project is by applying change to the situation. This can be done through amplifying an already existing tendency in the system or by artificially imposing change from the outside. These two solutions have very different outcomes and implementation techniques. In the first instance, by deciding to amplify the change in the current system, the project team is making the assumption that the organization will eventually (through self-direction) come to a workable solution to the problem being examined, but the solution will require time to decipher. A project of this type is, by its very nature, constrained to a very small initial area of order. In this situation it is best to adopt a methodology that lends itself to a high degree of change or positive feedback. An example of this would be a rapid application development (RAD) project. RAD doesn't attempt to get it right the first time: it schedules in iterations and allows the process to develop at the same time as the system. Obviously, RAD projects still need to keep to schedule and cost goals, but the final content of the system will not have been definable at the start of the project.

The second alternative of imposed change is the prototypical reengineering solution. The decision is made that the initial set of circumstances is so highly disordered that no amount of control (total quality management, or TQM, incremental process improvements, etc.) can achieve the organization's goals. Therefore, starting over with a clean sheet of paper is the only solution. An advantage of this from the point of view of the project team is that once the reengineered solution is defined, the project isn't constrained to the iterative cycle described earlier.

So as not to be accused of advocating a technique we haven't personally lived through, one of our clients hired us to assist in the implementation of a work-flow management system. They had recently centralized a function that had previously been internationally dispersed, and they wanted to develop a more formal infrastructure to ensure the efficacy of the new workflow. They had purchased some specialized software, had typed up a one-page requirements definition, and had budgeted six weeks to get a system up and running. After our initial evaluation of the situation it became clear that no amount of interviews or fact-finding missions would elicit a better set of requirements. The proposed system and process were too new for anyone to have anything more than a vague idea what the system should do. Our solution was to obtain funding to develop the system over a one-year period in approximately four iterations. The first version of the software was deployed in 12 weeks, and one month later we held our first user group meeting to find out what was working and what needed to be changed.

The key factors encouraging the "use of change" as a methodology on this project were:

1. All the people agreed the problem statement was vague and likely to remain so until they had worked with the new processes for a while.
2. Available (fourth generation) software allowed us to develop, deploy, and later modify the system in very short blocks of time.
3. Our funding wasn't tied to a release but covered a specific period of time instead.
4. Management and user expectations were reasonable.

Element 2: Using Change Effectively Requires Balancing at the Edge of Chaos

Complex systems tend to locate themselves at a place we call the "the edge of chaos." We imagine the edge as a place where there is enough innovation to keep a living system vibrant and enough stability to keep it from falling into anarchy. Only at the edge of chaos can a complex system flourish.

—Michael Crichton (1996), *The Lost World*

Operating on the edge of chaos says that you need people who can exist with a high degree of instability and change. One of the techniques that was most successful in enabling that environment was encouraging the concept of personal-mastery.

Psychologist Daryl Conner stated, "The single most important factor in managing change successfully is the degree to which people demonstrate resilience: the ability to absorb high levels of disruptive change while displaying minimal dysfunctional behavior." In order to respond with the requisite degree of resiliency individuals should have a positive view of life as challenging but still filled with opportunities; they should be focused on what they want to achieve but flexible in the demands they make on themselves and others while they're achieving their goals. Finally, individuals should be organized and proactive in engaging change rather than seeking to evade it.

To qualify for Dr. Conner's designation as a successful change agent, an individual would need to achieve a significant degree of personal-mastery. What can a project manager do to encourage this type of behavior short of hiring these miracle workers in the first place? Begin by rewarding results, not compliance; by encouraging initiative and risk taking, not goal tending; and by remembering that success breeds success. Tom Peters's 1987 book *Thriving on Chaos* recounts the story of a junior telecommunications engineer at Federal Express who, when faced with the loss of phone service for several days to the area he was supporting, simply rented a helicopter (using his own American Express card) and then, after being dropped on a snowbound mountaintop, trudged three-quarters of a mile through chest-deep snow to fix the phone line, all on his own initiative. If your own team members feel empowered to take that level of initiative without even your knowledge, you know you've created an environment that fosters personal-mastery.

A second tool available to the corporation and to a project manager for encouraging personal-mastery is an emphasis on professionalism. At the tail end of the ECRIS project our client made a very visible commitment toward project management by encouraging project team members to pursue the Project Management Institute's (PMI) certification. Approximately 25% of the project staff quickly signed up for the first classes offered after their last conversion, and there was a contagious level of enthusiasm. For some of them, especially the more junior members of the team and those who had spent the majority of their career out in the field, a new career opportunity had actually presented itself, and comments such as, "Now that I know this, I'll do it differently the next time" were not uncommon.

The flip side to this success was our failure with the support center's help desk. Help desk support service is one of the fastest growing components of the information technology field, with its own institute, national conference, and, at least in Massachusetts, a very active professional society. Unfortunately, we failed to communicate any excitement to the staff answering the phones. They perceived their job as essentially drudgery, that the only reason they were sitting there is that their value to the organization was less than that of the people we had in the field. Despite our best attempts, we were unable to communicate to them that the industry around them had changed, that instead of being sidelined, as they insisted in believing, they were in a prime area. A deeper analysis of this particular situation would lead us away from professionalism, back to personal mastery and the importance of having the right people on the project. The individuals in question were some of our weakest team members in terms of possessing the five attitudes of resilience we discussed at the beginning of this element.

Element 3: Create a D Channel for Communication

An organization can only exist in a fluid fashion if it has access to new information, both about external factors and internal resources. It must constantly process this data with high levels of self-awareness, plentiful sensing devises, and a strong capacity for self-reflection. Combing through this constantly changing information, the organization can determine what choices are available, and what resources to rally in response. This is different from the more traditional organizational response to information where priority is given to maintaining existing operating forms and information is made to fit the structure so that little change is required.
—Margaret Wheatley (1994), *Leadership and the New Science*

All communication consists of information (content that communicates something that requires a response) and noise (content reflecting disorder). A current review of management literature would include lots of little circles with lots of arrows showing the multitude of pathways information can take among the members of an organization. We fully concur with these models, but as a result of our project we have added two small, but critical, enhancements to the model.

Many models of group communication seem to be based on the child's game of telephone: one child says something to another, and that message is repeated through all the players until the last

Figure 12.2
Project Communication

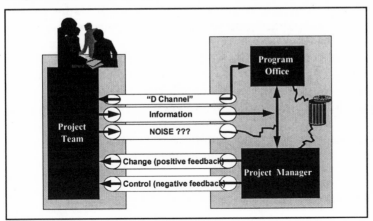

child repeats the message, and the group can then evaluate the distortion. The implicit emphasis is on making sure that the message is disseminated with as little distortion as possible. For the purposes of our model (see Figure 12.2) we would classify this as outbound communication. While not minimizing the importance of this, the area we found most important in contributing to our success was inbound communications.

While striving to articulate this concept, we realized that even though conventional models had bidirectional arrows showing communication paths between the individuals in a group, the model wasn't effective at portraying the fact that the communication of true information requires a response. We also realized that some mechanism had to be added to differentiate between noise and information when communicating inbound. The analogy we've settled upon is that of an ISDN line. ISDN technology provides three channels for carrying signals: an A and a B channel (both of which are 64k and dynamically allocatable) that can be turned on and off as traffic requires and a third channel (referred to as the D channel) that is a very narrow band that is always connected (i.e., never turned off) and that is used primarily for communicating status information and protocols. Using this concept, we've developed the model shown in Figure 12.2. This model is designed to illustrate three things:

1. All communication is a dynamic mixture of noise and information.
2. Because of filtering mechanism, information can sometimes become subsumed in the noise, and a secondary channel (the D channel) is needed as a reinforcing mechanism.
3. Once information is received, a response consisting of either change or control (positive or negative feedback) will be sent.

What does all this mean? It means fostering an environment of *active listening* within the project. Second, it means adding listening as a distinct line item to the list of responsibilities for certain team members (i.e., creating the D channel). Another analogy might be to create a hotline for the project team. The payback of using this technique is the speed of problem identification and resolution. An added benefit is that it encourages problem solving at the lowest level. If team members know their issues will be acted upon immediately when they communicate their needs, this knowledge will increase their reliance on their own problem-solving ability (self-organizing behavior) and results in a greater tendency to escalate the right problem at the right time.

CONCLUSIONS

By definition, a chapter such as this has an inherent linear and logical flow to it. The only problem is that since our message is one of nonlinearity and complexity, something seems to get lost in the translation. For that reason we've chosen to recapitulate our three elements in the format of a highly simplified mind map (Figure 12.3). Everything ties together and one thing flows naturally into the other.

Finally, it has been suggested to us that most of what we've discussed in this chapter is a post mortem analysis of an intuitive technique. While we did exactly what we claim to have done, we did it based on experience, and we weren't actually aware at the time of our project that we had shifted into a nonlinear paradigm. This criticism is partially valid in one sense. It is true that as a result of writing this chapter, we finally put words to our actions, thereby articulating our three elements. On the other hand, it would be wrong to assume we didn't consciously realize what we were doing, even if we couldn't have explained it at the time.

We've been asked repeatedly how we got management's authorization to use these techniques we've discussed, and again we want to stress that that's the wrong question. We never abandoned our project plans or our monthly forecast; we set dates, and we met them. What we did was create the right environment within our projects to allow for success, by creating an environment that fostered a constant flow of communication, by encouraging self-mastery and self-organizing behavior, and by rigorously understanding and enhancing our initial area of order.

It's our belief that we've touched only the tip of the proverbial iceberg in this chapter. We've chosen to focus primarily on project implementations, and we've hit only the high points. In the future,

Figure 12.3
Non-linear Project Management

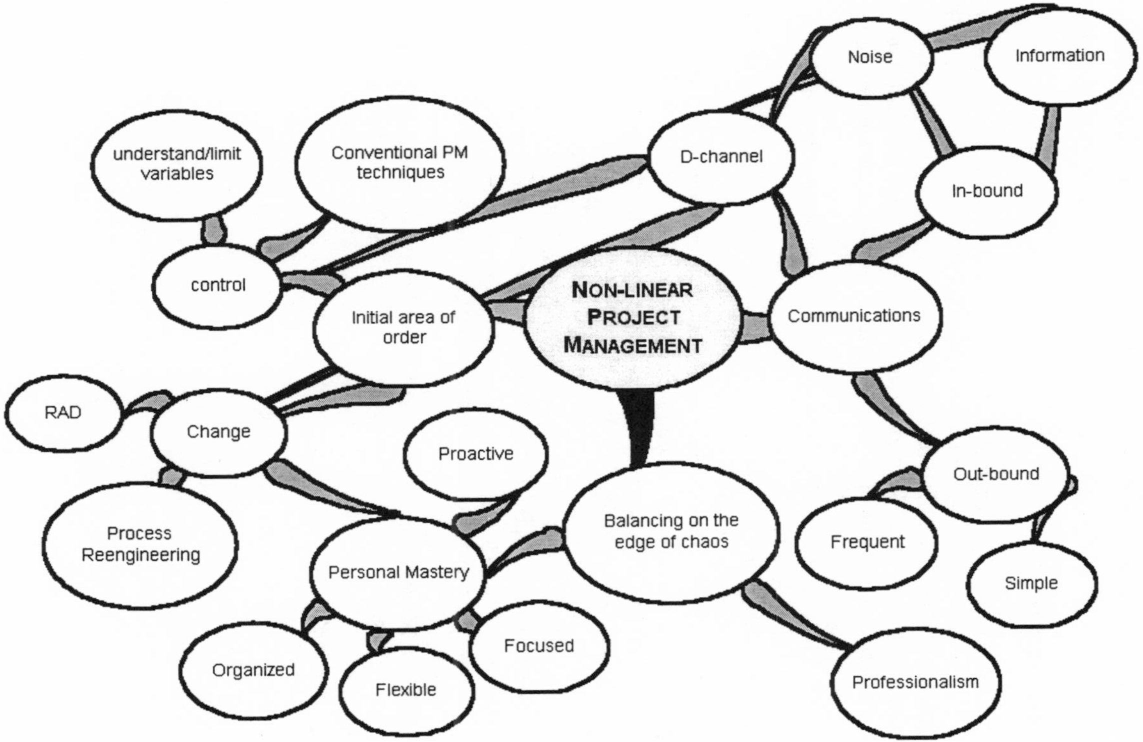

we hope to investigate applying the nonlinear paradigm to the software development process, and we'll continue to explore the implications of this model and its role in day-to-day project management.

REFERENCES

Arthur, Lowell Jay. *Rapid Evolutionary Development: Requirements, Prototyping, and Software Creation.* New York: John Wiley and Sons, 1992.

Bateson, Gregory. *Mind and Nature.* New York: Bantam, 1979.

Carr, David K. et al. *Managing the Change Process: A Field Book for Change Agents, Consultants, Team Leaders, and Reengineering Managers.* New York: McGraw-Hill, 1996.

Frame, J. Davidson. *The New Project Management: Corporate Reengineering & Other Realities,* San Francisco: Jossey-Bass, 1994.

Geyer, Felix. "The Challenge of Sociocybernetics." Proceedings, 13th World Congress of Sociology, Bielefield, 1994.

Gleick, James. *Chaos: Making a New Science.* New York: Penguin, 1988.

Goldstein, Jeffery. *The Unshackled Organization: Facing the Challenge of Unpredictability through Spontaneous Reorganization.* Portland, Oregon: Productivity Press, 1994.

Hammer, Michael and Stanton, Steven. *The Reengineering Revolution: A Handbook.* New York: Harper Business, 1995.

Keaten, James. "Chaotic Feedback Loops with Decision Making Groups: Toward an Integration of Chaos Theory and Cybernetics." Proceedings, Western States Communication Association, Portland, Oregon: 1995.

Lissack, Michael R. "Chaos and Complexity—What Does That Have to Do with Management?" www.lissack.com/writings/chaos.htm

Olsen, Dave. *Exploiting Chaos: Cashing in on the Realities of Software Development.* Van Nostrand Reinhold, 1993.

Peters, Tom. *Thriving on Chaos.* New York: Wings Books, 1987.

Senge, Peter M. *The Fifth Discipline: The Art and Practice of the Learning Organization.* New York: Doubleday, 1990.

Senge, Peter M. et al. *The Fifth Discipline Fieldbook: Strategies and Tools for Building a Learning Organization.* New York: Doubleday, 1995.

Wheatley, Margaret. *Leadership and the New Science: Learning about Organization from an Orderly Universe.* San Francisco: Berrett-Koehler, 1994.

Chapter 13

Complexity, IT, and the Interprise

Mark W. McElroy

The use of the term *paradigm shift* first appeared in 1962, when a young history of science professor at the University of California at Berkeley published a paper that he had originally conceived some 15 years earlier while still a graduate student at Harvard. In its final published form, *The Structure of Scientific Revolutions*, by Thomas S. Kuhn,[1] became a profoundly influential landmark of twentieth-century intellectual thinking on the history of science.

In his brilliant essay, Kuhn defined a paradigm as an "entire constellation of beliefs, values, techniques, and so on shared by the members of a given community."[2] The use of the term today is quite common in several different contexts, including science, technology, economics, and politics. In Kuhn's case, however, it was only the *scientific community* that he had in mind. But given the profound influence that science has historically had on society in general, the effects of Kuhn's paradigms can hardly be viewed as confined to science alone. Indeed, the very basis of contemporary organizational form can be traced to Newtonian mechanics, which has governed Western thought in general for the past 300 years.

Today, 25 years after Kuhn's essay was published, the use of the term *paradigm shift* has successfully transitioned from the ivory tower to the trade tower. Everyone in business uses the term freely, although very often inappropriately and to excess. But such is not the case with the present shift now under way, which most leaders in business and academia alike agree is of enormous proportions, and will change the way work happens and the manner in which businesses are organized to compete from now on.

The full extent of the present shift is just now beginning to come into focus. In its economic form, the transformation that we see is largely being driven by dramatic advances in information technology (IT) over the past 10 years. Understanding this transformation and the complexion of the new paradigm that lies behind it has become business imperatives for senior management at all levels of the enterprise, especially now the CIO (chief information officer).

Not only has information technology spawned the next paradigm in business, but the IT function internal to most organizations is itself now fully engaged in its own evolution *from infrastructure to product*. Information itself, whether in raw form or embedded in intelligent, customer-oriented product designs, *is* the product of the future. But it will not be the conventional enterprise that delivers such information-enriched products to the customer. The dominant organizational form that businesses will take in the future is the *interprise*.

THE SHIFT TO MASS CUSTOMIZATION AND AGILITY

The hallmark of true paradigm shifts is that they tend to be utterly counterintuitive, completely unpredicted. This is certainly true of the current shift from *product-centered* to *customer-centered* economics, a phrase that perhaps best captures the essence of the paradigm shift now in progress. The central orientation of business is changing from mass producing standard products, to mass producing nonstandard products. To be successful in the future, businesses will have to shift their emphasis from *mass production* to *mass customization*; from *lowering the cost of production* to *increasing the value of products* (see Figure 13.1).

In the new paradigm, *customer value perception* will be the primary driver of business strategy. Knowing what the customers' values are and having the ability to meet their needs will take precedence over lowering the cost and improving the quality of production. This changes everything.

Customizing products and services to meet the specific needs of individual buyers is rapidly becoming the standard modus operandi in business. Dramatic advances in information technology as applied to all stages of the value chain make this possible. Rapid turnaround of cycle times, such as *concept to cash*, with intimate inclusion of customers in the early stages of product design, is becoming the norm. But how can any one company that aspires to succeed in an economy marked by the mass production of individualized products (an oxymoron until now) position itself to be all things to all customers? The answer is that it can't!

What one player in the market can't do it alone, many players working together can. By combining the core competencies of sev-

Figure 13.1
A Concilience of Ideas Comes into Focus

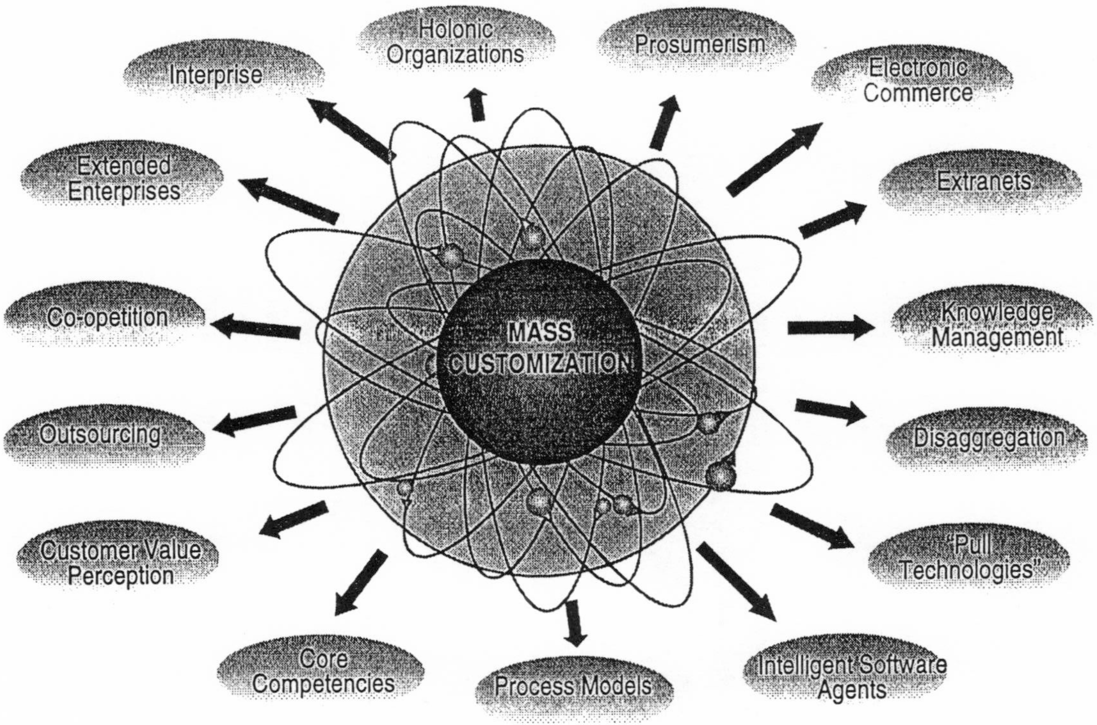

MASS CUSTOMIZATION

Electronic Commerce

Extranets

Knowledge Management

Disaggregation

"Pull Technologies"

Intelligent Software Agents

Prosumerism

Process Models

Holonic Organizations

Core Competencies

Interprise

Extended Enterprises

Co-opetition

Outsourcing

Customer Value Perception

Figure 13.2
The Virtual Web, a.k.a. The Interprise

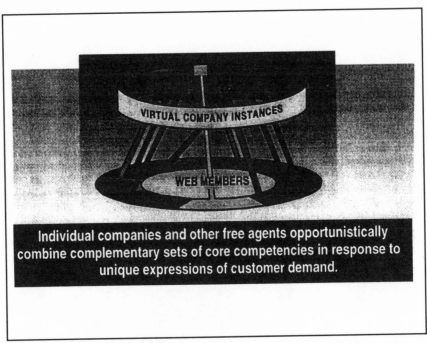

Individual companies and other free agents opportunistically combine complementary sets of core competencies in response to unique expressions of customer demand.

eral organizations in complementary alliances, businesses are able to meet the specific needs of individual customers and can produce highly customized products. These inter-enterprise, or *interprise*, collaborations are the organizational manifestations of the shift to *customer-centered economics* now unfolding in the marketplace.

This is classic systems thinking. By combining organizations in ways that blend their respective core competencies, or strengths, to the customer's advantage, the value of the result is unequivocally greater than the sum of its parts. The interprise exhibits certain emergent properties that no single organization can create by design. The interprise is more dynamic, is capable of taking whatever form is needed to fit the needs of individual customers, and can change its complexion over and over again as the unpredictable needs of new customers present themselves (see Figure 13.2). Indeed, what these unique forms of business possess when compared to the conventional enterprise is *unparalleled agility*.

In 1991, the U.S. Department of Defense commissioned a study of the United States' role and competitive position in the changing structure of worldwide industry. Awarded to the Iacocca Institute, the study concluded with a report entitled, *21st Century Manufactur-*

ing Enterprise Study: An Industry Led View.[3] Among the authors of this report, which was lauded by the *London Economist* as "the most significant report on manufacturing in a decade," was Dr. Kenneth Preiss, an authority on international competitiveness and coauthor of two recent books that introduced the twin concepts of the *interprise* and *agility* to the general public.

In what has become *the* watchword of customer-centered thinking, *agility* is the single most important feature of an interprise. Indeed, it is the raison d'etre for the interprise; it is *the* emergent property that all members of an interprise strive for, and that, in fact, gives it its considerable advantage in the marketplace. No other form of business organization can support the assembly of the right mix of core competencies, at the right time, for the right customer, as spontaneously and as effectively as the interprise.

In their groundbreaking book that closely followed their work on the Iacocca Institute's report to the federal government, the authors of *Agile Competitors and Virtual Organizations* (1995),[4] Kenneth Preiss, Steven L. Goldman, and Roger N. Nagel, defined "agility" as an emergent property of organizations that choose to cooperate with one another in the marketplace opportunistically rather than compete.

Sometimes referred to not as *competition* but as *co-opetition*, this deliberate bonding of complementary firms, according to Preiss et al., is not just "this month's good idea for how to gain a competitive edge....the evolution of agile competition is rooted in what is increasingly acknowledged as a new marketplace reality [a new paradigm], one that promises to determine the conditions under which companies and people will have to function for a long time to come."[5]

If it is true that form follows function, then the interprise logically follows agility. Companies that strive to achieve agility in market dexterity do so by becoming involved in collaborative interprises. In *Agile Competitors and Virtual Organizations*, Preiss and his colleagues provide a working definition of agility that includes the following elements[6]:

- *Dynamic and open-ended*: Agility is a process, an emergent property of a well-run interprise. Agile companies are marked by their ability to sense and respond to changing conditions in the marketplace on a real-time basis. Command and control over static hierarchies are replaced with a "continual readiness to change." The structure itself is fluid.
- *Context-oriented*: Agile companies are, by definition, market-driven, capable of placing themselves into different alignments and configurations with other firms in response to changes in market context or customer requirements. "Markets pull the acquisition of agile

business capabilities," and so the familiar, but product-centered, *supply chain* gives way to the emerging customer-centered *demand chain* (see Figure 13.3).

- *Change-embracing*: Agile companies embrace and dissipate change as a source of energy and are ideally suited for survival in a market-place increasingly characterized by uncertainty and rapid evolution. The interprise structure is inherently capable of withstanding changes of this kind; it thrives in a world of change and unpredictability because of its nonstatic form. It changes its com-plexion of constituent members and its blend of core competencies on demand, largely because it can.
- *Creatively proactive*: Agility enables the discovery of new opportuni-ties, the ability to be there first, to create new markets and to "pre-cipitate change" and respond with innovation. Like an organism's ability to replicate itself in a variety of forms that are ever so slightly different from each other but that continuously test the environment for new, more suitable niches, agile competitors are autopoetic, self-making, and self-regulating in their scope and composition. They are inherently capable of discovering new markets by constantly probing the outside world and by processing information about it.

Authors Preiss, Goldman, and Nagel sum up the challenge faced by management in surviving the transition to agility as follows: "To succeed in such an environment, companies must learn to *thrive* on change and uncertainty, not merely to cope with them. Senior management must reinvent the company repeatedly, the better to focus its core competencies on meeting the changing needs of its customers."[7]

But what of the transition itself? Exactly how does an organiza-tion transform itself from sole occupant of an enterprise with clearly defined boundaries, to one of many occupants in an interprise, with boundaries that never stand still? The answer may be surprisingly simple: tear down the boundaries!

PROCESS INTEGRATION AND DEMAND CHAINS

Recently, Dr. Preiss delivered a speech in Ascona, Switzerland, entitled, "The Emergence of the Interprise" at a conference which was entitled, *Organizing the Extended Enterprise*. In the paper that accom-panied his speech, Preiss described a working model of an interprise "in terms of the flows between the processes that comprise it."[8]

According to Preiss, three "primary flows" together account for the complex interactions required between members of a success-ful interprise. These flows are money, goods and services, and in-formation. In other words, processes within individual enterprises that revolve around the management of these three assets must

Figure 13.3
The Emergence of Demand Chains

- "Pull" Oriented
- Customer Integration
- Product Design
- Dynamic Relationships
- Serves Mass Customization
- Embryonic

DEMAND CHAIN

INTEGRATION

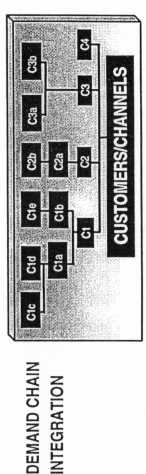

CUSTOMERS/CHANNELS

THE CUSTOMER

R&D → PROD. DES. → LOGIS. → MFTG. → MKTG → SALES → DIST. → CUST. SUPT.

THE VALUE CHAIN

- "Push" Oriented
- Supplier Integration
- Product Delivery
- Static Relationships
- Serves Mass Production
- Mature

SUPPLY

CHAIN

INTEGRATION

SUPPLIERS

DEMAND CHAIN THINKING BEGINS WITH THE CUSTOMER

be closely integrated among the members of an interprise. Moreover, Preiss argues, all three are closely interrelated with one another, "and one cannot be modeled separately from the others."

Tear down the process barriers around these three asset flows within and between a defined group of interprising partners, and you have the makings of an integrated interprise architecture; carefully combine them through cross-enterprise process integration, and the interprise then begins to take shape; enable the flow of information and electronic commerce across the interprise architecture via integrated application sets, EDI (electronic data interchange), and Internet-based technologies, and the form then begins to function.

Indeed, the integration of business functions across enterprise boundaries requires a somewhat less proprietary view of business processes than most managers are used to. Where business process reengineering ended in the waning days of the enterprise, business process *de*engineering and reintegration has begun in the age of the interprise.

The achievement of such cross-enterprise, or interprise, integration will most likely occur in two stages. The first stage will consist of the implementation of well-defined demand chains at an enterprise level. This will allow individual businesses to integrate with their customers' processes in the same way that many have already synchronized their manufacturing activities in well-orchestrated supply chains.

Once tightly coupled demand chains at the enterprise level have been established in the first stage, cross-enterprise process integration can begin in the second. This will occur across the entire value chain in such a way that distinctions made between *supply* and *demand* chains will all but disappear. As most firms adopt a more continuous view of themselves and their trading partners as integral members of fully integrated, circular value chains, the business boundaries of primary interest will gradually shift from the enterprise to *business processes*.

From this perspective, each link in the value chain will be bordered by demand influences, on one side, and supply considerations on the other, regardless of enterprise affiliations. In this modular view of the interprise, customers, too, will be deeply embedded in their suppliers' value chains, as they will be in *their* customers' value chains, and so forth (See Figure 13.4).

While the concept of demand chain integration is relatively new, several sources of seminal thinking on the subject warrant special mention. On the subject of customer integration and the notion of including customer processes in a more holistic view of the value chain, Frederick E. Webster, Jr., of the Amos Tuck Business School

Figure 13.4
The Trend Is Toward Total Value Chain Integration, or Virtual Integration, Driven by Customer Demand

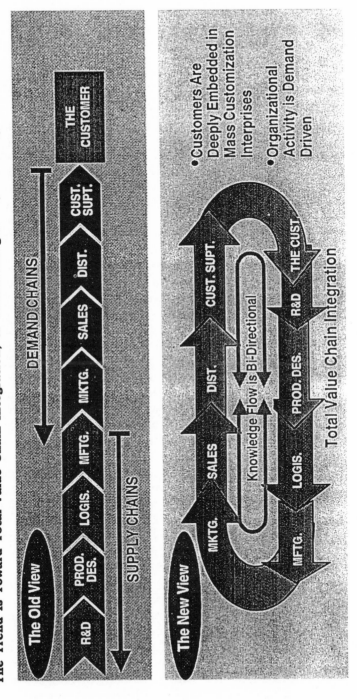

at Dartmouth says, "In companies with a mature commitment to total quality management, the quality process extends back into vendors' processes *and forward to those of the customer*"[9] (emphasis added). He goes on to state, "There is also a continuous flow of information from the customer back to the manufacturer, providing feedback on customer satisfaction, identifying the need for additional assistance, and suggesting the need for new products and services."[10]

But perhaps more than anyone else at this point, authors McHugh, Merli, and Wheeler, develop the concept of demand chain integration best in their book *Beyond Business Process Reengineering, Towards the Holonic Enterprise* (1995).[11] In this important work, the authors introduce the concept of the *holonic network,* on one hand, and *demand-driven logistics,* on the other. While the notion of holonic networks is essentially equivalent to what has been described in this chapter as the *interprise,* McHugh, Merli, and Wheeler do an impressive job of decomposing the operating model behind it into its constituent parts. Moreover, they do this in a way that is roughly comparable to how business processes were described earlier (i.e., as discrete functions that possess a certain degree of autonomy and that can be reconfigured and modeled with one another in a variety of ways).

The more interesting idea behind McHugh et al.'s work, however, is their notion of *demand-driven logistics.* In their view of the integrated value chain, demand-driven logistics "[i]s the backbone of the actual day-to-day execution of a virtual company."[12] They go on to explain, "In demand-driven logistics, rather than operating through a set of rules developed by the supply chain management group, the market sets the rules, and they are constantly changing."[13] Business activity in value chains of this kind, they argue, is triggered by "upstream demand signals...that emanate simultaneously from the point of sale via electronic data interchange [EDI]."[14] From there, demand travels throughout the entire value chain in one continuous stream and in the process renders our former preoccupation with supply chains woefully inadequate.

So, as individual businesses seek to establish interprise alliances with their trading partners, the integration of business processes, electronic commerce, and information between the constituent members of each alliance will be crucial to their mutual success. But most important and perhaps most challenging will be the deployment of IT within the new interprise environment. To this end, we have already seen the emergence of technology solutions to many of the issues that IT planners of interprise architectures will face. These include EDI and other standards-based transaction sets, intranets, the Internet itself, of course, and now, *extranets.* As a new class of "private Internets" that support self-defined communities of trading partners in interprise alliances, extranets are an important technology in the emerging field of interprise commerce.

Ultimately, the integration of business processes between companies in an interprise setting will require a new form of computing. In the *old* world of the enterprise, one used to say, "the network *is* the computer"; in the *new* world, the *interprise* has become the company, and the *extranet* is its computer.

A NEW ROLE FOR IT

Business and IT planners should realize that the drift toward interprise commerce is already under way; the train has left the station. The question of whether or not to embrace it is moot; the questions of *how to do so* and *how soon* are inescapable. From an IT perspective, the challenges inherent to making the switch from an enterprise model to the interprise will be enormous. Successful approaches for doing so, however, will begin with the adoption of a new *mental model* that has at its center *customer value perception*. Again, this stems from the incoming, customer-centered paradigm, as opposed to the outgoing, product-centered orientation. IT, along with all the other elements of the value chain, must ultimately enhance an organization's ability to achieve *agility*, that is, to optimize its ability to sense and respond to its customers' individual perceptions of value in creative ways.

In developing IT strategies for the customer-centered interprise, CIOs will need to rethink all of the fundamental principles that for the past 40 years have defined the role that IT should play in an organization. The IT function is moving from an *operations support* role to a *product delivery* role. Unlike in the past, when the makeup and content of IT logically followed the articulation of business needs, IT will be a business *driver* in the future. Enhanced IT will enable businesses to enter new markets, reach new customers, and offer new products and services that will be exclusively attributable to the value added by IT. In many organizations, IT has already become deeply embedded in the lines of business. Indeed, the IT function itself may well be on the verge of becoming a profit center!

One tends to view the IT domain as falling within the boundaries of the conventional enterprise, protected by elaborate security schemes and draconian firewalls. But these are precisely the walls that will prevent us from engaging in effective interprise commerce. The boundaries of the traditional enterprise, organizational and otherwise, will only serve to constrain the companies that they theoretically protect. The interprise *is* the company of the future, the *near* future no less, and its center of gravity is the customer's perception of value. What the interprise desperately needs is an IT function that makes cross-organizational information sharing and collaboration possible, not a patchwork of isolated IT domains whose keepers view the sharing of data with suspicion and distrust.

This vision of IT as an interactive undertaking at the heart of an interprise that focuses first and foremost on customer value perception, invokes a fundamentally new model of IT, its role in business, and even its governance. By the same token, the even more fundamental question of *what IT's role in the interprise should be*, versus its *modified role* in the domains of participating enterprises, must also be answered.

These are tough questions that all members of a potential interprise should address, and much work will be needed to do so. But when all is said and done, the true measure of success in an interprise-based IT environment will be the extent to which the following questions can be answered in the affirmative:

1. Does the interactive IT environment proactively enable the flow of information across the interprise in knowledge chains?
2. Does the interactive IT environment enable the inclusion of IT on the business side of the house as a driver of strategy?
3. Does the interactive IT environment support electronic interprise commerce by use of standards-based transaction sets?
4. Does the interactive IT environment support the integration of business applications across the interprise?
5. Most important, does the IT environment support the integration of business processes between trading partners, including customers, in demand-driven value chains?

Each of these questions points to a different aspect of a customer-centered world in which business revolves around the customer's perceptions of value as opposed to the producer's imposition of products. But they also point to the pivotal role that IT has played, and will continue to play, in the evolution of the interprise. Mass customization would simply not be possible if it were not for the ability to rapidly capture and convert customer needs into tailored products and services electronically, at the speed of light.

The primary challenge, then, that IT faces over the next several years, or its *mandate*, if you like, is how to transform itself from being enterprise-based to interprise-based in its orientation. IT's view of itself must fundamentally change, must turn inside out. IT strategies from now on should be crafted accordingly.

KNOWLEDGE MANAGEMENT

In the world of the interprise, information processing is very much a cross-organizational proposition. Information must flow freely between businesses if true interprise commerce is to occur. So, just as the notion of the value chain was important to the production orientation of an enterprise, so will the notion of *knowledge chains* be to the customization focus of the interprise. The real payoff in knowledge management strategies will therefore come in the context of intercompany relationships, more so than in the more familiar intracompany setting. Managing in-house knowledge will, of course, continue to be important, but the leveraging effects of interprise commerce will be realized only when knowledge is effectively managed *between* companies.

Before a business can be expected to share its information, however, it has to acquire it in the first place, and it must do so continuously. Successful members of an interprise will, therefore, be *learning organizations*. In this context, there are actually three forms of learning. The first is learning by individuals within an organization. Businesses must make it possible for their workers to continuously engage in meaningful training and individual development. Information technologies that make it easy for workers to *pull* and customize knowledge from a variety of sources will be key to this form of learning (i.e., *pull* versus *push* technologies).

The second and third forms of learning are at the organizational level. An organization must be capable of learning about itself and its business and production processes, on one hand, but must also be equally capable of learning about its customers' needs and its market opportunities, on the other. As Peter Senge put it in his successful book on learning organizations, *The Fifth Discipline* (1990), "Many now recognize the need for organization-wide learning capabilities not possessed by traditional authoritarian, hierarchical organizations."[15] Senge explains, "Team learning is vital because teams, not individuals, are the fundamental learning unit in modern organizations. This is where 'the rubber meets the road'; unless teams can learn, the organization cannot learn."[16]

Ultimately, the responsibility for creating effective knowledge management systems within the interprise may fall to the CIOs who serve its constituent members. If so, it will be the CIOs' responsibility to see to it that the IT functions within their respective organizations enable and support organizational learning in all three of its forms. But it will be the third form, however (learning about its customers' needs and its market opportunities), that businesses will find most challenging, because that form of learning will have to occur on a nearly real-time basis. Knowing what the customer wants *now*, not yesterday, will be of critical importance to the success of an interprise; if it can't connect with the customer on a real-time basis and instantly transfer knowledge of the customer's needs throughout its value chain, somebody else will.

QUANTUM ECONOMICS

Most businesses today are still organized in accordance with models drawn from the industrial age, which, in turn, were taken from the scientific community's prevailing worldview at the time (i.e., their paradigm). This Newtonian, reductionist perspective, in which the world and everything in it are viewed as a machine and can be explained in mechanical terms, has been with us for some 300 years now. It absolutely accounts for why we run our businesses the way we do. All of our hierarchical structures can be traced to the Cartesian view of the world, in which every living and nonliving system could be reduced to their constituent parts. In a world of that sort, hierarchy and the *command and control* approach to management make sense.

But this is classic mechanistic thinking, the opposite of systems thinking, and it lies at the very heart of the mind-set that gave birth to the assembly line, mass production, business process reengineering, total quality management, and just-in-time manufacturing. While the mechanistic model has arguably served us well for the past 100 years or so, its limitations are now starting to emerge in conspicuous ways. Business process reengineering has reached the point of diminishing returns; there's only so much to be gained by repeatedly attempting to fine-tune the machine. Businesses are at a loss to know what to do next; the next *big mechanistic idea* has yet to present itself.

Meanwhile, classical physics has turned out to be nothing more than a means of arriving at some very impressive approximations of reality, consistently reliable, but approximations nevertheless. Where certainty and conviction once prevailed, we now have the new science of chaos and complexity theory, an outgrowth of quantum physics. Science now expresses its views with axiomatic caveats such as the Heisenberg uncertainty principle, "which states that everything we can measure is subject to truly random fluctuations."[17]

In the new world of the interprise, however, the metaphor changes completely from the machine to the organism, from the factory to the ecosystem; and from certainty to estimation. While, to some, this may seem like frivolous musings in metaphors, others have concluded that we can learn a great deal about how best to manage the emerging interprise by observing the fall of the

Newtonian paradigm and the rise of quantum science, chaos theory, and the study of complexity. One can't help but notice the coincidence of timing between the emergence of these stunning insights into the capricious workings of the natural world and the dramatic departure from mechanistic thinking now under way in the *business* world. Scientific paradigms drive the prevailing worldview in almost every sector of society, and business is no exception.

With this in mind, it seems reasonable to suggest that the emergence of the interprise is at least partly attributable to the growing influence of quantum science and systems thinking in recent times. Indeed, if classical economic theory can be thought of as mechanistic in its predispositions, the *new* economics might best be described as quantum-oriented, or *quantum economics*, if you like. What can we learn from this?

COMPLEXITY AND THE INTERPRISE

One of the more fascinating aspects of the study of complexity is that the kind of behavior that marks nonlinear dynamical systems is by no means limited to the realm of the natural world. In other words, classically complex behavior can be found in a broad range of human social settings, such as politics, culture, our judicial systems, and the economy. All of these social constructs, say some, are subject to the laws of complexity, and their behavior should be regarded accordingly.

Among the proponents of this view is Stuart Kauffman, the well-known molecular biologist whose pioneering work at the Santa Fe Institute has contributed much to the unfolding story of complex systems and their curious behavior. In his important book on the nature of complexity, *At Home in the Universe* (1995), Kauffman states, "I suspect that the fate of all complex adapting systems in the biosphere—from single cells to economies—is to evolve to a natural state between order and chaos, a grand compromise between structure and surprise."[18]

This statement, of course, invokes Kauffman's now well known reference to the *edge of chaos*, or that place in a system's ontogeny that lies between order and randomness. He further asserts that "whether we are talking about organisms or economies, surprisingly general laws govern adaptive processes on multipeaked fitness landscapes."[19] For Kauffman and many others who think in similar terms, the laws of complexity absolutely apply to the world of human social affairs, not the least of which are its economic frameworks and the business systems therein. If complexity is the study of unstable, aperiodic behavior in nonlinear, dynamical systems, then surely the interprise falls within its scope.

Following completion of the earlier-mentioned study on global competition at Lehigh University, a group of that study's authors reorganized in the form of The Agility Forum to conduct a second study on the nature of agility. The results of this second study were published in January, 1997, under the title *Next Generation Manufacturing, A Framework for Action.*[20] What makes this second study so interesting is that it takes the vision of the agile enterprise as defined in the preceding work (again, by many of the same authors) and develops it further in terms that unmistakably evoke themes commonly found in chaos theory and the science of complexity. That this was intentional is doubtful; the similarities, however, are striking.

Among the "imperatives" that this second study concludes are essential if American industry is to remain competitive are the following: a*daptive, responsive information systems* that will "increase responsiveness, and mitigate many of the risks that now inhibit innovation." This imperative is clearly reminiscent of the concept of "structural coupling" as defined by Humberto Maturana and Francisco Varela, whose theory of *autopoiesis,* or self-making (discussed further later) seems just as applicable in a business context as it does in the wild. Moreover, the Nobel laureate Murray Gell-Mann's use of the term *complex, adaptive systems* to describe the evolutionary trajectories of natural systems can easily be applied to the interprise as well.

Other imperatives prescribed by the second study include the need to establish "knowledge supply chains" (or *knowledge management* systems), again, eerily reminiscent of the role of cognition in complex, adaptive systems, and the routine exchange of information and feedback within holistic systems (i.e., DNA exchange among bacteria, Rupert Sheldrake's theory of morphogenetic fields, etc.).

Yet another imperative cites the need for interenterprise collaboration and integration to enable "the rapid formation, morphing, and dissolution of extended enterprises that allow it to be dynamic without penalizing its partners." Here again, the language evokes parallel ideas of interdependency and coevolution in the natural realm (e.g., symbiotic organisms, or evolutionary *symbiogenesis* as formulated by Lynn Margulis).

SELF-ORGANIZATION

The interprise can further be described as a kind of self-assembling collection of businesses or *free agents,* which band together in opportunistic ways to satisfy the unique needs of individual customers. In addition to their tendency to self-organize, a feature that Stuart Kauffman sees as essential in the evolution of living systems, interprises can be viewed as classic examples of what the Russian-born chemist and physicist Ilya Prigogine called "dissipative structures." According to Prigogine, only the kind of nonlinear equations now routinely used to describe complex systems could characterize their behavior.

In discussing Prigogine's work in his own book, *The Web of Life* (1996),[21] physicist Fritjof Capra highlights another characteristic of dissipative structures as identified by Prigogine. He states, "Prigogine emphasizes that the characteristics of a dissipative structure cannot be derived from the properties of its parts but are consequences of 'supramolecular organization.'"[22] Surely this describes the attributes of an interprise, if not its very reason for being. The whole *is* greater than the sum of the parts!

Capra summarizes another of Prigogine's observations that, again, is reminiscent of the interprise. This time, the discussion centers around the nature of Prigogine's use of the word "dissipative." Capra points out that "a living dissipative structure, such as an organism, needs a continual flow of air, water, and food from the environment through the system in order to stay alive and maintain its order."[23] He goes on to state, "According to Prigogine's theory, dissipative structures not only maintain themselves in a stable state far from equilibrium, but may even evolve. When the flow of energy and matter through them increases, they may go through new instabilities and transform themselves into new structures of increased complexity."[24]

The analogy here to the interprise is undeniable. If Dr. Preiss is correct in his assertions of what flows through the dissipative structure of the interprise, then instead of air, water, and food from the environment, the interprise derives its energy from the flow of "money, goods and services, and information."[25]

Another manifestation of self-organization in living systems is the property of autopoiesis, or *self-making*. Originally formulated by Maturana and Varela, the theory of autopoiesis holds that all living systems continually experience structural changes while maintaining their internal patterns of organization. Of most significance in these relentless cycles of change is what Maturana and Varela refer to as *structural coupling*. Capra describes changes of this kind as "developmental rather than cyclical,"[26] changes, he asserts, that enable living systems to adapt, physically and organizationally, to their environment. "In other words," he says, "a structurally coupled system is a learning system. As long as it remains alive, a living system will couple structurally to its environment."[27]

If the interprise can be viewed as a kind of social organism that adapts to, and couples with, its environment, then it must also be regarded as a *learning system* for which knowledge acquisition and processing are both fundamental and imperative.

KNOWLEDGE *UN*-MANAGEMENT

The emergent cognitive property of the interprise is perhaps best explained in terms of what Fritjof Capra describes as "a systems theory of cognition."[28] Originally developed by Maturana and Varela, what has become known as the *Santiago theory* asserts that a brain per se is not necessary for a mind to exist. Mind, instead, is seen as a process-based phenomenon, with processes reflecting cognition itself.

Consider the process of self-organization as discussed earlier. To organize is to knowingly configure; to self-organize is knowingly to configure *oneself*. In the absence of cognition, then, how could a system carry out the act of self-organization? Without it, how could a system "know" what type of reorganization is needed, when to initiate it, or when it has been realized? *Process* in this context is really seen as a way of responding to information received from intimate contact with the environment, which, in turn, highlights the important role that feedback plays in building such awareness. Information, then, is the currency of self-organization.

In an example of how feedback serves to guide and inform single-celled organisms in ways that clearly suggest cognition, Capra describes the work of British biologist Brian Goodwin as follows: "Goodwin and his colleagues were able to identify feedback loops in a self-organizing process, in which structures of increasing order emerge at successive bifurcation points."[29] What this suggests is that complex organisms need not possess the singular type of mind that we associate with higher forms of life in order to have cognition per se. But some form of information processing is required. When applied to the interprise, this idea could have some very interesting implications in the evolution of knowledge management.

For example, rather than take the top-down approach of assembling information of a prescribed kind for employee retrieval (i.e., using so-called push technologies), perhaps a more fruitful approach would be to empower individual workers by providing them with tools that can be used to "pull" information of their *own* choosing from a *variety* of sources. The very idea of "managing" knowledge makes sense from the perspective of the command-and-control mechanistic mind-set, but in the new world of the self-organizing, dissipative structure, it has no place. If the interprise is truly subject to the laws of self-organization and complexity, its information and knowledge systems should be conceived accordingly.

One of the more interesting approaches to knowledge management is just now being formulated by two researchers, S.

Rasmussen and N. Johnson, of the Santa Fe Institute and Los Alamos National Laboratory, respectively. Rasmussen and Johnson are conducting experiments on a form of self-organized learning that they call *symbiotic learning*, or *emergent knowledge*. Thus far they have been able to demonstrate that measurable levels of collective learning take place in groups of otherwise independent agents in cases where all members of the group are interconnected by a network. Their experiments on the Internet, in particular, provide unequivocal evidence that collective knowledge can emerge from the interaction of autonomous agents in complex systems of a sort that no single member could predict or prescribe in advance.

This passive approach to knowledge management and its reliance upon the natural emergence of collective intelligence in self-organized systems is qualitatively different from most of the top-down, prescriptive strategies in wide use today. Perhaps it's time we learned to take a lesson from complexity.

CONCLUSION

If human economic systems are, in fact, subject to the laws of complexity, couldn't we safely conclude that business structures have always been exposed to these laws? What is it about the new paradigm of mass customization and the interprise that suddenly, somehow, as this chapter suggests, makes a difference today? The answer may lie in today's brand of information technology. One could argue, for example, that while business and commerce have always been subject to the external influence of complexity, their inability to sense and respond to its messages prevented them from behaving in kind. Until recently, they have been cognitively handicapped, operating in the myopic mode that we've come to know as the enterprise.

The ubiquitous presence of information technology in today's economy, however, pervades all aspects of the marketplace. Information accompanies every link in the value chain—or at least *can*—thereby enabling the capture and transfer of knowledge about each step of the process to whoever wishes to have it. The effects of this newfound awareness include susceptibility to the laws of complexity; that is, the ability, perhaps for the first time in the history of business affairs, to actually *know* what the customer wants, instead of guessing as much by way of traditional market research methods.

Information technology provides not only the cognitive framework required by business to *know* on a firsthand basis what specific customers want but also the means by which to respond accordingly. This is where mass customization and the interprise come into play. By unbundling the value chain into discrete processes in such a way that they can be reconstituted with one another, over and over again in limitless ways, businesses can free themselves from the prescriptive regimes imposed by calcified production systems originally designed to produce carbon-copied products in massive amounts.

In the IT-driven economy, customers will interact with these IT-enabled systems directly and will place orders for products or services that meet their *unique* specifications, using information systems that trigger demand-configured production chains at the point of sale. Businesses operating in this environment will be further freed from the pressure to build products and services under one roof. As long as the IT-enabled degree of process integration exists between companies that choose to do business in an interprise mode, it won't matter who the constituent players are in the fulfillment of individual orders. Interprises will thrive in this environment, and the laws of complexity will prevail.

So, if the interprise is, indeed, a manifestation of society's gradual shift away from mass production and mechanistic thinking toward the new realities of mass customization and systems thinking, and if we can all agree that the quantum view of the world has merit, then perhaps it has much to teach us in terms of how best to structure and manage our business affairs. Perhaps the key to the well-run interprise lies in understanding the way in which its analogue, the organism, achieves self-regulation and dynamic evolution.

In her widely acclaimed book, *Leadership and the New Science, Learning About Organization from an Orderly Universe* (1992) Margaret J. Wheatley says, "If organizations are machines, control makes sense. If organizations are process structures, then seeking to impose control through permanent structure is suicide."[30] If Dr. Preiss is correct in his assertion that "[a]n interprise is best modeled in terms of the flows between the processes which comprise it,"[31] then *process structures*, indeed, would seem to be an apt description of what we should focus on as we attempt to redefine the role of IT in the new context of the interprise.

The IT function must enable the flow of processes and information across the interprise. Its central role in the future will be to provide connectivity for ideas, knowledge, business transactions, trading partners, and customers across the extranet as the interprise seeks to evolve and find its niche in the emerging, nonlinear world of complex, adaptive systems.

But perhaps the biggest challenge we face in trying to determine how best to position and manage IT in the interprise is an attitudinal one. The conventional view of information is that it is a strategic asset, to be closely guarded and hidden from others for selfish gain by its owners. In the natural world of dissipative structures, however, this would be heresy. Likewise, it's hard to imagine how a collection of firms could collaboratively do business together without engaging in some form of meaningful information exchange as a way of enabling interprise commerce.

But certainly not all information needs to be shared; some will continue to be private and should be managed accordingly. Determining what information to share across the interprise will be a significant challenge faced by senior management when contemplating entry into an extended enterprise. The need to confront this challenge, though, has already led to recognition of the important role that *knowledge management* will play in the evolution of the interprise. Indeed, many organizations have already established *chief knowledge officers* within their ranks and have tasked these individuals with the development of knowledge management strategies at the both the enterprise and interprise levels.

In summing up her own view of the role of information in the quantum world of business, Margaret J. Wheatley offers the following sage advice: "In organizations, we aren't suffering from overload just because of technology, and we won't get out from under our information dilemmas just by using more sophisticated information-sorting techniques. Something much bigger is being asked of us. We are moving irrevocably into a new relationship with the creative force of nature. However long we may drag our feet, we will be forced to accept that information—freely generated and freely exchanged—is our only hope for organization. If we fail to recognize its generative properties, we will be unable to manage in this new world."[32]

The proactive exchange of information, coupled with sound knowledge management, will be the keys to success in the new world of mass customization and the interprise. How to do so in a way that rivals the effortless exchange of information in the natural world will be the central question that all IT strategies conceived from now on must answer.

NOTES

1. T.S. Kuhn. *The Structure of Scientific Revolutions*. Chicago: The University of Chicago Press, 1962.

2. Ibid., 175.

3. The Iacocca Institute, Lehigh University. *21st Century Manufacturing Enterprise Study: An Industry Led View*. 1991.

4. Goldman, S.L., R.N. Nagel, and K. Preiss. *Agile Competitors and Virtual Organizations*. New York: Van Nostrand Reinhold, 1995.

5. Ibid., 8.

6. Ibid., 42–43.

7. Ibid., xviii.

8. Preiss, K. "The Emergence of the Interprise," Keynote Lecture to the IFIP WG 5.7 Working Conference, *Organizing the Extended Enterprise*. Ascona, Switzerland, September 15–18, 1997.

9. Webster, F.E., Jr. *Market-Driven Management*. New York: John Wiley and Sons, 1994, 69.

10. Ibid.

11. McHugh, P., G. Merli, W. Wheeler. *Beyond Business Process Reengineering, Towards the Holonic Enterprise*. New York: John Wiley and Sons, 1995.

12. Ibid., 97.

13. Ibid., 122.

14. Ibid.

15. Senge, P.M. *The Fifth Discipline*. New York: Currency Doubleday, 1990, xiv.

16. Ibid., 10.

17. Davies, P. and J. Gribbin. *The Matter Myth*. New York: Simon and Schuster, 1992, 32.

18. Kauffman, S. *At Home in the Universe*. Oxford: Oxford University Press, 1995, 15.

19. Ibid., 27.

20. The Agility Forum. *Next Generation Manufacturing, A Framework for Action*, 1997.

21. Capra, F. *The Web of Life*. New York: Anchor Books, 1996.

22. Ibid., 181.

23. Ibid., 172.

24. Ibid., 89.

25. Preiss, K. *The Emergence of the Interprise*, 3.

26. Capra, F. *The Web of Life*, 174.

27. Ibid., 219.

28. Ibid.

29. Ibid., 191.

30. Wheatley, M.J. *Leadership and the New Science*. San Francisco: Berrett-Koehler, 1992, 23.

31. Preiss, K. "The Emergence of the Interprise," Keynote Lecture to the IFIP WG 5.7 Working Conference, *Organizing the Extended Enterprise*. Ascona, Switzerland, September 15–18, 1997, 3.

32. Wheatley, M.J. *Leadership and the New Science*. San Francisco: Berrett-Koehler, 1992, 145.

Chapter 14

Adaptive Corporations

Mark White

Corporations are tools that people use to discover and implement technologies—products, services, and processes—that offer relatively high economic fitness by effectively satisfying the needs and wants of paying customers. Viewed as tools, corporations are subject to design, with designers consciously or unconsciously trying to find better features to improve their corporation's utility in fulfilling its main mission. This chapter discusses corporate design from a complexity sciences perspective, discussing insights and methods that can help improve corporate utility in both technological discovery and implementation.

Complexity science offers important insights because it teaches us about autonomous agents adapting in a coevolving ecosystem with cooperation and competition intermingled. We can visualize patterns within the business ecosystem as a fitness landscape that associates fitness levels with the various technological combinations that make up products, services, and processes. Conflicting constraints among competing objectives make this landscape relatively rugged but still sufficiently correlated so that near technological neighbors typically enjoy similar fitness levels. New and changing technologies affect the fitness of neighbors near and far, so the agents themselves continually modify their landscape as their chosen technologies evolve and coevolve.

Since most new technologies are new combinations of existing technologies, the economic fitness landscape grows combinatorially—a feature of our complex, adaptive economic system that I have called Kauffmans' law in honor of Stuart A. Kauffman's (1988) early emphasis on the way it drives economic growth and adapta-

tion. Once an economy generates sufficient technological diversity to generate infinitely more diversity autocatalytically, that is,
once it is supercritical, then its combinatorial technology growth
explodes and creates valuable new investment opportunities far
faster than humanity's exponentially growing human and financial resources can exploit them. Nonetheless, the combinatorial
growth in technology means that humanity's exponentially growing population will have increasingly diverse ways of making a living—ways that they can discover and implement more effectively
by working in teams organized with effective corporate tools. The
accelerating change occasioned by combinatorial technology growth
makes discovery relatively more important and implementation
relatively less important than they were in the more leisurely
changing past. This gives an increasing comparative advantage to
the adaptive corporation.

The next section discusses the adaptive corporation's advantages in greater detail. Next the chapter presents some precur-
sors of the adaptive corporation. Then it derives important features an adaptive corporate design ought to include. Finally, this
chapter reflects on how adaptive corporations will likely change
the corporate population.

GOALS OF CORPORATE DESIGN

John Holland (1989) describes that the ideal corporation for the
supercritical economy "continue(s) to adapt to its environment while
using the capabilities it already has to respond, instant by instant,
to that environment. In so doing, the system is constantly trying to
balance exploration (acquisition of new information and capabilities) with exploitation (the efficient use of information and capabilities already available)." In truth, Holland was explicitly writing
about the behavior of his own invention, classifier systems driven
by genetic algorithms, rather than corporations for the twenty-first
century, but his design indeed points the way implicitly toward corporations that properly balance exploration and exploitation, rather
than leaning heavily toward exploitation, as most current corporate designs do. As Holland goes on to say about classifier systems:
"The cognitive system that results is well founded in computational
terms, and it does indeed get better at attaining goals in a perpetu-
ally novel environment." That would constitute a significant improvement over existing corporate designs.

Existing corporate designs have prospered in a relatively stable
environment with relatively low technological diversity and innovation rates. In this slowly changing economic environment, ex-

ploitation skills frequently mattered far more than exploration skills since the long persistence of technologies meant a firm had plenty of time to recoup its investment in optimizing a particular process, service, or product. Firms prospered with command-and-control approaches that mobilized all their capital and human resources to do one thing particularly well, rather than looking for better things to do. Even when change agents discovered better things to do, the dominant players in command-and-control corporations had little trouble maintaining the resource flows that supported the status quo within the corporation. Merchant banks might finance outsiders with significant prospects, but internal threats to dominant technologies were minimal, so technological patterns persisted even when change was appropriate.

This command-and-control legacy means existing corporate designs have a very difficult time generating the sequence of technological breakthroughs that sustainable adaptation in a supercritical economy requires. James Utterback (1995) notes: "As a general rule, competency-enhancing innovations come equally from established firms and outsiders. Competency-destroying innovations, however, nearly always come from outsiders." When established firms fail to introduce competency-destroying innovations, they leave the field open for new firms to discover and implement the technological breakthroughs that reorder industries—and often bankrupt established firms. (See Arthur [1996] on the economics of reordering industries and Lane and Maxfield [1995] on managing a technological transition.)

Adaptive corporate designs should accelerate the firm's progress on learning curves (local hill climbing on the economic fitness landscape, which Utterback calls competency-enhancing innovations) and enable the firm's progress on adaptation curves (technological breakthroughs involving long jumps across the economic fitness landscape, which Utterback calls competency-destroying innovations because they accomplish client objectives with new technologies quite distinct from the firm's current technologies). This acceleration is crucial to a firm's sustainability for, as Utterback (1995) notes, "The idea of competency is critical to the survival of all firms as they encounter incremental and discontinuous technological change. As we have seen, it took just four decades for the whole of the photographic industry to be transformed. In the process, many previously successful companies disappeared. In an era of far more rapid and radical technological change, it remains to be seen how today's businesses will fare." Indeed, we can expect that businesses with adaptive corporate designs will drive technological change and will fare very well as they do so.

TOWARD THE ADAPTIVE CORPORATION

While the vast majority of existing corporations follow a command-and-control approach that effectively mobilizes resources to implement a given technological discovery and the incident innovations that stem from climbing its associated learning curve, a few corporations have managed to incorporate design features that have led to multiple breakthroughs on the adaptation curve. These multiple-breakthrough firms include 3M, HP, Koch Industries, Thermo Electron, and Great Harvest. Their successes provide empirical content for theories of corporate design.

As Ken Baskin (1998) observes, 3M succeeds at innovation because its corporate DNA revolves around the identity "innovation." Their corporate legends battled the odds to bring breakthrough technologies to market—one hero even kept working for a year on a personal project after his boss fired him when he refused to drop it! The project created a major new business for 3M, and the intrapreneur rose to a vice presidency. Together with a willingness to accept failed experiments as an integral part of the innovation process, this lionizing of successful innovators who bucked the odds is a key design feature for adaptive corporations. Every firm has its entrenched interests, even 3M, and innovators must overcome internal resistance if they are going to significantly change the way the firm does business. 3M has institutionalized this aspect of adaptability.

In its heyday, Hewlett-Packard generated a constant stream of unique products as well. David Packard (1995) wrote that "right from the beginning, Bill and I knew we didn't want to be a me-too company merely copying products already on the market." Just as much as 3M, HP recognized the need to value its mavericks. Packard tells the story of awarding a medal to an engineer for "extraordinary contempt and defiance beyond the normal call of engineering duty," an engineer who "later became director of a department...with his reputation as a maverick intact." Management there had at least an intuitive understanding of economic fitness landscapes, with an implicit interest in unique fitness peaks. Packard quotes Bill Hewlett always advising: "Don't try to take a fortified hill, especially if the army on top is bigger than your own."

Koch Industries treats central planning as a fatal conceit (see Petzinger, 1997a). Inspired by Austrian economists such as Hayek, chairman and CEO Charles Koch endeavors to apply free market principles inside the firm. Over 30 years, the firm has developed a tool kit incorporating 80 models that employees use, as Koch (1997) puts it, "first, to identify the problem and root causes, then, to develop a course of action, and, finally, to create measures of progress."

He calls the system market-based management, and it incorporates five important elements: vision, virtue and talents, knowledge systems, decision rights, and incentives. Decision rights let employees change the procedures for running the firm's assets as they see fit, and incentives let them share in the value they create with their decisions.

Thermo Electron founder George Hatsopoulos (1996) likes to quote a stock analyst who called his firm "a perpetual idea machine." He also likes to say he's never had an employee leave to start up a new technology firm. With his spinouts invention, employees can start up new firms without leaving Thermo Electrons corporate family. Spinouts are new firms with their own stock held by key employees and the public but majority-owned by Thermo Electron and supported by its financial, administrative, and technological resources. With spinouts, Thermo Electron can reward innovative employees with equity tied very closely to the value that they add, rather than equity that responds to a whole mix of projects. Spinouts also allow Thermo Electron to continue focusing on its main strengths without losing opportunities to pursue additional markets or technologies that may arise as it evolves. The firm's original spinouts have spun out additional firms, which have spun out still more, and those still more in a few cases—making Thermo Electron a corporate great-grandmother. No conglomeration of low-growth firms, every firm that Thermo Electron and its progeny spin out is designed to capitalize on an attractive innovation.

Pete and Laura Wakeman have created what they call the first free-network franchise, Great Harvest. Their franchise contract begins with the statement: "ANYTHING not expressly prohibited by the language of this agreement IS ALLOWED." Their objective was freedom for franchisees, but innovation is the strength that emerged. Given the liberty to experiment, their franchisees constantly discover new ways to add value to a whole-wheat bread store, and those methods rapidly diffuse through the organization through informal contacts among franchisees rather than changes to the store manual. Indeed, while they are all identifiably Great Harvest stores, each store has its own distinct personality—like ordinary siblings, rather than identical twins—since Great Harvest stores evolve rapidly by continually incorporating a mix of proven successful innovations from all across the network. Petzinger (1997b) quoted Pete Wakeman's attitude toward competitors' trying to copy Great Harvest's methods: "They be left holding a blueprint of what Great Harvest was, and will be out of view."

Each of these adaptive corporations has its own unique history, mixing together many important elements to create the formulas for their successes. Yet each of them incorporates at least one key element for adaptive corporations. First among these elements is permitting what you don't prohibit—a concept I call common law practice to distinguish it from prohibiting what you don't permit, which I call Roman law practice after the Latin bureaucracies that require legal underpinnings for each and every activity. If you prohibit what you don't permit, then innovators must argue their case before they can run an experiment, which would make sense if deduction could tell how experiments will turn out, but, in fact, only experiments can tell us whether innovators can achieve their goals. Whether common law is explicit, as in Great Harvest's franchise contract, or implicit, as in the stories that lionize the mavericks at 3M and HP, prior permission for experiments is crucial for successful innovation, and innovation is crucial for successful adaptation in a changing world.

Beyond simply permitting experimentation, firms can improve their innovative capacity by teaching employees how to seek breakthroughs at undefended fitness peaks, by motivating employees to innovate with direct and substantial incentives that reward innovators with a substantial share of the value that their innovations create and by creating an organizational structure that uses patches and spinouts to flexibly incorporate breakthrough opportunities. John Holland's work on classifier systems adds value here because it suggests improved methods over the best current practices for teaching and motivating innovators.

CORPORATIONS AS CLASSIFIER SYSTEMS

Corporations are complex systems with many features that interact nonlinearly to produce emergent outcomes. From a financial perspective, relevant corporate features include cash flows, real options, and capital structure. From a management perspective, relevant features include strategies and tactics; from an engineering perspective, plant, equipment, and processes; from a marketing perspective, products, services, and brands; from a human resources perspective, employees and policies; and so forth across various disciplines and features. Taken together, the interactions among these various features determine the corporation's responses to its environment. If the responses are appropriate, the corporation prospers, as do its shareholders and stakeholders. Corporate designers, then, should seek out methods that comprehensively integrate the various corporate features to create a responsive system. John Holland's classifier systems do precisely that.

Holland (1989) says, "Classifier systems are a particular class of message-passing, rule-based systems." They consist of performance systems, which determine how the classifier system interacts with its environment, and adaptive mechanisms, which modify the performance systems based on results from its environmental interactions. In a typical corporation today, the performance system consists of employees, plant and equipment, and standard operating procedures, while the adaptive mechanisms consist of managers, supervisors, and their committees that decide how to modify the standard operating procedures. This typical command-and-control, Roman law approach to the adaptive mechanism keeps employees from changing standard operating procedures unless they receive explicit permission to do so—a situation that not only leads to big differences between the operating manuals and the way employees really do things but also retards improvements in the way employees really do things. When the environment changes slowly, retarding improvements in standard operating procedures does only modest damage to a firm's competitiveness. When the environment changes quickly, retarding improvements in standard operating procedures may prove fatal.

Holland (1989) notes, "It is a central tenet of our approach that all rules serve as hypotheses, more or less confirmed, rather than as incontrovertible facts." A laissez-faire, common law approach to the adaptive mechanism embodies this central tenet by permitting what it doesn't prohibit. New procedures are simply hypotheses, and their interactions with the environment confirm them more if they are successful hypotheses or less if they are unsuccessful hypotheses. Hard-and-fast prohibitions may exist—don't give bookkeepers single-signature authority over checking accounts—but employees are generally free to propose marginally or radically new procedures in any area of the firm and generally free to implement new procedures in their own area. This common law approach not only doesn't discourage the experiments that can generate continuous improvements in the firm's standard operating procedures as successful new rules diffuse but also keeps the operating manuals in line with the way employees really do things. This makes it easier for innovators to compare their ideas to current procedures in search of improvements—and if the standard operating procedures are on-line in an Intranet, easier still.

Common law must be at the heart of any corporate adaptation mechanism, but better adaptation mechanisms will also take into account Holland's work on credit assignment and rule discovery—especially genetic algorithms, Holland's ingenious contribution to rule discovery. In neither case do I propose here a direct one-to-one translation of Holland's mechanisms to corporate practice, but rather mechanisms that capture the spirit of Holland's work, if not its precise content.

In assigning credit, Holland proposes a bucket-brigade algorithm where rules active at the time the system gains a payoff from the environment share in that payoff and, in turn, pay off the stage-setting rules that provided messages fulfilling their conditions. I highly recommend that those interested in the details refer to Holland (1989, 1997) and give some thought to how to implement Holland's system of bids and payments. In corporate practice, though, my own analysis suggests that the objective of strengthening successful rules is best served by awarding equity to innovators who propose successful new rules. The amount of equity should constitute some fraction of the marginal value the innovator adds to the corporation. To the extent that innovations build on prior art, the new innovator should receive part of the value, and the innovator who created the prior art should receive part of the value—this helps achieve Holland's objective of strengthening not only active rules, but stage-setting rules as well.

Equity makes more sense than cash for paying the innovators who create new procedures or technologies. First, equity means that current innovators will share in the marginal value generated by subsequent innovators, giving them a reason to capitalize on part of the value of their innovative procedure within the adaptive corporation, rather than capitalizing on the full value by leaving the corporation to start up their own business. This sharing in the value of future innovations, plus the advantages of diversification by sharing in the value of other projects, divisions, and spinouts, can make staying in the corporation more attractive than going it alone. Conversely, to the extent that creative destruction overtakes the adaptive corporation and devalues earlier innovations (a distant, but nonetheless real, possibility), the reduced equity values tend to automatically reduce any excessive prior awards.

The committees making equity award decisions should do so conservatively through time, since it is easier to keep awarding more equity in the future than to take away equity already awarded. Still, equity awards should be essentially unlimited, since the innovator discovering a true breakthrough technology may create far more new value than the corporation's entire prior value. Fairness is paramount, since innovators' motivation to stay in the system rather than opt out for a startup depends on their confidence that the system won't abuse them. Since successful innovations create new value, the system should have plenty of raw material to keep innovators happy. The corporation should also keep noninnovators happy by providing generous salaries and cash bonuses to people for fulfilling their performance system roles well, but equity dividends and the decision rights in a direct shareholder democracy will go to the proven innovators who provide the corporation with the valuable new procedures it needs to successfully coevolve with its rapidly changing environment. Proven innovators should be the decision makers most likely to vote their shares for those new ideas with the greatest potential for adding value. I call this credit assignment mechanism, my own invention, an innovator stock ownership program, or ISOP.

Genetic algorithms provide an immensely powerful tool for rule discovery, making John Holland justly famous for their discovery. With them, computers can quickly find very good rules for certain well-defined, nonlinear optimization problems, such as pipeline operations, shop floor scheduling, or gas turbine designs. Some day, computers may even rival the human brain's power in such poorly defined nonlinear optimization problems as generating new products, services, and processes with high economic fitness. For the time being, though, corporate rule discovery will probably benefit more from training employees in using such creativity-enhancing concepts as genetic algorithms, fitness landscapes, and parsing and recombining (aka associations/improvisation) than it would benefit from trying to computerize such algorithms. Humans still have a tremendous advantage in parsing elements out of a combination, so while computers can do a wonderful job in combining elements already given, they are unlikely to systematically parse elements in new ways that lead to new perspectives and technological breakthroughs. This doesn't mean that computerized algorithms can't help people discover new procedures—on the contrary, the story of Marsh Fisher's combination of real estate and franchising to create the concept behind Century 21 suggests that computers indeed have the potential to help people uncover valuable combinations of known elements—but it does mean that any firm relying solely on computers may leave itself vulnerable to blindsiding by people parsing elements more effectively.

Beyond the classifier system's adaptive mechanisms of credit assignment and rule discovery, adaptive corporations need to find ways to effectively organize around valuable new procedures. Self-organization by employees creating their own procedures in teams works very well, but self-managing teams should understand such concepts as patches (see Kauffman, 1995), which can help teams determine their appropriate size and the connectedness of their tasks with other team's tasks, and spinouts (see Hatsopoulos, 1996), which give organizations an option for capitalizing on attractive technologies or markets that nonetheless seem tangential to the organization's main thrust. Still, without the valuable new procedures that come from common law, credit assignment, and rule discovery, patching a demotivated Roman law performance system would add very little value on its own, and spinouts would be pointless. Treating corporations as classifier systems helps create the innovations that justify flexible organizations.

DIFFUSION

Command-and-control corporations have prospered because slowly changing environments favored attention to performance systems at the expense of adaptive mechanisms. As long as opportunities for technological improvements were relatively limited, and few corporations pursued them, the environment rewarded this emphasis on exploiting known procedures rather exploring for improved procedures. Adaptive corporations would not have prospered in earlier centuries or decades, for the same reason that technological start-ups were exceedingly rare compared to present days. This situation is changing rapidly. Combinatorial technology growth is accelerating the potential for economic change so dramatically that, as adaptive corporations begin to systematically turn that potential into new products, services, and processes, all corporations will have to pay more attention to their adaptive mechanisms. They will likely use Holland's principles.

Critics, especially traditional academic critics, could denigrate this work based on its suggestive empirical evidence on the importance of common law and adaptive mechanisms to corporate success, rather than definitive evidence. Furthermore, the suggested corporate applications for classifier systems are general descriptions, not precisely detailed plans. However, their criteria would be deductive, rather than inductive. There's no attempt here at a deductive proof that designing corporations as classifier systems will enhance their adaptability. Rather, by proposing a new combination of complexity science with management practices, this work follows classifier systems in spirit—creating new rules that serve as interesting hypotheses, not supposedly incontrovertible facts.

Indeed, this work is a long jump on the economic fitness landscape, but with sufficient elements in both theory and practice to provide a valid basis and guide for testing. The best way to test the corporation as classifier system is through real-world experimentation, not deduction, and the best experiments will likely come from setting up new corporations in green fields, not in trying to transform existing organizations. Starting up a diversified portfolio of ISOP corporations would test the concept and, to the extent that certain corporations succeeded more than others, provide the experience that could guide improved implementations. Further research would involve studying more corporations that incorporate the crucial elements in adaptive mechanisms, as well as studying 3M, HP, and so on from a classifier systems viewpoint. However, the best research would set up new corporations explicitly designed to incorporate these elements. As Charles Koch (1997) notes: "The brutal irony is the more we try to avoid specific failures, the more we ensure overall failure." We must experiment.

REFERENCES

Arthur, Brian W. 1996. "Increasing Returns and the New World of Business." *Harvard Business Review* (July–August), 100.

Baskin, Ken. 1998. *Corporate DNA*. New York: Butterworth-Heinemann.

Hatsopoulos, George N. 1996. "A Perpetual Idea Machine." *Daedalus* (March), 81.

Holland, John H. 1988. "The Global Economy as an Adaptive Process." In *The Economy as an Evolving Complex System*, edited by P. W. Anderson, K. J. Arrow, and D. Pines. Redwood City, CA: Addison-Wesley, 117.

Holland, John H. 1989. "Using Classifier Systems to Study Adaptive Nonlinear Networks." In *Lectures in the Sciences of Complexity*, edited by D. Stein. Redwood City, CA: Addison-Wesley, 463.

Holland, John H. 1995. *Hidden Order*. Redwood City, CA: Addison-Wesley.

Kauffman, Stuart A. 1988. "The Evolution of Economic Webs." In *The Economy as an Evolving Complex System*, edited by P. W. Anderson, K. J. Arrow, and D. Pines. Redwood City, CA: Addison-Wesley, 125.

Kauffman, Stuart A. 1995. *At Home in the Universe*. New York: Oxford University Press.

Koch, Charles. 1997. "How to Succeed in Interesting Times." Speech delivered at Wharton School, University of Pennsylvania.

Lane, David and Robert Maxfield. 1995. "Foresight, Strategy, and Complexity." Santa Fe Institute working paper 95-12-106.

Packard, David. 1995. *The HP Way*. New York: Harper Business.

Petzinger, Thomas Jr. 1997a. "Charles Koch Teaches Staff to Run a Firm like a Free Nation." *Wall Street Journal*, January 18.

Petzinger, Thomas Jr. 1997b. "Bread-Store Chain Tells Its Franchisees: Do Your Own Thing." *Wall Street Journal*, November 21.

Utterback, James M. 1995. "Developing Technologies: The Eastman Kodak Story." *McKinsey Quarterly* (January), 130.

Chapter 15

Complexity in the Dynamics of Organizational Founding and Failure

Joel A. C. Baum and Brian S. Silverman

There has been a great deal of interest recently in the application of complexity theory to a variety of real-world, time-dependent systems, driven by the promise of this new branch of mathematics to untangle and bring forth order from seeming disorder. Many time series, most notably in the natural sciences and business finance, have proven difficult to analyze with conventional linear methods, which are now beginning to be modeled using nonlinear and nonparametric methods. Complex systems are understood by looking for patterns within their complexity—patterns that describe the potential evolution of the system.

The unraveling of these adaptive systems has been aided by the discovery of mathematical expressions that exhibit similar tendencies. Mathematical techniques and methods for studying nonlinear dynamics have been developed to characterize and, to some extent, analyze noisy time series by analyzing these expressions (Tong, 1990). Many adaptive systems in the natural world are now known to exhibit chaotic or nonlinear behavior, the complexity of which is so great that they were previously considered random. Chaotic systems have now been recognized and studied in biology, physics, economics, and management (e.g., Anderson, Arrow, and Pines, 1988; Baum and Silverman, 1998; Brock and Malliaris, 1989; Brown and Eisenhardt, 1998, Cheng and Van de Ven, 1996; Kauffman, 1993; McKelvey, 1996; Waldrop, 1992). In the contemporary management literature, however, complexity theory tends to be invoked at a metaphorical level (e.g., Morgan, 1997; Nonaka, 1988; Peters, 1988; Vinten, 1992), with increased turbulence and accelerating pace of change in the business world sufficient to motivate the label "chaotic."

Chaos theory suggests that adaptive systems steer themselves to "the edge of chaos" by regulating their level of autonomy/mutual dependence (1) among components and (2) between the system as a whole and other systems in the environment with which it interacts (Baum, 1998; Brown and Eisenhardt, 1998; Levy, 1994; McKelvey, 1996; Phelan, 1995; Stacey, 1995, 1996; Thietart and Forgues, 1995). The advantage of operating at the edge of chaos stems from the system's ability to achieve both close relations and stability. If organizations have no ties, they do not influence each other. If ties are very close, there may be too much interdependence between them—every act of one will influence the pattern of relationship, and this might become extremely uncertain and unstable because of the imploding repercussions of every act. Too much interdependence leaves no room for individual autonomy. Systems need to find a balance between interdependence and autonomy.

How complex are competitive interorganizational systems? Individual organizations appear often to stray far from the edge of chaos into stable configurations of strategy, structure, and process (Miller, 1986), which may generate excessive stability at the expense of exploration of new ways of doing and acting (Levinthal and March, 1993). Interorganizational systems, by comparison, are far less constrained by systems of goals and incentives and authority structures, permitting the proliferation of new ideas and technologies (Miner and Haunschild, 1995). Evidence supports the idea that competitive interorganizational systems are complex systems poised at the edge of chaos. In competitive situations, organizations must continuously coevolve, adjusting to the adaptations of their rivals (Barnett and Hansen, 1996; Baum and Silverman, 1998; Sorenson, 1996). Each organization must be able to adapt rapidly if the competitive environment changes in such a way as to make their behavior suboptimal. Thus, a change in the environment may cause an "arms race" or evolutionary spurt (Barnett, 1997; Schumpeter, 1934). Consistent with this view, industries typically evolve through long periods of incremental change in which organizations and their leaders tend to hold their position for relatively long periods of time (often for decades), interrupted by occasional discontinuous change or punctuated equilibrium (Chandler, 1990; Miller and Friesen, 1984; Tushman and Romanelli, 1985). These shocks are just as likely to make the system less turbulent as more turbulent (Tushman and Anderson, 1986). This suggests that competitive interorganizational systems follow a power-law distribution or punctuated equilibrium indicative of a complex system (Bak and Chen, 1991).

The stream of organizational ecology research on rates of founding and failure in competitive interorganizational systems has strong, but to date unexplored, ties to complexity theory. For example, among the oldest and most famous examples of simple, deterministic, nonlinear equations that produce complex aperiodic behavior are the Logistic and Lotka-Volterra equations, which were originally conceived as models of population growth. The currently popular density-dependence model of organizational founding and failure (Hannan and Carroll, 1992; Hannan and Freeman, 1989) is derived directly from these equations. Modeling efforts in organizational ecology, however, fail to address a crucial implication of this connection: analytic approaches typically employed in organizational ecology research may not be well suited to modeling complex, nonlinear, dynamical systems (Morrison, 1991).

Complexity theory provides a rich theoretical framework as well as techniques for detecting nonlinear dynamics that can describe (and potentially help account for) the dynamics of organizational founding and failure. Our empirical strategy is to analyze historical patterns of organizational founding and failure in 12 diverse organizational populations using techniques for detecting and describing nonlinear dynamics (e.g., Lyapunov exponent, correlation dimension, surrogate testing, Hurst exponent). The populations are[1]:

1. Manhattan hotels, 1898–1980 (Baum and Mezias, 1992)
2. U.S. labor unions, 1835–1985 (Hannan and Freeman, 1989)
3. San Francisco newspapers, 1845–1975 (Hannan and Carroll, 1992)
4. U.S. trade associations, 1900–1982 (Aldrich et al., 1994)
5. Massachusetts railroads, 1825–1922 (Dobbin and Dowd, 1997)
6. Manhattan banks, 1791–1980 (Banazak-Holl, 1992)
7. Brooklyn banks, 1823–1980 (Banazak-Holl, 1992)
8. International nongovernmental organizations, 1875–1973 (Boli and Thomas, 1997)
9. New York State life insurance companies, 1812–1985 (Ranger-Moore, 1997)
10. New York City commercial newspapers, 1725–1989 (Blau, 1998)
11. New York City ethnic newspapers, 1784–1989 (Blau, 1998)
12. New York City political newspapers, 1781–1989 (Blau, 1998)

Our results provide a characterization of these populations' founding and failure dynamics, including an assessment of the extent to which orderly, chaotic, or random behavior is apparent. If sequences of organizational founding and failure produced by competitive, interorganizational systems are characterized by chaotic behavior, we will identify a potentially consequential methodological shortcoming of past empirical work in organizational ecology and a myriad of innovative techniques for gaining new insight and understanding that may render complex interorganizational systems (more) predictable.

A TYPOLOGY OF DYNAMIC SYSTEMS BEHAVIOR

How can differences in the behavior of dynamic systems be characterized? Research in physics and biology reveals complex systems as progressing through stages of order and chaos from highly ordered, regular, predictable, and controllable states through conditions of differing mixes of order and disorder. Importantly, research reveals that systems do not tend to gravitate toward random behavior but, rather, toward an area of complexity "at the edge of chaos" that lies between randomness and order. Studies of phenomena as disparate as sandpiles, earthquakes, and artificial life have found that systems move toward complex behavior (Bak and Chen, 1991; Kauffman, 1991, 1993; Langton et al., 1992). Complex behavior enables the system to maximize benefits of stability while retaining a capacity to change (Kauffman, 1993; Waldrop, 1992).

Dynamic systems exhibit three basic patterns of behavior—*orderly, chaotic,* and *random*—whose features and predictability are summarized in Table 15.1. Each pattern is characterized by the dominance of specific *attractors,* which differ among themselves in terms of the mix of order and disorder. An attractor is a set of points that represents the possible states, or phase space, that a time series generated by a dynamic system tends to take over time.

Table 15.1
Patterns of Behavior in Dynamic Systems

Pattern	Attractor	Behavior	Micro-Trajectory Predictable?	Macro-Attractor Predictable?
Orderly	Point Limit Cycle	Behavior repeats itself exactly	Yes	Yes
Chaotic	Strange	Behavior repeats itself a little differently each time and bifurcates into different behaviors	No	Yes
Random	Random	Disorder	No	No

Orderly behavior: point and limit cycle attractors. The orderly pattern coincides with *point* and *limit cycle* attractors in which behavior repeats itself exactly; the behavior of the system is both stable and predictable at both microtrajectory and macroattractor levels. In the p*oint* attractor behavior repeats itself like a free-falling pendulum that always comes to rest at the same point. Innovative behaviors always revert to a particular state. In the *limit cycle* attractor behavior is drawn to a cyclically changing set of 2, 4, 8, or 16 states. Behavior repeats itself like a streetlight that goes on and off according to the amount of daylight. Limit cycle behavior can be found in examples of populations of animals that oscillate in a cyclic manner. These are simple, linear, near-equilibrium systems, typical of physical and mechanical systems, in which a limited number of behaviors are repeated continually. When disturbed by environmental change, the system always returns to the same behavior(s).

Chaotic behavior: strange attractor. The chaotic pattern is reflected in *strange* attractors. In this pattern, the system applies a variety of behaviors that develop and change as need arises. Systems characterized by the chaotic pattern show the greatest adaptability to changing environmental conditions (Kauffman, 1993; Waldrop, 1992). Change in chaotic systems tends to be small most of the time, but, occasionally, large-scale change occurs (Bak and Chen, 1991; Phelan, 1995). In strange attractors, behavior is characterized by irregularity, uncertainty, and difficulty in predicting and planning ahead. Behavior bifurcates from similar, uniform behavior to an array of possible behaviors. Strange attractors can bifurcate between 2, 4, 8, or 16 patterns. Chaotic systems display a strong sensitivity to initial conditions that makes accurate predictions of future conditions virtually impossible. Nevertheless, the overall behavior does have a discernible attractor that can be identified throughout time and that bounds possible behavior.

Random behavior: random attractor. In the random pattern unpredictability characterizes the dynamics of events. Orderly behavior does not develop. Novelty is at its extreme, and the system appears to be in a constant agitation. The pattern that borders and constrains the behavior of chaotic processes disappears, and behavior faces no limitations imposed of order and regularity. The behavior of strange attractors is called chaotic because prediction at the microscale is limited, but, nevertheless, there is a macrolevel pattern behind the disorder (i.e., the attractor is predictable) (Kellert, 1993). Chaotic processes are not random; they follow rules, although the rules (even simple ones like the logistic equation) can produce extreme complexity. In the random attractor, disorder reigns and allows no place for order.

MEASURING AND MODELING COMPLEXITY

One way to represent the complexity of time series data is algorithmic information content (AIC) (e.g., Chaitin, 1987; Gell-Mann, 1995; Gell-Mann and Lloyd, 1996). AIC measures the compressibility of a time series (e.g., the series "123123123" could be compressed to repeat "123" three times). An orderly system with a point attractor has minimal AIC—a complete description of the system can be given with a single number. A periodic system following an orderly limit cycle has a somewhat greater AIC defined by the set of points along its deterministic path. A chaotic system has a still larger AIC related to the fractal dimension of its strange attractor. As random noise is added to the system, the data become less compressible. Random behavior has maximum AIC: the shortest description of a random time series is the series itself. Table 15.2 shows the kinds of models that are appropriate depending on AIC (adapted from Dooley, 1994).

Systems that yield time series with a high degree of order (linear deterministic) or disorder (random noise) are simple to model. Systems having a moderate degree of disorder can be modeled with linear differential or difference models. Systems with intermediate values of (dis)order—at the edge of chaos—are the most difficult to model. The conclusion: appropriate modeling of time series generated by complex, adaptive systems depends on correctly ascertaining AIC levels. If competitive, interorganizational systems exist at the edge of chaos (Kauffman, 1993) or in a low dimensional state of chaos, then assumptions of standard analytical techniques are inappropriate. Once we know this, however, we have a better idea of what models to apply to understand the dynamics: (1) use stochastic models to explain random processes; (2) use linear deterministic models to explain orderly behavior; (3) use nonlinear dynamic modeling to explain chaotic processes (Morrison, 1991).

DETECTING CHAOS AND COMPLEXITY

While orderly behavior (point and low-order limit cycle attractors) is quite easily detected, we need a way to differentiate between chaotic and random behavior. Two features of chaotic processes provide a basis for rendering such a differentiation. One is the sensitivity of chaotic processes to initial conditions—in contrast to orderly processes, where different starting points converge to the same sequence of points on a simple attractor, and random processes, where there is no impact of initial conditions on subsequent behavior. The second is that chaotic processes display predictable attractors that bound possible system behavior, while purely

Table 15.2
AIC and Time Series Model Types

AIC (Attractor)	Model	Example
Low (Point)	Linear deterministic	Linear regression Exponential, sine/cosine Moment matching
Moderate (Limit Cycle)	Linear differential Linear difference	Fourier analysis Spectral analysis ARIMA linear time series
Intermediate (Strange)	Nonlinear differential Nonlinear difference	Lorenz equations Exponential time series
High (Random)	Random noise	Normal distribution Probability density function

random processes do not. The diagnostic tests described later have been developed to measure these characteristics—sensitivity to initial conditions and attractor predictability—of dynamic systems.

Sensitivity to initial conditions. Complex systems exhibit a sensitive dependence on initial conditions, as first pointed out by Lorenz (1963: 133): "two states differing by imperceptible amounts may eventually evolve into two considerably different states. If, then, there is any error whatever in observing the present state—and in any real system such errors seem inevitable—an acceptable prediction of an instantaneous state in the distant future may well be impossible." He termed the generator of sensitivity to initial conditions "the butterfly effect."

For a dynamic system to be chaotic, it must have a large set of initial conditions that are highly unstable. No matter how precisely initial conditions are measured, predictions of subsequent behavior become radically wrong after a short time. It is thus considered proof of the presence of chaos if sensitivity of the system under analysis to initial conditions can be demonstrated (Wolf et al., 1985). The standard method of identifying this attribute is by the calculation of the *Lyapunov exponent.* This exponent measures the rate at which neighboring points on the attractor diverge as they are moved forward in time. Roughly speaking, the (maximal) Lyapunov exponent is the time average logarithmic growth rate of the distance between two neighboring points, that is, the distance between two points grows as $e^{(t \cdot l)}$, where l is the exponent. The trajectories on the attractor are embedded in a multidimensional space, and so the divergence is represented as the difference between 2 n-tuples. There are as many Lyapunov exponents as there are dimensions in the state space of the system, but the largest is usually the most important. The dominant average Lyapunov exponent, 1, is defined as:

$$\lambda = \log_2 \{[\Sigma^l_{n-1} (n + 1/ l)_n]/n\text{-}1\},$$

where n indexes the samples and l is the Euclidean distance between a trajectory and its nearest neighbor. With very large amounts of data, the density of points in a region of the attractor permit calculation of local Lyapunov exponents—since the rate of divergence is not necessarily constant over the whole attractor. In practice, data limitations typically permit measurement of only the first exponent, however. Positive Lyapunov exponents, which indicate sensitivity to initial conditions, are considered evidence either of chaos, since the distance grows (on average in time and locally in phase space) exponentially over time, or of randomness, negative exponents of mean reverting behavior, and the value zero is characteristic of cyclic behavior.

   Correlation dimension. Given a positive Lyapunov exponent, a second measure of chaos, the correlation dimension, can be used to distinguish chaotic from random time series (Dooley and Van de Ven, 1997). It is a measure of spatial correlation of scatter points in d-dimensional space. The correlation dimension indicates the attractor's dimension. For example, a point has $d=0$; a line has $d=1$, a plane has $d=2$, and a cube has $d=3$. The point is to determine whether the attractor for a seemingly random time series has low or high d. A major difference between chaotic and random processes is that, although both *appear* random to the eye and to standard linear time series methods, chaotic behavior stretches and folds within a low-dimensional space defined by its attractor, while random behavior is unbounded and completely fills the phase space. Thus, for a random time series, d will be slightly less than, or equal to, the embedding dimension.

   For orderly or chaotic time series, however, the attractor has a finite dimension. If such a series is embedded in a dimension less than its true dimension, it will appear random and thus have a d near the embedding dimension. If the series is embedded in a dimension equal to, or greater than, its true dimension, it will have d near its true dimensionality. For example, a time series for which the true dimension is 4.5 would exhibit d equal to 3 and 4 when plotted in embedding dimensions 3 and 4, and 4.5 for embedding dimensions 5 and higher. Thus, in general, random processes will have high d, and chaotic processes will have low d, substantially lower than 10, in the range of 5 or 6 (Brock, Hsieh and LeBaron,

1991: 17). Hence, identification of chaotic behavior involves testing whether or not a seemingly random time series trajectory exhibits low d (Cheng and Van de Ven, 1996).

Surrogate testing. The validity of the conclusion that a time series is chaotic based on its Lyapunov exponent and correlation dimension can be evaluated empirically using surrogate testing (Theiler et al., 1992). In surrogate testing, additional time series are created that have similar properties to the time series in question. To test the null hypothesis that the time series is linear (periodic), phase randomization is used to generate surrogate time series (Kaplan and Glass, 1995). A phase-randomized surrogate time series has the same length, distribution and linear dynamical structure as the original. The only aspect altered is the *nonlinear* structure of the data. If a time series has low d because it is periodic in nature, then surrogates will also have low d. If, however, the time series has low d because of *nonlinearity*, then surrogate series will have high d since phase randomization will have removed the low dimensional nonlinear structure.

The color of noise. What if a time series is determined to be random based on the foregoing tests (e.g., $l>0$ but $d>6$)? In that case, additional diagnostics can be performed to determine whether the noise is *purely random* (white noise), *persistent* and mean drifting (brown/black noise), or *antipersistent* and mean reverting (pink noise). Hurst (1965) developed a time series measure that is a useful diagnostic of noise color. The *Hurst exponent* can be thought of as a measure of autocorrelation that estimates nonlinear and long-term persistence (not linear dependencies). It is derived using so-called R/S analysis. Given a time series X containing n points and an integer divisor p, where for convenience, $10 \pounds p < n/2$, the data can be divided into n/p blocks. For each block the average value is calculated, then the maximum range of each block and the standard deviation of each block. The value (range/standard deviation) is calculated for each block and then averaged. This average value, rs, is related to the Hurst exponent by the following formula:

$$rs = (p/2)^H,$$

where H is the Hurst exponent. Hurst exponent values range between 0 and 1. A value of 0.5 indicates a true random walk (white noise). A value $0.5 < H < 1$ indicates persistent behavior (brown/black noise), in that one can expect with increasing certainty as the value moves toward 1 that whatever direction of change has been current will continue. Similarly, values $0 < H < 0.5$ indicate antipersistent behavior (pink noise), in that one can expect that whatever direction of change is current is unlikely to continue. A straight line with nonzero gradient would have a Hurst exponent of 1, and at the limit of 0, the time series must change direction every sample.

ORGANIZATIONAL FOUNDING AND FAILURE TRAJECTORIES

Identifying complex dynamics entails knowing what to look for. As the foregoing discussion indicates, however, looking at time series trajectories may not be very helpful in distinguishing complex, yet predictable, dynamics from those that are essentially random. As can be seen in the panels of Figure 15.1, which gives detrended, three-year moving average counts of founding and failure, this is true of the 12 sample populations.[2]

We now turn to using the methods we outlined earlier for detecting complex dynamics to analyze organizational founding and failure time series. For each time series we

1. Compute l for embedding dimensions 3-6.[3]
2. Compute d for embedding dimensions 3-7.[4]
3. Compute surrogate ds to check the validity of conclusions based on l and d.
4. Compute H to determine the color of noise for series that turn out to be random.

The end result is a dynamic characterization of the multiple organizational founding and failure trajectories underlying the evolution of nine populations of organizations. The characterization includes an assessment of the extent to which complex dynamics have become apparent in each interorganizational system. Table 15.3, on pages 302–303, summarizes the findings.

Lyapunov exponents. l is positive across embedding dimensions 3–6 for all founding and failure time series indicative of either chaotic or random (not periodic) behavior that is sensitive to initial conditions.

Correlation dimension. With only three exceptions, values for d stabilize for each trajectory across embedding dimensions 3–7 indicating a relatively low-dimension attractor characterized by either periodic or chaotic (not random) behavior. Combined with the positive ls, the stable ds imply *chaotic* founding and failure time series. For the three exceptions (international nongovernmental organization failure, San Francisco newspaper founding, New York City ethnic newspaper failure), the positive ls and unstable ds imply *random* behavior.

Surrogate testing. Surrogate testing provides more mixed results. Surrogate ds that increase approximately linearly with the embedding dimension reinforce the implied *chaotic* behavior and indicate that the low ds for the original time series resulted from chaotic dynamics. For founding and failure of Brooklyn and Manhattan banks, founding of international nongovernmental organizations, failure of San Francisco newspapers and founding of New York City ethnic newspapers, however, surrogate ds stabilize across embedding dimensions 3–7, suggesting that the low ds for the original founding and failure time series resulted from *orderly* dynamics. Taken together, the three analyses indicate that of the 24 time series analyzed, 7 (29.2 percent) are orderly, 3 (12.5 percent) are random, and 13 (54.2 percent) are chaotic.

Hurst exponents. The final step in the analysis is to estimate H for the three random series to determine the color of their noise. $H>0$ for international nongovernmental organizations' failure and San Francisco newspaper founding series, which indicates brown/black noise—persistent behavior in which the current direction of change tends to continue. $H=.5$ for NYC ethnic newspaper failure, indicating a purely random (white noise) series.

DISCUSSION AND CONCLUSION

Complexity theory provides a model of three different, basic behavioral patterns of dynamic systems: ordered, chaotic, and random. The states describe systems from a highly ordered condition that can be predicted and controlled through varying mixes of order and disorder, culminating in a state of randomness. The states differ from each other in terms of their dominant attractors. The first and third patterns are problematic for adaptive functioning of competitive interorganizational systems. Within the chaotic mode, however, sustainable adaptive functioning is achieved when the system is at the edge of chaos. In this mode the system balances itself between order and disorder, and between path dependence and path creation, so as to maximize organizational learning. The evidence we presented suggests that founding and failure trajectories underlying the evolution of organizational populations may be the result of complex, competitive, interorganizational systems poised at the edge of chaos, opening new theoretical opportunities for understanding organizational evolution.

If, as complexity theorists assert, much of the interesting and adaptive behavior in human social systems *does* exist at the edge of chaos, then this poses a serious research challenge because modeling complexity increases with data complexity (Dooley, 1994; Morrison, 1991). Interorganizational systems that yield time series with a high degree of order (linear deterministic) or disorder

Figure 15.1
Detrended, Three-Year Moving Average Founding and Failure Counts (Panels A-D)

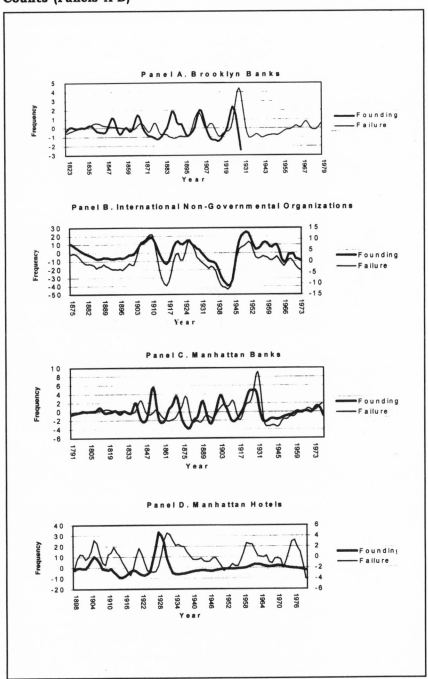

Figure 15.1
(Panels E-H)

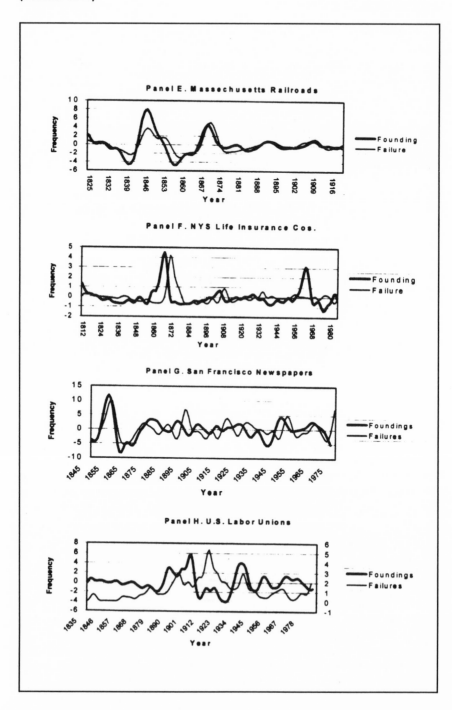

**Figure 15.1
(Panels I-L)**

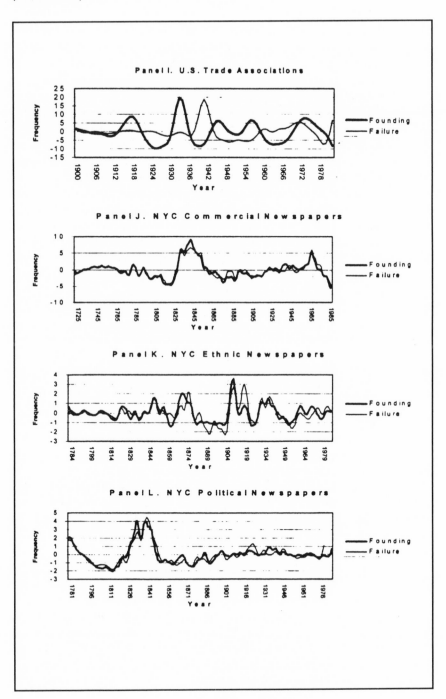

(random noise) are simple to model. Those having a moderate degree of disorder can be modeled with linear differential or difference models. Systems with intermediate values of (dis)order—at the edge of chaos—are the most difficult to model. The conclusion: appropriate modeling of time series generated by complex, adaptive systems depends on correctly ascertaining AIC levels. If competitive, interorganizational systems exist at the edge of chaos, or in a low dimensional state of chaos as our analysis suggests may frequently be the case, then assumptions of standard analytical techniques employed in research on such interorganizational systems may be inappropriate for modeling these complex, nonlinear, dynamical systems. Once we know this, however, we have a better idea of what models to apply to understand the dynamics: (1) use stochastic models to explain random processes; (2) use linear deterministic models to explain orderly behavior; (3) use nonlinear dynamic modeling to explain chaotic processes (Morrison, 1991).

Adaptive behavior in human social systems at the edge of chaos poses major theoretical and conceptual challenges as well. A diagnosis of chaos imposes the challenge of theorizing about phenomena that "are neither stable and predictable nor stochastic and random; that unpredictability of behavior does not imply randomness; that [behavior] may be extremely sensitive to different initial conditions and that learning processes may be much more complex than simple cybernetic mechanisms imply" (Dooley and Van de Ven, 1997: 42). Moreover, by definition, a chaotic system is a deterministic system: behavior that appears random, in fact, is determined by precise laws. Finding chaos in social systems is thus potentially a challenging proposition to defend for human systems. Such a claim will have to overcome the common tendency to mistakenly contrast *determinism* with *voluntarism* rather than with *probabilism* (Baum, 1996).

Implications for practicing managers are also apparent—and equally challenging. Emergent order in an interorganizational system—the kinds of organizations surviving—is the result of the interrelated dynamics of organizations being favorably selected ecologically (downward causation) (Hannan & Freeman, 1989) and of evolutionary BVSR (blind-variation-and-selective-retention) processes percolating up from within organizations (upward causation) (Campbell, 1994). Under ecological conditions at the edge of chaos such as those suggested by our findings, however, even though functioning properly, evolutionary BVSR processes within organizations may fail to produce the kinds of intraorganizational behaviors necessary for survival and growth in the competitive context (Kauffman, 1993). Complexity effects at the interorganizational

Table 15.3
Dynamic Behavior Diagnostics Results Summary

Population	Event	$l>0$	d stable (value)
Brooklyn banks, 1823-1980	Founding	Yes	Yes
	Failure	Yes	Yes (3.4)
International non-government organizations, 1875-1973	Founding	Yes	Yes (1.6)
Manhattan banks, 1761-1980	Founding	Yes	Yes (3.1)
	Failure	Yes	Yes (2.8)
Manhattan hotels, 1898-1980	Founding	Yes	Yes (2.6)
	Failure	Yes	Yes (3.8)
Massachusetts railroads, 1822-1925	Founding	Yes	Yes (3.3)
	Failure	Yes	Yes (3.3)
NYS life insurance cos., 1812-1985	Founding	Yes	Yes (3.3)
	Failure	Yes	Yes (3.5)
San Francisco newpapers, 1845-1975	Founding	Yes	No
	Failure	Yes	Yes (5.1)
U.S. labor union, 1835-1985	Founding	Yes	Yes (4.4)
	Failure	Yes	Yes (4.0)
U.S. trade associations, 1900-1982	Founding	Yes	Yes (3.3)
	Failure	Yes	Yes (4.9)
NYC commercial newpapers, 1725-1989	Founding	Yes	Yes (2.9)
	Failure	Yes	Yes (3.2)
NYC ethnic newspapers, 1784-1989	Founding	Yes	Yes (2.5)
	Failure	Yes	No
NYC political newspapers, 1781-1989	Founding	Yes	Yes (3.8)
	Failure	Yes	Yes (3.5)

Table 15.3 (continued)

Population	Surrogate *d* stable	Implied Behavior	Color
Brooklyn banks, 1823-1980	Yes	Orderly	
	Yes	Orderly	
International non-government organizations, 1875-1973	Yes	Orderly	
Manhattan banks, 1761-1980	Yes	Orderly	
	Yes	Orderly	
Manhattan hotels, 1898-1980	No	Chaotic	
	No	Chaotic	
Massachusetts railroads, 1822-1925	No	Chaotic	
	No	Chaotic	
NYS life insurance cos., 1812-1985	No	Chaotic	
	No	Chaotic	
San Francisco newpapers, 1845-1975	No	Random	Brown/ Black
	Yes	Orderly	
U.S. labor union, 1835-1985	No	Chaotic	
	No	Chaotic	
U.S. trade associations, 1900-1982	No	Chaotic	
	No	Chaotic	
NYC commercial newpapers, 1725-1989	No	Chaotic	
	No	Chaotic	
NYC ethnic newspapers, 1784-1989	Yes	Orderly	
	No	Random	White
NYC political newspapers, 1781-1989	No	Chaotic	
	No	Chaotic	

system level may thus create ecological conditions in which selected firms and strategies are little better than those selected against. Consequently, managers working in complex ecological contexts may need to become experts in "tuning" competitive landscapes—as well as internal BVSR—to foster joint optimization of adaptive processes at intraorganizational and interorganizational levels (McKelvey, 1998).

NOTES

1. We are most grateful to Howard Aldrich (U.S. trade associations), Jane Banazak-Holl (Manhattan and Brooklyn banks), Judith Blau (New York City newspapers), and Jim Ranger-Moore (New York State life insurance companies) for helping us to compile several of these time series.

2. Often chaotic behavior is superimposed on some slowly varying periodic function. Effective study of chaos requires that the smooth function, which represents the slow trend, be subtracted from the data before a detailed analysis is performed. A polynomial fit is one way to accomplish this (Sprott and Rowlands, 1995). We used a fourth-order polynomial fit to detrend each time series.

3. We examine embedding dimensions 3–6 since series with $d>6$ are generally considered random.

4. We examine embedding dimensions 3–7 since real time series rarely have $d<3$ and time series for which $d>7$ are generally considered random.

REFERENCES

Aldrich, H. E., C. R. Zimmer, U. H. Staber, and J. J. Beggs. 1994. "Minimalism, Mutualism, and Maturity: The Evolution of the American Trade Association Population in the 20th Century." In J. Baum and J. Singh (eds.), *Evolutionary Dynamics of Organizations*, 223–239. New York: Oxford University Press.

Anderson, P. W., K. J. Arrow, and D. Pines (eds.). 1988. *The Economy as an Evolving Complex System*. Redwood City, CA: Addison-Wesley.

Bak, P., and K. Chen. 1991. "Self-Organized Criticality." *Scientific American*, Vol. 264, No. 1, 26–33.

Banazak-Holl, J. 1992. "Historical Trends in Rates of Manhattan Bank Mergers, Acquisitions and Failure." Working paper, University of Michigan.

Barnett, W. P. 1997. "The Dynamics of Competitive Intensity." *Administrative Science Quarterly*, Vol. 42, 128–160.

Barnett W. P., and M. T. Hansen. 1996. "The Red Queen in Organizational Evolution." *Strategic Management Journal*, Vol. 17 (summer special issue), 139–158.

Baum, J.A.C. 1996. "Organizational Ecology." In S. Clegg, C. Hardy, and W. Nord (eds.), *Handbook of Organization Studies*, 77–114. London: Sage.

Baum, J.A.C. 1999. "Whole-Part Coevolutionary Competition in Organizations." In J. Baum and B. McKelvey (eds.), *Variations in Organization Science: In Honor of Donald T. Campbell*. Thousand Oaks, CA: Sage.

Baum, J.A.C., and S. J. Mezias. 1992. "Localized Competition and Organizational Failure in the Manhattan Hotel Industry." *Administrative Science Quarterly*, Vol. 37, 580–604.

Baum, J.A.C., and B. S. Silverman. 2000. "Complexity, (Strange) Attractors, and Path Dependence in Innovation Trajectories." In Raghu Garud and Peter Karnøe (eds.), *Path as Process*. Hillsdale, NJ: Lawrence Erlbaum. In press.

Blau, J. R. 1998. "Immigrant Communities and Their Newspapers in America, 1850–1930." *Sociological Analysis*.

Boli, J., and G. M. Thomas. 1997. "World Culture in the World Polity: A Century of International Non-Governmental Organization." *American Sociological Review*, Vol. 62, 171–190.

Brock, W. A., D. A. Hsieh, and B. LeBaron. 1991. *Nonlinear Dynamics, Chaos, and Instability: Statistical Theory and Economic Evidence*. Cambridge, Mass.: MIT Press.

Brock, W. A., and A. G. Malliaris. 1989. *Differential Equations, Stability and Chaos in Dynamic Economics*. Amsterdam: North Holland.

Brown, S. L. and K. M. Eisenhardt. 1998. *Competing on the Edge*. Boston: Harvard Business School Press.

Chaitin, G. J. 1987. *Algorithmic Information Theory*. Cambridge: Cambridge University Press.

Chandler, A. D. 1990. "The Enduring Logic of Industrial Success." *Harvard Business Review* (March–April), 130–140.

Cheng, Y-T., and A. H. Van de Ven. 1996. "Learning the Innovation Journey: Order Out of Chaos?" *Organization Science*, Vol. 7, 593–614.

Dobbin, F., and T. J. Dowd. 1997. "How Policy Shapes Competition: Early Railroad Foundings in Massachusetts." *Administrative Science Quarterly*, Vol. 42, 501–529.

Dooley, K. 1994. "Complexity in Time Series Modeling." *Society for Chaos Theory in Psychology and the Life Sciences*, Vol. 2, No. 3.

Dooley, K., and A. H. Van de Ven. 1997. "A Primer on Diagnosing Dynamic Organizational Processes." Working Paper, Arizona State University and University of Minnesota.

Gell-Mann, M. 1995. "What Is Complexity?" *Complexity*, Vol. 1, 16–19.

Gell-Mann, M., and S. Lloyd. 1996. "Information Measures, Effective Complexity, and Total Information." *Complexity*, Vol. 2, 44–52.

Hannan, M. T., and G. R. Carroll 1992. *Dynamics of Organizational Populations: Density, Competition, and Legitimation*. New York: Oxford University Press.

Hannan, M. T., and J. Freeman. 1989. *Organizational Ecology*. Cambridge: Harvard University Press.

Hurst, H. E., Black, R. P., and Simaika, Y. M. 1965 *Long-Term Storage: An Experimental Study*. London: Constable.

Kaplan, D., and L. Glass 1995. *Understanding Nonlinear Dynamics*. New York: Springer-Verlag.

Kauffman, S. A. 1991. "Antichaos and Adaptation." *Scientific American*, Vol. 265, No. 2, 64–70.

Kauffman, S. A. 1993. *Origins of Order: Self-Organization and Selection in Evolution*. Oxford: Oxford University Press.

Kellert, S. H. 1993. *In the Wake of Chaos: Unpredictable Order in Dynamical Systems.* Chicago: University of Chicago Press.

Langton, C. G., J. D. Farmer, S. Rasmussen, and C. Taylor (eds.). 1992:Artificial Life II: *A Proceedings Volume in the Santa Fe Institute,* Vol. 10. Reading, Mass.: Addison-Wesley.

Levinthal, D. A., and J. G. March, 1993. "The Myopia of Learning." *Strategic Management Journal,* Vol. 14, 94–112.

Levy, D. 1994. "Chaos Theory and Strategy: Theory, Application and Managerial Implications." *Strategic Management Journal,* Vol. 15 (summer special issue), 167–178.

Lorenz, E. 1963. "Deterministic Nonperiodic Flow." *Journal of the Atmospheric Sciences,* Vol. 20, 130–141.

McKelvey, B. 1996. "Complexity vs. Selection among Coevolutionary Firms: Factors Affecting Nash Equilibrium Fitness Levels." Paper presented at INFORMS College on Organization Science, Atlanta, GA, October.

Miller, D. 1986. "Configurations of Strategy and Structure: Towards a Synthesis." *Strategic Management Journal,* Vol. 7, 233–249.

Miller, D., and P. H. Friesen. 1984. *Organizations: A Quantum View.* Englewood Cliffs, NJ: Prentice-Hall.

Miner, A. S., and P. R. Haunschild. 1995. "Population-Level Learning." In B. Staw and L. Cummings (eds.), *Research in Organizational Behavior,* Vol. 17, 115–166. Greenwich, CT: JAI Press.

Morgan, G. 1997. *Images of Organizations,* 2d ed. Thousand Oaks, CA: Sage.

Morrison, F. 1991. *The Art of Modeling Dynamic Systems.* New York: Wiley.

Nonaka, I. 1988. "Creating Order out of Chaos: Self-Renewal in Japanese Firms." *California Management Review,* Vol. 30, 57–73.

Phelan, Steven E. 1995. "From Chaos to Complexity in Strategic Planning." Paper presented at the 55th Annual Meeting of the Academy of Management, Vancouver, British Columbia, Canada, August.

Ranger-Moore, J. 1997. "Bigger May Be Better, but Is Older Wiser? Organizational Age and Size in the New York Life Insurance Industry." *American Sociological Review,* Vol. 62, 903–920.

Schumpeter, J. 1934. *The Theory of Economic Development.* Cambridge, Mass.: Harvard University Press.

Sorenson, O. 1996. "The Complexity Catastrophe and the Evolution of the Computer Workstation Industry." Paper presented at the INFORMS College on Organization Science, Atlanta, GA, November.

Sprott, J. C., and G. Rowlands. 1995. *Chaos Data Analyzer: The Professional Version.* New York: American Institute of Physics.

Stacey, R. D. 1995. *Strategic Management and Organizational Dynamics.* Pitman.

Stacey, R. D. 1996. *Complexity and Creativity in Organizations.* San Francisco: Berrett-Koehler.

Theiler, J. et al. 1992. "Testing for Nonlinearity in Time Series: The Method of Surrogate Data." *Physica D,* 58, 77–94.

Thietart, R. A., and B. Forgues. 1995. "Chaos and Organization Theory." *Organization Science,* Vol. 5, 19–31.

Tong, H. 1990. *Non-Linear Time Series—A Dynamical System Approach.* New York: Oxford University Press.

Tushman, M. L., and P. Anderson. 1986. "Technological Discontinuities and Organizational Environments." *Administrative Science Quarterly,* Vol. 31, 439–465.

Tushman, M. L., and E. Romanelli. 1985. "Organizational Evolution: A Metamorphosis Model of Convergence and Reorientation." In B. Staw and L. Cummings (eds.), *Research in Organizational Behavior*, Vol. 7, 171–222. Greenwich, CT: JAI.

Vinten, G. 1992. "Thriving on Chaos: The Route to Management Survival." *Management Decision*, Vol. 30, 22–28.

Waldrop, M. M. 1992. *Complexity: The Emerging Science at the Edge of Order and Chaos*. London: Penguin Books.

Wolf, A., J. B. Swift, H. L. Swinney, J. A. Vastano. 1985. "Determining Lyapunov Exponents from a Time Series." *Physica*, Vol. 16D, 285–317.

Chapter 16

Evaluating Performance in a Complex, Adaptive System (CAS)

Glenda H. Eoyang and Thomas H. Berkas

Individuals, programs, and teams at all levels of an organization are expected to assess and report on their performance. Groups choose to evaluate performance for a variety of reasons. Evaluation data establish a foundation for continuous improvement and build frameworks for fact-based decision making. Such data establish individual and group accountability and support the effective use of resources. Organizations in education, nonprofit public service, government, and business recognize the need for effective formative and summative evaluation. Funders, participants, elected leaders, stakeholders, and other constituencies expect organizations to be able to evaluate performance.

Most evaluation processes are based on performance against predicted goals. Increasingly, institutions that are not able to provide such basic evaluative information risk losing the support of their funders and other stakeholders. Historically, evaluation programs were developed to work in organizations that were assumed to be closed, stable, and predictable. In many situations, linear, low-dimension evaluation systems provided adequate data to represent organizational performance approximately. Such evaluation approaches were close enough to meet the needs of organizations and their supporters.

To be effective, however, an evaluation program must match the dynamics of the system to which it is applied. Recent research in organizational management, behavior, and psychology indicates that human systems behave as complex, adaptive systems. Organizational systems that were once stable are moving outside the range of linear, predictable behaviors and entering into the regime of chaotic or complex adaptive behavior. Prediction and controlled performance toward a goal, like those assumed by traditional evaluation methods, cannot be expected from a complex, adaptive system (CAS). For this reason, new tools, techniques, and methods must be designed to meet the needs of constituencies that request evaluation of organizations while they are in the more dynamic phases of complex adaptation.

Recent research reflects two approaches to applications of complexity in the evaluation of human systems. The first focuses on new descriptions of the evaluation process. It pulls metaphors from various CAS applications to explain the evaluation process as emergent and complex. As heuristic tools, these studies may encourage constructive conversations about the roles and strategies of program evaluation. They do not, however, offer integrated theory or pragmatic suggestions to improve the practice of evaluation. The second approach provides new measurement techniques to support data collection and analysis in complex systems. The most promising of these techniques is nonlinear time series analysis, which allows the evaluator to investigate patterns of behavior that emerge in a complex system over time.

This chapter seeks to build a third type of bridge between complexity science and evaluation of performance of human systems. By bringing together the complex and adaptive characteristics of human systems and the aims of evaluation, the chapter seeks to identify new theoretical grounding and new practical approaches that will improve the effectiveness of evaluation of human systems. It describes the characteristics of CASs that relate to evaluation design and implementation. It defines some principles that should guide evaluation in a CAS and introduces five tools and techniques to support evaluation in a CAS. Finally, it outlines the role of the evaluator in a complex environment. The purpose is to use complexity theory to bridge the gap between the assumptions of traditional, linear evaluation systems and the dynamical behavior of the human systems they are designed to assess.

CHARACTERISTIC BEHAVIORS OF CAS

A CAS is defined in terms of its parts, the behavior of those parts, and the emergent behavior of the whole. A complex, adaptive system (CAS) consists of interdependent agents. The behavior of each agent conforms to a short list of simple rules, and the group of agents exhibits emergent, systemwide patterns of behavior.

All CASs have some features and behaviors in common. A subset of those characteristics, specifically, ones that are relevant to evaluation, are addressed later. Each is defined, and its effect on evaluation systems is described. These characteristics include

- Dynamic
- Massively entangled
- Scale-independent
- Transformative
- Emergent

Dynamic

A CAS exists in a state of dynamic flux. Because of the number of agents, their interdependence, and their openness to external influences, a CAS changes constantly and discontinuously.

Constant change in a CAS is driven by the number of agents, their association with their own rules of behavior, and the interdependence between the agents and their environments. These complex interactions generate a system that is roiling with change. At no point does the system come to a natural equilibrium or stopping point. Many different metaphors have been used to describe this dynamic phenomenon in human systems. You can imagine such action to be permanent whitewater, a sandpile, shifting sands, unshackled action, coupled fitness landscapes, or any number of computer simulation models. All of these images connote the ever-changing nature of a CAS.

This change does not always follow a smooth, predictable pattern. Change happens at every point in time, but it may bring surprising outcomes. From a traditional point of view, any continuous change implies a smooth curve of effects over any given interval. This constraint does not affect the behavior of the CAS. While change in a CAS is continual (the system is always in motion), the change may not be continuous because it may not follow a smooth, predictable curve. It may come in bursts that are apparently random. Random jumps and discontinuities (bifurcations or punctuated equilibria) shape the emergent dynamics of the CAS.

For this reason, the evaluator cannot expect a smooth, linear path between project start and project end. System performance does not improve along a straight line or even a smooth curve. Bursts of activity may be preceded by long periods of apparent stasis. There may be no correlation between the percentage of time or resources consumed in a project and the percentage of distance moved toward a goal. Such unpredictable patterns cannot be assessed by means of periodic sampling or end-point evaluation only.

These temporal and dynamical characteristics challenge many of the assumptions of the traditional evaluator. The evaluator cannot realistically consider an organization or a program to be moving in a predictable way toward a predetermined end point. This means that social systems do not move inexorably toward a project's end point. They may not come to rest even when the end of a project is reached. An evaluator may be able to assign an arbitrary beginning and end date of an intervention, but the system itself recognizes no such boundaries in time. For this reason, the whole concept of projected and predictable outcomes is an artificial construct when evaluating performance in a CAS. An evaluator may be able to frame expectations, but the self-organizing nature of the system may result in completely different outcomes from those expected.

Evaluators and evaluation plans must adjust to the perpetual, but unpredictable, dynamic behavior of a CAS. The changing patterns within the system must be captured and described, without depending on natural end points of behavior or extrapolation or interpolation from timed samples.

Dynamic evaluation principles. Because a CAS is dynamic, evaluation systems should incorporate flexible and dynamic features. Specifically, they should

- Capture an emerging model of causal relationships. Assessment captures and describes change in a system based on current understanding of the context and causes for that change. Change can be acknowledged only when compared to some baseline or starting point. Because the patterns of causation are one of the things that change in a CAS, it is critical to capture baseline representation of those causal relationships, but it is necessary to revise that image frequently. Evolution of the causal model over time can provide a powerful and simple description of the systemic aspects of change.
- Evaluate and revise the evaluation design often. Because the CAS baseline is constantly shifting, the evaluation plan should include options for frequent and iterative reconsideration and redesign. Data about the redesign of the evaluation program can also become a rich source of information about the developing patterns of the system.
- Capture, preserve, and learn from the "noise" in the system. Most evaluation programs focus on the relatively narrow range of expected behaviors. In a CAS, much of the meaningful information about system future, patterns, and dynamics comes instead from the unexpected system behaviors. For this reason, evaluation should capture the unexpected as well as the expected, the long- and short-term outcomes, and the close and distant points of view. Only from these diverse data can an evaluation emerge that is sophisticated enough to reflect the complexity of the system being evaluated.

Dynamic evaluation tool. In the dynamics of a CAS, even the relationships of causes and effects change over time. As described earlier, for maximum utility, an evaluation approach needs to capture the changes in causation during the course of an intervention. For example, consider a causal diagram, which is one option for representing the causal logic of a system. A variety of other symbol sets would work as well. Other potentially useful methods include stocks and flows modeling from system dynamics, process modeling from information systems design techniques, or mind mapping from creativity methodologies.

Regardless of the systems used, to be most effective the representation should be

- Graphic and well-labeled
- As simple as possible
- Generated by a group of concerned and involved stakeholders
- Widely distributed for use throughout the system
- Reviewed and revised frequently

A causal diagram provides many different benefits to an evaluation program. Conversation about basic cause-and-effect reasoning in the system will help surface and reconcile divergent mental models. The causal diagram can establish the foundation for other aspects of the evaluation system by defining major variables, indicators, and hoped-for outcomes. Periodic review and revision provide natural points of evaluation and assessment. Major shifts in the causal diagram signal discontinuities in the dynamically changing CAS environment.

Massively Entangled

Relationships in CASs are complicated and enmeshed. Kontopolous (1993) describes CASs as massively entangled because the component parts of the systems and the variables describing those parts are large in number and interrelated in complicated ways. Two kinds of entanglement relate directly to evaluation: among the large number of variables that determine system behavior and among system participants.

Many CASs are driven by a large number of interdependent variables. The behavior of most CASs is influenced by a wide variety of factors. (The exception, of course, is deterministic chaos, in which system behavior emerges from a small number of nonlinear relationships.) In addition to being numerous, variables can be nonlinear and discontinuous. Some dimensions vary in their influence over time. They may lie dormant for long periods until some control parameter reaches a critical value and sparks them into action.

One way to respond to these multiple and unruly variables is to look for those "differences that make a difference" in the system. The number of potential differences is quite large and virtually unknowable in social systems. For example, adolescents' behavior may depend on age, gender, physical type, family stability, relationships with peers, and so on. In addition, over time, the relevance, power, or interrelationships among differences may change. Such a complex interaction of variables makes it unrealistic to expect to represent the system with a finite number of independent and dependent variables. Though some current trends in psychological assessment respond to multidimensionality of system response, most traditional evaluation systems seek to identify a small number of key variables that affect change and to establish the relationships among those variables. Unfortunately, these strategies are insufficient to represent the complicated interdependencies in a CAS.

In addition to being intractable (if not infinite) in number, the dimensions that drive behavior of a CAS have nonlinear relationships with each other. A small change in one variable may generate exponential change in another. This pattern is exacerbated because CASs depend on iterative processes. They repeat the same processes over and over again. The output of a previous process becomes the input for the next one. Iteration magnifies the effects of the nonlinearity, so that simple, causal relationships are virtually impossible to detect, measure, control, or evaluate.

These complex interrelationships demonstrate that the entanglement of variables in a CAS involves both their number and nonlinearity. These complex relationships limit the value of traditional causal reasoning, making it difficult to do at best and counterproductive at worst.

Another level of entanglement, however, introduces a different set of complexities to assessing behavior in a CAS. The parts of the system (individuals, groups, institutions) are related to each other in complicated and unpredictable ways. These systems demonstrate cross-current causality, which complicates analysis. Kontopoulos describes this characteristic of CASs as heterarchy, saying that their structures lie somewhere between the extremes of anarchy and hierarchy.

In Kontopoulos' model, anarchy allows for causality only from the part to the whole. Individuals are free to take action, and their actions determine the behavior of the whole group. Hierarchy, on the other hand, assumes only top-down causality. (Whatever is determined at the top of the organization will be carried out in all its parts.) Neither of these alternatives is rich enough to describe the range of behaviors of the CAS, whose interactions are driven by multidirectional causality. Sometimes the part determines the whole. Sometimes the whole determines the part. Sometimes parts determine each other. In a social system, for example, an unruly individual may necessitate a change in the rules, or pressure from peers may be sufficient to constrain the behavior of this individual. Each level of organization has a definite, though incomplete, causal relationship with all others.

In addition, the parts of the system are not related in simple, logical patterns. The structure of the system is not a simple arrangement of circles in a concentric set, with each higher level encompassing the lower ones completely. Rather, the system performs as a set of nonconcentric, interlocking spheres of influence. For example, in a simple pattern a child might be described as a member of a class within a grade level in a school in a district in a geographical area. In this logical, concentric model, each of these sets is totally encompassed in the next larger one. Though such a description is possible, it overlooks the rich interdependencies of other heterarchical relationships of family, friendships, religious associations, neighborhoods, reading groups, Scout troops, and so on. Such messy and multilevel causal relationships determine the behavior in a CAS and make it difficult for the evaluator to establish clear units of analysis or lines of causality.

Most traditional evaluation methods, both quantitative and qualitative, make assumptions to constrain the system and build a simple model of cross-scale relationship. Some assume that the system is based on concentric levels of organization to avoid the issue of complex crossing of boundaries between organizational levels. The evaluator may define the individual participant as part of an age cohort, which is part of a treatment group, which is part of a program, and so on. Each part of the system has its mutually exclusive definition with regard to all the rest.

Other evaluation methods focus on a single organizational level to bypass the issues of heterarchy altogether. These methods choose either the individual or the group as the unit of analysis and ignore the other levels to avoid cross-scale concerns and patterns.

Unidirectional causality is also a fundamental assumption for most evaluation programs. This approach identifies a simple, causal pattern as fundamental to its work. An evaluator will define a small set of causes and measure effects that are perceived to follow from those causes. Such a focus on predetermined causality denies the essential multicausal patterns in a heterarchical system. When an evaluator identifies variables and describes them as having dependent or independent relationships, the cross-causal nature of the system is ignored.

In a CAS, these simplifying assumptions are not valid. Because a CAS is heterarchical, linear methods of problem definition or methodological simplification are inadequate.

Entangled evaluation principles. CASs involve multiple "differences that make a difference" and complex interrelationships among system components. For this reason, evaluation systems should

- Incorporate multiple strategies, cycle times, time horizons, dimensions, and informants. Because a CAS has a structure that is non-linear, open, and high-dimensional, an evaluation design cannot predetermine all factors that will be of interest. For this reason, it is critical that a variety of data be collected to reflect the variability of the system. The practice of triangulation, which is common in qualitative research methods, is an example of such a strategy. Triangulation of informants, strategies, and time frames will help the evaluation program represent the complex dynamics of the system better. Such a diverse design will allow the evaluator to collect a wide range of information and to determine in hindsight what was most relevant. An effective CAS evaluation design will even incorporate linear evaluation strategies in short time frames and closed parts of the system where prediction appears to be possible.
- Be explicit about the language and meanings of evaluation findings. Interpretation in a CAS depends intimately on its heterarchical context. Evaluation will be distorted when the method is designed in one context, the data collected in another, and findings reported in still another. The complex interdependencies and unique dynamics of each environment require that context-specific identifying information be associated with all data and analysis that are used for evaluation.

Entangled evaluation tool. Iterative redesign generates an evaluation program that reflects the massive entanglements of the system. It also allows the evaluation design to coevolve with the system under investigation. Iterative redesign establishes a plan for periodic review and revision of the evaluation design throughout the life of the project. The practical problem with iterative redesign is that it is time-consuming and difficult to document and manage. This section suggests an approach that simplifies the process without losing its critical self-reflective advantages. It focuses on time horizons and collection/reporting scales of the system, which are the two main "differences that make a difference" in a dynamical system. It consists of a schedule of planned evaluations and a structured process to be repeated at regular intervals during the project.

The structured process consists of a small number of questions to be addressed by each group at each point in the schedule. At points designated on the plan, individuals or groups determine goals, evaluate performance against previously defined goals, and review projections for outcomes for each future time period by responding to the following questions:

- How did we perform against the projected outcomes for this time frame?

- What outcomes do we project for the next iteration of each time frame (indicators, data collection, and analysis methods)?
- What action should we take to move toward those outcomes?
- To whom and how should we communicate the results of this discussion?

A sample schedule of evaluation activities appears in Figure 16.1. Any particular project team will design the schedule to meet its needs. Because the points at which data are collected, analyzed, and reported will vary from project to project, the arrangement presented here is illustrative only. It is based on the following assumptions:

- The near-term time frames (week, month) can be varied to match the natural cycle time for the project. Some project outcome and long-term outcome frames should always be included, however. At each of these regular intervals, the evaluation design and performance against plan will be reviewed and revised. The shorter cycle times would represent more informal analysis of the plan and the longer times a more formal one. For example, the weekly redesign might consist of a five-minute discussion in a staff meeting, while the project review may involve a formal evaluation document.
- The arrows represent the collection and reporting patterns. Data are collected at the tail of the arrow, and findings are reported at the arrow's head. The thoroughness and formality of each of the data collection and distribution cycles would be determined by the team before the beginning of the intervention and modified as needed.
- The numbers indicate how many different evaluation contexts are included in the plan. This number will change with the needs of individual projects.
- The four levels of stakeholders (participant, project team, funder, and community) represent the scaled nature of the CAS. The names and the number of the groups can be varied as needed for the specific evaluation context. These groups can even be intersecting and entangled if the complexity of the project demands it.

This process involves an iterative schedule of evaluation and redesign and a simple set of questions to be used in each iteration. Such a structure can ensure that intended outcomes will be defined for each time period and that performance will be measured against those outcomes. The approach, however, does not lock the system into an unrealistic expectation for prediction or control, which is unrealistic in a CAS.

Scale-Independent

A CAS functions simultaneously at many different levels, or scales, of organization. Complex systems gain coherence across

Figure 16.1
Causality in Anarchy, Hierarchy, Heterarchy

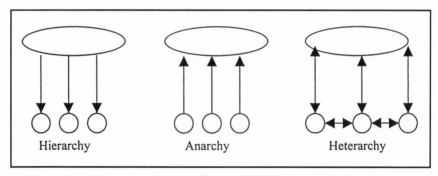

Source: Eoyang (1997).

levels because the same patterns appear at various levels. For example, the angles between the veins in a leaf are the same as those between twigs, branches, and roots. This self-similar structuring provides an integrity and comprehensibility to the system. The same scale-independent patterning can be observed in human systems. Individual agents take relatively independent actions; various groupings of agents emerge in the dynamical course of events; and the whole system exhibits identifiable behaviors. Behaviors in each of these domains are both similar to, and different from, behaviors in the other domains. An individual child may reflect the tension felt in an entire school, groups or gangs may form in response to this tension, and rumors may move through the faculty in response to specific incidents. Each of these domains is intimately associated with the others and exhibits both similarities and differences from them.

The complex outcome behaviors of a CAS may be the result of the iterative application of a "short list of simple rules." A cellular automaton, which is a type of computer simulation model, demonstrates most clearly the effect of a "short list." In a cellular automaton, a collection of interdependent agents is generated and represented as patches of light or darkness on a computer monitor. The agents can change their state by turning their light on or off. Each agent watches its neighbors and follows a short list of simple rules to determine its own local behavior. Over time, collections of these interdependent agents mimic a variety of complex behavior patterns (including the flight of a flock of birds, the life cycle of a bacterial colony, or the spread of infectious disease). The short list of simple rules is one mechanism that connects the parts to each other and to the whole and brings the coherence of scaling to the otherwise apparently orderless behavior of a CAS.

Traditional evaluation methods make basic assumptions about the relationships between the part and the whole in a human system. They do not depend on patterns that appear at multiple scales or on the possibility that complex patterns of behavior emerge from short lists of simple rules. Quantitative approaches to evaluation assume that uncontrolled interdependence among participants is minimal. The behavior of the whole group is seen as the sum of the behaviors of its parts. The coevolving, scale-independent nature of the CAS makes such an assumption unrealistic. In some CAS situations, the individual can act as proxy for the whole because certain patterns are constant across scales of the system. When behavior is driven by a short list of simple rules, observations of an individual provide clues to the behavior of the whole. In other situations, the emergent patterns are different in kind from the summation of the parts. New and unexpected, systemwide behaviors emerge from the complex interactions of the agents. Traditional evaluation systems are not designed to deal with self-similarity or the radical emergence that is evident in scaling phenomena of CASs.

Scaling evaluation principles. Because a CAS incorporates many self-similar levels of organization, an evaluation program must incorporate both micro- and macropatterns and structures. A specific evaluation program should

- Make information about the evaluation process open and accessible to all stakeholders. When information moves smoothly between and among organizational levels, self-similarity and its resultant coherence are encouraged. By being explicit about decisions and processes, evaluation becomes an effective, transforming feedback loop. As a process with multiple stakeholders, evaluation can support change and transformation efforts by participants in all parts of the system. Used in this way, evaluation becomes a part of the intervention, rather than some irrelevant activity.
- Be sensitive to both the similarities and the differences between contexts within the same system. Design and develop evaluation processes at the level where they will be used. Because certain system patterns are independent of scale, systemwide evaluation will uncover systemwide patterns. General rules and short lists of simple rules can be developed to apply to the entire system. On the other hand, each context has its own unique context, so specific evaluation plans must be designed to meet the unique needs of the local context. Not only will the measures be more relevant and meaningful, but also the process of defining the evaluation plan will contribute to the system transformation process.

Scaling evaluation tool. A short list of simple rules gives coherence across scales of a complex system. Given this dynamic of a

CAS, it is possible to develop a short list of simple rules that could generate a complex and effective evaluation program across many different parts of a complex human system. Such a strategy would use the inherent dynamics of the CAS to establish an evaluation program. This approach would involve developing a short list of simple rules that will help each individual and group in the system design and implement their own evaluation plans.

The systemwide evaluation plan that would emerge from this process would not be predictable because it would evolve as the system evolved. This approach provides a practical framework for the constructs of microdesign and microevaluation. Microdesign and microevaluation acknowledge that the system is changing too quickly to support large-scale planning or assessment. As an alternative, designers and evaluators focus on the smallest stable element (time, organizational unit, or functional component). An intervention or assessment is designed for each small unit. A consistent short list of simple rules would provide some coherence at the macrolevel as a foundation for microdesign. Such an evaluation system would emerge and integrate with the ongoing evolution of the system under observation.

Every part of the system would be expected to follow the same short list of simple rules for evaluation. The following rules might be sufficient to establish such a reflective evaluation process:

- Evaluate to inform action.
- Communicate findings to others in terms they care about and understand.
- Focus on "differences that make a difference."

If all stakeholders of a program followed these three rules, they would generate a cluster of evaluation activities that would look different from many traditional evaluation plans. One certainly could not predict the activities or the findings of the evaluation process, but all participants in the CAS would be informed productively about their performance and the performance of others in the system. The role of the professional or external evaluator in such a situation would be to help everyone involved watch the evaluation program emerge and to follow the same short list of simple rules to assess and improve the emerging evaluation process as a whole.

Transformative

The interdependent agents of a CAS are transformed and transforming in their interactions. Because a CAS and its agents are open systems, transformation occurs across the system's external boundaries. Feedback loops generate both change and stability in the system. Because each CAS is unique, its behavior is context-dependent. All of these transformative behaviors have major implications for the design and implementation of effective evaluation systems.

The agents that constitute a CAS are indefinite in number and are acted upon by forces external to the system. Bertalanffy (1968), in his seminal work *General System Theory: Foundations, Development, Applications* acknowledged that open systems were different in kind from the closed, well-behaved systems that were his focus. Weick (1979) applied the ideas of open systems and unplanned interdependencies to articulate a model of organizational behavior. Open systems are unpredictable, and their behaviors are dependent on context. System boundaries must be defined arbitrarily, and factors outside those boundaries may have as much influence on system behaviors as the dependent and independent variables defined within it. Agents and causal factors that lie outside the system at one time or place may be an integral part of the system at others. Because these systems are dependent on context and because each context is unique, CASs are themselves each unique. Two apparently similar systems may demonstrate profound differences over time. Even the same system, after the passage of time, may bear little resemblance to its previous configuration.

The transformative nature of a CAS influences evaluation in three ways. First, the evaluator cannot identify with any confidence which factors will influence outcomes. What appears to be relevant may become irrelevant, and the accidental may become causal in the course of an intervention. Second, participants in a system cannot be identified with any level of confidence. Sources of evaluation data may be inaccessible as they move in and out of the system of focus. While this feature complicates process evaluation, it makes longitudinal, individual study designs unfeasible. Finally, an evaluation system must be adaptable to the unique situation of each individual system. No matter how well a generic evaluation process is designed, it will be ineffective unless it is adapted to the unique situation of each local system under evaluation. A CAS cannot be evaluated in isolation from the environment in which it is embedded.

In the absence of a rigid external boundary, agents in a CAS are connected to each other by a complex network of transforming feedback loops. These loops carry resources (material, information, and energy) from one agent to another. When an agent receives a resource, it adapts and sends out responding messages to other agents in the system. These transforming feedback loops serve to give both stability and changeability to the CAS. They fuel the interdependence of the system by keeping the parts synchronized.

They support evolution of the system by providing impetus and resources for adaptation.

Feedback loops relate to evaluation in three distinct ways. First, evaluation is a powerful feedback loop. Designing an evaluation system and then collecting, analyzing, and reporting findings generate a tremendous amount of potentially transforming information. This information may generate a variety of change, especially if it is accessible to individual agents, emerging groups, and the system as a whole. The second way that feedback loops affect evaluation is as an object of evaluative focus. If feedback loops are the mechanism of transformation, it is logical to evaluate their effectiveness as a way to assess the performance of the organization as a whole. Finally, the evaluation process introduces a new set of feedback relationships in the system. By collecting and analyzing data, the evaluation process itself becomes a player in the complex emergence of behavior in a CAS. An evaluator must acknowledge this intimate interaction with the system.

Transformative evaluation principles. The CAS transforms and is transformed over time. Evolutionary change can be observed in individual and systemwide behavior over the course of an assessment period. Effective evaluation systems respond to this concern because they

- Make evaluation a part of the intervention. As a transforming feedback loop, assessment activities should enrich and enhance the intervention activities. To support this goal, the evaluation design should be as simple and self-documenting as possible. It should include simple, iterative activities, and it should be totally understood by as many stakeholders as possible.
- Involve as many members of the system as possible in the design of the evaluation system. Because each CAS is unique, any effective evaluation system will need to be adapted in situ. The evaluator increases understanding of the system and its dynamics when changes in the evaluation program are made during the design stage and before implementation begins. Discussion of the design can be a time of tremendous learning and adaptation on the part of all stakeholders. With effective and continuing feedback, the whole system can coevolve and adapt to the needs and aspirations of participants and the community.
- Use evaluation as a reinforcing, rather than damping, feedback mechanism. Especially early in a project, use evaluation procedures to find things to celebrate. Use the feedback to amplify the energy and commitment in the system.

Transformative evaluation tool. This approach represents an effort to identify and simplify the transforming feedback patterns for the evaluation process. It may also be used to identify the feedback loops that are intended to be part of the intervention. The entities in the system are represented in a Venn diagram. Lines between the components indicate the exchange of information, energy, and/ or resources. Each arrow can be described in terms of

- What information, energy, or other resource flows each way along the arrow?
- What transformation can be observed as a result of the exchange?
- How might the feedback loop be adapted to be more transforming?
- Should new feedback loops be added to the system? If so, where and how?
- What should be included in reflective feedback loops (not shown in the diagram) within each of the component parts?

Each feedback loop, then, becomes a focal point for observation, measurement, assessment and intervention in the system.

Emergent

CASs exhibit emergent, or self-organizing, behavior. New patterns are generated by the interaction of the agents. New structures are established, and old ones disappear. These structural changes are not designed and imposed by some force outside the system. They self-organize as the internal dynamics of the system play out over time. Two aspects of emergence in a CAS are of particular interest to evaluators: sensitive dependence on initial conditions and attractors' regimes.

A CAS is sensitive to small changes in initial conditions. An apparently trivial difference in the beginning state of the system can result in enormously different outcomes. This phenomenon is sometimes called the "butterfly effect."

The implications of the butterfly effect for evaluation in social CASs are many. Traditional evaluation tools assume the effectiveness of an intervention to be a direct result of the intervention itself. In a CAS, however, the results of the same intervention may vary widely because of small variations in initial conditions.

One of the implications of sensitive dependence is a need for a shift in thinking about outcome evaluation. Traditionally, outcome evaluation depended on a prediction of outcome, behavior required to move toward the outcome, and the measurement of progress to determine success or failure. Because of the butterfly effect, such a theory of "outcome evaluation" is not feasible in a CAS. Prediction is not possible, and controlled performance toward a goal is unrealistic, so evaluation based on performance against such a goal is meaningless. It is feasible to define an outcome in a CAS when it is recognized as a possible scenario result rather than a predicted outcome. It is perfectly reasonable to have hopes for the future of a CAS, to take action in each subsequent moment in the context of that hope, then to evaluate whether the hope became a reality in a given amount of time. This CAS approach to outcome evaluation, however, does not imply the model of prediction and control assumed by many traditional outcomes evaluators.

In addition to concerns about outcome definition and evaluation, many common assessment techniques use reliability as a measure of quality. Reliability requires that the same evaluation process be used multiple times with the same results. Because a CAS is sensitive to initial conditions, however, it is impossible to reproduce the same evaluation environment twice. For this reason, reliability is not a logical possibility in a CAS, so some other criterion is required to assess the effectiveness of evaluation programs.

Because of the butterfly effect, the future of a CAS is unpredictable, but not all of the future is equally uncertain. The near-term future can be relatively knowable; midterm will be less predictable; and far-term future will be uncertain at best. As the time horizon moves out, uncertainty increases because there will be more opportunities for various conditions and more time for those variations to magnify uncertainty. Because of this dynamic, an evaluation program must have distinct strategies for assessing a range of possible short-, medium- and long-term goals.

Sensitive dependence is one aspect of emergence in CASs, and it drives concerns about outcomes, reliability, and time horizons for evaluation systems. A second aspect of emergence deals with patterns that appear over time in the behavior of CASs. These patterns, called "attractors," provide some insight into the emerging relationships in a CAS.

Systems exhibit certain classical patterns of behavior over time. Scientists describe these patterns as attractors. An attractor is not like a magnet—it does not literally constrain the behavior of individuals in the system. Instead, an attractor is the pattern that forms as the individuals in the system interact. The individual behaviors form the pattern, and then other individuals are constrained to perform within the pattern. In this way, an attractor is emergent and self-reinforcing. Wherever an agent enters the system, it will move toward the established pattern of behavior, which is the predominant attractor regime. In this way, the activities of the agents in a complex system are patterned, though they are not predictable for any specific individual at any particular time.

Systems in motion generate one of four distinct patterns. The four categories of attractor are generally recognized to be point, periodic, strange, and random. A point attractor emerges when all parts of the system tend to converge to a single point. The common example of a point attractor is a marble rolling around in a round-bottomed bowl. Wherever the marble starts out, it will eventually reach the lowest point in the bowl. A periodic attractor emerges when the system oscillates from one value or position to another. Examples include a driven pendulum, the swimming suit industry, or the monthly financial reporting cycle. In all of these cases, the cycle is defined, and the system moves from one orderly position to the next. A strange attractor, which is characteristic of the behavior of a deterministic chaotic system, represents system behavior that stays within a bounded region without ever repeating the same sequence twice. A random attractor shows no discernible pattern at all. Each one of the attractor regimes describes an emergent pattern of behavior that is exhibited by a system, even though the behavior of the individual agents is unpredictable from one moment to another. By collecting time series data, the evaluator can reconstruct a portrait of the attractor regime for a particular system. The attractor is the primary method of "seeing" systemwide changes in behavior over time.

Studies of system maturity and creativity indicate that as systems mature, they tend to move from one attractor regime to another, beginning with random and moving through periodic, strange, and point attractor regimes in sequence. Discerning systemic patterns of behavior through attractors should be a standard technique for evaluation. The problem is that traditional techniques of evaluation do not provide the kind of data required for reconstruction of the system attractor. Attractor patterns can be discerned only from carefully designed time series analysis. The series must be of sufficient length. The sampling interval must be constant and scaled to the dynamical behavior of the system. Traditionally, many evaluation efforts collect data only at long and discrete intervals, such as the beginning and ending points of an intervention. These techniques do not capture the emerging patterns over time, so they are unable to reconstruct the attractor portrait for the system. Because the emerging attractor is the most trustworthy picture of systemwide behavior, evaluation methods should be designed to ensure that they capture and analyze the data that would reveal such patterns.

Emergent evaluation principles. The systemwide behaviors of a CAS emerge over time. For this reason, the evaluation system should focus on developmental and emergent patterns of behavior that

- Match the developmental stage of the system. Some evaluators refer to this as readiness assessment or evaluability assessment. They ask the question, Is this system mature enough to provide useful data during an evaluation? A CAS working in the regime of a random attractor may not provide information about systemwide progress toward outcomes, even though individual agents are progressing well. Such a system will require different evaluation techniques than a system that has matured to a point attractor regime. Consider the dynamical pattern that the system exhibits over time to design an evaluation program to capture the "differences that make a difference."

- Track patterns and pattern changes over time, rather than focusing exclusively on behaviors of specific individuals or groups. While it may be unreasonable to expect a particular path of development or a predetermined outcome from a CAS, emergent patterns of behavior can be expected outcomes. An effective evaluation system must be able to capture and report on these evolving patterns.

Emergent evaluation tool. The emergent nature of a CAS unfolds over time, so the only way to observe this emergence is through the use of time series analysis. In time series analysis, quantitative data are collected at regular intervals over a period of time. The sequence of numbers is analyzed to determine what patterns emerged in the data. A variety of analysis and modeling techniques can be used to discern patterns in time series data. Both linear and nonlinear techniques are available, and valuable information can be collected from both. Time series analysis has been used to assess various human systems behaviors in business, government, and industry. This approach has also been used to evaluate psychological behavior in humans.

This approach has many benefits as a method to identify and describe the emerging patterns of behavior in a CAS, but it also has its drawbacks. Specifically, the approach

- Requires a long time series for analysis. It is difficult to generate a time series of sufficient length from a human system.
- Is very sensitive to sampling rates. The sampling interval must be small enough to reveal the underlying pattern but not frequent enough to introduce irrelevant noise. Often, a sampling rate that is frequent enough for analysis makes unrealistic demands on the participants to collect and report data.
- Requires experienced analysts. Given the current technology, time series analysis is as much an art as a science. Analysts must have extensive experience with the tools and some familiarity with the context that generated the data before they can interpret the data realistically.
- Depends on mathematical algorithms that may not be valid or reliable. The tools for time series analysis are relatively new and are based on a variety of assumptions about the stability, stationarity, and distribution of the system under study. They are not appropriate for all applications with human CASs.
- Works best on systems with few dimensions. Current tools are unable to distinguish between a very high-dimension attractor and ran-

domness. Because most human CASs exist in high-dimension space, the tools may be ineffective.

In spite of its drawbacks, time series analysis and reconstruction of attractors promise to give real insight into the complex, entangled dynamics of evaluation of human systems. All of these tools and techniques (causal diagrams, iterative redesign, shorts and simples, feedback analysis, and time series analysis) provide ways for the evaluator to capture and interpret information about the performance of a human CAS. When these approaches are used in conjunction with more traditional quantitative and qualitative evaluation methods, it will be possible to generate an assessment of a CAS that matches the variety and richness of the system itself. Such an assessment will yield information that can be used by all participants of the system to improve performance, even when prediction and control are not possible.

This section has presented a summary of CAS behaviors that are most closely related to evaluation. As CASs, human systems are dynamic, entangled, scale-independent, transformative, and emergent. These characteristics challenge the basic assumptions of traditional evaluation methods. They necessitate new evaluation approaches that are as rich and varied as the human systems they are designed to assess. The next section suggests a new role for the evaluator of such a dynamic system.

ROLE OF THE EVALUATOR

Complex, adaptive dynamics do more than just require new tools and techniques for evaluation. They also transform the evaluator's role. Rather than being concerned with defining and measuring performance against specific outcomes, the evaluator takes on the task of designing and implementing transforming feedback loops across the entire system. This role of transforming agent falls into two primary categories: absorbing uncertainty and making learning the primary outcome.

Absorbing uncertainty. Change unfolds continually in a CAS. Individuals and their organizations express anxiety during times of change and uncertainty. Evaluators have an opportunity to mediate this anxiety in three ways. They can help the system understand and make sense of the CAS dynamics they observe. By explaining the basics of CAS, the evaluator can help the organization be reflective about its experiences and fears. Second, evaluators can help articulate the CAS dynamics within a given, local context. By stating, and encouraging others to state, the dynamic patterns in the environment, the group can begin to build mechanisms to cope in the future. Finally, the evaluator can lower the cost of failure. By framing an evaluation method as experimentation and learning, the evaluator can encourage individuals and groups to value their mistakes and to learn from them. All of these intervention approaches can help the evaluator absorb the pain of uncertainty and lack of control that are hallmarks of the CAS.

Making learning the primary outcome. Effective adaptation is the best indicator of success in a CAS. Evaluators can use their experiences and expertise to focus on learning as an adaptive mechanism. To do this, the evaluator should

- Emphasize the importance of variety in a system.
- Distinguish between exploitative and exploratory learning and help groups find the appropriate uses of each.
- Encourage the use of scenario planning and creative approaches to planning for the future.
- Encourage every individual in the organization to think about the multiple, heterarchical levels of organizational structure.

From this perspective, the evaluator is less an instrument of assessment in the organization and more an instrument of transformative change. Evaluators can provide a valuable service to the CAS organization by designing, implementing, and maintaining effective feedback loops between and among system components.

CONCLUSION

As long as human systems behaved in linear and predictable patterns, traditional methods of evaluation were sufficient. As human systems move toward complex, adaptive behavior, however, the assumptions that are the foundation for evaluation are no longer valid. In some circumstances, the traditional evaluation approaches are effective, and in others they are woefully lacking. A CAS perspective on evaluation opens the door to approaches that truly reflect the complexity and adaptation of the human systems they represent. Such an approach integrates divergent techniques of the past and presents new alternatives for the future.

As described in this chapter, a CAS approach to evaluation does not replace more traditional approaches. Rather, it provides a theoretical framework that incorporates many tools and techniques that were previously considered to be at odds with each other. Qualitative and quantitative approaches of all kinds can play significant roles in the evaluation of a complex, adaptive system. A CAS model of evaluation is most useful when complexity renders other methods of evaluation ineffective; when evaluation will be used to challenge existing assumptions of linear causality; or when the interventions to be evaluated are designed to reflect the complex, adaptive nature of the system.

This chapter has outlined the behaviors of CAS and related those behaviors to the issues of evaluation. It has also identified principles and tools for an evaluation program that would be effective in a CAS. Finally, it has outlined the role of the evaluator in a healthy CAS.

REFERENCES

Bak, P. (1996). *How Nature Works: The Science of Self-Organized Criticality.* New York: Copernicus.

Bertalanffy, L. (1968). *General System Theory: Foundations, Development, Applications.* New York: George Braziller.

Briggs, J. and F. D. Peat. (1989). *Turbulent Mirror: An Illustrated Guide to Chaos Theory and the Science of Wholeness.* New York: Harper and Row.

Cooperrider, D. and S. Srivastva. (1987). "Appreciative Inquiry in Organizational Life." *Research in Organizational Change and Development,* Vol. 1, 129–169.

Cowan, G. D. Pines and D. Meltzer. (1994). *Complexity: Metaphors, Models, and Reality.* New York: Addison-Wesley.

Deming, E. (1986). *Out of the Crisis.* Boston: Massachusetts Institute of Technology.

Devore, J. and R. Peck. (1994). *Introductory Statistics.* 2d ed. St. Paul, MN: West.

Dooley, K. (1996). "A Nominal Definition of Complex Adaptive Systems." *The Chaos Network,* Vol. 8, No. 1, 2–3.

Dooley, K. (1997). "A Complex Adaptive Systems Model of Organizational Change." *Nonlinear Dynamics, Psychology, and Life Sciences,* Vol. 1, No. 1, 69–97.

Eoyang, G. (1997). *Coping with Chaos: Seven Simple Tools.* Cheyenne, WY: Lagumo.

Fetterman, D., S. Kaftarian, and A. Wandersman (eds.). (1996). *Empowerment Evaluation: Knowledge and Tools for Self-Assessment and Accountability.* Thousand Oaks, CA: Sage.

Fink, A. and J. Kosecoff. (1996). *How to Conduct Surveys: A Step-by-Step Guide.* Newbury Park, CA: Sage.

Gell-Mann, M. (1994). *The Quark and the Jaguar.* New York: W. H. Freeman.

Gleick, J. (1988). *Chaos: Making a New Science.* New York: Viking Penguin.

Goldstein, J. (1994). *The Unshackled Organization.* New York: Productivity Press.

Gray, P. (ed.). (1994). *Decision Support and Executive Information Systems.* Englewood Cliffs, NJ: Prentice-Hall.

Guastello, S. (1995). *Chaos, Catastrophe, and Human Affairs: Applications of Nonlinear Dynamics to Work, Organizations, and Social Evolution.* Mahwah, NJ: Lawrence Erlbaum Associates.

Guba, E. and Y. Lincoln. (1989). *Fourth Generation Evaluation.* Newbury Park, CA: Sage.

Guess, D. and W. Sailor. (1993). "Chaos Theory and the Study of Human Behavior: Implications for Special Education and Developmental Disabilities." *The Journal of Special Education*, Vol. 27, No. 1, 16–34.

Haynes, S. (1995). "Introduction to the Special Section on Chaos Theory and Psychological Assessment." *Psychological Assessment*, Vol. 7, No. 1, 3–4.

Haynes, S., D. Blaine, and K. Meyer. (1995). "Dynamical Models for Psychological Assessment: Phase Space Functions." *Psychological Assessment*, Vol. 7, No. 1, 17–24.

Heiby, E. (1995a). "Assessment of Behavioral Chaos with a Focus on Transitions in Depression." *Psychological Assessment*, Vol. 7, No. 1, 10–16.

Heiby, E. (1995b). "Chaos Theory, Nonlinear Dynamical Models, and Psychological Assessment." *Psychological Assessment*, Vol. 7, No. 1, 5–9.

Kantz, H. and T. Schreiber. (1997). *Nonlinear Time Series Analysis*. New York: Cambridge University Press.

Kaplan, D. and L. Glass. (1995). *Understanding Nonlinear Dynamics*. New York: Springer-Verlag.

Kauffman, S. (1995). *At Home in the Universe*. New York: Oxford University Press.

Kellert, S. (1993). *In the Wake of Chaos*. Chicago: University of Chicago Press.

Kelly, K. (1994). *Out of Control*. New York: Addison-Wesley.

Kerlinger, F. (1985). *Foundations of Behavioral Research*. 3d ed. New York: Holt, Rinehart, and Winston.

Kibel, B. (1996). "Evaluation Using Results Mapping." *New Designs for Youth Development* (Winter), 9–15.

Kiel, L. D. (1994). *Managing Chaos and Complexity in Government: A New Paradigm for Managing Change, Innovation, and Organizational Renewal*. San Francisco: Jossey-Bass.

Kontopoulos, K. (1993). *The Logics of Social Structure*. New York: Cambridge University Press.

Lewin, R. (1992). *Complexity: Life at the Edge of Chaos*. New York: Macmillan.

Lorenz, E. (1993). *The Essence of Chaos*. Seattle: University of Washington Press.

Mainzer, K. (1994). *Thinking in Complexity: The Complex Dynamics of Matter, Mind, and Mankind*. New York: Springer-Verlag.

March, J. (1994). *A Primer on Decision Making: How Decisions Happen*. New York: Free Press.

Morgan, G. (1997). *Images of Organization*. 2d ed. Thousand Oaks, CA: Sage.

Morrow, K. (1990). "Evaluating Communicative Tests." Annual Meeting of the Regional Language Centre Seminar, Singapore.

Olson, D. and J. Courtney. (1992). *Decision Support Models and Expert Systems*. New York: Macmillan.

Pandit, S. and S. Wu. (1983). *Time Series and Systems Analysis with Applications*. New York: John Wiley and Sons.

Patton, M. (1990). *Qualitative Evaluation and Research Methods*. 2d ed. Newbury Park, CA: Sage.

Patton, M. (1997). *Utilization-Focused Evaluation: The New Century Text*. 3d ed. Newbury Park, CA: Sage.

Paulson, F. and P. Paulson. (1991). "The Ins and Outs of Using Portfolios to Assess Performance." Revised. Joint Annual Meeting of the National Council of Measurement in Education and the National Association of Test Directors, Chicago.

Prigogine, I. and I. Stengers. (1988). *Order Out of Chaos*. New York: Bantam New Age Books.

Richey, R. (1994). "Design 2000: Theory-Based Design Models of the Future." Proceedings of Selected Research and Development Presentations at the 1994 National Convention of the Association for Educational Communications and Technology, Nashville, TN.

Stacey, R. (1993). *Managing the Unknowable*. New York: Jossey-Bass.

Stacey, R. (1996). *Creativity and Complexity in Organizations*. San Francisco: Berrett-Koehler.

Strauss, A. and J. Corbin. (1990). *Basics of Qualitative Research: Grounded Theory Procedures and Techniques*. Newbury Park, CA: Sage.

Stringer, E. (1996). *Action Research: A Handbook for Practitioners*. Thousand Oaks, CA: Sage.

Vaill, P. (1996). *Learning as a Way of Being: Strategies for Survival in a World of Permanent White Water*. New York: Jossey-Bass.

Van de Ven, A. (1993). "The Emergence of an Industrial Infrastructure for Technological Innovation." *Journal of Comparative Economics*, Vol. 17, 338–365.

Waldrop, M. M. (1992). *Complexity: The Emerging Science at the Edge of Order and Chaos*. New York: Simon and Schuster.

Weick, K. (1979). *The Social Psychology of Organizing*. New York: Random House.

West, B. and W. Deering. (1995). *The Lure of Modern Science: Fractal Thinking*. River Edge, NJ: World Scientific.

Wheatley, M. (1992). *Leadership and the New Science*. San Francisco: Berrett-Koehler.

Wheatley, M. (1997). *A Simpler Way*. San Francisco: Berrett-Koehler.

Chapter 17

Complexity Metaphors and the Process of Small Business Foresighting

Ted Fuller

The context of this chapter is ways of thinking about the future state of a present phenomenon. Thinking about "the future" is a rather abstract idea, whereas contemplating what changes might occur to a certain defined object is conceptually possible. The particular object of study in this context is the population of small firms in the United Kingdom.

The notion of a "population" of small firms is in itself a constructed concept. However, it is not without meaning, as government policy and the business strategies of those who interact with numbers of small firms as a market are directed by notions of aggregate ontological homogeneity.

On the surface at least, the population of small firms seems to resemble the characteristics Holland ascribes to a complex, adaptive system (see Chapter 16). They can also be conceptualized to fit John Casti's working definition of a complex, adaptive system (Casti, 1998). First, the firm needs to be thought of as an "individual agent," and the population as a collection of individual agents. Second, each firm is in receipt of local information, which means that it does not share the precise information that all agents have in the space in which it exists, nor does it have an overview of the whole of that space. Third, it is "intelligent," that is, uses mechanisms to direct what it does (often called "rules" in this domain). Fourth, it is adaptive, that is, able to change what it does and the rules it follows.

If the population (or subpopulations) of small firms are analogous with notions of a complex, adaptive system, then in what ways can complexity theory inform an understanding of the behavior of small firms? How can it help in anticipating change in the population of small firms?

This case study illustrates the weaving of a complexity discourse into an enterprise that sought to contemplate the future of small firms in the U.K. It first discusses the metaphors of complexity and the epistemological limitations that any modeling approach has inherently. It notes, however, that meaning and actions can arise from the language grounded in abstract models.

The domain of futures studies is introduced, and the analogies between that and complexity are drawn. The conjunction between these theoretical principles and the substantive domain of the small firm is discussed. The way that these ideas were operationalized in a scenario-building process, involving human experts as the mechanisms for "structural coupling," is then described. The resulting scenarios, formed from the "edge of chaos" metaphor, are described. A discussion then reflects on the meaning of this approach with respect to anticipating alternative futures, if not to prediction per se.

COMPLEXITY METAPHORS

Complexity theory provides metaphors that give meaning to observed and simulated reality. Complexity theory, or studies, is founded on observed similarities in diverse dynamical patterns. The essence of dynamical systems is that they are open and dissipative, and they do not follow the predictable, entropic path of closed systems tending to chaos; rather, they move in patterns at the edge of order and chaos.

Complexity is a systemic concept. Its purpose is in understanding the behavior of interconnected phenomena (which we call systems). The similarities of different dissipative systems, such as ecologies, insect populations, brains, and so on, give rise to a number of linguistic schema or metaphors by which similarities in these different phenomena can be compared. These metaphors provide a language to describe patterns of behavior in complex, adaptive systems. The metaphors are of dynamics and form.

If a "system" under investigation is assumed to behave as a dissipative system or as a complex, adaptive system, then metaphors of the general dynamics of these systems may provide a conceptual framework for understanding the dynamics of that specific system. That is, general features of a dynamical system can explain specific corresponding instances. Complexity studies as a general enterprise is one in which system worlds are created, their dynamics observed, and inferences drawn about real-world behavior and explanations for this. System worlds are created at varying levels of abstraction from the reality of the objects they represent. In computer simulations, for example, properties of real-world objects are abstracted, represented, and used as building blocks, becoming, in effect, the theory (future) of the represented world.

There are difficulties, in epistemological principles, with this approach. It is open to a fallacy that metaphors are the same as reality. Theoretically, models are fictitious constructions, the language of "as if," not "what is" (Harvey and Reed, 1996: 309). Complexity is a discourse of models and abstractions. Models, as opposed to theories, are well-formed metaphors and analogies. They do not claim to express the truth of the world, merely to provide heuristic insights. For example, how can the completeness of a "system" be verified? Critical theorists, for example, assume the existence of causal mechanisms of power whose workings can be observed or inferred but also assert the existence of liabilities and latent capacities that are unobservable (Bhaskar, 1989). Similarly, as Cohen and Stewart argue, similar forms of order can be the result of quite different initial conditions and different rules. They call this "complicity," and it alludes to a process where simple systems interact in a way that both changes and erases their dependence on initial conditions (Cohen and Stewart, 1994: 417).

However, such is the power of metaphor in language that the meaning taken from these systemic studies is, arguably, "what is," not "as if." Understanding through language is one way in which the human interpreting mechanisms are "coupled" to the environment. Inferences about the real world have real meaning; they cause particular sense-making (Weick, 1995) and particular behavior. Meanings are culturally shaped, and the power of conceptual ideas transmitted by particular linguistic allusions is important. Reflecting on phenomena through a particular languaging gives those phenomena meaning, which, in turn, guides behavior.

Complexity theory contributes to an understanding of dynamics. It has been suggested that causes of specific instances of behavior in a domain cannot be discovered from the metaphors of complexity. For example, Lissack in a substantial discussion on complexity metaphors suggests that complexity theory provides descriptive power, but no means of "proof" (Lissack, 1996). Quoting Scott Barton (1994) in *American Psychologist*:

These [metaphorical] definitions bear little resemblance to the definition of chaos in the physical sciences....[they] offer no cure for the profound difficulty faced in the establishment reliability and validity of their research....

Concepts of chaos, nonlinear dynamics, and self-organizing systems can allow investigators to explore a variety of areas from new and promising angles, ones that many may have never before considered.

It is argued here that devices of complex, adaptive systems research, in particular, simulation, may assist the identification of causality or influence. As will be shown, the language of complexity is a coordinating mechanism. Meaning is made through language. Languaging, as Maturana suggests, is the "coordination of coordinations" (Maturana and Varela, 1994). So, while metaphors or models are incomplete, fallible descriptions or explanations of the world, they do direct behavior. If they direct behavior, they are mechanisms for creating futures and therefore for anticipating futures.

FUTURES STUDIES—WAYS OF ANTICIPATING CHANGES IN "PHASE SPACE"

A key relationship between complexity theory and futures studies is with time. Futures studies assumes that the future is a continuation from the present, though it will not be the same as the past or present, and that future events and outcomes cannot be predicted accurately (Bell, 1997). This is analogous to ideas in complexity theory that the explanation of events has a strong temporal element, that is, that events are caused by previous events.

The notion of time in complexity is not linear "clock" time. The meaning of time in this domain is one of phases, for example, periodicy of events or generations of objects. However, the underlying "arrow of time" is one-way, irreversible. Future studies is concerned with the relationship of the present with the future, that is, to identify future implications of today's actions. In principle it situates the human agent as being in a phase or cycle of events or as a precursor to, and cause of, future generations.

The proximity of futures studies to the ideas of complexity studies, for example, evolutionary theory, has been noted previously, (e.g., Mannermaa, 1992). Complexity theory is not the futures studies paradigm. Futures studies embraces a number of paradigms and is frequently humanistic in its motives. For instance, foresight is seen as an individual skill or social/cultural principle, rather than an analytical enterprise. Nor do all theories that anticipate or explain changes in human behavior rely on systems thinking.

One important similarity of the two sets of ideas is the shared perspective that explanations of phenomena and their behavior and hence predictions about their future cannot be based solely on the analysis of observed, empirical evidence. The nature of the relationships between the present and the future is fundamental to both futures studies and complexity theory. We do not study "the future," we study (presearch?) the future of something that exists now. If certain features of the phenomenon under study are analogous to a "dynamical" system, then expectations of patterns of behavior of those features can be informed by the metaphors of complexity.

Complexity theory offers dynamical patterns and metaphors for these patterns, for example, patterning of time, such as the notion of phase space, and patterning of paths or trajectories in time (to the future), for instance, bifurcation and attractors. These patterns, as it is shown, can inform meaning or significance in a substantive domain.

SCENARIOS

Scenario writing is a technique that simulates reality to explore possible futures. Scenarios are a central plank of futures studies, "one of the most productive and durable of all futures tools" (Slaughter, 1997: 338). They are constructed from building blocks of known ontological features extrapolated to a common (future) time period. They are essentially metaphorical. Bijl (1992) defines a scenario as "a description of the present situation in society and of a possible and desirable or possible situation in the future, as well as a description of the events that can lead to that future. A scenario study, in other words, means delineating possible alternatives for the present." Such scenarios take a well-defined set of assumptions, then develop an imaginative conception of what the future would be like if these assumptions were true, thus presenting a number of possible alternatives, each one based on certain assumptions and conditions (Grainger, 1980). They thus rely on commonly accepted regularity of features (or, in Gell-Mann's terms, schemata) for their validity (Gell-Mann, 1994).

Scenarios are produced from simulations of the interaction of known features of a domain at a particular ontological level. The possible substantive values of the features of that system, at the ontological level under analysis, are interpreted through the known (present) metaphors of that system or analogous systems. The value of scenarios themselves is that alternative, extreme cases can yield unexpected illuminations of phenomena. The processes of scenario building are valuable as a form of theory building and communication.

The nature of simulations that yield scenarios varies widely. For example, in some cases the simulation is computed from highly explicit rules and equations, and in some cases the simulation is analogical, using chemical or physical artifacts. Scenarios in the social science domain tend to be created by "soft simulation," that is, the intervention of human interpretation in the creation of nonmathematical metaphorical schemata.

The creation of scenarios of whatever kind requires theory about what salient features exist in the domain in question and the nature of the dynamical relationships between agents in that domain.

The following section relates the experience gained from adopting ideas from complexity theory to the enterprise of scenario building with respect to the future for small firms.

THE LANDSCAPE OF SMALL FIRMS

The population of small firms in the U.K. is economically and socially important. Government statistics indicate that small firms account for about 30 percent of GDP and about half of private sector employment (DTI, 1997). The future of this population is likely to be important to the U.K. economy and society, but there is limited study on this future aspect of small firms. Small firms themselves in general do not have a long-term perspective. There are good reasons for this. As individuals they have very little power to influence even their own future. Their "flexibility" may be their greatest economic strength, though this notion of flexibility is not what it may seem. As a population, they are flexible. The births and deaths of firms are high. Entrepreneurs start new ventures on the back of old ones. Rates of start-up (and death) are higher in emerging fields of activity. For individual firms, the meaning of flexibility may be a rather painful and costly demise.

The notion of a "population" of small firms is in itself a constructed concept. The population is heterogeneous. That is, it apparently has different observed characteristics and dynamics. The population as such takes on meaning to the observer through diverse constructs. Some businesses exist (can be counted) as "registered" for value-added tax, some as limited companies having a "legal status." Some businesses are self-employed people or are what families do to earn a living. Entrepreneurs may own or run one or more businesses. Some businesses have property or business premises, and businesses produce economic "added value" in various forms, in relationship with other businesses.

It is suggested that the analogy of a complex, adaptive system can be applied to the population of small firms. Each business is different. Each has its own "initial conditions," and each incurs a number of "accidents" in its temporal path. Given that entrepreneurs are "innovative," then many businesses will operate with their own "rules," as well as complying (more or less) with more general rules. There is a great deal of "replication" in the population as one firm copies another's ideas, and government policy encourages firms to adopt "best practice."

Evolutionary metaphors of emergence, fitness, and replication resonate with observations of the large number of smaller firms in the economy. Small businesses are not a homogeneous population. They vary considerably in size and sector activity, their ownership, their location and the markets served and so on. Some of the features of their domain are shared in common. Most businesses interact with key economic stakeholders, such as banks and government agencies. Businesses operate in a regulated environment, providing at least some of the "rules" of behavior. The fundamental "energy" or resource of most businesses is cash, without which activities usually cease.

The nature of the relationship between the environment and the small firm or various aggregations of small firms is a complex issue and not explained by any single theory. Naman and Slevin (1993) identified a relationship between organizational complexity and environmental complexity. Gibb (1993) provides a descriptive model of the firm as having various "relationships" with a range of organizations. Mitchell and Agle (1995) set these relationships in a theoretical framework as "stakeholder relationships." Stakeholders include owners, employees, customers, suppliers, investors, and lenders. Small firms are theorized as operating in "networks" by a number of researchers, including Johannisson (1987), Jarillo (1988), Lorenzoni and Ornati (1988), and Larson (1992). These studies stress the importance of both social and economic rationale for the relationships.

This discourse on the importance of relationships between the individual firm and other "agents" in its environment is resonant with ecological metaphors, or the "multiagent space" of artificial life simulations, such as SWARM (Hiebeler, 1994). However, the nature of the relations and "coupling" between small firms and their environment is not well enough understood to have yet produced plausible complex, adaptive models.

At this stage in our research, the notion of the firm in a nexus of stakeholder relationships is used as a conceptual basis for a "theory of the firm." The nature of these relationships is not well articulated in the literature. For example, its representation in agency theory (Williamson, 1991) as a nexus of contracts does not adequately take account of qualitative or noneconomic factors. These ideas are further developed elsewhere in the context of understanding the variety in small firms as a range of business styles (Fuller, Lewis, et al., 1997).

The landscape for the small firm, then, is one of flows of many interagent (stakeholder) relationships over time. The terrain changes rapidly as each stakeholder changes, such that the "whole" picture, if such a notion is realistic, is highly unpredictable. What, then, is an appropriate ontology or ontological level to assume for the purposes of scenario building in this environment?

The choice of ontology was informed by the notion of emergence from conditions. The dynamics of the small enterprise is characterized by rapid change, with "halflives" of around three years. Not only is there a high churn rate (births and deaths) of enterprises, but also existing businesses are in continuous change and adaptation to new environments. Such is their dependence on their stakeholders that it was assumed that the path of coevolution could be reduced to a consideration of the nature of emergence from the stakeholder environment. This notion is that the future of an agent can be simulated by simulating the environment upon which it depends, rather than by following the path of an individual agent. The question to ask is what the meaning of "fitness" is in a defined environment, rather than trying to track the unpredictable path of a particular agent. The conceptual unit of analysis is, therefore, "fitness" or some notion of what the characteristics are of an agent surviving in a particular nexus of relationships.

There is an obvious flaw in this principle, which is that the agents themselves influence the evolution of the landscape. Small firms shape the future of their stakeholders. It is recognized that this flaw may be important but is ignored because of the relative weakness of the small firm in its influence on the landscape. Small firms are individual and have relatively little power. Bolton noted this definitional characteristic in his influential report (HMSO, 1971). Nor do small firms act as a group on their stakeholders. Each operates individually. Therefore, the forces that might shape overall stakeholder response are more likely to be cultural rather than a function of collectivism of small firms. This does not ignore that an individual entrepreneur or business type can make a "symmetry-breaking" change in landscape, as exemplified by Howard Sherman's "Supercuts." It assumes that these interfirm or sectoral symmetries are not at the same ontological level that we are considering, that is, the overall shape of the population.

THE DEVELOPMENT OF "COMPLEX" SCENARIOS

Using the preceding principles, scenarios were created through a process of simulation to investigate possible emergent properties of small firms. Three stages were used in the process of "simulation." The first was to identify the building blocks, or schemata, for the construction of a "world" of conditions. This was done using notions of agents and trajectories. These were combined to inform human experts. The second stage was to mentally immerse human experts in these conditions and allow them to create notions of "fitness" through the articulation of viable "agents" (i.e., small firms). The third stage took these various ideas as empirical data to abstract a sense of order implied by the existence of these agents.

The process began with the identification of agents and trajectories. The initial building blocks of the future environment for small firms were chosen, and the possible alternative paths of these articulated. The choice of features was informed by the substantive body of theory existing in the domain (of small firms). While this may be considered inadequate, the common discourse in the research domain cannot be ignored and is the best we have. As with all "futures" thinking, the critical issue is whether what constitutes the features of the environment today will exist or have the same causal powers at some time in the future. Part of the role of the human experts was to critique each feature as to its relevance in their future environment.

Examples of agents or stakeholders in the small firms' domain that have causal powers over small firms included consumers, corporate organizations, financial institutions, national government, regional governance, European Union, world governance—advanced countries/less developed countries (LDCs).

The trajectories of agents were generated as alternative possibilities. At this stage, the process closely resembles typical scenario developments (Schwartz, 1991), where alternative paths of a few major "driving forces" are mapped out. For example, three alternative paths with respect to "consumers" were developed thus:

1. A widespread diffusion of popular technology takes place. This means widespread adoption of satellite and cable television, as well as increasing use of the computer-based Internet. A universalization of consumer type takes place. However, the deployment of new technologies in production and service delivery allows mass customization to take hold. This results in particular consumer patterns (e.g., based on a matrix of locality, religions, and ages) to be serviced, from a wide source.

2. The morality of materialism becomes a major political and cultural issue. Initially, this is an extreme view; however, it increasingly draws on a wide support base. Religious groups from a broad political spectrum are at the forefront, but then the environmental movement, the Church of England, and traditional political groups all pick up this issue as one of consequence.

3. A combination of environmental legislation and political instability in the less developed countries means that there are shortages of certain goods. Personal transport is affected, and shortages prompt changing patterns in food consumption (e.g., toward more root vegetable and red meat consumption). Arguments emerge for central government to intervene as wholesalers turn to new sources for supplies. (Source: Foresight Research Centre internal working papers)

It is clear from the preceding trajectories that no particular "complexity" notions or ideas were present at this stage of analysis. The descriptions were substantive and concerned with real possibilities. The trajectories were storylike and implicated causal structures in their construction.

EMERGENCE OF NEW ENTERPRISES AND THE MEANING OF FITNESS

The second stage was to simulate emergence in alternative implied environments. To effect this, a generative process was engineered. This involved "coupling" to these alternative trajectories combined human expertise in the shape of eclectic groups of entrepreneurial people. The people were chosen for their strategic awareness and their position in the small business environment. Each person worked in or with the major stakeholders of U.K. small firms or in small firms themselves. Over the course of 24 hours about 20 people in this group were asked to situate themselves in the environments that (1) might be created by a combination of the trajectories and (2) combined their own expectations of the trajectories from their experience.

The reasoning behind this approach is informed by the ideas of Maturana and Varela (1994). The idea is that knowledge is formed from within and that an appropriate metaphor of knowledge is direct shaping of the world and meaning by the structural capacity of the organism.

The group had two main roles arising from their "structural coupling" with the small firm's environment, first as sensors of changes in their own environments and, second, as the human simulation or sense-making of what might emerge in these alternative futures. These debates focused on the concrete, substantive issues and behavior, not on any abstract simulations. The discussions created their own natural abstractions. Following are examples from these discussions:

1. People are living longer in the advanced countries, meaning increased expenditure on personal health. This results in less disposable income being spent on other goods. There may be a need to explore new funding methods for this. It could be that SMEs can provide local pockets of health care.
2. By 2006 the increased numbers of people who have come to the end of their traditional working life will have vastly increased. Will these emerge as a substantive pressure group? The class of 1968 has the potential to emerge as a new social movement.
3. Large firms will direct their marketing spending toward their nonusers and attempt to gather data about them. As direct marketing will

give firms a better/more efficient outcome, there will be a consequent decline in large firms' undertaking mass media advertising.

4. The notion of global marketing will really start to make sense, as
    firms will address small numbers of customers in many locations to
    make up their target audience.

5. There will be gaps left between these product specifications, leaving
    niches for smaller firms. Leaving aside the neural networks and the
    new, smart marketing, smaller firms will increasingly get involved
    with very localized niches. (Source: Foresight Research Centre inter-
    nal working papers)

In other words, a very diverse and rich picture, exactly as if one
were painting it now, for the environment is rich and diverse, with
meaning created through language and by mediated accounts and
analysis, as well as by individual experience.

SCENARIOS—MAKING COHERENCE OF THE CONDITIONS

The third task was to make some broad sense of the rich picture unfolding in the discourse, if that was possible. Here,
Kauffman's metaphor that the most "productive" systems are those
located at the "edge of order and chaos" (Kauffman, 1993) was applied as a structure. This metaphor, on the edge of chaos, was used
to frame three possible scenarios for small business in the future.

The first scenario is labeled "positive diversity." This is the
first of two scenarios in which the apparently increasing levels of
complexity identified today actually reduce through the introduction of new ontological layers, or symmetry breaking (Anderson,
1972). In this first scenario, the "attractor" for the more ordered
patterns is human values. There is an "emergent" integrative social order, the acceptance of diversity, or pluralism. Overall, the
result is a sense of confidence in the sustainability of human actions. This scenario assumes a greater degree of social, political,
and economic cohesion. Diversity among political, ethnic, and
lifestyle groups is recognized and tolerated, and society is confident in the value of integration and learning through educational
and training innovations. Such confidence leads to investment and
trust, providing a virtuous circle of economic and social development. In this scenario, small firms would be seen as important
contributors and as a focus for financial and human investment.
The numbers of self-employed and small firms and, in particular,
medium-sized firms would grow, with a slight decrease in numbers
of larger firms. This scenario, rather utopian perhaps, is that of
the "future confident." New forms of citizenship or communit-
arianism might exemplify this. (These scenarios are given in de-

tail in other publications; cf. Foresight, 1997; Fuller, Jenkins, et al., 1997.)

The second scenario is "natural selection." In this scenario, again bringing increased order, the "attractor" is the corporate state, or corporate ecology. Global businesses have wealth and power beyond nations. Their record on ethics and morality is not good. Thus, in this scenario the features are ordered on accentuated corporate political and economic power. Societies become more polarized between rich and poor (the poor are "dissipated entropy"). There is a simplification of conditions as corporations become extremely "fit" in this landscape, thus reducing the nature of diversification. In this scenario, the increasing economic power of global corporations and a lack of social investment exacerbate the current trend in polarization of minority groups and income levels. For many people, there is a sense of fear about the future. The role of small firms in this environment is mainly the provision of services (including manufacturing and distribution services) to corporations in relationships, which become analogous with the role of employed persons in the 1970s. Other small firms would exist as a form of activity and underemployment in the "uneconomic" voids. The numbers of medium-sized and large firms would probably reduce in this environment, given a trend toward near corporate monopolies in large niches. Self-employment and smaller firms would increase in number in this very tough competitive environment. This distopian scenario, from a human development perspective, is "future fearful."

The third scenario is "opportunistic survival." Here, complexity increases with no symmetry breaking creation of new layers. The fluid state of order and reorder is maintained in a complex economic system with many interdependent power relationships. This is the domain of the global brand and the "incredible" (small, concentrated) niche as firms demonstrate all the characteristics of agents in a rich ecology. The niche is the attractor; there are many peaks of value or basins of energy. Diversity is the main feature. In this scenario we explore the nature of opportunistic coexistence of small and large firms. The environment is competitive, but increased diversity of needs and demands by consumers, along with an increased ability for businesses to meet those demands, creates a market of niches. Some are large, being met by global brands. Others are very small, local or specialized, and certainly temporary. Niche thinking dominates society, in cultural and economic terms. Members develop strong niche identities and ignore those outside their niche. Some niches are wealthier than others are. Within each market niche the working practices of large and small business would interconnect as semi-independent economic ecologies. The overall balance of firms would move toward the smaller size as more work was placed in smaller units, but often under the control of the larger firm, either directly or through licensing arrangements. This is the domain of the "future uncertain."

DISCUSSION

Do complexity theory and notions of complex, adaptive systems add anything to the enterprise of anticipating future states through soft simulation and scenarios? The thesis is that they do. They provide an explanation of patterns through analogy with known dynamical patterns. Concepts of ordering, such as attractors, paths, niches, and fitness, can be used to make sense and meaning of rich, complex pictures. The theories can provide a conceptual form for a narrative structure. The metaphor at the edge of chaos can be utilized to construct different scenarios, according to the anticipated degree of order in an environment. A broad language of metaphors enables the analogies to be given meaning in action.

The meaning of structural coupling in social systems is as yet unclear. It is situated in a discourse of autopoiesis—self-producing systems (Maturana and Varela, 1973; Luhmann, 1986). In this particular enterprise, the concept of structural coupling was operationalized as being the immersion of people in a new set of ideas and the articulation of responses. Its significance here is that the ideas emerged from a flow of discourse about concrete phenomena. As an approach this does not strike one as particularly novel, but rather as quite a normal way of developing ideas. The experiment is repeatable, but is not replicable, nor is it reversible. Those people's thinking has been altered, and a different set of people would create a different set of meaning from the conjunction of the data and their experiences. The linking of notions of structural coupling to this exercise and therefore the interpretation of the process are perhaps novel.

The exercise was informed by substantive theory, by empirical evidence, by personal experience, and by complexity theory. The role of complexity theory was to coordinate disparate substantive theories. Without substantive theory and empirical evidence of the domain, no sense could have been made of the domain. However, the coordinating role of complexity theory created new insights about alternative structures of the domain.

Complexity studies have no meaning without a notion of time phases but are not associated with present, past, or future. The dynamical metaphors are as applicable in a (present) discourse of the future as in a discourse of the present or past. They may appear as a "postdictive" mechanism, that is, for identifying previously known patterns in observed behavior. It is argued that the complexity metaphors have greater power than this. They facilitate an anticipation of future states by enabling the contemplation of a range of patterned possibilities though are not predictive in a substantive sense.

The ontology or ontological (structural) level that was being modeled in this exercise was not that of the individual small firm. The ontological feature of the stakeholder was dominant in the theorizing of the domain, and thus the ultimate meaning of the scenarios developed was applicable to such stakeholders. The flow of interactions between ideal types of firms and the stakeholder environment created notions of typicality of firms, but not predictions of actual small firms. This reasoning is sensitive to critiques of "ecological fallacy," that is, assigning meaning to an agent from a study of an aggregation of agents.

There is still much to learn and understand about the nature of dynamical social systems, but further experimentation in the context of complexity with the interrelationships between simulation, language, expectations, and actions is suggested as a fruitful arena for further research.

SUMMARY

This chapter illustrates how the language of complexity studies has helped to create meaning in the process of anticipating the future of a substantive domain, namely, the small firm. It demonstrates how the language of dynamical patterns assisted in the ordering of concepts drawn from substantive theory. Substantive theories and complexity metaphors have been used together to make a richer discourse of meaning than either would yield on its own. With regard to time, these dynamical patterns are phase-oriented but not date-oriented. They are legitimate in contemplating an unknown future.

The nature of small firms was conceptually modeled as a complex, adaptive system. Metaphors that describe the dynamical properties of these systems were used to underpin a method of anticipating and articulating alternative future scenarios for small firms.

The central modeling concept was the emergence of fitness characteristics in alternative landscapes ordered by different overt causal powers. The method by which these scenarios were created and critiqued was informed by ideas of "structural coupling" between people with deep knowledge of the domain and a set of novel ideas.

The results led to a better understanding of types of firms that might exist in such landscapes and the influences on their formation.

REFERENCES

Anderson, P. W. (1972). "More Is Different: Broken Symmetry and the Nature of the Hierarchical Structure of Science." *Science,* Vol. 177, 393–396.

Bell, W. (1997). "Assumptions of Futures Studies. Foundations of Futures Studies: Human Science for a New Era." *Transaction,* Vol. 1, 115–164.

Bhaskar, R. (1989). *The Possibility of Naturalism: A Philosophical Critique of the Contemporary Human Sciences.* Hemet Hemstead, Harvester Wheatsheaf. Routledge: New York.

Bijl, R. (1992). "Delphi in Future Scenario Study on Mental Health and Mental Health Care." *Futures,* 232–241.

Casti, J. (1998). "Would Be Worlds and Sim Stores." Paper presented at London School of Economics Complexity Seminar.

Cohen, J. and L. Stewart. (1994). *Complicity and Simplexity: Discovering Simplicity in a Complex World. The Collapse of Chaos.* New York: Penguin, 396–473.

DTI. (1997). *Small and Medium Enterprise Statistics for the U.K. 1996.* London: Department of Trade and Industry, SME Policy Division.

Foresight. (1997). *Visions of the Small Business Landscape in 2006.* Durham, NC: Durham University Business School.

Fuller, E., A. Jenkins, et al. (1997). *Visions of the Small Business Landscape in 2006.* Durham, England: Durham University Business School.

Fuller, E., J. Lewis, et al. (1997). *The "Business Style" Interactions of Small Firms.* Belfast: U.K. Small Firms Policy and Research, Institute for Small Business Affairs.

Gell-Mann, M. (1994). *The Quark and the Jaguar.* London: Little, Brown.

Gibb, A. A. (1993). "Key Factors in the Design of Policy Support for the Small and Medium Enterprise Development Process: An Overview." *Entrepreneurship and Regional Development,* Vol. 5, 1–24.

Harvey, D. L. and M. Reed. (1996). "Social Science as the Study of Complex Systems." In *Chaos Theory in the Social Sciences,* edited by L. D. Kiel and E. Elliot. Ann Arbor: University of Michigan Press, 295–323.

Hiebeler, D. (1994). *The Swarm Simulation System and Individual-Based Modeling.* Santa Fe Institute, 94-12-065.

HMSO. (1971). *Bolton Report. Report of the Committee of Inquiry on Small Firms.* London: HMSO.

Holland, J. (1995). *Innovation, Risk and Lever Points. Complexity and Strategy.* London: Santa Fe Institute and Praxis Group.

Jarillo, J. (1988). "On Strategic Networks." *Strategic Management Journal,* Vol. 9, 31–41.

Johannisson, B. (1987). "Anarchists and Organizers: Entrepreneurs in a Network Perspective." *International Studies of Management and Organization,* Vol. 17, No. 1, 49–63.

Larson (1992). "Network Dyads in Entrepreneurial Settings: A Study of the Governance of Exchange Relationships." *Administrative Science Quarterly,* Vol. 37, 76.

Lissack, M. R. (1996). "Complexity Metaphors and the Management of a Knowledge Based Enterprise." http://www.lissack.com/writings/proposal.htm: 37.

Lorenzoni, G. and O. Ornati. (1988). "Constellations of Firms and New Ventures." *Journal of Business Venturing,* Vol. 3, 41–57.

Luhmann, N. (1986). *The Autopoesis of Social Systems. Socio Cybernetic Paradoxes,* edited by F. Geyer and J. van de Zouwan. London: Sage.

Mannermaa, M. (1992). "In Search of an Evolutionary Paradigm for Futures Research." *Futures,* Vol. 231, No. 4, 358 et seq.

Maturana, W. and F. Varela. (1973). "Autopoetic Systems: A Characterisation of the Living." In *Autopoesis and Cognition: The Realisations of the Living,* edited by H. Maturana and F. Varela. Dordrecht: Reidel, 63–134.

Maturana, H. R. and F. J. Varela (1994). *The Tree of Knowledge, the Biological Roots of Human Understanding.* London and New York: Shambhala.

Mitchell, R. K. and B. R. Agle. (1995). *Toward a Theory of Stakeholder Identification: Defining the Principle of Who and What Really Counts.* University of Victoria.

Naman, J. L. and D. P. Slevin (1993). "Entrepreneurship and the Concept of Fit: A Model and Empirical Tests." *Strategic Management Journal,* Vol. 14, 137–153.

Schwartz, P. (1991). *The Art of the Long View.* New York: Doubleday.

Slaughter, R. (1997). *The Knowledgebase of Futures Studies.* Hawthorn, Australia: DDM Media Group.

Weick, K. E. (1995). *Sensemaking in Organizations.* Thousand Oaks, CA: Sage.

Williamson, O. (1991). "Comparative Economic Organization: The Analysis of Discrete Structural Alternatives." *Administrative Science Quarterly,* Vol. 36, 269–296.

Chapter 18

Gorbachev as CEO Roadkill: Lessons for the Modern Corporation from the Soviet Foreign Policy Establishment's Failure to Manage Complexity

Robert M. Cutler*

Western specialists on the Soviet Union during the Cold War encountered, without realizing it, many issues under current discussion in management science. Those issues presented themselves as problems in understanding the cognitive aspects and organizational development of the Soviet political system. Indeed, the first major political interpretation of the post-Stalin Soviet system (Meyer, 1965) literally characterized it as "USSR, Inc.," in order to make the point that it was organized as a large bureaucratic institution. The political disintegration of the USSR can be regarded as a failure by the Soviet system to adapt successfully to demands from increasingly complex international and domestic environments. As such, there is direct relevance to the situation encountered by managers in complex bureaucracies today.

In a nutshell, the organizations in the Soviet foreign policy establishment autocomplexified in response to the increasingly complex global environment. By the time Gorbachev finally accelerated changes in Soviet foreign policy doctrine, the complex multiplica-

* I wish to thank Michael Lissack and Steve Maguire for detailed comments on an early version of this manuscript. Various stages of this research were supported by the Social Science Research Council, New York; the Social Science and Humanities Research Council, Ottawa; and the International Research and Exchanges Board, Princeton. The work presented here also draws on 20 years of interviews by the author with participants in the foreign policy-making process of the once and former Soviet Union.

tion of political resources and incentive structures in Soviet society had already made that society effectively part of the global environment external to the Soviet political system. Consequently, the constituent parts of the USSR self-organized their own foreign policies independent of Moscow (Matlock, 1995). In the end, what impeded Soviet foreign policy adaptation was preexisting doctrinal constraint upon organizational cognition and interest articulation. People were not allowed to say they saw things that, according to the doctrine, were not permitted to exist; even the ideology could not be modified enough (Remington, 1985). That is why, for example, to discuss the nationalities questions in the late 1980s, it was necessary in the USSR to invent a whole new language with new analytical terms having meanings that the previous rules of discourse did not permit to be recognized. The Soviet system imploded and collapsed due to accumulated structural inertia, under the force of being required to deal with too much cognitive change and consequent organizational chaos too fast.

This collapse holds lessons for the modern North American corporation. Most prominent among these lessons are strategies for dealing with the tension of stress and its duration. With this in mind, it is easy for an organizational observer to find analogies between the Gorbachev era of Soviet politics, on one hand, and, on the other hand, IBM's failure to exploit the personal computer, American auto manufacturers' inability to deal with changing markets, Apple's failure to develop its market niche, Microsoft's initial response to the Internet, and even the quick demise of "New Coke." All such analogies are based on the presence of cognitive dissonance between different organizational levels: what management understands as "fact" may mean little to the folk in the field, and vice versa.

The Soviets had some awareness of this cognitive dissonance. Under Khrushchev in the late 1950s, the party's Central Committee sent fact-finding propaganda groups into the regions to find out exactly what was happening on the ground (Hoffmann, 1968). At first, these fact-finding missions talked only with the local officials and administrators. Only a few years later, in the early 1960s, did Moscow realize that this was insufficient and sent such groups back out into the field to see what was really happening. When Khrushchev was overthrown in 1964, his successors redirected these developments in organizational feedback and denied scarce political resources to those interested in "framing" the new information with the help of new ideas. The resulting failure of the central control mechanism of the system to receive and properly interpret feedback meant that the system was increasingly fallible and unable to respond to demands emanating from the society at large. The latter thus became radically divorced from communications with the "elite," and this ultimately led to collapse.

DOCTRINE, IDEOLOGY, AND STRATEGY

A few terms that are critical to the discussion that follows; moving from the abstract to the concrete, they are "doctrine," "ideology," "strategy," and "tactics." Doctrine refers to immutable historical destiny defining the basic actors, their relations, and how these will turn out. Ideology concerns the particular combination and succession of themes of conflict and cooperation. Strategy concerns overarching patterns of conduct animated by those themes. Tactics are situational moves designed to achieve specific and immediate goals, the succession of which forms a strategic pattern. In specific examples of Soviet Marxist-Leninist reference:

1. *Doctrine is the immutable teleology* dictating how to define the dramatis personae of international politics and plotting the script of their theater. For example, the conflict between the Soviets and the Chinese in the late 1950s and early 1960s was a dispute over doctrine, because it concerned the number and the composition of different "camps" in world politics and whether the use of nuclear weapons could hasten the victory of world socialism (Zagoria, 1962).
2. *Ideology consists in the ensemble of idea-elements* defining the categories of cognition. It is the vocabulary that expresses eternal doctrinal truths.
3. *Strategy is the goal-oriented line* of action prescribed by ideology. When the categories of ideology concatenate to define what really exists, they limit the set of possible futures because what is inexpressible in their language becomes a priori impossible. Specific, conceivable futures imply goal-oriented lines of action to attain them, and each goal-oriented line of action is a strategy.
4. *Tactics operationalize strategy* at the level of actions, intentions to act, and preferences for actions to be taken, with reference to concrete issues in particular policy fields.

An example of the interplay among these levels of cognition is how altered perceptions cause attitudinal change. Take the example of Soviet attitudes toward world politics in general and toward other international actors in particular. By 1970 a large number of Soviet experts on international affairs regarded the European Economic Community (EEC) as an economic "center of imperialism" equal in stature to the United States. A new "three centers" theory of imperialism proposed that, at least economically, Western Europe and Japan had freed themselves from American tutelage and actually competed with Washington for influence within the international capitalist system (e.g., Mel'nikov, 1972). The "three centers" theory was nothing less than a revision of the *ideology*. As such, it had important implications for the *strategy* of the international communist movement.

If world capitalism had three centers, then socialist revolution might occur in one of them (such as Western Europe) long before it did in another (the United States or Japan). Various strategies could promote this. For example, the slogans "united front" and "popular front" are drawn from the history of the Communist International between the two world wars. Historical experience links the united front to the image of revolution as cataclysm, a maximalist image in which revolution is foremost a political act, and great strides are made through a limited number of earth-shaking changes. By contrast, the popular front strategy emphasized numerous minor tremors in the political landscape and promoted incremental, rather than cataclysmic; social change. The united front and popular front policy tendencies animated an internal Soviet policy dispute in the early 1970s over the proper strategy for West European communist parties, linked to the debate over the "three centers" theory of world capitalism.

For the model of the international environment based on the "three centers" theory, the paramount value was to split Western Europe from the United States, and West European unification could be a means to that end. The Soviets sought to use left-wing influence in national parliaments to prevent the consolidation of a united Western Europe. However, they looked favorably on West European communist participation in a consolidated European Parliament, because under the "three centers" theory this would be a natural concomitant to EEC political integration. That being so, incrementalist Soviet analysts supposed that a West European communist party coming to power in coalition with other parties need not mean the immediate installation of the dictatorship of the proletariat.

The "three centers" theory of world capitalism made it again possible for the communists to consider incremental tactics toward the acquisition of power by electoral rather than violent means in Western Europe. When West European communists renovated their domestic alliance tactics, they supported this new model of the international environment. The united front entailed an exclusionary, "three-class alliance" strategy comprising only workers, peasants, and left-wing radicals. The alliance strategy of the popular front was an inclusionary, "four-class alliance" that also comprised certain strata of the national bourgeoisie (Rasputins, 1980). The code words "socialism" and "democracy," respectively, expressed the united front and popular front tendencies. To pursue "socialism" meant accelerating the near-at-hand collapse of capitalism and catalyzing the political revolution that would bring its final downfall. To pursue "democracy" meant emphasizing social change and promoting it gradually, through such measures as extended economic planning, nationalized industry, and enhanced workers' control over economic production (Zaretskii, 1973).

To give but one example, In spring 1974, during the period before the French presidential election, the Soviets had a value conflict between continued, businesslike relations with a French government dominated by "bourgeois parties" and the political uncertainties that would result from a success of the "Union of the Left" of the socialists and communists (with the communists uncharacteristically in the minority). Yet a status quo conservatism first led them to favor a Gaullist candidate. When the French communists objected to this, the Soviets shifted toward the socialist Mitterrand, whom the communists supported. However, after the first round of the elections eliminated the Gaullist from the runoff, the underlying dynamic of Soviet détente interests in Europe led them to support the candidate of the "bourgeois parties" Giscard d'Estaing over the left-wing coalition that could have destabilized their delicate European diplomacy (Cutler, 1990). The Soviets made this choice because they believed it increased the chances of realizing their long-range goal to separate Western Europe political from the United States. This was the same reason they refused to support the revolutionary maximalism of the Portuguese communist leadership in late 1975. However, such incrementalism in Soviet foreign policy failed when unanticipated consequences spilled over into Eastern Europe in the mid-1980s and began to unravel the Soviet bloc.

There are various explanations for the failure of Brezhnevian incrementalism in Europe and Gorbachev's response to it. For example, consider the "new blood" argument (Etheredge, 1981) that "resources are needed to continually hire skilled new people who bring fresh ideas or first-hand knowledge of what other people are doing." Or consider communication flow theory, according to which "much innovation . . . is embedded within the changing quality of communication," and "innovation rates are increased by particular patterns of communication and by networks of intra-institutional structures that create and support them" (Etheredge, 1981). For our purposes, what is pertinent is the distinction among what Steinbruner (1974) has called "uncommitted," "grooved," and "theoretical" thinkers. Clashes among such members of the Soviet foreign policy establishment created the context for foreign policy-making. The differences among them are shown in Table 18.1.

THE POLICY-MAKING HIERARCHY

In the policy-making hierarchy, uncommitted thinkers were concentrated in the higher echelons, grooved thinkers in the lower,

Table 18.1
Differences among "Uncommitted," "Theoretical," and "Grooved" Thinkers, with Examples from the Complex System of the Soviet Foreign Policy-making Establishment

	Uncommitted Thinking	Theoretical Thinking	Grooved Thinking
Chief Cognitive Characteristic	Consistency and stability principles prevent overall integration foe divergent patterns of thought, each urged on the decision maker by a different "sponsor."	When highly generalized conceptions become established, they provide the mind with a basis for handling the uncertainty of the immediate decision problem.	Stability is established by long exercise over extended sequences of decisions. Experience offers powerful analogues for new decisions.
Other characteristics	Due to the organizational setting, the reality principle forces a more abstract intellectual framework than for the grooved thinker. But abstraction is made difficult by uncertainty. The time frame is relatively more extended, with a greater range of problems and greater scope of individual problems. There is oscillation among competing belief patterns, compromising stability somewhat, in favor of simplicity.	Beliefs are generally organized around a single transcendent value, inferentially related to specific objectives. Since thought processes are less dependent on incoming information to establish coherent beliefs, inconsistency mechanisms are widely employed to cope with it.Likely to be found in small, closely knit groups which interact regularly over issues of common concern. This pattern of interaction provides social reinforcement.	Operates in a very short-range time frame and with a quite low level of abstraction. Attention is given only to that small number of variables which are pertinent to a decision problem.Simplicity principle organizes problem conceptions around a single value. Reality principle provides well-anchored, ready-made structure for new problems.

Table 18.1
(continued)

Organizational condition in propaganda-making organizations	Within a particular information channel in an organizational unit, formal or informal, having a restricted scope of concern. *Soviet examples*: Newspaper editorial board members, Political Observers, Special Correspondents.	Levels where intersecting information channels carry relatively abstracted, aggregated information. *Soviet examples*: Propaganda planners and ideologists, Central Committee propaganda specialists.	Levels where problems nearly always fall readily into a small number of basic types. *Soviet examples*: Operational propagandists, press secretaries.
Organizational condition in policy-making organizations	Levels where intersecting information channels carry relatively abstracted, aggregated information. *Soviet examples*: Politburo, Central Committee policy departments, Central Committee Secretariat	Within a particular information channel in an organizational unit, formal or informal, having a restricted scope of concern. *Soviet examples*: Academy of Science institute researchers, members of social organizations.	Levels where problems nearly always fall readily into a small number of basic types. *Soviet examples*: "Staff" bureaucrats in the field, information-collectors at headquarters.

Source: Based on Cutler (1981, 1990), drawn from Steinbruner (1974); c.f. Haas (1991).

and theoretical thinkers in the middle. The low-level functionaries in the Ministry of Foreign Affairs were grooved policymakers. The Ministry of Foreign Affairs applied the general foreign policy line to specific circumstances, consulting with different segments of the Central Committee and with specialists from the Academy of Sciences. The chief decision makers in the country, including the Politburo and the Secretariat and, to some degree, the Central Committee departments, were uncommitted policymakers. Uncommitted thinkers use a more abstract framework and a more extended time frame than do grooved thinkers. They deal with a greater range of problems and have a greater scope in which to address individual problems. The institute-based advisers and ministerial consultants were theoretical policymakers (Eran, 1979; Glassman, 1968; Meissner, 1977; Petrov, 1973; Schapiro, 1975, 1977).

There were three ways in which individual "theoretical-thinking" specialists exerted influence. The first was to air ideas in institutional journals. Journal articles had greater immediacy than lengthy monographs and so carried more influence in policy circles. Ideas could also be aired at roundtables and conferences held in the institutes themselves. Officials from the Ministry of Foreign Affairs, cadres from the Central Committee, leading journalists, and other political observers participated in these exchanges of views (Löwenhardt, 1981). A specialist's choice between the second and third instruments of influence depended on the nature of the problem: an analyst could submit either a policy-planning report or a situation report. In a policy-planning report the Soviet analyst of international affairs did not express a policy preference. He established the available options only in general terms, laying out broad policy alternatives. Very much as in other countries, he could discuss the results he foresaw for each alternative and the differing situations to which he sees them variously leading. This was frequently a means for expressing a covert policy preference (e.g., Inozemtsev, 1972, analyzed in Legvold, 1974). Situation reports, on the other hand, were submitted on request by specialists at research institutes to one or another Foreign Ministry desk (e.g., Kudriavtsev, 1974, analyzed in Cutler, 1985). Due to the often fast-moving nature of events, they were usually contracted on an ad hoc basis through informal and personal contacts.

THE PROPAGANDA-MAKING HIERARCHY

The allocation of roles in the propaganda-making hierarchy differed from that in the policy-making hierarchy. In particular, theoretical thinkers occupied the highest echelons, and uncommitted thinkers occupied the intermediate ones. The "theoretical" thinkers were propaganda planners and ideologists, because they worked with highly generalized conceptions within a restricted scope of concern. They established the system's general propaganda strategy through regular meetings with high-echelon operational propagandists such as the editors in chief of the principal newspapers, to whom they issued directives. Some theoretical propaganda makers also constituted a subset of theoretical policymakers.

Directives issued by propaganda planners ("theoretical thinkers" in the propaganda apparatus) were aimed at individuals who had competence over a limited range of tasks, which they executed according to standard operational procedures. These operational personnel, such as low-level media commentators or Tass correspondents stationed overseas, addressed uncomplicated problems that nearly always fell readily into a small number of types and therefore were "grooved" thinkers. Their scope of responsibility was limited to expressing others' evaluations, such as may be received via propaganda directives, and to collecting and transmitting raw information for such evaluations. At this level of hierarchy in the information channel, there was the least scope for the expression of independent judgment and evaluation. Staff correspondents stationed overseas for individual newspapers fell partly into the category of grooved thinkers, because collecting and transmitting raw information are an important part of their duties. Their authority to evaluate this information independently and to communicate those evaluations varied with the individual journalist, depending on his experience and his relations with the editorial board back home in Moscow.

Uncommitted thinkers used a more abstract framework and a more extended time frame than did grooved thinkers. They dealt with a greater range of problems and had a greater scope in which to address individual problems. In the policy hierarchy these individuals occupied roles at the highest levels of organizations, but in the propaganda hierarchy they occupied intermediate roles between theoretical and grooved thinkers. The most important uncommitted thinkers occupied middle-ranking roles such as political observers, special correspondents, and editors of the international section in the newspapers' own offices. Journalists holding the title of political observer and special correspondent were able to articulate publicly their more personally held views. As a Soviet sociologist of the Soviet press observed, commentators holding the rank of political observer in particular had "the right not only . . . to evaluate [international] events for which no official position ha[d] yet been established but also, taking the changing situation into account and based on independent analysis . . ., to bring new nuances into the existing official position" (Popov, 1984). On occasion, therefore, some uncommitted and theoretical propaganda makers also acted as theoretical policymakers or expressed their views.

NORMATIVE CONSIDERATIONS

The differences between these policy and propaganda hierarchies are very much like the differences between engineering and marketing in the modern North American corporation. For example, vaporware may be perfectly acceptable to the marketing types (as a means of either holding the competition at bay or "bribing" consumers to hold off the next purchase), but unbackable promises are anathema to the engineers. Still, such a disagreement does not prevent the two groups from using similar lexicons to describe activities. A complex-system approach to the corporate context allows an observer the tools to ascertain the nuances of such disagreements.

Similarly, a complex-system approach to Soviet foreign policy-making provides a nuanced understanding of how the recombination of ideas is conditioned by the relationships among the individuals who carry them. These relationships, in turn, are constrained not only by the norms of the organizations in which those individuals work but moreover by the differentiation of their roles (set out in Table 18.1) in the overlapping propaganda-making and policy-making systems. Consider the individual, such as a newspaper's special correspondent, who believes that the model of the international environment implicit in the dominant policy tendency does not coincide with newly received information. (This occurs in noncrisis situations where the highest political elite are not involved in policy micromanagement.) Such a special corresponsdent could write an article that expressed an alternative view on the issue, thereby questioning the dominant view and generating either implicitly or explicitly a policy alternative.

Indeed, unexpected international events motivated organizations and people in them to evaluate new information at hand, on the basis of their preferred models of the international environment. Normally, the standard operating procedures of the overlapping policy-making and propaganda-making organizations resolved spontaneous differences in the line to be taken. Yet although an authoritative decision might resolve the disagreement, the next unexpected international event would bring the overall "definition of the situation" into question again. Decisions on propaganda strategy thus not only expressed consensus about what to tell the people who read newspapers inside and outside the country but also resolved very real differences of interpretation among press observers. In specific situations it is possible to identify specific journalists who performed this task of resolving such conflicts of interpretation (Cutler, 1982, 1990). Usually, but not always, these were "theoretical thinkers" in the propaganda-making system who also had other roles in the policy-making system.

Those whose focus is on organizational structures (Aspaturian, 1966, 1972) would suppose that a difference of opinion between the party's Central Committee and the government's Ministry of Foreign Affairs may have been reflected, at some point, a difference between the two principal press organs representing foreign policy views, the party's newspaper, *Pravda*, and the government's newspaper, *Izvestiia*. They would, however, normally have tended to be close to one another and to the main line of Soviet foreign policy. Other press organs having a special role reflected institutional positions derived either from political function (e.g., *Krasnaia zvezda* and the military) or from specialized readership targeting. A complex-system approach would add that *Pravda* and *Izvestiia* had specific functions in the propaganda-making system that may have influenced their articulated policy preferences and that other major press organs could also assume certain systemwide roles under special circumstances (Cutler, 1982, 1985, 1990).

The complex-system approach's loose concept of an "organization" further implies that differences between such institutions as the party's Central Committee and the government's Ministry of Foreign Affairs were no longer necessarily even the most salient, because the institutions (and the people in them) were no longer "impermeable." This was especially true at the intersection of the Soviet policy-making and propaganda-making systems in foreign affairs. Since individual career paths were no longer made within a single institution after Stalin, it became easier for people in foreign policy-making organizations and people in the propaganda-making organizations to coalesce into transinstitutional "tendencies of articulation" (Griffiths, 1971).

A complex-system approach thus allows for the fact that institutional boundaries were more permeable than supposed by those whose focus is on organizational structures. Indeed, the notion of permeable boundaries became the dominant theme in understanding what happened to Gorbachev. They may also be the dominant theme in understanding what is happening in corporations today.

LESSONS FOR COMPLEX ORGANIZATIONS TODAY

In all organizations, organizational learning is affected by the character of the external environment and how it is experienced. The environment thus can be characterized not only by objectively determined qualities (in particular, the length of a situation's duration) but also by subjective qualities perceived by the organizational actor (in particular, the amount of tension experienced). The two most salient such characteristics are the duration of the external situation and the tension in the environment it represents.

The interaction of these two variables represents the degree of stress: short-duration and low-tension situations are lowest in stress, and long-duration and high-tension situations are highest. Cutler's (1990) study of response to stress by the Soviet foreign policy establishment reveals:

1. In general the least stressful situations (those characterized by short duration and low tension) engender incremental responses to the environment that are of a mainly tactical nature and concern the relation between tactics and strategy.
2. Long-duration, low-tension situations principally invoke relations between strategy and ideology, leading to the possibility of revision at the ideological level in the medium or long term.
3. Still more stressful situations, typically characterized by short duration and high tension, instantiate relations between doctrine and ideology.
4. The most stressful situations (long duration and high tension) tend to freeze and institutionalize existing relations among all levels in the cognitive hierarchy.

A complex-system approach implies that institutions at varying levels may be as affected and driven by the international environment as by their own domestic political environment. The extent of Soviet institutional subordination to the political system as a whole and to the political elite led to the overall failure of ideology and doctrine to adapt. That failure, in turn, blocked the ability to motivate strategic changes. This failure created the situation where things collapsed, because superrigid institutions at many levels were unable to deal with the sudden unleashing of hyperfluid forces.

Gorbachev's most striking doctrinal innovations in foreign policy were of a nature that only the supreme political leader could make. Not even Khrushchev was entirely successful in his attempt to do the same, since the ideological constraints on strategy made it very difficult for the ideology itself to be revised on the basis of aggregated tactical lessons translated through strategy. Yet those ideological constraints, particularly the USSR's image of its role in world history, interfered with the long-run viability of the system as a whole. Thus, self-image can be a brake on environment-driven learning, especially if one sees oneself as being resource-rich, in a position of strength, or even invincible.

If we look at the Brezhnev era (between Khrushchev and Gorbachev from roughly the mid–1960s to the mid–1980s), it was not quite that case that organizations in the Soviet foreign policy establishment could not say what they thought because of official doctrinal constraint, although this was, of course, to some extent true. The situation was a bit more nuanced. More precisely, it was the

case that those to whom they might articulate these views had incentive structures that made them deaf. The danger came from the
"theoretical propaganda-makers" who were stuck in old ways of thinking and who imposed these upon "uncommitted propaganda-makers"
as well as upon the "uncommitted policymakers" whom they advised.
In a corporate environment, the doctrine is often reflected in "corporate culture." Moreover, "theoretical propaganda-makers" are often
themselves also playing roles as "uncommitted policymakers" when,
for example, they are board members inherited from earlier organizational developments within the corporation. These individuals have
an established way of doing things that can be anchored in the past
as far back as the very founding of the organization.

Now consider Apple and its policy of hardware manufacture with
no software licenses. This strategy, conceived by the two Steves,
was essential in the company's early days. By maintaining complete control, they minimized the risk of misconceived hardware
or software interfering in Apple's relationship with its customers.
But the external market changed; unfortunately, the internal Apple
culture did not. The established way of doing things thereby shielded
the organization from responding to change in the environment. A
potential 30 percent market share was allowed to fritter to less
than 5 percent. Some people saw this at Apple, and they were either silenced or drummed out. Apple's images of self and of environment (i.e., market) were prevented from evolving, much like
Soviet foreign policy.

An approach focusing on the production of shared cognitive
norms rather than on organizational structure—call it
"interactionist"—would suggest that learning in Soviet foreign policy
was driven by the international environment and that this learning manifested in changes in Soviet images of that environment
and of other actors in it (Griffiths, 1972, 1991). The complex-system
approach goes further to imply that these predispositions are learned
not only on a strategic level but moreover with respect to specific
policy issues on a tactical level. Learning therefore occurs under
hierarchical cognitive constraint and must be studied in this hierarchical context (Abelson, 1973; Cutler, 1990; Peffley and Hurwitz,
1985). An aggregate of things that are learned on the tactical level
may "bubble up" to the strategic level; on rare occasions, an aggregate of things learned on the strategic level can bubble up to the
ideological level. This occurred in the 1920s, when the first historical precursor of the "popular front" appeared in Soviet ideology
under conditions of a high-stress international environment
(Degras, 1967). If, during the "Star Wars" nuclear-weapon era of
the early 1980s, a high-stress environment militated against Soviet foreign policy learning, what facilitated apparent learning at

the earlier time? The answer seems to lie in the capabilities of Soviet power and in the leadership's assessments of those capabilities, for in the earlier period, the Bolshevik position in world politics was precarious. To return to the Apple analogy, when Jobs was in charge and perceived strength, cloning was forbidden (both in the 1980s and in 1998); when Spinler and Amelio were in charge and perceived weakness, the market was allowed a voice.

We seem justified in concluding that when stress is high, countries and corporations alike learn necessary survival behavior under conditions of institutional weakness relative to the environment, than under conditions of strength. It appears that self-awareness of one's own resource weakness automatically decreases the tension experienced: one spends less energy trying to rigidify useless or nonexistent internal structures. This, in turn, facilitates learning on the ideological level, even without excluding bubble-up to the doctrinal level. In practical terms, that means that it becomes permissible to redefine the entire organizational mission. When the organizational actor judges itself to have sufficient resources to withstand "psychological assaults" from the environment, an organization is more likely to attribute its own real failures to aspects of the environment. It may then misallocate those resources in seeking to control that environment rather than in promoting necessary organizational change.

In the Soviet context, domestic reforms in the Russian empire and the Soviet Union historically tended to follow upon defeats in international politics. The ultimate lesson for governments may be that their countries do not have a function so transcendent in international affairs as to map into null-space their neighbors far and near. Germany required two world wars to learn this lesson, and it seems that Russia is slowly reconciling itself to it after centuries of being the regional hegemon. The consistent overestimation of one's own resources leads only to overextension, which, in the best case, produces defeat, and, in the worst case, disintegrative collapse.

The world of business has unfortunately all too many parallels with this analysis. "Perils of excellence" and the "Icarus paradox" (after Daedalus' mythological son who used wax to bind feathers to his arms and fly, succeeded, but flew too close to the sun, melting the wax so that he plunged into the sea) are a real concern for strategists (Lant and Montgomery, 1987; Miller, 1990, 1994). Successful "builders" can become unsuccessful "imperialists" without noticing it: this was the case with ITT and the unwieldy heterogeneous empire it ruled in the late 1970s.

After lengthy intervals of continued success, firms exhibit increased inertia and insularity and fail to adapt to changing environments. Not only do resources accumulated over time buffer the organization from variation in the environment (reducing the perceived need for change), but also the open and eager commitment of powerful leaders to what have been proclaimed to be successful policies makes challenges by lower-ranking members in the organization less likely, even if the latter's position "in the field" or "at the heart of the action" might uniquely qualify them to offer such a critique.

Consider IBM and the losses it endured early this decade. Despite being the inventor of the personal computer, IBM sat back and allowed others to reinvent that industry, losing control over the direction and pace of technical change. "Big Blue went into denial, channeling its massive resources into bucking the market rather than facing it" (*Economist*, June 6, 1998, 66). Not only did it lose talented people, but the loyal who remained were frustrated and disheartened. The radical transformation required and eventually implemented by Lou Gerstner was, in fact, an organizational "cultural revolution" (Allaire and Firsirotu, 1985) that revised the assumptions, terminology, and normative aspects of organizational discourse at the highest levels of the cognitive hierarchy (doctrine and ideology). "Products" became "services," and "sales" became "solutions." The newly empowered Global Services division acts as an efficient intelligence-and information-gathering mechanism, "out there" with customers and having an incentive structure encouraging brutal honesty when IBM products do not meet its clients' needs.

COMING TO GRIPS WITH WHAT CANNOT BE GRASPED

There may be a trade-off between, on one hand, survivability within established structures and, on the other hand, performance. Maximization of performance may sometimes be impossible under conditions of optimized survivability within a structure of subordination. Anyone who has ever worked for anyone else probably knows this from personal experience. There is no reason that organizational performance should be any different in this respect. Indeed, the more complex any environment becomes, the more likely this may be, and the more frequently the contradictions may appear. The long (i.e., continuous) duration of unpredicted and unfamiliar decisional situations and the experience of high tension in the contemporary business environment then combine to increase the stress on decision makers. As pointed out earlier, all other things being equal, this decreases their ability to learn from the environment against which their very success or failure will be judged. Such a condition today seems characteristic, if not fundamental.

One solution is for organizational adaptation through learning to cease being a mechanism for responding to the environment and for mergers and acquisition to predominate in an attempt to control the environment. Yet merger and acquisition in the corporate world today are barely survival tools by which corporations and their components are driven—driven, moreover, not necessarily by any internal logic about the environment but by the environment itself unreflectively. Prominent chief executive officers (CEOs) frequently face, with respect to their subsidiaries, much the same problem Gorbachev faced with the republics. However, if merger-and-acquisition becomes the dominant ideology, then corporate executives become less able to respond optimally to new problems that require solutions other than merger and acquisition. In the history of international politics, the examples of Napoleon and Hitler suggest themselves as analogies.

Consider Lithuania, for example, as a division of another company that was acquired by "USSR, Inc.," under Stalin's stewardship. The military occupation of Lithuania was for Stalin a rational decision. Yet after a visit to Lithuania, already self-organizing to take itself out of the Soviet Union, Gorbachev began talking about "socialist pluralism" and began planning to institute changes in the party's rules that legitimated factions and erased its "leading role" from the long-standing doctrine. This would probably have happened in any event, given Gorbachev's intents for reform; but in the absence of the annexation of the Baltic states nearly a half century earlier by Stalin, it could well have happened differently, with different results. There is an argument to be made that Stalin's annexation of the Baltic states strongly contributed to the ultimate disintegration of the Soviet Union. In political terms, then, Lithuania was a "loss-making center" that should have been divested. But doctrinaire ideologues at corporate headquarters (the Kremlin) enforced a political inertia making such change impossible until it was too late.

Even in the late 1980s, an effective response would not necessarily have entailed the breakup of the Soviet Union. Gorbachev tried "downsizing" the USSR by drafting a new treaty to replace the 1922 agreement that formed the USSR—a "new Union Treaty"—and as many as nine republics would have signed it as late as summer 1991. By rejecting the so-called Shatalin plan for economic reform, however, Gorbachev denied the leaders of those republics any incentive to stay in a reformed USSR, which he proposed to call the Union of Sovereign States (Matlock, 1995). With no centrally generated rationale for remaining part of the parent organization, these divisions of "USSR, Inc.," driven by the international environment, including their own electorates (which had become part of the Soviet Union's international environment while the Kremlin was not looking), spun themselves off. They found the international environment to be extremely receptive to this self-initiated antitrust action.

Much the same logic animates the idea of "spin-offs." This has been key to the wealth of leveraged buyouts (LBOs) and to the success of such conglomerates as 3M and Thermo-Electron. These firms encourage the direct addressing of cognitive dissonance between headquarters and the field, while other firms (the old AT&T and the big three carmakers come immediately to mind) encourage the disavowal of even the possibility that such dissonance is important. On one hand, corporate subsidiaries have to have a fair amount of freedom to respond to the environment, both for their own efficiency and to guarantee the survival of the overall system. If that does not happen, then a corps of ideologues can form in the corporate headquarters that has a vested interest in the continuation of a dysfunctional corporate culture. Such a corporate culture is like a "field," invisible on organizational charts but exerting an influence on perceptions and decisions much as Marxism-Leninism did in the Soviet Union. In the end, either key engineers may leave and began their own spin-off, start-up firms, or entire divisions may become unprofitable and subject to hostile takeovers and buyouts, all because the corporate ideologues have exerted such a pull that even a "reformist" CEO like Khrushchev may be unable to escape their influence.

On the other hand, if the subordinate managers are empowered to respond as necessary to their immediate business environment, relatively free of central direction, then there is no guarantee a priori that they will not decentralize themselves out of the system. That is what some of the Soviet republics began doing even in late 1980s, before the entire Soviet system came crashing down after the failed coup attempt in August 1991.

The difficult question for managers at the highest level is how to allow the subsidiaries the freedom to survive and be viable, while at the same time providing them incentives to stay within the overall corporate institution yet without imposing upon them constraints that suboptimize their survivability. Gorbachev tried and failed. Steve Jobs failed and returned. What happens to the reader of this chapter is not merely up to that reader. These days, all people not only need all the help they can get but also can get all the help they need. However, only a complex-system approach can help figure out which of the many answers available is the right one. The CEOs of "USSR, Inc.," did not learn this soon enough. And you?

REFERENCES

Abelson, Robert P. 1973. "The Structure of Belief Systems." In *Computer Models of Thought and Language*, edited by Roger C. Schank and Kenneth Mark Colby. San Francisco: W. H. Freeman, 276–339.

Allaire, Y., and Firsirotu, M. 1985. "How to Implement Radical Strategies in Large Organizations." *Sloan Management Review*, Vol. 27, 19–34.

Aspaturian, Vernon V. 1966. "Internal Politics and Foreign Policy in the Soviet System." In *Approaches to Comparative and International Politics*, edited by R. Barry Farrell. Evanston, Ill.: Northwestern University Press, 212–287. Reprinted in Aspaturian, 1971, 491–551.

Aspaturian, Vernon V. 1972. "The Soviet Military-Industrial Complex— Does It Exist?" *Journal of International Affairs*, Vol. 26, No. 1, 1–28.

Cutler, Robert M. 1981. "Decision Making and International Relations: The Cybernetic Theory Reconsidered." *Michigan Journal of Political Science*, Vol. 1. No. 2 (Fall 1981), 57–63.

Cutler, Robert M. 1982. "Soviet Debates over Foreign Policy toward Western Europe: Four Case Studies, 1971–1975." Ph.D. diss., University of Michigan.

Cutler, Robert M. 1985. "Domestic and Foreign Influences on Policy-making: The Soviet Union in the 1974 Cyprus Conflict." *Soviet Studies*, Vol. 37, No. 1 (January), 60–89.

Cutler, Robert M. 1990. "Participation and Learning in Soviet Foreign Policy-making: The Press and Information-Processing under Brezhnev." Book manuscript.

Degras, Jane. 1967. "United Front Tactics in the Comintern, 1921–1928." In *International Communism in the Era of Lenin*, compiled by Helmut Graber. Ithaca, N.Y.: Cornell University Press, 491–497.

Eran, Oded. 1979. *The Mezhdunarodniki: An Assessment of Professional Expertise in the Making of Soviet Foreign Policy.* Jerusalem: Turtledove.

Etheredge, Lloyd S. 1981. "Government Learning: An Overview." In *The Handbook of Political Behavior*, Vol. 2, edited by Samuel L. Long. New York: Plenum Press, 73–161.

Glassman, Jon D. 1968. "Soviet Foreign Policy Decision-Making." In *Columbia Essays in International Affairs*, Vol. 3: *The Dean's Papers, 1967.* New York: Columbia University Press, 373–402.

Griffiths, Franklyn. 1972. "Images, Politics, and Learning in Soviet Behaviour toward the United States." Ph.D. diss., Columbia University.

Griffiths, Franklyn. 1991. "Attempted Learning: Soviet Policy toward the United States, in the Brezhnev Era." In *Learning in U.S. and Soviet Foreign Policy*, G. N. Breslauer and Tetlock, P. E., (ed.), 1991.

Haas, Ernst 1991. "Collective Learning: Some Theoretical Speculations." In Breslauer and Tetlock, 1991.

Hoffmann, Erik. P. 1968. "Communication Theory and the Study of Soviet Politics." *Canadian Slavic Studies*, Vol. 2, No. 4 (Winter), 542–558.

Inozemtsev, N. N. 1972. "Les relations internationales en Europe dans les années 1980." In *Europe 1980: L'avenir des relations intra-européennes; Rapports presentés à la Conférence des Directeurs et Représentants des Instituts européens de relations internationales, Varna, 3–5.X.1972.* Leiden: A. W. Sijthoff, 121–136.

Kudriavtsev, Vik. 1974. "Vokrug 'kiprskogo krizisa'." *SShA*, No. 9 (September), 72–75.

Lant, T. K., and Montgomery, D. B. 1987. "Learning from Strategic Success and Failure." *Journal of Business Research*, Vol. 15, 503–518.

Legvold, Robert. 1974. "The Problem of European Security." *Problems of Communism*, Vol. 23 (January–February), 13–33.

Löwenhardt, John. 1981. *Decision Making in Soviet Politics*. New York: St. Martin's Press.

Matlock, Jack M., Jr. 1995. *Autopsy on an Empire: The American Ambassador's Account of the Collapse of the Soviet Union*. New York: Random House.

Meissner, Boris. 1977. "Der Auswärtige Dienst der UdSSR." *Aussenpolitik*, Vol. 28, No. 1, 47–61.

Mel'nikov, D. 1972. "Zapadnoevropeiskii tsentr imperializma." *Mirovaia ekonomika i mezhdunarodnye otnosheniia*, No. 1 (January), 14–30.

Meyer, Alfred G. 1965. *The Soviet Political System*. New York: Knopf.

Miller, D. 1990. *The Icarus Paradox: How Exceptional Companies Bring About Their Own Downfall*. New York: HarperBusiness.

Miller, D. 1994. "What Happens after Success: The Perils of Excellence." *Journal of Management Studies*, Vol. 31, 325–358.

Peffley, Mark A., and Hurwitz, Jon. 1985. "A Hierarchical Model of Attitude Constraint." *American Journal of Political Science*, Vol. 29, No. 4 (November), 871–890.

Petrov, Vladimir. 1973. "Formation of Soviet Foreign Policy." *Orbis*, Vol. 17, No. 3 (Fall), 819–850.

Popov, V. P. 1984. *Na glavnom napravlenii (O rabote politicheskogo obozrevatelia)*. Moscow: Mysl'.

Rasputins, B. I. 1980. *Sovetskaia istoriografiia sovremennogo rabochego dvizheniia*. Chast' 2, *Sotsial'no–politicheksie problemy*. L'vov: Vishcha shkola, Izdatel'stvo pri L'vovskom gosudarstvennom universitete.

Remington, Thomas F. 1985. *The Truth of Authority: Ideology and Communication in the Soviet Union*. Pittsburgh: University of Pittsburgh Press.

Schapiro, Leonard. 1975. "The General Department of the CC of the CPSU." *Survey*, No. 96, 53–65.

Schapiro, Leonard. 1977. "The International Department of the CPSU: Key to Soviet Policy." *International Journal*, Vol. 32, No. 1 (Winter), 41–55.

Steinbruner, John D. 1974. *The Cybernetic Theory of Decision: New Dimensions of Political Analysis*. Princeton, N.J.: Princeton University Press.

Zagoria, Donald S. 1962. *The Sino–Soviet Conflict 1956–1961*. Princeton, N.J.: Princeton University Press.

Zaretskii, V. A. 1973. "Vzaimosviaz' demokraticheskikh i sotsialisticheskikh zadach na sovremennom etape klassovoi bor'by v razvitykh kapitalisticheskikh stranakh". In *Problemy rabochego, kommunisticheskogo i natsional'no–osvoboditel'nogo dvizheniia (Nauchnye trudy)*, edited by A. A. Koval'skii and M. M. Solntseva. Moscow: MGIMO, 102–119.

Chapter 19

The Emergence of Technological Fields

Raghu Garud, Peter Karnøe, and E. Andres Garcia

Among organizational scholars, there is a growing appreciation of the complexities associated with the emergence of technological fields. At one level, complexity is manifest in the components that constitute a technological system. At another, complexity is manifest in the interactions between agents with diverse perspectives. At a deeper level, however, complexity resides in the generative forces or rules that shape manifest phenomena (Drazin and Sandelands, 1992).

How do agents constituting a technological field navigate the complex landscapes that they confront? Given complexity, and indeed because of it, it is very likely that agents will adopt different approaches to guide their choices and behaviors based on beliefs of what is and what is not possible (Nelson and Winter, 1982; Dosi, 1982). These approaches can have dramatically different consequences as initial choices become amplified through learning processes that generate knowledge in a recursive manner. Consequently, complexity is as much about how we deal with nature as it is about nature itself.

We attempt to illustrate this proposition with a comparative study of wind turbine fields in Denmark and the United States. While a wind turbine could be considered just an extension of the age-old windmill, in its modern incarnation it is a sophisticated, "systemic" technology that, like aircraft, automobiles, and computers, comprises numerous interacting subsystems and components (Winter, 1987; Rosenberg, 1982; Sahal, 1985). Wind turbines meld knowledge from diverse streams such as electronics, mechanics, hydraulics, advanced materials, and aerodynamics to create a system that can transform the kinetic energy in wind to rotational energy and then to electromagnetic energy. A drive train of shafts and gears connects to a generator. A yaw system holds the rotor or propeller in the direction of the wind, and an electronic system comprising sophisticated software and sensors makes automatic adjustments to a changing environment of wind and weather.

The interactive complexity (Perrow, 1984) that is part of the logic implicit in such technology often makes it hard to design the "best" system a priori—there are simply too many variables and issues to be considered. These challenges are magnified if the system itself is poorly understood and, furthermore, is put to use in varying and poorly understood environmental contexts. In such a situation, it becomes difficult, if not impossible, to design a system that takes into account all the contingencies that might arise (Rosenberg, 1982). Further ambiguities about the production and use of complex technological systems are introduced by a new field's emerging institutional structures.

Of interest here are the different approaches adopted by wind turbine innovators in the United States and Denmark to confront this complex phenomenon. Using a baseball metaphor, we can describe the American approach as aiming to "hit a home run" via a theoretical breakthrough. In contrast, we can characterize the Danish approach as aiming to "hit singles and doubles" based on practical incrementalism. Interestingly, as history testifies, the Danish approach led to the development of wind turbines that are superior in performance to ones developed in the United States (Karnøe, 1993; Gipe, 1995).

COMPLEXITY AND TECHNOLOGICAL FIELDS

Previous attempts at understanding technological change show us how even the simplest of questions can become elusive; for example, how do technological fields emerge? While cursory observations into this question may suggest a simple linear progression from the conception of an innovative idea, through its technical development, and to its commercial adoption, a more probing examination exposes a complex web of reciprocal interactions between those developing, using, and regulating the technology.

Each of the constituents, as illustrated in Figure 19.1, brings a different "frame" to the situation (Bijker, Hughes, and Pinch, 1987; Karnøe and Garud, 1997). For instance, frames about production may include beliefs about the future potential of a technological system and how best to actualize that potential. Frames about use may consist of the multiple meanings that can be attributed to a technological system when in use. Governance frames may include, on one hand, beliefs about the social consequences of a technological system and, on the other, the effect that specific policy instruments can have to shape the system's development (Jørgensen and Karnøe, 1995). When considered separately, each of these perspectives encourages a microanalytic view, downplaying or ignoring the dynamic interaction among different frames that could result in certain approaches being pursued over others.

At a microlevel of analysis, interactions between agents with different perspectives are "chaotic" at best (Polley and Van de Ven, 1996). Indeed, what one set of actors may think is appropriate, another may not even understand. At a macrolevel though, these interactions generate "observable" patterns. For instance, a pattern is often revealed in the selection of a technological "dominant design" (Tushman and Anderson, 1986; Anderson and Tushman, 1990), which, in chaos theory terms, may represent a type of "strange attractor." Surrounding and supporting these dominant designs are certain sociotechnical arrangements, patterns of use, and wider institutional structures.

These observable patterns usually become apparent only after the fact with the benefit of time and distance. However, it is seldom possible to wait for meaningful structures to emerge, espe-

Figure 19.1
Frames Constituting and Constituted by a Technological Field-in-the-Making

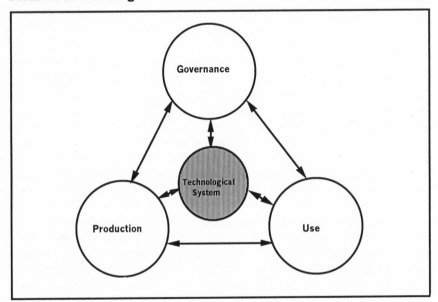

cially if we as practitioners or as scholars are a part of the phenomenon-in-the-making. How, then, should we navigate the treacherous, complex road on a real-time basis?

Concepts from the science of complexity offer a useful framework. Drazin and Sandelands (1992) make a distinction between a complex system's observable structure, elemental structure, and deep structure. Observable structure represents perceived macrolevel, supraindividual patterns or structures generated by the interactions of the system's constituent agents, often manifesting emergent properties not evidenced at the individual level. Elemental structure consists of microlevel, individual social behaviors and interactions manifested in time and space. Deep structure consists of the generative grammar, rules, or logics that produce the social behaviors and interactions in the first place (see also Tsoukas, 1989).

This framework is readily applicable to technology management. Technological fields are emergent structures driven by the underlying logics of various actors who enact their realities depending on their frames of reference (Bijker, Hughes, and Pinch, 1987; Garud and Rappa, 1994). In doing so, actors with differing frames of reference influence each other. An interactional debate ensues between the actors, the outcomes of which are institutionalized in practices and meanings (Berger and Luckman, 1966) that, in turn, feed back to affect individual actors by shaping their frames of reference and their actions. These dynamic, intersecting processes provide technological systems with the potential to evolve in different directions, depending on initial conditions and subsequent interactions between agents perceiving and interpreting through particular frames of production, use, and governance.

Other concepts from the science of complexity such as feedback loops and accumulated stocks (Senge, 1990) can be mapped into the realm of technology management as concepts of learning and knowledge accumulation. Agents engage in intersecting learning processes: learning-by-doing, learning-by-using and learning-by-testing (Garud, 1997; Rosenberg, 1982). Learning-by-doing is an experiential process of knowledge accumulation regarding how a technology is produced (Arrow, 1962; Argote and Epple, 1990). Learning-by-using, is a process that explores and creates knowledge of what is of value through the actual use of a product (Rosenberg, 1982; Karnøe, 1993). Learning-by-testing is a process of systematic experimentation and simulation to accumulate knowledge of the principles underlying the functioning of a technological system (Dutton and Thomas, 1985). Together, these learning processes generate knowledge about specific problems, choices, environments, and outcomes. Such knowledge, generated through production, use, practical experimentation, and thoughtful reflection, eventually becomes codified in a field's evolving communities of practice and other institutional bodies (Brown and Duguid, 1991).

An interesting aspect of these learning processes is the possibility of knowledge's developing in a recursive way. Indeed, the underlying logics of actors in a technological field are partly shaped by their existing stock of knowledge, forming the basis for their beliefs of what is and is not possible. Over time, feedback from production, use and testing drives and directs the buildup of knowledge in a path-dependent, cumulative manner. Eventually, these transformational processes manifest themselves in the form of "technological trajectories" (Dosi, 1982), paths along which a technology develops based on previous choices and on future expectations (Dosi, 1982; Nelson and Winter, 1982; Arthur, 1989). Once set in motion, each trajectory progresses with its own developmental logic that recursively feeds upon itself via learning processes that lead to the accumulation of knowledge (Cohen and Levinthal, 1990).

The notion of trajectories is useful to explain a puzzling facet of wind turbines. Specifically, despite their best efforts, technological innovators in the United States failed to create a robust wind turbine field, whereas their Danish counterparts succeeded. We think that unraveling the generative forces that have constituted the wind turbine fields in Denmark and the United States may help us understand these outcome, and, in the process, suggest that complexity is as much about how we as humans deal with nature as it is about nature itself.

TECHNOLOGICAL FIELD IN THE MAKING

In this study, we focus on the private market (i.e., nongovernmental) wind turbine fields in both Denmark and the United States. Our observations are based on historical archives of the development of the fields in the two countries as well as a real-time study of their evolution over a period of more than 10 years. Surprisingly similar circumstances existed in both countries between 1975 and 1990. For instance, entrepreneurs in both countries started out at about the same time, in the mid-1970s. Entrepreneurs in both countries also were stimulated by market incentives at about the same time, in the late 1970s and early 1980s. Finally, the emerging wind turbine industry in both countries was supported by newly established test and research centers focusing on small-scale wind turbines. A natural experiment, in effect, unfolded during the 1975–1990 time period, the initial and early consolidation phases of the development of modern wind power technology.

Despite the similarities, however, actors in the two countries pursued significantly different paths. American innovators adopted a "high-tech" breakthrough approach, while Danish innovators adopted a "low-tech" incremental approach. Despite their best efforts, the Americans failed to create a robust wind turbine field, whereas their Danish counterparts succeeded. We think that unraveling the generative forces that have constituted the wind turbine fields in the two countries may help us to understand these outcomes. An explanation for these diverging paths lies in ways of thinking and doing institutionalized over time in the two countries. We reflect on these institutionalized ways of thinking and doing in our comparative description of the evolution of the two fields. We will also reflect on how learning and knowledge accumulation processes amplified these paths into distinctive trajectories with dramatically different outcomes. Through this reflection, we will offer a tentative proposition—complexity may be more a state of mind than a state of nature.

Today, the Danish wind turbine field is robust and viable, with Danish firms holding almost 60 percent of the global market share. The market leader, Vestas, is a Danish firm with a 24 percent market share. Four of the 5 largest wind turbine firms in the world are Danish, as well as 6 of the 10 largest. Danish firms' sales come primarily from tough export markets requiring flexibility, adaptability, and resourcefulness, not from a familiar, comfortable home market (BTM Consult, 1997). Yet, in the early days, becoming the global market leader was probably the furthest aspiration imaginable by anyone. After all, the origins of the Danish wind turbine field can be traced to unglamorous, low-tech, agricultural equipment. Participants were "hands-on" engineers, machinists, and skilled workers without a lot of fancy degrees and credentials, unlike their high-tech American counterparts. They worked on developing simple designs and incrementally improving them over time. The dominant design that emerged early on had even been christened an "ugly duckling" for its ungainly solidity and simplicity. This is a story of how an ugly duckling was transformed into a beautiful swan.

Meanwhile, the lead article in a recent edition of a wind turbine trade journal showed a photograph of an American-designed wind turbine with its blades hanging at an unnatural angle, the victim of blade failure. It was a fitting image, as the journal was reporting the sad demise of Kenetech Windpower, the last big American turbine manufacturer and once the largest wind power company in the world. Kenetech was filing for bankruptcy after having spent millions of dollars developing wind turbines over the past two decades (Davidson, 1996). The high-profile bankruptcy dramatized the steady decline over time in the viability of the American wind turbine field. With Kenetech gone, none of the top 10 wind turbine firms in the world are American. Yet, only a few years earlier, there was much optimism that the American field would become a powerhouse and prevail in global competition. It had a high-tech, glamorous aerospace pedigree. It had academically trained engineers with a highly theoretical problem-solving orientation that had their sights set on discovering technological breakthroughs. There was confidence that the development of novel, sophisticated, breakthrough designs would leapfrog over the competition, making the Danish field's "pedestrian" approach obsolete. This is therefore also a story of how defeat was snatched from the jaws of victory.

PRODUCTION FRAMES IN DENMARK

Practical engineers and skilled workers. The Danish wind turbine industry originated in a region of Denmark where a particular type of work organization was prevalent: the small and medium-sized craft shop or factory (Kristensen, 1990, 1992). Early development was organized by small bands of practical engineers, mechanics, fitters, and other skilled workers. The flat, flexible, craftlike organization of these firms encouraged the kind of communication and coordination among different groups required for learning to take place. Design, production, operational experience and maintenance, and redesign took place in an organic, collaborative, integrated manner. Problems would be communicated and tackled directly without too many bureaucratic formalities or hierarchical approvals, further improving the capacity for learning. The "craft-educational complex" (Kristensen, 1992) of technical schools, established before the turn of the century by local craft associations, also played an important institutional role in helping Danish skilled workers to reproduce craft-based, high autonomy social roles within organizations (Kristensen, 1990).

From agricultural equipment to wind turbines. In contrast to the high-tech Americans, participants in the Danish wind turbine field had low-tech backgrounds. All three small companies that helped to create the field had originally produced agricultural equipment. Their accumulated stock of pragmatic, often tacit craft knowledge was primarily embedded in practices and routines (Nelson and Winter, 1982) that had coevolved with the technology of the manufacturing process and the social organization of the shop floor. Upon entering the new field of wind turbines, they naturally used an approach they were familiar with and good at, namely, their core competency of designing and constructing equipment that was durable and reliable enough to operate for many years with little maintenance or downtime. Learning-by-doing was an integral and familiar part of achieving that reliability.

Practical problem-solving orientation. Danish wind turbine participants did not define the problems they faced in terms of the formal, theoretical language of aerodynamics and structural dynamics. Rather, they defined them in practical terms as mechanical or material challenges discovered through hands-on experience, especially through technical failure. They struggled to get turbines to work reliably by designing and redesigning components that failed or could be improved. Many a problem was solved by "throwing metal on it." Ironically, the stodgy, heavyweight Danish designs lessened the negative effects of the severe vibrations that gave the elegant, lightweight American designs poorer reliability and a shorter life (Stoddard, 1986). Development work on the early Danish turbines was thus characterized by pragmatic, ad hoc efforts with often serendipitous results. Design and construction were guided by simple rules of thumb and by trial and error. Over time there accumulated a large amount of practical, hands-on, often tacit knowledge that gradually, yet steadily, improved turbine-specific competencies.

Incremental simplicity. Danish wind turbine participants pursued much more simplicity and much less sophistication and novelty than their American counterparts. Their preferred innovation approach has been one of incremental improvements to simple, sturdy designs as experience is gained with them. In the 1950s a Dane, Johannes Juul, developed a turbine, eventually christened the "Danish design," whose simplicity and robustness fitted well with the practical orientation and aversion to novelty of the field's early firms. It was quickly adopted by them, becoming the dominant design and, to a great extent, fixing the Danish technological trajectory going forward. Danish firms also patiently built on existing knowledge and refrained from taking design risks that might be too great. For instance, in a gradual, step-by-step upscaling, the size of Danish wind turbines grew from the 10–30 kW range in the mid-1970s to the 500 kW range by the early 1990s. This incremental approach was ideally suited to fostering learning-by-doing, allowing firms to concentrate on solving, and learning from, a small number of manageable problems within each incremental step.

PRODUCTION FRAMES IN AMERICA

Design engineers and unskilled workers. The American wind turbine firms generally perceived design-oriented engineering as their primary activity, with production being of secondary concern. The firms' design and production functions therefore tended to be poorly integrated, with little internal communication and collaboration between them. Design engineers became insulated from the hands-on problems encountered in turbine construction and maintenance, making it very difficult for this practical knowledge to feed back and revise the engineers' more theoretical knowledge base.

In comparison to the Danish educational system, the American educational system has been much weaker at educating workers. It has tended to conform to prevalent managerial conceptions of efficient mass production as requiring a narrow set of worker skills and a strict segregation of workers away from "thinking" tasks such as the solution of production problems (Noble, 1984). There has also been a steady decline in American companies' technical apprenticeship programs (Piore and Sabel, 1984). The resulting lack of skilled workers also hampered the learning-by-doing process of American wind turbine firms.

From aerospace to wind turbines. Most participants in the American wind turbine field had aerospace engineering backgrounds. However, wind turbines were different enough in their functioning and conditions of use to make much of the knowledge from the aerospace field inapplicable and downright misleading. Rather than serving as a core competency, that knowledge base instead became a core rigidity (Leonard-Barton, 1992). It prevented American designers from perceiving new possibilities and different alternatives and directly contributed to low reliability and poor performance of many American turbines. American engineers perceived the creation of a lightweight, aerodynamically efficient turbine as the only rational and appropriate option for increasing performance and decreasing costs. However, there was no compelling technical reason to build a light turbine, since it would normally not be airborne. A heavier design approach would have increased turbine sturdiness and stabilized its performance. American engineers thus needed to "unlearn" (Hedberg, 1981) many of the lessons of their old aerospace field in order to be able to learn in the new wind turbine field.

Theoretical problem-solving orientation. American design engineers valued and sought mostly theoretical knowledge. Design problems were mainly perceived in terms of engineering "science." Aerodynamic and structural forces had to be modeled and dealt with in advance, in great detail, and with a high degree of accuracy. Technical problems were to be solved by advances in theory and embedded in advanced CAD/CAM equipment, rather than by practical means such as prototype construction and trial-and-error learning. The overemphasis on developing the basic science underlying wind turbines was also consistent with the changed characteristics of American engineering education, which over time had moved away from its traditional practical orientation toward a more "scientific" engineering based on fundamental theoretical principles (Dertouzos and Solow, 1989; Seely, 1993).

Breakthrough approach. American wind turbine designs were typically quite sophisticated. The goal of many American engineers seemed to be a breakthrough innovation, or at least a design that had radically changed features compared to existing technology (F. S. Stoddard, personal communication, January 5, 1993). American designers generally hoped that lightweight, high-tech, high-risk designs would leapfrog over the simpler, but safer and sturdier, Danish designs (Davidson, 1993). This tendency to aim for radical changes can be seen in American firms' strategies for upscaling the size of their turbines. For example, three firms whose largest turbines were in the 25–100 kW range decided to ramp up by several orders of magnitude to 300 kW for their next generation of machines. The large number of major, novel, and complex problems encountered when employing a breakthrough approach made it difficult to engage in learning-by-doing; some constellations of problems turned out to be simply intractable.

USE FRAMES IN DENMARK

Critical early users. The Danish industry began by selling its early, small turbines to individual users and cooperatives; by the early 1980s several hundred of them had been installed. The presence of many dispersed installations, experiencing possibly different conditions of use, created multiple learning points. Geographical proximity enabled producers to learn quickly from their mistakes and to keep turbines in operation (Gipe, 1995). Mistakes thus came to be viewed as market probes creating opportunities for learning, rather than as evidence of failure. The learning-by-using that took place with these small turbines formed the basis for the gradual design scale-up to the larger turbines now being deployed by utilities.

Concerned with safety and reliability, early users put critical pressure on producers to improve turbines. These user demands created a relatively strong "selection environment," resulting in market-driven adaptation. The Danish Wind Mill Owners' Association played a particularly important role. Its insistence on a fail-safe braking system turned out to be a key factor in furthering technological development, since "it attempted to ensure the survival of the wind turbine when something went wrong" (Gipe, 1995:59). By regularly publishing reliability and performance data on most turbine models, it also created market "transparency" and forced producers to compete on market-defined evaluation criteria (van Est, 1996a).

Feedback from foreign markets. Generous federal and state tax credits in California during the mid-1980s for large, centralized arrays of wind turbines known as "wind farms" resulted in an export boom known as the "California wind rush." While providing fantastic growth opportunities, it also presented tremendous technological and organizational challenges (Karnøe, 1991). Danish firms assumed their technology could be easily transposed into other environments. However, the wind regimes in California and Denmark differed significantly; the new wind regime tended to be more turbulent, with higher speeds and greater variability, subjecting Danish turbines to greater stresses than they had previously encountered. There quickly arose an unexpected need for repairs on a sizable number of them. Danish manufacturers soon began to realize the magnitude of effort required to service capital equipment in a distant export market under much different conditions of use. Government market subsidies expired just as service obligations were increasing. Export sales plummeted, and Danish firms, most of which were small and undercapitalized, were not prepared organizationally and financially to cope with the squeezes brought on by rising costs, falling revenues, and overcapacity. The field experienced a shakeout, with a number of firms merging or undergoing bankruptcy reorganization.

The Danish firms, however, absorbed some hard-learned lessons from the California export experience (van Est, 1996b). They continued to develop and incrementally scale up a new generation of more powerful, more efficient turbines. Slowly, new markets began emerging in response to increased concern over environmental problems and as developing countries began to realize the attractiveness of small-scale distributed energy generation. When global wind turbine markets began to take off in the mid-1990s, Danish firms found themselves in the enviable position of having a proven, robust technology and experience in export markets. They solidly established themselves as market leaders.

USE FRAMES IN AMERICAN FIRMS

Lack of critical early users. Unlike Denmark, in the United States during the 1970s and 1980s a "home" market of smaller, distributed wind turbine users did not develop. American firms' fixation on sophisticated, breakthrough technology made their wind turbines too expensive, complicated, and unreliable for most small users. Producers did not perceive the distributed market as all that promising or appealing, focusing on the centralized "wind farm" concept instead. Their aerospace roots, where government would buy large quantities of a certain model of aircraft or helicopter, appeared to constrain their thinking to only a "wholesale" and not a "retail" sales mentality. Consequently, there was not the type of critical feedback or demand for reliability from small users that could have provided the necessary inducements (Rosenberg, 1976) for American firms to learn, develop better designs, and gradually upscale them to larger users. There was also little pressure for the development of independent mechanisms for information disclosure and evaluation that could have made the market more "transparent" and helped to protect users from buying poor technology. Neither producers nor government agencies made much effort to provide accurate, reliable, and timely performance data. The result was a dramatically muted learning-by-using process.

Wind farm excesses. The trend toward generating wind energy from centralized wind farms that had begun in the late 1970s dramatically accelerated in the early 1980s (Gipe, 1995), due to the lure of easy profits from tax credits provided by the federal government and the state of California. The speculative fever of wind farm development that was unleashed almost ended up destroying the nascent wind turbine field. Existing American (and Danish) firms cranked up their production capacity, and new firms rushed into the industry in an attempt to cash in on wind farms' apparently limitless demand for what was at the time, particularly from the American firms, an immature, untested technology. Extremely generous public subsidies encouraged "projects where money was made mostly in the financial wheeling and business dealing before anything was in the ground, regardless of whether the turbines actually worked" (Davidson 1996: 4). Wind farm developers thus had little incentive to be critical of turbine performance. Eventually, American turbines began to fail in large numbers. The unrealistic expectations created by manufacturers' hyped-up performance projections, the technology's subsequent poor record, the negative image portrayed by the media of wind farms as a tax scam (van Est, 1996a), and publicized criminal fraud cases against "fly-by-night" developers combined to cause a backlash against wind power that resulted in long-lasting damage to the field. As one participant put it: "It seems. . .that the only feedback we really got was from the lawyers and lawsuits" (F. S. Stoddard personal communication, January 5, 1993). The dysfunctional effects of the artificially induced speculative boom practically short-circuited the learning-by-using process.

GOVERNANCE FRAMES IN DENMARK

Test and research center model: technological institutes. The Danish Wind Turbine Test Station (DWTS) was established in 1978 by a $1 million grant from the Danish Energy Agency to specifically support the emerging wind turbine industry. The craft-educational complex discussed earlier was supplemented by another important institution that served as a model for the test center. Established at the beginning of the century, the Danish Technological Institute supported the diffusion of knowledge, methods, and the latest technologies among small and medium-sized craft firms. It also provided independent testing of particular technical products and industrial processes. Over time a number of specialized technical institutes sprang up to support specific industries. The establishment of the DWTS thus followed an institutionalized Danish model of providing testing and consulting support for smaller firms. From the beginning, research activity at this test center thus had a strong practical orientation regarding how problems were defined, prioritized, and addressed, with the research agenda primarily shaped by design engineers from the wind turbine industry itself.

Test center approval for market subsidies. In 1979 a Danish government act established a market subsidy, payable to buyers, for 30 percent of the total cost of a wind turbine. In order for a turbine to qualify for the subsidy, though, it had to be evaluated and approved by the test center. This approval responsibility quickly became the dominant factor in shaping the type of problems addressed and the type of knowledge developed by the test center. Consistent with the practical problem solving orientation and conservative attitude toward innovation that categorized the field, operating reliability and safety became the center's primary evaluation criteria. The center, however, only determined some minimum standards needed for qualification for the subsidy and did not "select" any particular design. The DWTS thus played an extremely important role in helping the industry to successfully develop its technology base. The extensive contact between turbine firms and the test center that occurred during numerous iterations of designing, constructing, testing, reviewing, and problem-solving prior to approval of a new turbine contributed immensely to the cumulative building of a shared knowledge base and research agenda within the industry (Andersen, 1993), and consequently to the continuous incremental improvement of turbine performance.

GOVERNANCE FRAMES IN AMERICA

Test and research center model: national laboratories. Governmental research and development (R&D) support for small-scale wind turbines began in 1977 with the establishment of a research center. Originally known as the Solar Energy Research Institute (SERI), its name was later changed to the National Renewable Energy Laboratory (NREL), which more closely reflected its institutional roots, the government-directed U.S. National Laboratories program (e.g., Los Alamos, Brookhaven, Livermore). Perceiving its mission as engaging in fundamental engineering science research, it shied away from the very kind of systematic testing of commercial turbines under simulated or actual conditions of use that would have identified, evaluated, and measured progress on practical industry problems. The research center thus did not provide much support for market-driven innovative activities. By focusing its research on finding the "best" (i.e., breakout) turbine design based on scientific principles, the center generated knowledge that was too abstract and theoretical to provide the kind of simulation and testing feedback that the industry most needed.

Military R&D contracting. Military and aerospace R&D contracts have dominated U. S. government-funded research in the postwar period (Mowery and Rosenberg, 1989; Noble, 1984). A desire for breakthrough innovations also tended to be an important criterion in awarding these contracts. NREL's mission to search for the best wind turbine embodied this attitude. Pressure to achieve breakthroughs translated into a direct coercive force on firms applying to the center for small-scale development contracts. The center defined the standards or evaluation criteria that had to be met, biased toward designs that offered the promise of a technological breakthrough (Nelson, 1984). The upshot was the creation of an artificial selection mechanism bearing little resemblance to actual or potential conditions of use for wind turbines. This usurped the role of the marketplace in selecting suitable technologies and resulted in "false" or incorrect learning taking place by American wind turbine firms.

DISCUSSION

It is not surprising that participants from two different institutional contexts adopted very different "navigational" approaches to wind turbine development that either enabled or constrained learning processes and knowledge accumulation. As previously discussed, technological fields are emergent structures driven by the underlying logics of the participants, who interactively enact their realities based on their frames of reference (Bijker, Hughes, and Pinch, 1987). The outcomes of their interactions become institutionalized in taken-for-granted practices and meanings (Berger and Luckmann, 1966), which, in turn, feed back to influence those very participants by shaping their frames of reference, thus closing the hermeneutic circle. Depending on the initial conditions and subsequent interactions between participants perceiving and interpreting through particular frames of production, use, and governance, technological systems have the potential to evolve in a number of unpredictable directions.

The frames of production, use, and governance employed by the Danes influenced them to adopt a "transformative" approach of adapting competencies, materials, and policy instruments at hand to create a robust wind turbine field. The process of transformation itself appears to have been one of continual negotiation and sense-making between producers, users, and regulators, leading wind turbine firms to develop sensitivity and responsiveness to feedback from multiple constituencies. Progress was made on the basis of these small, yet continual, feedback signals. Practical experimentation coupled with incremental modifications allowed for the evolution of the field in an emergent way. Indeed, in the evolution of the Danish wind turbine field there was no set of grand plans, on central coordination. Instead, the evolution of this field seems to have been supported by an institutional capacity for a high degree of mutual learning and knowledge accumulation that melded processes and outcomes into a collective act of resourcefulness, adaptation, and sense-making. Such a collective act is similar to processes observed in other settings. For instance, recognizing the challenges of navigating through complexity, scholars have offered complementary notions such as the "science of muddling through" (Lindblom, 1959), "logical incrementalism" (Quinn, 1978), or "emergent strategies" (Mintzberg, Raisinghani, and Theoret, 1976).

In contrast, these emergent properties appear to have been missing in the evolution of the American field. The frames of production, use, and governance employed by the Americans encouraged them to pursue a "breakthrough" approach of wanting to invent something completely new. They attempted to design an "optimal" wind turbine by employing sophisticated theory and lightweight materials to achieve high aerodynamic efficiency. The superordinate goal of leapfrogging the competition via an extreme reliance on theory resulted in designers' becoming insensitive and unresponsive to feedback from multiple constituencies, thereby constraining essential learning processes. Reflecting on this situation, one American participant summed it up as follows: "We trusted our engineering tools too much...and we simply didn't believe that the engineering problems were as hard as they were.... We thought in a typical American fashion that there would be inevitable breakthroughs that would make the 'pedestrian' Danish approach obsolete overnight."

Learning represents the deeper structures (Drazin and Sandelands, 1992) that drove the evolution of the technological fields in the two countries. In Denmark, the confluence of learning-by-doing, learning-by-using, and learning-by-testing appears to have generated a virtuous cycle. This coupling of different bases of learning to create a virtuous cycle is similar to the observations by Cheng and Van de Ven (1996) on the development of two biomedical technologies. They found that large, built-up repertoires of action experiences, outcome preferences, and institutional practices acted as amplifying processes, increasing the probability of discovering creative means-ends connections. It is also similar to observations that Rosenbloom and Cusumano (1987) offer in their study of the video cassette recorder (VCR) industry. Firms that were able to harness all these knowledge components as an overall system were the ones that were successful in developing and commercializing the VCR.

In contrast, in the United States wind turbine field learning-by-doing, learning-by-using, and learning-by-testing were either muted or decoupled from one another, resulting in the creation of a vicious cycle. For instance, efforts to develop a breakthrough design reduced the capability and/or motivation to engage in learning-by-doing and learning-by-using. A breakthrough was sought on theoretical grounds; consequently, feedback and therefore learning opportunities from production and use were not considered to be as important as they were in Denmark. This is consistent with the observation by Cheng and Van de Ven (1996) that having experience with only one outcome preference or agreed-upon end (in this case, a desire for a breakthrough innovation) and one course of action (e.g., a theoretically based engineering approach) provides little opportunity for learning.

CONCLUSION

Complexity is a key facet of many dynamic phenomena, including the emergence of technological fields. We have offered a comparative study of wind turbine fields in Denmark and the United States. Our summary observation is that the evolution of a technological field must be understood as a complex system having emergent structures or patterns shaped by initial conditions, random historical events, institutionalized frames of reference, and learning processes that are either enabled or constrained by these frames. The confluence of learning processes may ultimately result in either virtuous or vicious cycles of technology development for the field. These observations lead us to tentatively conclude that complexity is as much about how we deal with nature as it is about nature itself.

REFERENCES

Anderson, P. and M. L. Tushman. (1990). "Technological Discontinuities and Dominant Designs: A Cyclical Model of Technological Change." *Administrative Science Quarterly*, Vol. 35, 604–633.

Argote, L. and D. Epple. (1990). "Learning Curves in Manufacturing." *Science*, Vol. 247 (February 23), 920–924.

Arrow, K. (1962). "The Economic Implications of Learning by Doing." *Review of Economic Studies*, Vol. 29 (June), 155–173.

Arthur, W. B. (1989). "Competing Technologies, Increasing Returns, and Lock-In by Historical Events." *The Economic Journal*, Vol. 99, 116–31.

Berger, P. L. and T. Luckmann. (1966). *The Social Construction of Reality*. New York: Doubleday.

Bijker, W. E., T. P. Hughes, and T. J. Pinch. (1987). *The Social Construction of Technological Systems: New Directions in the Sociology and History of Technology*. Cambridge: MIT Press.

Brown, J. S. and P. Duguid. (1991). "Organizational Learning and Communities of Practice: Toward a Unified View of Working, Learning, and Innovation." *Organization Science*, Vol. 2, 40–57.

BTM Consult ApS. (1997). *International Wind Energy Development: World Market Update 1996* (March).

Cheng, Y. and A. Van de Ven. (1996). "Learning the Innovation Journey: Order Out of Chaos?" *Organization Science*, Vol. 7, No. 6, 593–614.

Cohen, W. M. and D. A. Levinthal. (1990). "Absorptive Capacity: A New Perspective on Learning and Innovation." *Administrative Science Quarterly*, Vol. 35, No. 1, 128–152.

Davidson, Ros. (1996). "Kenetech Files for Bankruptcy Protection." *Windpower Monthly* (June) 4, 20–21.

Davidson, Ros. (1996). "A New Start." *Windpower Monthly* (June), 4.

Davidson, Ros. (1993). "In Search of Wisdom." *Windpower Monthly*, (July), 25–29.

Dertouzos, M., R. Lester, and R. M. Solow. (1989). *Made in America: Regaining the Productive Edge*. MIT Commission on Industrial Productivity, Harper Perennial.

Dosi, G. (1982). "Technological Paradigms and Technological Trajectories." *Research Policy*, Vol. 11, 147–162.

Drazin, R. and L. Sandelands. (1992). "Autogenesis: A Perspective on the Process of Organizing." *Organization Science*, Vol. 3, No. 2 (May), 230–249.

Dutton, J. M. and A. Thomas. (1985). "Relating Technological Change and Learning by Doing." In Richard D. Rosenbloom (Ed.), *Research on Technological Innovation, Management, and Policy*, Vol. 2. Stamford, CT: JAI Press, 187–224.

Garud, R. (1997). "On the Distinction between Know-How, Know-Why and Know-What in Technological Systems." In J. Walsh and A. Huff (Eds.), *Advances in Strategic Management*. Stamford, CT: JAI Press.

Garud, R. and M. Rappa. (1994). "A Socio-Cognitive Model of Technology Evolution." *Organization Science*, Vol. 5, No. 3, 344–362.

Gipe, P. (1995). *Wind Energy Comes of Age*. New York: John Wiley and Sons.

Hedberg, Bo. (1981). "How Organizations Learn and Unlearn." In P. Nystrom and W. Starbuck (Eds.), *Handbook of Organizational* Design. London/ New York: Oxford University Press, 3–27.

Jørgensen, U. and P. Karnøe. (1995). "The Danish Wind Turbine Story: Technical Solutions to Political Visions?" In A Rip, T. J. Misa, and J. Schot (Eds.), *Managing Technology in Society: The Approach of Constructive Technology Assesment.* London/New York: Pinter.

Karnøe, P. and R. Garud. (1997). "Path Creation and Dependence in the Danish Wind Turbine Field" In J. Porac, and M. Ventrusca, *The Social Construction of Industries and Markets.* New York: Pergamon Press.

Karnøe, P. (1993). "Approaches to Innovation in Modern Wind Energy Technology: Technology Policies, Science, Engineers and Craft Traditions." Center for Economic Policy Research Publication # 334, Stanford, CA.

Karnøe, P. (1991), *Danish Wind Turbine Industry—A Surprising International Success: On Innovations, Industrial Development and Technology Policy* (in Danish). Copenhagen: Samfundslitteratur.

Kristensen, P. H. (1992). "Strategies against Structure: Institutions and Economic Organization in Denmark." In R. Whitley (Ed.), *European Business Systems: Firms, Markets and Their National Contexts.* San Francisco: Sage.

Kristensen, P. H. (1990). "Denmark's Concealed Production Culture, Its Socio-Historical Construction and Dynamics at Work." In F. Borum and P. H. Kristensen (Eds.), *Techonological Innovation and Organizational Change.* Copenhagen: New Social Science Monographs.

Leonard-Barton, D. (1992). "Core Capabilities and Core Rigidities: A Paradox in Managing New Product Development," *Strategic Management Journal,* Vol. 13, 111–126.

Lindblom, C. E. (1959). "The Science of 'Muddling Through.'" *Public Administration Review,* Vol. 19, 79–88.

March, J. G. (1991). "Exploration and Exploitation in Organizational Learning." *Organization Science,* Vol. 2, No. 1, 71–87.

Masuch, M. (1985). "Vicious Circles in Organizations." *Administrative Science Quarterly,* Vol. 30, 14–33.

Mintzberg, H., O. Raisinghani, and A. Theoret (1976). "The Structure of Unstructured Decision Processes," *Administrative Science Quarterly,* Vol. 21, 246–275.

Mowery, D. C. and N. Rosenberg. (1989). *Technology and the Pursuit of Economic Growth.* London and New York: Cambridge University Press.

Nelson, R. R. and S. G. Winter. (1982). *An Evolutionary Theory of Economic Change.* Cambridge: Belknap Press of Harvard University Press.

Nelson, V. (1984). "A History of the SWECS Industry in the U.S." *Alternative Sources of Energy,* Vol. 66, (March/April).

Noble, D. (1984). *Forces of Production: A Social History of Industrial Automation.* New York: Knopf.

Perrow, C. (1984). *Normal Accidents: Living with High-Risk Technologies.* New York: Basic Books.

Piore, M. and C. Sabel. (1984). *The Second Industrial Divide: Possibilities for Prosperity.* New York: Basic Books.

Polley, D. and A. H. Van de Ven. (1996). "Learning by Discovery during Innovation Development." *International Journal of Technology Management*, Vol. 11, No. 7/8, 871–882.

Quinn, J. B. (1978). "Strategic Change: Logical Incrementalism." *Sloan Management Review*, Vol. 20, No. 1, 7–21.

Rosenberg, N. (1982). *Inside the Black Box: Technology and Economics*. New York: Cambridge University Press.

Rosenberg, N. (1976). *Perspectives on Technology*. London and New York: Cambridge University Press.

Rosenbloom, R. S. and M. A. Cusumano. (1987). "Technological Pioneering and Competitive Advantage: The Birth of the VCR Industry." *California Management Review*, Vol. 29, No. 4, 3–22.

Sahal, D. (1985). "Technical Guideposts and Innovation Avenues." *Research Policy*, Vol. 14, 61–82.

Seely, B. (1993). "Research, Engineering, and Science in American Engineering Colleges: 1900–1960." *Technology and Culture*, Vol. 34, 2.

Senge, P. (1990). *The Fifth Discipline*. New York: Doubleday/Currency.

Stoddard, F. S. (1986). "The California Experience." *Proceedings of the Danish Wind Energy Association Wind Energy Conference*.

Tsoukas, H. (1989). "The Epistemological Status of Idiographic Research in the Comparative Study of Organizations: A Realist Perspective." *Academy of Management Review*. Vol. 14, No. 4, 551–561.

Tushman, M. L. and P. Anderson. (1986). "Technological Discontinuities and Organizational Environments." *Administrative Science Quarterly*, Vol. 31, 439–465.

Usher, A. P. (1954). *A History of Mechanical Inventions*. Cambridge: Harvard University Press.

Van de Ven, A. H. and R. Garud. (1993). "The Co-evolution of Technical and Institutional Events in the Development of an Innovation." In J. Baum and J. Singh (Eds.) *Evolutionary Dynamics of Organizations*. New York: Oxford University Press, 425–443.

van Est, R. (1996a). "Common Sense Wind Energy: The Development of Wind Energy Policy, Technology, and Economy in California." Unpublished paper.

van Est, R. (1996b). "Living Sense Wind Energy: The Development of Wind Energy Policy, Technology, and Economy in Denmark." Unpublished paper.

Winter, S. G. (1987). "Knowledge and Competence as Strategic Assets." In D. J. Teece (Ed.), *The Competitive Challenge: Strategies for Industrial Innovation and Renewal*. Cambridge, MA: Ballinger, 159–184.

Chapter 20

An Almost Last Word

Michael R. Lissack

Thirty years ago, Thompson (1967) was able to write "Uncertainty appears as the fundamental problem for complex organizations, and coping with uncertainty, as the essence of the administrative process." The intervening three decades have marked little progress. Connell and Nord (1996) write of the "Infiltration of Organization Science by Uncertainty and Values" making note of the increased emphasis on language and meaning. Gergen and Thatchenkery (1996) note that methods may be sought to generate "new realities." Jacobson and Jacques (1997) can write of "Destabilizing the Field" by introducing a post-structuralist approach to the questions of meaning within organizations. If the study of organizations is itself plagued by uncertainty and doubt, that is a reflection of the uncertainties felt by organizations themselves and the members thereof. Perhaps what is occurring is that, as time marches inexorably forward, we are encountering more of what Rittel described as "wicked problems—a class of social system problems which are ill formulated, where the information is confusing, where there are many clients and decision makers with conflicting values, and where the ramifications in the whole system are thoroughly confusing" (Churchman, 1967). Or perhaps we just feel like we are.

A central concern of organization science is that of understanding how people construct meaning and reality, and exploring how that enacted reality provides a context for action. When managers 'enact' the environment, they as Weick (1995) put it: "construct, rearrange, single out, and demolish many 'objective' features of their surroundings ... they unrandomize variables, insert vestiges of orderliness, and literally create their own constraints." Through this process of sense making and reality construction, people in an organization give meaning to the events and actions of the organization. A challenge to the modern day manager (among many others) is to perform the same trick, that is, to recognize the pertinent features of a situation, develop or apply a theory explaining the relationships between the pertinent features, and then make a decision based on the predictions/understanding the application of the theory derives. Yet, because of the complexity inherent in many such situations it is impossible to know beforehand what is important to consider, and therefore what mental model to apply and what will happen if you get it wrong.

Management is hard work. It involves strategy and drudgery, fame and fear of exposure. As many a HR chieftain has said, much of it is less than glamorous. Managers have to deal with people and people are very much more difficult to understand and deal with than machines (though many theories attempt to model people simply as machines). Managers will fail and they will succeed. Before the interdependent, cell-phoned, interneted, networked world, life *was* simpler for the manager. Change was slower. A manager not only had a simpler system to deal with, but also he or she generally had more time to make decisions, and also more time to realize whether the decision was correct or not, and then still more time to put things right if they were wrong. In a simpler world the gap between what theory prescribed and what managers experienced was less apparent, and far less important.

Nowadays, however, things are very different. Primarily as a direct result of the rapid development of IT, systems are more connected and the geographical boundaries of old are no longer physically bound (or close) to a region from the rest of the world. The ability to connect to the rest of the world allows an organization to influence and to be influenced by a greater network of organizations, societies, and so on. Connectivity has grown exponentially. In this global, complex world life moves quickly (partly as the ability to generate and make use of information grows), that is, the tempo of business has increased significantly and is continuing to do so. The manager no longer has the luxury of time for many decisions. This combination of increased complexity and tempo means that the gap has grown and become plainly more apparent than ever before.

Because organizing is so complex, there has been a prejudice in the management literature to reduce it to hierarchical rational procedures. Management has been presented as a top-down rational process where actions are derived from more general principles and overall coordination is determined by a first cause (the vision, CEO, whatever). Consider Henry Mintzberg's classic comment: "If you ask managers what they do, they will most likely tell you that they plan, organize, co-ordinate and control. Then watch what they do. Don't be surprised if you can't relate what you see to those four words." If organizing is self-emerging, then its point of departure is its interactive processes and not any first principle or basic managerial thesis of action.

During the two years that it took to put this book together, the linkage between complexity and management has become more firmly established in the public eye. A wide variety of conferences, books, articles and the like are available. A new journal has appeared from the New England Complex Systems Institute called *Emergence: A Journal of Complexity Issues in Organization and Management.* Even the management consulting firms have chimed in. Together too many complexity and management presentations have a common litany:

1. Managers now find themselves in a qualitatively different world. It is more *uncertain, turbulent, complex, nonlinear, unpredictable, fast-paced, dynamic,* and even *postmodern.* The *old* or *traditional* models employed by managers, founded as they are on Newtonian science, are not (or will not be) adequate in this new world. By *old* or *traditional* models are meant: hierarchical command-and-control structures; bureaucratic organizational routines; centralization of power and decision-making; planning and forecasting; attempts at the reduction of uncertainty; and the use of machine and mechanical metaphors.

2. Science has developed something new and improved, a *New Science* that deals with chaos, complexity, complex adaptive systems, self-organization and autopoiesis. From New Science can be derived a new set of managerial tools, models, principles or even entire philosophies that, if applied, will bring organizational success. Once translated into organizational terms, these commonly involve: the flattening of hierarchies; decentralization of power, authority and decision-making; empowerment of employees; embracing uncertainty; and the use of organic and ecological metaphors. (excerpted from Maguire and McKelvey, 1999)

This book and the research of the authors herein have gone beyond this standard argument. For the mere translation of science terms into managerial jargon is not enough to lead managers to fruitful action.

For example, complexity science renders the traditional management concept of vision obsolete. What is wrong with vision? Vision is only based on what has been incorporated into your sense making, yesterday. You certainly only know about yesterday while you are trying to envision not just tomorrow but some medium term future. By naming it "vision" (an outcome) you reify it and thus, preclude changes in it. This is of course perfectly okay if your world is stable, but what if it isn't? Having locked in an outcome, it is all too tempting to work backwards from it not focusing on the potential interactions that could happen along the way. The very process of working backwards, of needing to have a defined game plan for achieving set goals, will restrict your "possibility space" and may interfere with your ability to adapt to changes going on around you and seize new opportunities when they arise. In this way, having an articulated vision works to silence your company's scouts—the staff members who are always probing for new ideas, new markets, and new possibilities. The strategic vision makes no room for emergence, thus whatever emerges would not have been accounted for in the game plan and may go unexplored or unexploited. Although vision has no tolerance for emergence, as the Internet has shown, in the twenty-first century, emergence will be the name of the game.

Unlike vision, coherence will be increasingly important. What coherence can do is enable actions to be grounded in certainty of purpose, identity, context, and further actions. Incoherence and decoherence reveal themselves by uncertainty, shame, or actions which defy sense making. Coherence is only a part of culture—in society or in an organization. Cultures provide context for being coherent or not. An organizational culture which thrives on inducing shame is incoherent. By contrast, an organization whose actions make sense to its members and stakeholders must have found a coherent viewpoint from which to guide such actions. (For more on coherence, see *The Next Common Sense: Mastering Corporate Complexity Through Coherence*, by myself and Johan Roos).

Boisot's (1999) learning cycles concept describes an endless process of value creation, exploitation, and erosion. To the extent that emergent change has intervened in the cycle to cause erosion where exploitation might otherwise have occurred, it seems that an offsetting intervention is called for. In response, the complexity school argues that the nature of management's tasks must change. It is not that traditional advice such as Tom Hout's (1999) is wrong, but that alternative explanations exist for how to get there.

create the right conditions for thinking and learning...select and nurture the best talent, set the right rules for the organization, wire people into appropriate networks, distribute rewards properly, resolve conflicts, and usher out the wrong people. Do these better than competitors do.

As Pondy put it in 1976:

The effectiveness of a leader lies in his ability to make activity meaningful for those in his role set—not to change behavior but to give others a sense of understanding what they are doing and especially to articulate it so they can communicate about the meaning of their behavior.... If in addition the leader can put it into words then the meaning of what the group is doing becomes a social fact.... This dual capacity...to make sense of things and to put them into language meaningful to large numbers of people gives the person who has it enormous leverage.

The possibility space of the organization (the boundaries of the potential for action) is constrained by the language of interpretation available to it and its members—for it is in that language that their reality will be constructed. Managers choose the environments they attend to, and their internal views shape these choices. The choice of frames (which endow meaning) and metaphors (which can provoke new images) within an organization can be determinative of what an organization can both extract and absorb from the environment around it. Kauffman (1996) refers to nearby possibilities as "the adjacent possible." The sequence of activities within and by an organization represent both movement within the possibility space and an enactment of how it defines the adjacent possible. In the interplay between language and activity, one finds both meaning and tension. Organizations must not only act, but their understanding of those actions—their sense making—must be coherent, if identity is to be preserved.

In the assertion and preservation of identity lies the greatest challenge to management and the greatest potential contribution of complex systems thinking. By tackling problems from a complex systems perspective, new understandings, and thus new possibilities for action emerge. What one should do, see, understand, or communicate are not governed by absolutes—so much for the dictates of the *One Minute Manager*—but by the demands of the local situation rooted in an understanding of that situation's innate complexity. Coherence is a socially tested awareness of a situation where the group has found a way for the parts of their narration (facts, observations, data) to fit together meaningfully. Coherence is not embedded in an organization. Coherence is an on-going social process wherein shared values support it and make it possible. The willingness to accept on-going and not static truth, the ability to live in process and not need hierarchy are crucial to sense making. Of course one can question how much of the time managing needs sense making. One can argue that much of the time managing functions by not seeing problems and by avoiding or repressing change in order to maintain routines. But in a globalized economy of rapid change and short product life cycles management's task to stabilize circumstances and repress change is becoming less and less effective, and the need to manage meaning and identity more and more important.

In terms of complex systems, at NECSI we like to say that the study of complex systems with regard to management is the study of how to resolve the paradox of intentional emergent coherence. Coherence is an alignment of context, viewpoint, purpose and action that enables further purposive action. That notion of purposive is reflected in our use of the term "intentional." Emergence, however, is a reflection of the idea that not only do things change but also that new and different entities can emerge from the interactions and intersections of existing things, people, and relationships. All three notions are processes. All are temporary at best. All are situational. But, when combined, intention, emergence and coherence can be a potent force and the foundation for the bricolage tools needed by organizations in a complex age.

And it is these words with which I leave the readers of this volume. Consider intention, emergence, and coherence as the building blocks for a new management style constructed around sense making and identity. It is in these domains where complex systems thinking can add value. And, I believe, will do so.

WEB SITES

- http://necsi.edu
- http://emergence.org
- http://coherence.org
- http://Lissack.com

REFERENCES

Boisot, M. (1999). *Knowledge Assets*. London: Oxford University Press.

Churchman, C. (1967). "Wicked Problems." *Management Science*, Vol. 4, No. 14.

Connell, A. and Nord, W. (1996). "Infiltration of Organization Science by Uncertainty and Values." *Journal of Applied Behavioral Science*, Vol. 32, No. 4.

Gergen, K. and Thatchenkery, T. (1996). "Organization Science as Social Construction, Postmodern Potentials." *Journal of Applied Behavioral Science*, Vol. 32, No. 4.

Hout, T. (1999). "Are Managers Obsolete?" *Harvard Business Review* (March-April).

Jacobson and Jacques (1997). "Destabilizing the Field, Poststructuralist Knowledge-Making Strategies in a Postindustrialist Era." *Journal of Management Inquiry*, Vol. 6, No. 1.

Kauffman, S. (1996). "Investigations." Santa Fe Institute Working Paper 96-08-072.

Lissack, M. and Roos, J. (1999). *The Next Common Sense: Mastering Corporate Complexity Through Coherence*. London: Nicholas Brealey Publishers.

Maguire, S. and McKelvey, W. (1999). "Complexity and Management: Moving From Fad to Firm Foundations." *Emergence: A Journal of Complexity Issues in Organizations and Management,* Vol. 1, No. 2.

Pondy, L. (1976). "Leadership Is a Language Game." In Mccall, M. and Lombardo, M. (eds.). *Leadership, Where Else Can We Go?* Greensboro, NC: Center For Creative Leadership.

Thompson, J. (1967). *Organizations in Action, Social Science Bases of Administrative Theory.* New York: McGraw-Hill.

Weick, K. (1995). *Sensemaking in Organizations.* Thousand Oaks, CA: Sage Publications.

Concluding Remarks

Michael R. Lissack and Hugh P. Gunz

This volume has taken the reader through numerous models and a wide variety of industries. From telecommunications and the Internet to windmills and Soviet power politics, one message stands out: a complexity theory-based perspective has the potential to change how managers conceive of their world and, from that change in perspective, to affect further the actions they take in creating that world.

What, for us, is the essential message in this statement? Complexity theory may have the potential to change perspectives, but is there a simple message to be distilled from this thought that translates into practice? We believe there is. For us, it has to do with serendipity: *complexity theory suggests a means for corporate organizations and individual managers to increase the amount of serendipity in their lives.*

Serendipity, as the term is typically used today, is the faculty of making happy and unexpected discoveries by accident. But this loses a key part of Horace Walpole's original 1754 definition. In his formulation, serendipity is a lot more than just stumbling over a happy discovery: he focused as well on the need for the discoverer's mind to be suitably prepared. Serendipity, as he defined it, is the art of making discoveries, by accidents *and sagacity*, of things the searcher is not in quest of. Sagacity is derived from the Latin noun *sagicitatem* ("keenness of perception") and means, according to the Oxford English Dictionary, gifted with acuteness of mental discernment; having special aptitude for the discovery of truth; penetrating and judicious in the estimation of character and motives; and the devising of means for the accomplishment of ends. Serendipity occurs when fortunate accidents happen to sagacious people. When this meaning is restored, the actions that companies can take to promote serendipity become clear. Complexity theory in its managerial application suggests that serendipity is more likely when companies take an approach of *bricolage* and not of planning toward their day-to-day activities.

Bricolage is a term described by Claude Levi-Strauss to describe the concrete thought of not-yet-civilized people. It is a French word naming the activity of the *bricoleur* (a man who undertakes odd jobs, a sort of jack-of-all-trades, or more precisely, a committed, do-it-yourself man). The essential idea of *bricolage* is the looseness of commitment to specific goals, the idea that materials, structures, and competences developed for one purpose are transferable and can very easily be used to advantage in the satisfaction of alternative objectives. Levi-Strauss' use of the term is sufficiently profound to be worthy of extended quotation:

The bricoleur is adept at performing a large number of diverse tasks; but, unlike the engineer, he does not subordinate each of them to the availability of raw materials and tools conceived and procured for the purpose of the project. His universe of instruments is closed and the rules of his game are always to make do with "whatever is at hand"...in the continual reconstruction from the same materials, it is always earlier ends which are called upon to play the part of means.... This formula, which could serve as the definition of "bricolage," explains how an implicit inventory or conception of the total means available must be made...so that a result can be defined which will always be a compromise between the structure of the instrumental set and that of the project.... The bricoleur may not ever complete his purpose but he always puts something of himself into it.

Perhaps *bricolage*, and not planning, is the best characterization of objective-related human behavior in everyday situations. Clearly, only *bricolage*, and not planning, can deal with the terrain within every organization that is not and cannot be managed, in which people, both individually and in groups, engage in unsupervised, spontaneous activity such as talking and fantasizing. *Bricolage*, with its focus on the interaction of pre-existing tools and available materials, helps to explain the power of the particular in determining the course of development. The resources of the corporation and its environment can be viewed as the tools and materials of the bricoleur constraining our undertaking and accomplishing any activity.

So what is the role of complexity theory in all this? It is the tool kit of the modern-day manager-turned *bricoleur*. Complexity theory offers new insights into day-to-day management issues and suggests new paths to "make do" with what the environment has made available. Complexity theory emphasizes the need for adaptiveness and the need for environmental information—factors of which any *bricoleur* is keenly aware. With complexity theory as part of the tool kit and with *bricolage* as an attitude, the modern-day manager can be better prepared and, thus, more sagacious. To return to Walpole, the more sagacious the manager, the greater the chances of serendipity. Anyone trained in the tradition of the Boy Scouts would immediately recognize in this echoes of Baden-Powell's famous admonition to his followers. Complexity theory, in short, is about being better prepared.

REFERENCE

Levi-Strauss, Claude (1996), *The Savage Mind*. Chicago: University of Chicago Press, 17, 21.

Recommended Readings

Allison, M.A., and Kelly, S. (1999). *The Complexity Advantage; How the Science of Complexity Can Help Your Business Achieve Peak Performance*. New York: McGraw-Hill.

Axelrod, R.M. (1997). *The Complexity of Cooperation: Agent-Based Models of Competition and Collaboration*. Princeton, N.J.: Princeton University Press.

Baskin, K. (1998). *Corporate DNA: Learning from Life*. Boston: Butterworth-Heinemann.

Bar-Yam, Y. (1997). *Dynamics of Complex Systems*. Reading, Mass.: Perseus Press.

Bechtel, W., and Richardson, R.C. (1993). *Discovering Complexity: Decomposition and Localization as Strategies in Scientific Research*. Princeton, N.J.: Princeton University Press.

Boisot, M.H. (1995). *Information Space: A Framework for Learning in Organizations, Institutions and Culture*. London: International Thomson Business Press.

Boisot, M.H. (1998). *Knowledge Assets: Securing Competitive Advantage in the Information Economy*. New York: Oxford University Press.

Brown, S., and Eisenhardt, K. (1998). *Competing on the Edge: Strategy as Structured Chaos*. Cambridge, Mass.: Harvard Business School Press.

Byrne, D. (1998). *Complexity Theory and the Social Sciences*. New York: Routledge.

Childre, D.L., and Cryer, B. (1998). *From Chaos to Coherence: Advancing Emotional and Organizational Intelligence through Inner Quality Management*. Boston: Butterworth-Heinemann

Cilliers, P. (1998). *Complexity and Postmodernism: Understanding Complex Systems*. New York: Routledge.

Clement, S.D., and Jaques, E. (1991). *Executive Leadership: A Practical Guide to Managing Complexity*. Malden, Mass.: Blackwell Publishers.

Cohen, J., and Stewart, I. (1995). *The Collapse of Chaos: Discovering Simplicity in a Complex World*. New York: Penguin USA.

Connor, D.L. (1998). *Leading at the Edge of Chaos: How to Create the Nimble Organization*. New York: John Wiley and Sons.

Elkins, D.J. (1993). *Manipulation and Consent: How Voters and Leaders Manage Complexity*. Vancouver: University of British Columbia.

Flood, R.L., and Carson, E.R. (1993). *Dealing with Complexity: An Introduction to the Theory and Application of Systems Science*. New York: Plenum Publishing Corporation.

Friedman, L. (1997). *The Dynamic Enterprise: Tools for Turning Chaos into Strategy and Strategy into Action*. San Francisco: Jossey-Bass Publishers.

Furze, D., and Gale, C. (1994). *Interpreting Management: Exploring Change and Complexity*. London: International Thomson Business Press.

Gleick, J. (1988). *Chaos: Making a New Science*. New York: Penguin USA.

Gottinger, H.W. (1983). *Coping With Complexity: Perspectives for Economics, Management and Social Sciences*. Berlin: D. Reidel Publishing.

Hock, D.W. (1998). *The Chaordic Principle: Mixing Chaos and Order to Jump Start the Twenty-First Century*. New York: Bantam Doubleday Dell.

Holland, J.H. (1996). *Hidden Order: How Adaptation Builds Complexity*. Reading, Mass.: Perseus Press.

Holland, J.H. (1998). *Emergence: From Chaos to Order*. Reading, Mass.: Perseus Press.

Hurst, D.K. (1995). *Crisis & Renewal: Meeting the Challenge of Organizational Change*. Cambridge, Mass.: Harvard Business School Press.

Jervis, R. (1997). *System Effects: Complexity in Political and Social Life*. Princeton, N.J.: Princeton University Press.

Kauffman, S.A. (1993). *The Origins of Order: Self-Organization and Selection in Evolution*. New York: Oxford University Press.

Kauffman, S.A. (1996). *At Home in the Universe: The Search for Laws of Self-Organization and Complexity*. New York: Oxford University Press.

Kelly, K. (1994). *Out of Control: The New Biology of Machines, Social Systems, and the Economic World*. Reading, Mass.: Perseus Press.

Kelly, K. (1998). *New Rules for the New Economy: 10 Radical Strategies for a Connected World*. New York: Viking Press.

Kiel, L.D. (1994). *Managing Chaos and Complexity in Government: A New Paradigm for Managing Change, Innovation, and Organizational Renewal*. San Francisco: Jossey-Bass Publishers.

Marion, R. (1999). *The Edge of Organization: Chaos and Complexity Theories of Formal Social Systems*. Thousand Oaks, Calif.: Sage Publications.

Maruyama, M. (1992). *Context and Complexity: Cultivating Contextual Understanding*. Berlin: Springer Verlag.

McMaster, M.D. (1996). *The Intelligence Advantage: Organizing for Complexity*. Boston: Butterworth-Heinemann.

Merry, U. (1995). *Coping with Uncertainty: Insights from the New Sciences of Chaos, Self-Organization, and Complexity*. Westport, Conn.: Praeger Publishing.

Oshry, B. (1996). *Seeing Systems: Unlocking the Mysteries of Organizational Life*. San Francisco: Berrett-Koehler Publishers.

Pascale, R.T. (1991). *Managing on the Edge: How the Smartest Companies Use Conflict to Stay Ahead*. New York: Touchstone Books.

Perrow, S. (1986). *Complex Organizations: A Critical Essay*. New York: McGraw-Hill.

Price Waterhouse Change Integration Team (1995). *The Paradox Principles: How High-Performance Companies Manage Chaos, Complexity, and Contradiction to Achieve Superior Results.* Chicago: Irwin Professional Publishing.

Priesmeyer, H.R. (1992). *Organizations and Chaos: Defining the Methods of Nonlinear Management.* Westport, Conn.: Quorum Books.

Pryer, F.L. (1996). *Economic Evolution and Structure: The Impact of Complexity on the U.S. Economic System.* Cambridge: Cambridge University Press.

Reeves, W.W. (1996). *Cognition and Complexity: The Cognitive Science of Managing Complexity.* Baltimore, Md.: Scarecrow Press.

Sanders, T.I. (1998). *Strategic Thinking and the New Science: Planning in the Midst of Chaos, Complexity, and Change.* New York: Simon & Schuster.

Scott, W.R., and Meyer, J.W. (1994). *Institutional Environments and Organizations: Structural Complexity and Individualism.* Thousand Oaks, Calif.: Sage Publications.

Sherman, H., and Schultz, R. (1998). *Open Boundaries.* Reading, Mass.: Perseus Books.

Sifonis, J.G. (1996). *Corporation on a Tightrope: Balancing Leadership, Governance, and Technology in an Age of Complexity.* New York: Oxford University Press.

Stacey, R.M. (1992). *Managing the Unknowable: Strategic Boundaries between Order and Chaos in Organizations.* San Francisco: Jossey-Bass Publishers.

Stacey, R.D. (1996). *Complexity and Creativity in Organizations.* San Francisco: Berrett-Koehler.

Stevens, R., Jackson, K., Brook, P., and Arnold, S. (1998). *Systems Engineering: Coping with Complexity.* Upper Saddle River, N.J.: Prentice-Hall Trade.

Stewart, I., and Cohen, J. (1997). *Figments of Reality: The Evolution of the Curious Mind.* Cambridge: Cambridge University Press.

Von Glinow, M.A., and Albers Mohrman, S. (Eds.) (1990). *Managing Complexity in High Technology Organizations.* New York: Oxford University Press.

Waldrop, M.M. (1993). *Complexity: The Emerging Science at the Edge of Order and Chaos.* New York: Touchstone Books.

Weick, K.E. (1995). *Sensemaking in Organizations.* Thousand Oaks, Calif.: Sage Publications.

Wheatley, M.J. (1994). *Leadership and the New Science: Learning about Organization from an Orderly Universe.* San Francisco: Berrett-Koehler.

Wheatley, M.J., and Kellner-Rogers, M. (1998). *A Simpler Way.* San Francisco: Berrett-Koehler.

Youngblood, M.D., and Renesch, J. (Eds.) (1997). *Life at the Edge of Chaos: Creating the Quantum Organization.* Dallas: Perceval.

Zohar, D. (1997). *Rewiring the Corporate Brain: Using the New Science to Rethink How We Structure and Lead Organizations.* San Francisco: Berrett-Koehler.

Index

About the Contributors

PEKKA AULA is a researcher at the Department of Communication, University of Helsinki, Finland. His research interests include information society's organization as a complex evolving system and organizational communication as means to manage organizational complexity and chaos. He has also conducted studies in the domain of the new media and information networks.

JANET BARDYN is a project manager with Oracle Corporation and a member of the New Grange Center for Project Management. Her professional practice and research aim is to further the discussion of project management as its own professional discipline. Bardyn was a project manager at NYNEX prior to joining Oracle.

KEN BASKIN is a writer, consultant, and speaker whose firm, Life Design Partners, specializes in helping client organizations improve productivity, enhance innovation, and grow market share by taking advantage of life's design principles. His book, *Corporate DNA: Learning from Life*, reflects the 15 years he spent writing for such organizations as Bell Atlantic, ITT, Monsanto, Sun Company, and the U.S. Department of Energy.

JOEL A. C. BAUM holds the Canadian National Chair in Strategic Management in the Rotman School of Management at the University of Toronto, Ontario. He is editor-in-chief of the journal *Advances in Strategic Management*. His research focuses on the "institutional ecology" of organizations, including working on possible applications of complexity theory concepts and techniques to the dynamics of interfirm competition and innovation.

THOMAS H. BERKAS is a research scientist with the Search Institute in Minneapolis. The Search Institute develops, conducts, and reports on research and evaluation projects related to specific areas of adolescent development with a goal of informing programs, organizations, policy, and community initiatives about how they can best meet the needs of young people.

ROBERT M. CUTLER is a fellow of the Institute of European and Russian Studies, Carleton University, Ottawa, and an international consultant. He has spent most of his career concerned with organizational analysis and design, information, and communications within and among organizations and how cross-cultural issues affect those concerns. His other professional experience is in negotiation, conflict resolution, and policy analysis, development, and implementation.

GLENDA H. EOYANG is the author of *Coping with Chaos: Seven Simple Tools* and the president of Chaos Limited. She is also president of Excel Instruction, Inc., a technical training and documentation company located in Minneapolis. Her current professional interests include applications of complexity theory to integration of technology, leadership, evaluation, information and knowledge management, and organizational change. Her current research interests include emergent communication and computer simulation models for decision support.

DONNA FITZGERALD is a project manager with Oracle Corporation and a member of the New Grange Center for Project Management. Her professional practice and research aim is to further the discussion of project management as its own professional discipline. Fitzgerald was a co-founding principal of an information systems consulting firm prior to joining Oracle.

TED FULLER is director of the Knowledge Systems Research Centre at Durham University Business School and also deputy chairman of Durham's Small Business Centre. He has published widely on entrepreneurship development, including a number of expert systems for enterprise guidance and manuals for business trainers. His current research is on strategic environmental trends and applications of information technology and telecommunications to enterprise learning and development.

E. ANDRES GARCIA is an international management consultant whose clients have included firms in financial services, advertising, beverage bottling, cosmetics, packaged goods, pharmaceuticals, software, and telecommunications. His research interests revolve around "social dilemmas," a class of situations which individual rationality and collective rationality are in conflict (encompassing well-known models such as the "prisoners' dilemma" and the "tragedy of the commons") and that appear to be at the heart of most major societal problems.

RAGHU GARUD is an associate professor of management at the Leonard N. Stern School of Business, New York University. He is an editor of *Technological Innovation: Oversights and Foresights*. His teaching and research interests lie in exploring the intersection between technology, organizations, and strategy. In his current research, he, along with Peter Karnøe, is exploring path creation as a process of mindful deviation.

HUGH P. GUNZ is an associate professor in organizational behavior at the Joseph Rotman School of Management of the University of Toronto, Canada. He is the author of *Careers and Corporate Cultures: Managerial Mobility in Large Corporations*. A former Chair of the Careers Division of the Academy of Management, his research has focused on managerial careers and business strategies. He has written extensively on subjects such as downsizing and the management of professionals and has expanded his research to include the effects of complex systems theories on the concept and management of a "career."

PETER KARNØE is an associate professor in the Department of Organization and Industrial Sociology, Copenhagen Business School, Denmark. His current research interest is exploring such conceptions as path creation and path dependence with respect to understanding the generation of such techno-social orders that become the path we create. Theoretic insights from complex adaptive systems, actor-network theory, and symbolic interactionism are used to understand the material and symbolic dimensions (selection criteria in use) in the constitution of temporal orders in an open-ended evolutionary space.

HAROLD E. KLEIN is an associate professor in general and strategic management at Temple University in Philadelphia. He served as contributing editor to the *Journal of Business Strategy*. His research focuses on strategic planning methodology, strategic environmental scanning function, strategic decision support systems, management cognition, scenario planning techniques, and development planning systems.

ADAM J. KOCH is a lecturer at the Swinburne University of Technology in Melbourne, Australia. His research has focused mostly on competences, capabilities, and skills considered critical in contemporary international business, on the competence-based business strategies, on critical evaluation of the current marketing management practice in Australia, and on the evolution of the Central European markets.

MICHAEL R. LISSACK is the director of the Institute for the Study of Coherence and Emergence and of its Networking, Emergence, and Complexity Studies Initiative. He is the moderator of the Complex-M complexity and management discussion group on the Internet. He is the coauthor of *The Next Common Sense* and of a textbook, *Management Redefined*. Formerly an investment banker with Smith Barney, he spent 14 years financing state and local government infrastructure projects. He has become actively involved in web-related companies both as an initial investor in Tripod (now a part of Lycos) and as a board member for Intelligenesis.

STEVE MAGUIRE is an assistant professor of strategy and organization at McGill University in Montreal. An editor of the journal *Emergence*, his research focus is on sustainable development and business strategy. He investigates how socio-economic systems react to environmental "surprises," produce new ecological understanding, then incorporate it into their functioning.

MARK W. McELROY is a twenty-two year veteran of management consulting including time spent at Price Waterhouse, KPMG Peat Marwick, and AnswerThink Consulting Group. He is currently a Principal in the Knowledge Management Practice at IBM Consulting. In addition to his affiliation with NECSI, Mark has been deeply involved with attempts by the Knowledge Management Consortium to apply principles of complexity theory to the field of knowledge management. Mark is also a board member of the Sustainability Institute, a think-tank in New England that uses system dynamics tools to study and develop environmentally and socially sustainable economic models for business and industry.

TOM PETZINGER is the author of the column "Front Lines" in the *Wall Street Journal* and of two books, *The New Pioneers* and *Hard Landing: The Epic Contest for Power and Profits That Plunged the Airlines into Chaos*. His columns on how businesses cope with the complexities of the modern economy are a must-read every Friday.

IF PRICE is a visiting professor in innovation management and director of research programs at Sheffield Hallam University's Facilities Management Graduate Centre and a coauthor of *Shifting the Patterns*. He spent more than 18 years with British Petroleum (BP) including serving as manager of research and then head of business process review for BP Exploration. His research and consultancy focus on the processes of innovation and change in organizations, including the application of modern evolutionary theory to organizational design.

BRIAN S. SILVERMAN is an assistant professor of business administration in the competition and strategy area at Harvard Business School. His research focuses on the strategies and structures through which firms access and exploit technological capabilities. His research also applies concepts and techniques from non-linear dynamics to understand and model technological change.

MARK WHITE is a partner in the Mexico City firm White and Associates and the author of a weekly business column in *The News*, Mexico City's English-language daily. His research and consulting practice focuses on applying complex adaptive systems theory to strategy and finance.

ROBIN WOOD is an executive consultant in Ernst & Young's adaptive strategy consulting practice. In this capacity he advises international organizations on the development of adaptive strategies, organizations and operations using new science and complexity-based approaches. He is currently working on his next book, entitled "Managing Complexity: How the New Sciences Can Help Businesses Adapt and Prosper." Prior to joining Ernst & Young, Wood helped form four other firms, including Genesys, a strategy consulting firm, where his clients included 3M, Hewlett Packard, Shell, State Farm Insurance, Unilever, Jardine Matheson, and a variety of multinational pharmaceuticals, computing, and telecommunications corporations.

ARNOLD J. WYTENBURG is president of Wytenburg Management Inc., a strategy and management planning consultancy. He is a veteran business leader with more than 25 years of experience assisting many global Fortune 500 and small to midsized companies in their efforts to optimize organizational performance. He is also a researcher, methodologist, educator, and commentator specialized in exploring the management implications of the new sciences with a focus on such theories as complexity, emergence, system dynamics, and information dynamics.

ISBN 1-56720-285-3